The Journal of Decorative and Propaganda Arts

25

THE AMERICAN
HOTEL

The Wolfsonian–Florida International University Miami Beach, Florida

Issue 25,
The American Hotel
The Journal of Decorative and Propaganda Arts, published by The Wolfsonian–Florida International University.
ISBN 1-930776-17-9

Editorial Offices:
The Journal of Decorative and Propaganda Arts
The Wolfsonian–Florida International University
1001 Washington Avenue
Miami Beach, Florida 33139
Telephone: (305) 535-2612
Fax: (305) 531-2133
e-mail: dapa@thewolf.fiu.edu
www.wolfsonian.org

The Journal of Decorative and Propaganda Arts Issue 22, Cuba Theme Issue; 23, Florida Theme Issue; and 24, *Design, Culture, Identity: The Wolfsonian Collection* are also distributed by
The MIT Press
Cambridge, Massachusetts
London, England
http://mitpress.edu
For information on the availability of other back issues, contact *The Journal's* editorial offices.

Cover:
Schultze and Weaver, Waldorf-Astoria Hotel, New York, final study of a tower lantern, presentation drawing by Lloyd Morgan, color pastel and tempera on board, 45 x 29 in. (114.3 x 73.7 cm), c. 1930. The Wolfsonian– Florida International University, Miami Beach, Florida, The Mitchell Wolfson Jr. Collection. WFIU-67.

Printed in Spain by Grafos S.A.

25

Exploring the period 1875 – 1945

The Journal of Decorative and Propaganda Arts

Publisher and Wolfsonian–FIU Director
Cathy Leff

Guest Editor
Molly W. Berger

Senior Editor
Leslie Sternlieb

Copyeditor
Ellen Hirzy

Art Director
Peter Roman
Inkbyte Design

Millionaires' Elysiums: The Luxury Apartment Hotels of Schultze and Weaver
Andrew S. Dolkart
10

The Rich Man's City: Hotels and Mansions of Gilded Age New York
Molly W. Berger
46

Early Twentieth-Century Hotel Architects and the Origins of Standardization
Lisa Pfueller Davidson
72

The New South in the Ancient City: Flagler's St. Augustine Hotels and Sectional Reconciliation
Reiko Hillyer
104

Revisiting Hotels and Other Lodgings: American Tourist Spaces through the Lens of Black Pleasure-Travelers, 1880-1950
Myra B. Young Armstead
136

Princes and Maids of the City Hotel: The Cultural Politics of Commercial Hospitality in America
A. K. Sandoval-Strausz and Daniel Levinson Wilk
160

William Price's Traymore Hotel: Modernity in the Mass Resort
George E. Thomas and Susan Nigra Snyder
186

Merchandising Miami Beach: Morris Lapidus and the Architecture of Abundance
Alice T. Friedman
216

Living Large: The Brash, Bodacious Hotels of Dorothy Draper
Mitchell Owens
254

"Wrecking the Joint": The Razing of City Hotels in the First Half of the Twentieth Century
Bernard L. Jim
288

Director's message Cathy Leff

With this twenty-fifth issue of *The Journal of Decorative and Propaganda Arts*, we tell the story of American hotels and how they evolved into some of the world's most significant and interesting buildings. The ten essays contained in this book explore the design and culture of this most complex urban institution and demonstrate how the social and technological developments of the late nineteenth through the mid-twentieth centuries found their expression in luxury lodgings.

This volume also reflects our connection to the seaside leisure traditions of our Miami Beach home, better known as a vacation retreat than as a study center for material culture. We celebrate the Wolfsonian's tenth anniversary with the exhibition *In Pursuit of Pleasure: Schultze and Weaver and the American Hotel* during the fall of 2005. Both projects have enabled us to appreciate the legacy of this architectural firm, visible across the skylines of New York and South Florida. We could think of no better way to celebrate this decade of growth and achievement than to dedicate this volume and the upcoming exhibition and accompanying catalog to a subject—the American hotel—that has defined our community.

Since its inception in 1986 *The Journal* has been committed to fostering new scholarship across a variety of disciplines. The serious study of hotels—apart from what you might find in trade journals or coffee-table books—is an emerging discipline, and this was one of the most challenging theme issues we have ever assembled. Our contributors are among the new generation of hotel scholars and have produced a volume that not only functions as an introduction to the fascinating complexities of hotel design but also sheds new light on the surrounding culture and social conditions. We hope their work will encourage many more scholars to consider this a fertile area for investigation.

Molly W. Berger, our guest editor, is one such serious student of the hotel, and she devoted considerable energy to assuring the excellence of the content. Her dedication to the long unfolding of this project never flagged, even as she maintained the dual positions of instructor of history and assistant dean of the College of Arts and Sciences at Case Western Reserve University in Cleveland.

We are deeply appreciative of the continued strong support of the Cowles Charitable Trust and to Wolfsonian board member Charles Cowles for his personal commitment to *The Journal*. Sincere thanks to the Graham Foundation for Advanced Studies in the Fine Arts for its generous funding of this publication.

A project like this requires the intelligence and capability of many people. Concurrent with the production of this journal was the research ultimately leading to the museum's hotel exhibition. Sincere thanks to Marianne Lamonaca, chief curator and assistant director for exhibitions and curatorial affairs; Jonathan Mogul, research associate; and Lisa Li, curatorial assistant, for offering their assistance to *The Journal* in the midst of significant preparation.

The registration department and library were essential to providing images for many of the essays and were instrumental in coordinating research occurring in the Schultze and Weaver collection. Thanks to Kimberly Bergen, registrar; Debbye Kirschtel-Taylor, assistant registrar; and Amy Silverman, registration assistant, for their investigative prowess, as well as Francis X. Luca, associate librarian, and Nicholas Blaga, assistant librarian, for their solid support of this effort.

Thanks also to Regina Bailey, assistant director for planning and special initiatives, for stepping in at a moment's notice to ensure the timely receipt of images. Silvia Ros, visual resources manager, brought her considerable photographic skills to documenting the challenging variety of Wolfsonian objects used in this volume. Sheila Thomson, former public information officer, cheerfully offered her computer expertise to access difficult digital images. Michael Hughes, visitor services manager, provided helpful reviews in matters of local history.

We are grateful to art director Peter Roman of Inkbyte Design, who designed *The Journal*. His dedication to excellence is evident on every page, and he not only produced a superb publication but did so with grace and good humor. Ellen Hirzy, copyeditor, offered an extra measure of clarity to every manuscript and maintained a rigorous attention to style.

Foremost, I am indebted to Leslie Sternlieb, senior editor of *The Journal*, whose steadfast intellectual and personal commitment to this project made this publication possible. Overseeing all aspects of the editorial and design processes, working with our guest editor and contributors alike, Leslie has once again delivered a volume that distinguishes our institution.

I would also like to express my gratitude to Mitchell Wolfson Jr. for having the vision to acquire for The Wolfsonian the Schultze and Weaver collection, which will provide future scholars with an extraordinary array of materials unavailable anywhere else.

On a more personal note, I would like to thank our readers, who have remained loyal for nearly two decades, Florida International University, and Roger Conover and Lisa Reeve of the MIT Press for their commitment to our success.

The American Hotel Molly W. Berger

Americans "invented" the large urban luxury hotel in the early nineteenth century, and since that time these buildings have proven to be a source of fascination for the world's traveling public. We tend to think of our cities' gilded palaces as democratic imitations of the aristocratic palace homes in England and Europe and, like them, something beyond the realm of "real" life. But a lively new history of American hotels is emerging from researchers and scholars that establishes the hotel as not only homegrown but even characteristically American, arising from an evolving political economy's needs for new kinds of public spaces to accommodate America's particular blend of democracy and commerce. Boldly conceptualized, hotels represented their cities as progressive and sophisticated and often marked their place in the world.

The essays in this issue of the *Journal of Decorative and Propaganda Arts* showcase the hotel as a complex site of social and cultural production characterized by a host of competing ideas and ideologies. These grand buildings were at once commercial and domestic, egalitarian and restrictive, and the site of both production and consumption. Nonetheless, they shared a common architectural program that organized their operations and continues to make them readily recognizable and accessible to all who come.

New York City's Waldorf-Astoria is perhaps the best-known hotel in the nation, if not the world. Temporary home to kings, queens, and presidents, to well-heeled tourists and business travelers, its famed towers and flag-draped portico are icons in the popular media of print, film, and television. It also serves as the point of entry for this issue. The Wolfsonian–Florida International University includes in its holdings the Schultze and Weaver collection, an archive of the architectural firm that designed the 1931 Waldorf-Astoria, one of the most esteemed of the firm's many preeminent commissions. The collection is a bounty of presentation drawings, linens, photographs, and correspondence that allows us insight into understanding the meaning of the Waldorf and other hotels like it. As you read the essays, though, you will begin to understand from a number of varying perspectives the significance of the Waldorf-Astoria and its late nineteenth-century predecessor of the same name. Most of the essays, whether explicitly or implicitly, refer to one or the other as a landmark in the history of the American hotel. As part of its mission to investigate how design shapes and represents human experience, The Wolfsonian can claim a unique position to focus on the hotel as a significant point of inquiry for American society and culture.

The *Journal of Decorative and Propaganda Arts* focuses primarily on the period 1875 to 1945, and these decades are also appropriate ones for studying the American hotel. They coincide with the maturation of American industrial capitalism and the expansion and consolidation of enormous wealth. American hotels were both a product and an agent of those economic and organizational processes. The first Waldorf-Astoria (1891–1893) represented the culmination of seventy years of design evolution, yet it also took the first bold steps into the new world of the scientifically managed skyscraper hotel that addressed the needs of reorganizing economic, political, and professional classes. Large American cities began to build similarly grand hotels—often featuring as many as one thousand or more rooms—that served not only the wealthy traveling public but also extended luxuriously extravagant accommodations to the rising middle and upper middle classes. In addition, these hotels addressed the requirements of new national professional, fraternal, and social organizations for meeting and banquet facilities. Resort hotels developed in parallel, responding to the legions of vacationers traveling by train or automobile who sought respite from the exigencies of industrial America and at the same time constructed consumer-based identities of self through the fantastical worlds that resort hotels created.

The essays in this volume are grouped into three sections arranged under broad concepts. The first group of essays looks at hotels from the perspective of architects and developers, an approach that privileges design, ownership, and management. Andrew S. Dolkart draws on the Wolfsonian's Schultze and Weaver collection and focuses on the firm's development of the luxury residential apartment hotel, including the Waldorf-Astoria towers. This development in urban living appealed to investors, who could take advantage of loopholes in building regulations, and to wealthy families, who appreciated the release from the responsibilities of maintaining huge townhomes and their requisite staffs. While analyzed through the lens of the architectural historian, the buildings' plans shed light on the everyday needs and organization of upper-class New York life and how those requirements shaped the city's landscape. My essay follows and approaches the connection between luxury hotels and upper-class life from a different architectural association: that of elite Gilded Age mansions and luxury hotels. I argue that these two kinds of wealthy urban residences were the same building type, existing on opposite ends of a design continuum of size and ownership. Many of the elite families whose residences lined upper Fifth Avenue also invested in and built similarly conceived and decorated hotels. Thus, they extended the spoils of industrial capitalism to the middle classes, who joined with elite forces in support of the industrial practices that produced such great wealth by eagerly renting bedrooms and other spaces in the hotel. Lisa Pfueller Davidson's essay rounds out this section, focusing on the intersection between architectural design and the scientific management principles that produced the nation's first standardized hotels. Davidson's essay serves as a corrective to assumptions that place these processes in post–Second World War hotel chain development by examining the early hotels of E. M. Statler. Governed by the gospel of efficiency and principles of mass production, Statler blended managerial and architectural expertise with his own instincts about the needs of a vast traveling public.

In the second section, social and cultural historians look at the nation's hotels through the perspectives of race, class, and gender. Reiko Hillyer examines Henry Flagler's hotel development in St. Augustine, Florida, as a project of post–Civil War reconciliation between northern and southern economic interests. Flagler reproduced northern standards of luxury for visitors from that region to create a familiar and comfortable environment, made more attractive by an exotic southern location. However, this development relied on and was complicit with an intentional revision of Florida's history that imagined and perpetuated a romanticized Spanish heritage while nearly erasing the history of Florida's participation in the Civil War, the persistence of which would alienate the northern clientele necessary for the resort's success. The underlying racial discourse in Hillyer's essay is explicitly analyzed by Myra B. Young Armstead, who alerts us to the absence of African Americans in most narratives of luxury and commercialized elitism. Denied access to hotels by vicious segregationist customs and laws, upper- and middle-class blacks developed comparable hotels and resorts throughout the nation, as well as information networks that eased the burdens of travel imposed by racism. These primarily black-owned establishments enabled African Americans to participate in widespread national practices such as leisure travel and vacation escapes in a way that was parallel to white Americans and, as important, to do so in a deracialized environment. Moving from issues of race to those of class and gender, Andrew K. Sandoval-Strausz and Daniel Levinson Wilk take us behind the scenes in American hotels to explore the relationship between labor and capital. They look at the service sector through the experiences and cultural representations of hotel clerks and chambermaids and argue that service transformed during the nineteenth and twentieth centuries from a model based on the traditional patriarchal household to a new mode of commercial hospitality. They find their evidence in popular culture: as hotels became ubiquitous and romanticized settings for novels and films, the status of hotel workers was concomitantly elevated.

In the third section, we focus on design and look at three of the twentieth century's pacesetting designers, all of whom understood modern consumer culture and the way in which sophisticated and outré design could lure customers and thus ensure profits. George E. Thomas and Susan Nigra Snyder's essay examines William Price's Atlantic City Traymore Hotel as the first to employ total design principles that linked exteriors and interiors, including furniture, menus, dishes, and other material objects, into a unified, "branded," recognizable, and marketable concept. Thomas and Snyder credit Price's ideas for influencing modernists such as Morris Lapidus, and they trace a direct evolutionary line from Price through Lapidus to the drama of today's Las Vegas hotels. Alice T. Friedman explores these ideas further through the work of Lapidus, whose post–Second World War Miami Beach hotels earned the savage scorn of cultural critics. Nonetheless, Lapidus understood the bewitching attraction of glamorous theatricality and the way in which his outrageous interior spaces met the needs of consumers who, after two decades of depression and war, longed to be carried away from everyday experience. Mitchell Owens's essay on Dorothy Draper continues these themes, capturing the exuberance of Draper's imagination as she transformed developers' expectations and travelers' experiences with her outsized trendsetting designs. Draper's interiors were the antithesis of the standardized hotels that Davidson describes, as they appropriated and challenged traditional historicisms and led the design world in new and unexpected directions. In combination, these three essays instruct us in the hotel's significance as perhaps the only public venue that could successfully entertain the execution of these kinds of larger-than-life ideas.

The final essay in the volume, by Bernard L. Jim, challenges us to think about the way the public constructs the relationship between hotels and cities and the tensions that exist between developers and citizens as each claims ownership of established buildings. Jim's essay scrutinizes the demolition of two beloved hotels, New York's first Waldorf-Astoria, whose site gave way to the Empire State Building, and Cleveland's Weddell House, which yielded to the Rockefeller Building. Jim employs theories of progress, development, and commoditization to interpret their destruction and the effect the demolitions had on the respective communities. The absence of the material record—the buildings them-selves—reminds us how difficult it is to recover a lost past and compels us to examine the value we place on buildings. Hotels are particularly important institutions to study if we are to fully understand our nation's past because they bind the material, economic, social, and cultural worlds in ways that are perhaps unique. These essays are an important first step toward recovering a heretofore unwritten national story. Happy traveling!

Andrew S. Dolkart

Millionaires' Elysiums: The Luxury Apartment Hotels of Schultze and Weaver

Andrew S. Dolkart holds the James Marston Fitch Professorship and is associate professor of historic preservation at the Columbia University School of Architecture, Planning, and Preservation. Dolkart has written extensively on the architecture and development of New York City, including *Morningside Heights: A History of Its Architecture and Development*, which won the 1998 Association of American Publishers' Award for best scholarly book on architecture and urban planning. He is presently completing a book on the redesign of row houses and the evolution of urban neighborhoods in the early twentieth century.

An affluent New Yorker of the early 1930s could wake up in an elegant suite in the Sherry-Netherland Hotel, take luncheon with friends in the luxurious Tapestry Room of the Park Lane Hotel, have tea at the refined Hotel Pierre, and then spend the evening at a formal affair in the palatial ballroom of the Waldorf-Astoria. Unless this peripatetic New Yorker was a careful reader of the real estate columns of local newspapers, he or she would not realize that all of these hotels had been designed by the same New York City architecture firm—Schultze and Weaver. Even today, few visitors to the three surviving hotels—the Sherry-Netherland, Pierre, and Waldorf-Astoria—appreciate that they were all designed by the preeminent American hotel designer of the 1920s and early 1930s. The firm earned an international reputation by using modern skyscraper construction techniques, but embellishing these advanced structures with traditional ornamental forms. This approach enabled the architects to perfect urban hotels that were more luxurious in their appointments and services than any previously erected.

Leonard Schultze, S. Fullerton Weaver, and the Firm of Schultze and Weaver

Leonard Schultze and S. Fullerton Weaver established their architectural partnership in 1921. Schultze had been a design architect and planner with the prominent firm of Warren and Wetmore, while Weaver was a trained engineer and successful real estate developer. These distinctly different professional backgrounds and areas of expertise would prove to be perfect complements in their new enterprise. Although little has been written about Schultze and Weaver, a remarkable archive of the firm's work is part of the collection of The Wolfsonian–Florida International

All architectural design by Schultze and Weaver, except where noted.

All Wolfsonian collection photographs by Silvia Ros, except where noted.

Detail of Schultze and Weaver's final study for the Waldorf-Astoria Hotel, New York, rendered by Chester B. Price, c. 1930 (see fig. 24).

University in Miami Beach, Florida. While few archives of American architects survive, the Schultze and Weaver office records, photographs, and an extensive collection of drawings, including many of partner Lloyd Morgan's extraordinary presentation drawings, provide an especially rich resource for understanding not only this firm's important commissions, but also the architectural profession in early twentieth-century America.

Unlike other successful architects of his generation, Chicago-born Leonard Schultze (1877–1951; fig. 1) did not attend a university architecture school, nor did he study at the École des Beaux-Arts (although he frequently traveled to Paris). Rather, he studied in one of the first Beaux-Arts-inspired ateliers in America, that of the French immigrant Emmanuel Masqueray. Schultze was hired by the architectural firm of Warren and Wetmore in 1903. According to Schultze, he served as chief of design and construction for Grand Central Terminal and its related structures.[1] He was involved in the creation of "Terminal City," the group of masonry office buildings, apartment houses, and hotels that rose above the railroad tracks along Park Avenue. Schultze created a complex that reflected his ideal of a uniform building ensemble where the individuality of each structure was subsumed into a uniform scale and aesthetic, such as he had seen on Haussmann's Parisian boulevards.

A major component of the Terminal City plan was the construction of new hotels close to the railroad terminal, six of which were designed by Warren and Wetmore when Leonard Schultze was chief designer. Two were large transient hotels catering to tourists and business visitors. The Biltmore (1912–1913) was commissioned by the New York Central Railroad and Gustav Baumann, founder of the Biltmore chain. Baumann died a few months after the opening of the hotel and was succeeded by John Bowman. Several years later, Bowman commissioned the Hotel Commodore (1918–1919). Schultze also worked on Bowman's Biltmore in Providence, Rhode Island. Schultze's relationship with Bowman, established during the construction of these hotels, would play a crucial role in the success of his own architectural firm only a few years later.[2]

Schultze was also responsible for Warren and Wetmore's Hotel Ambassador (1919–1921), on the east side of Park Avenue between Fifty-first and Fifty-second streets, one of the earliest apartment hotels that included amenities to attract wealthy households (fig. 2). Designed in a restrained Renaissance style, with street facades clad in white cast stone that imitated limestone—in contrast to the red brick of almost all of the surrounding apartment buildings—the hotel was visually distinctive in the midst of what was rapidly becoming a wealthy residential neighborhood. Elegant public rooms and individual suites were furnished with authentic and repro-

duction antiques, chosen so that the rooms would escape "the stigma of commonplaceness" and provide an environment of "at-homeness."[3] The lessons that Schultze learned while working on the Ambassador provided the basis for the even grander apartment hotels that his own firm would design a few years later, two of which would rise on Park Avenue in the Terminal City zone.

S. Fullerton Weaver (1880–1939; fig. 3) was born in Philadelphia and graduated from the University of Pennsylvania with a degree in civil engineering in 1902. He worked for a steel firm on Staten Island for a few years before establishing the Fullerton Weaver Realty Company, which specialized in the construction of the apartment buildings that were just beginning to lure New York's wealthiest residents

fig. 4
Lloyd Morgan, *Buildings Designed by Schultze and Weaver, Architects, from 1921 to 1936*, photograph of a lost oil painting, 1936. The Wolfsonian–Florida International University, Miami Beach, Florida, The Mitchell Wolfson Jr. Collection. WFIU-147. From left to right, the Hotel Pierre, the Waldorf-Astoria Hotel, and the Sherry-Netherland Hotel.

away from their townhouses. Weaver built at least six apartment buildings, including three palatial structures on Park Avenue in the Terminal City zone. In 1914 and 1915 he commissioned two apartment buildings from Warren and Wetmore, at least one of which—420 Park Avenue (1915–1916; demolished)—was supervised by Schultze. In 1921, following his war service as a major in the army, Weaver joined with Leonard Schultze to form Schultze and Weaver.[4]

The new Schultze and Weaver office was initially staffed almost entirely with architects who had been employed at Warren and Wetmore. In 1926 the staff was augmented by Lloyd Morgan, a graduate of Pratt Institute and the École des Beaux-Arts; two years later he became a partner. Besides playing a major role in the design of the firm's buildings, Morgan was a brilliant delineator, responsible for many of Schultze and Weaver's spectacular large-scale charcoal and watercolor presentation drawings.[5] Staff architects were not Warren and Wetmore's only loss to Schultze and Weaver. The firm also took a major client—John Bowman and his Biltmore hotel chain. Indeed, during the firm's first years in practice, Biltmore projects in Los Angeles, Atlanta, Havana, and Coral Gables, Florida, accounted for over half of their work.[6]

During the 1920s and 1930s Schultze and Weaver gained a reputation as leading hotel designers, not only of apartment hotels, but also of transient hotels, such as the Lexington on Lexington Avenue and Forty-eighth Street (1928–1929), and of luxurious resort hotels, most prominently the Biltmore in Coral Gables (1924–1926) and the Breakers in Palm Beach, Florida (1925–1926). Architect and critic Kenneth Murchison claimed that they "know the hotel problem better than do any architects of this country."[7] However, Schultze and Weaver designed a wide variety of buildings— apartment houses, clubs, office buildings, and homes—as is evident in a spectacular painting by Lloyd Morgan that illustrates all of their buildings designed between 1921 and 1936 (fig. 4). The painting is dominated by the towers of their three great New York City apartment hotels.

The Apartment Hotel in New York

During the nineteenth century, a few wealthy New Yorkers had made their homes in hotels. Andrew Carnegie, for example, moved into the Windsor on Fifth Avenue in 1867 and remained there for more than twenty years.[8] Few hotels, however, catered exclusively or even primarily to permanent or semipermanent residents. It was only in the early years of the twentieth century that a significant number of developers took advantage of the economic potential of apartment hotels, which generally had larger suites than traditional transient hotels. Although these suites lacked the kitchen facilities common in apartments, most included a warming pantry where meals prepared in the hotel's kitchen could be delivered and served by the hotel's staff. Residents could also eat their meals in the hotel's dining room or go out to a restaurant or club. Contemporary commentators saw these hotel suites as "modernized and improved" versions of the respectable boarding houses where many middle-class people had lived in earlier decades, but offering residents the privacy "which neither the boarding house nor the ordinary hotel can furnish."[9] Both the public and private rooms in the first generation of residential hotels were often lavishly decorated with heavy European revival–style furnishings, such as those in the "Looey"-style drawing room at the aptly named Hotel Stentorian rented by the Spragg family in Edith Wharton's *Custom of the Country*.[10]

Proponents of the apartment hotel argued that it solved the "servant problem," since the hotel staff took care of most chores, thus freeing women from "supervising a thousand and one petty details" of domestic life.[11] Others, however, including a critic writing in *Architectural Record* in 1903, warned that the popularity of the apartment hotel was the "enemy [of] American domesticity," causing women to sacrifice the "dignity of their own lives and their effective influence over their husband and children."[12] Nonetheless, the apartment hotel was popular with affluent, upper middle-class households, especially those without children. It also appealed to real estate developers. Since the suites did not have legal kitchens, apartment hotels were classified as commercial buildings and were, therefore, exempt from New York City's stringent housing laws regarding height, lot coverage, fireproofing, and other potentially costly investments. The advantages of building residential hotels rather than apartment buildings became especially evident after the passage of the Tenement House Act of 1901, which strictly regulated the size and character of apartment buildings. In fact, apartment hotel construction surged after the passage of this law, since these hotels could be taller and bulkier than apartment houses.

The peak years for apartment hotel construction in New York came in the 1920s, just after Leonard Schultze and S. Fullerton Weaver established their practice. The popularity of Schultze and Weaver's apartment hotels and similar, if less famous, examples designed by other architects reflected the changing nature of urban life for the wealthy and new realities in speculative real estate in the years just before and after the stock market crash of 1929. Prior to the First World War, most wealthy New Yorkers lived in private townhouses maintained by large staffs. However, by the 1920s architectural critic Matlock Price noted that "the situation has changed, and these houses, no longer an essential part of a changed social fabric, are burdensome, and … uncongenial to their owners."[13] Increasing land values in the townhouse neighborhoods and the difficulty of finding adequate numbers of servants led many to find alternative accommodations. Luxurious apartment houses on Fifth Avenue and Park Avenue (such as those designed by Warren and Wetmore or built by S. Fullerton Weaver) attracted many wealthy households, as did the small and relatively inexpensive row houses in the deteriorated neighborhoods of the far East Side, which were transformed into fashionable homes. Many other families took advantage of improved rail transportation and new automobile parkways, moving to the suburban countryside; in 1924 one architectural critic reported, "Many are leaving [New York] to make their permanent homes in the country, where estates are constantly increasing in size and number, as country life occupies more and more the time and interest of city people."[14]

Some of these converts to country life also kept city apartments, but others maintained suites in the new class of apartment hotel that catered to the requirements of the wealthy. These hotels, built on the city's most fashionable thoroughfares, also attracted city residents who gave up their townhouses or apartments and moved full-time into suites, as well as guests who rented suites for a few weeks or a few months. In 1929, when the popularity of hotel living was at its peak, one writer described its appeal:

> A family with means to pay for the service may close the town or country house, dismiss the servants and by simple process of arriving at one of a score of apartment hotels an hour behind the trunks and bags, may dress for dinner with a full complement of maids and valets—members of the house staff—and therefore continue their accustomed mode of life without the slightest break in the calm course of their living.[15]

Apartment hotels were a popular option for developers in the 1920s since they continued to be unregulated by New York's housing laws and thus could still be far larger than apartment houses. In addition, although most suites only had pantries with refrigerators and sinks, they had carefully placed electrical outlets where residents often installed stoves, illegally converting them to "housekeeping" units, that is, apartments with kitchens. City regulators were well aware of the fact that developers were taking advantage of this loophole in the housing laws.[16] After a 1929 change in the law permitted taller apartment buildings, developers lost

fig. 5
Park Lane Hotel, New York,
view from the northwest,
1924. The New York Public
Library, Astor, Lenox,
and Tilden Foundations,
United States History,
Local History and
Genealogy Division.
945 D4. Photograph
by Omomee.

interest in all apartment hotels except those catering to the very wealthy—
the clientele for whom Schultze and Weaver designed their hotels. During
the 1920s apartment hotels also became important social centers at a time
when the profits from traditional hotels and restaurants were declining
due to Prohibition. In an apartment hotel, residents could be served dinner in their private suites while drinking their own bootleg liquor. These
apartment hotels also frequently included vast rooms for large public
entertainments—weddings, debutante balls, commemorative dinners,
fund raisers, and so forth—that could be profitable even without alcohol.
Schultze and Weaver designed four of the most lavish of this new breed of
residential hotel, where they demonstrated their mastery at combining
elegantly furnished private suites and expansive entertainment spaces.

The Park Lane Hotel

In 1922, only a year after the Schultze and Weaver office opened, S. Fullerton Weaver established a real estate syndicate, with Leonard Schultze as an investor, which took a long lease on the New York Central's property on the east side of Park Avenue between Forty-eighth and Forty-ninth streets.[17] The syndicate intended to build a thirteen-story apartment hotel named Park Lane "to convey to New York all the meaning which London's famous Park Lane conveys to the visitor to that city."[18] At the rear of the lot, the syndicate created a fifty-foot-wide private street dubbed "Park Lane," which provided for off-street deliveries and assured light and air to east-facing apartments. The design of the Park Lane was not innovative. The facades were in a simple Italian Renaissance–inspired style and were constructed of brick and limestone that harmonized with the character of Terminal City (fig. 5). It succeeded, as Matlock Price reported, "in being impressive without being conspicuous."[19] The H-shaped mass of the building, with light courts above the second story facing east and west, broke the street wall of Park Avenue, but maximized the amount of light and air that reached each room.

The Park Lane was planned with suites of two to six rooms laid out to appeal to a wealthy clientele. Rooms were relatively large and, in what Weaver considered an important innovation, even the smallest suite was provided with its own service pantry so that hotel staff could prepare and serve meals, thus "reliev[ing] the hostess of all responsibility."[20] Apartments could be rented either unfurnished or furnished in a simple and traditional manner, much like the suites at the earlier Hotel Ambassador. As at most apartment hotels, the lobby of the Park Lane was relatively small, but richly decorated to resemble the entrance foyer of a palatial private home, with travertine walls, a painted wood-beam ceiling, Persian rugs, and revival-style furniture. Such decor, not unlike that which many of the residents used to furnish their own homes, assured guests that this was an establishment of the highest order.

The Park Lane differed from the Ambassador and most other elegant apartment hotels in that it provided grand public entertainment spaces, including an enormous Renaissance-inspired dining room, the Tapestry Room, extending along most of the Park Avenue frontage (fig. 6). In this "unusually quiet and satisfying environment" residents could take their meals.[21] However, the hotel owners did not rely solely on the fees paid by residents, since the dining room was also open to the public. In addition to the dining room, Schultze and Weaver provided an elegant Louis XVI ballroom at the rear of the building. This room was available for rental to both residents and the general public and had its own entrance on Forty-eighth Street so that revelers would not disturb the hotel's residents.

fig. 6
Park Lane Hotel,
New York, Dining or
Tapestry Room, 1924.
From *Arts and Decoration*
21 (September 1924): 42.
Avery Architectural
and Fine Arts Library,
Columbia University,
New York. Photograph
by Amemya.

The Park Lane opened at an opportune time, with the economy booming and many wealthy households seeking accommodations. In its early years the hotel was extremely profitable. Weaver reported success in renting suites to "acceptable families to whom social atmosphere and environment are prerequisites." The public rooms immediately became popular venues for exclusive social activities. Articles and listings in the social columns reported on both residents and social events: "Mr. and Mrs. Clarence M. Woolley [president of the American Radiator Company] have come from Sunridge Farm, their place at Port Chester, and are at the Park Lane, where Mrs. Maude Emery Smith, widow of the former President of the New York Central Railroad, has also taken an apartment"; "Mrs. Clinton Mackenzie will give a tea and dance … in the ballroom of the Park Lane to introduce her daughter, Miss Cornelia Mackenzie."[22]

The Sherry-Netherland

The success of the Park Lane Hotel and similar buildings encouraged the construction of a wave of new and even larger apartment hotels. Several of these were erected on enormously valuable property along Park and Fifth Avenues, the city's two most exclusive thoroughfares. Developers sought to maximize profits by erecting skyscraper hotels of ever-increasing height. Zoning rules required setbacks as a building rose, but permitted slender towers to rise on one-quarter of a lot. The first of these luxury tower hotels was the Ritz, designed by Emery Roth and Thomas Hastings and built in 1925 and 1926 at Park Avenue and Fifty-seventh Street. This forty-one-story structure was, for a brief time, the world's tallest hotel. Developer Arthur Brisbane hired the Ritz-Carlton chain to manage the hotel and, through its name, lend an association of elegance and refinement.[23]

However, the Ritz was soon overshadowed by an even taller and more luxurious apartment hotel located on an even more highly visible site—Schultze and Weaver's Sherry-Netherland on the corner of Fifth Avenue and Fifty-ninth Street, immediately across from Grand Army Plaza and the main entrance to Central Park (fig. 7).

By the early 1890s Grand Army Plaza had become a center for luxury hotels, with the original Plaza to the west and the Savoy and the Netherland to the east. The Netherland had been erected by William Waldorf Astor in 1892, a few years before he erected the Astoria portion of the original Waldorf-Astoria. Astor and his heirs retained ownership of the Netherland until 1924, when they sold the property to a developer who intended to convert it into apartments and stores. That plan was replaced when developer S. Keller Jacobs acquired the property early in 1926 in order to erect a thirty-five-story apartment hotel. Demolition soon began, but a plan to disassemble the steel frame of the old hotel and reerect it in Florida never materialized.[24]

Schultze and Weaver, working with Buchman and Kahn, a firm active in the design of large industrial lofts and showrooms as well as of modest skyscraper office buildings, filed plans for the 570-foot-tall New Netherland apartment hotel in May 1926. With their experience designing skeleton-frame skyscrapers, Buchman and Kahn probably advised on the structure of the new hotel. However, the conservative exterior design and the interior plan and provision of amenities are quintessential examples of Schultze and Weaver's work.[25]

Jacobs was a builder with no interest in actually running a hotel. Thus, in March 1927, with construction well under way, he transferred ownership to the Sherry-Netherland Company, a subsidiary of Louis Sherry Inc., which was part of the extensive hotel and restaurant interests of the Boomer-du Pont Properties Corporation. Among Lucius Boomer (1878–1947) and General T. Coleman du Pont's (1863–1930) other holdings were the Waldorf-Astoria Hotel and the Louis Sherry restaurant and catering business. The relationship that developed between Boomer and Schultze and Weaver on this project would lead, a few years later, to the commission for the new Waldorf-Astoria. Almost immediately after purchasing the New Netherland, Boomer and du Pont added "Sherry" to the hotel's name. Just as Arthur Brisbane had exploited an association with the Ritz to provide glamour to his hotel, Boomer and du Pont brought to their new apartment hotel the cachet of being associated with Sherry's, a business that had served New York's elite for more than forty years. A little over a month after their purchase of the hotel, a spectacular fire burned the tower scaffolding and damaged the exterior brickwork.[26] Nevertheless, construction was delayed only a few weeks, during which every damaged or even slightly discolored brick was replaced.

The Sherry-Netherland was planned as the tallest residential building in the world, rising 573 feet. At the time of its opening in November 1927, the Sherry-Netherland was the fourth-tallest building in New York. Schultze and Weaver's design, taking full advantage of its height and highly visible site, was one of the first buildings to exploit the setback massing requirements of the city's zoning law to dramatic effect. Its distinctive towered profile advertised the hotel's presence, attracting attention away from both the Ritz, located only two blocks to the east, and the huge mass of McKim, Mead, and White's new Savoy-Plaza rising just across Fifty-ninth Street. Although the massing was innovative, the hotel's design recycled the traditional Italian Renaissance ornament favored by the conservative clientele that was expected to patronize the establishment.

fig. 8
Sherry-Netherland Hotel, New York, presentation drawing by Chester B. Price, view from the southwest, graphite, ink, and colored pencil on board, 40 ¾ x 26 in. (103.5 x 66 cm), 1926. The Wolfsonian– Florida International University, Miami Beach, Florida, The Mitchell Wolfson Jr. Collection. WFIU-77.

The three-story base of the hotel, clad in rusticated, ochre-colored limestone, is pierced by large arched openings, most filled with delicate storefronts of cast iron, polished plate glass, and green marble. The inclusion of stores along the street was possible because of the hotel's location near the northern boundary of the area zoned for commercial activity. Above the base, the building is clad in brick with terra-cotta trim matching the stone in color. The mass of the building rises through a series of setbacks to a soaring slender tower culminating in a steep pyramidal roof crowned by a slender terra-cotta flèche, often described at the time of the building's completion as a "minaret." This crown was originally highly colored. "The brightest point [in the city], at the moment, is the freshly gilt minaret of the new Sherry Netherland Hotel, piercing the sky like a gold needle, shot through the bright new gilt-edged green roof," wrote critic H. I. Brock shortly before the hotel's official opening.[27] The dramatic mass of the hotel, rising from the open space of Grand Army Plaza, created a powerful image, evident in architectural delineator Chester B. Price's spectacular drawing of a sun-bathed Sherry-Netherland rising above the plaza (fig. 8).

fig. 9
Sherry-Netherland Hotel,
New York, lobby, 1927.
From *Architecture* 56
(December 1927): 327.
Avery Architectural
and Fine Arts Library,
Columbia University,
New York. Photograph
by Amemya.

The Sherry-Netherland was planned as one of the most exclusive residential offerings in New York. In the announcement of his purchase of the hotel, Lucius Boomer declared, "It will be the last word in city dwelling places, so exclusive that only about 100 families can be accommodated, and so luxurious that every door will have a gold-plated door knob and every bathroom will have silver-plated fixtures."[28] Indeed, following its opening, architect and critic Kenneth Murchison claimed that the interiors were "undoubtedly the most elaborate and the most costly in this country."[29] As at the Park Lane, the small lobby of the Sherry-Netherland was decorated to create the impression of a palatial private residence (fig. 9). This effect was evident the moment one walked into the outer vestibule, where two relief panels salvaged from the Fifth Avenue mansion of Cornelius Vanderbilt II were installed. In the main lobby, painted panels also from

Vanderbilt's mansion were incorporated into the lavish decor, creating the effect of a Florentine palace, with a groin-vaulted ceiling painted in the manner of a fresco, marble pilasters, bronze grills, sculpted rondels, and Renaissance-inspired furniture.

Unlike the earlier Park Lane and the later Pierre and Waldorf-Astoria, the Sherry-Netherland was not planned with large rooms for public entertainment. Since the site was relatively small, measuring only one hundred feet on Fifth Avenue and 125 feet on Fifty-ninth Street, there was no room for a ballroom. Instead, Schultze and Weaver designed an elegant restaurant of modest scale set on the first story below the level of the lobby at the base of a rear light court. Guests entered by descending a staircase into the skylit room (artificially lit at night), with an arcaded terrace, real and artificial travertine walls, and ornate detailing creating the illusion of a Renaissance courtyard. Typical of apartment hotels of the era, a less formal grill room with a low vaulted ceiling was located in the basement along the Fifth Avenue lot line. The treasure of this lost room was a series of nine tile murals illustrating Aesop's fables designed by Schultze and Weaver and produced in vivid color by Gladding, McBean, and Company of California (fig. 10).[30]

The actual apartment suites were the most important aspect of the Sherry-Netherland design. "It is ideal," proclaimed a prospectus, "for those families who spend much of the year on country estates, but wish a *pied-à-terre* in town … ideal for those who flit about with the social season on both continents."[31] Suites ranged from two to six rooms, with a few single-room units that could be rented by resident's guests and a few small maid's rooms for those with their own staff. A typical floor in the

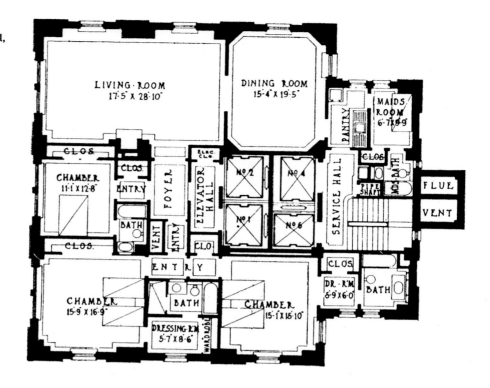

base of the building contained six suites ranging from two to four rooms,
while each tower floor had only a single apartment with living room,
dining room, three bedrooms, three baths, and a maid's room (fig. 11).
At the top of the tower was an eight-room duplex with a double-height
living room, described by Greta Palmer, the *New Yorker* critic known as
"Duplex," as "a stately residence for any millionaire who is not liable to
dizzy spells."[32] It rented for a phenomenal $35,000 per year. The most
desirable apartments were those just above the setbacks, which had
private terraces where a resident could, according to the initial marketing
campaign, host a private tea or an outdoor banquet.[33] The residential
terrace was a new idea in New York in the 1920s, introduced at the Ritz
but even more appropriate at the Sherry-Netherland where the terraces
overlooked Central Park (fig. 12).

The living and dining rooms in many of the apartments were comparable
in size to those in the luxury apartment buildings rising farther north
along Fifth Avenue, although Duplex found the bedrooms to be rather
small.[34] Amenities included wood-burning fireplaces in the tower apartments; gas fireplaces in the units below; modern bathrooms with marble
and tile finishes and newly fashionable built-in shower stalls; and serving
pantries supplied with electric refrigeration and warming closets, conveniently entered by staff from the hall or the apartment foyer so that
residents would not be disturbed while food was being prepared. Although
suites could be rented unfurnished, most were filled with traditional
colonial-inspired furnishings.

		The Management's SERVICE CHART		
			Date October seventeenth	
Apartment	Tenant	Service	Hour	Servant
7 B	Smith	Valet	9:00am	Hawkins
36	Brown	Luncheon 6 covers	1:30pm	Gadd Mously Etwas
12 D	Jones	Dinner 2 covers	7:30pm	Marston
30	Hemingway	Hang Curtains	10:00am	Schwarz
21 E	D'Andrea	Lady's maid	8:00pm	Elise
24	Thompson	Polish personal silver	10:00am	Judd
2 H	Moore	Flowers	11:00am	Marcel
34	Leavenworth	Tea (4)	4:15pm	Behr
23 B	Tripp	Hair-dresser	5:00pm	Agnes
22 A	Snow	Laundress	8:00am	Cecile
18 C	Morgan	Vacuum	8:00am	Humfeld

**fig. 12
(above)
Drawing of Central Park viewed from a terrace of the Sherry-Netherland Hotel, New York. From "The Sherry-Netherland," advertising brochure, c. 1927. Illustrator unknown. The Wolfsonian–Florida International University, Miami Beach, Florida, The Mitchell Wolfson Jr. Collection. WFIU-149.**

**fig. 13
(above, right)
Management's service chart for the Sherry-Netherland Hotel, New York. From "The Sherry-Netherland," advertising brochure, c. 1927. The Wolfsonian–Florida International University, Miami Beach, Florida, The Mitchell Wolfson Jr. Collection. WFIU-149.**

Most important to the hotel's image was the "Sherry service," not only in the restaurants but also in the apartments where a resident could have a meal served, her hair styled, or personal chores performed by chambermaids, valets, ladies' maids, butlers, or other hotel employees. In addition, the staff accommodated residents' transient lifestyles by opening and closing apartments on a few hours' notice. Each day a clerk prepared a service chart that assured that each resident's needs would be met (fig. 13). "Sherry," proclaimed the hotel's original prospectus, "can command the highest quality of service staff…. The Sherry tradition of perfection is drilled into every member of the personnel."[35]

The Sherry-Netherland was an immediate success, in part due to Lucius Boomer's extensive advertising campaign in upscale magazines such as *House and Garden, Vanity Fair*, and the *New Yorker*. These advertisements proclaimed the hotel as "more than a place to live; it is a way of living." They not only boasted of the quality of the hotel's amenities and services but also assured potential residents, "There are economic advantages…. No permanent staff to maintain. No service-quarter rent to pay."[36] Early residents were largely the wealthy bankers, brokers, and merchants that Boomer had hoped to attract, including, in 1930, chemical magnate Dwight Church and Vere S. Smith, manufacturer of Crayola crayons.[37]

fig. 14
Hotel Pierre, New York,
presentation drawing by
Chester B. Price, view
from the southwest with
Grand Army Plaza and the
Metropolitan Club, pastel
on board, 45 ³/₄ x 30 in.
(116.2 x 76.2 cm), 1929.
The Wolfsonian–Florida
International University,
Miami Beach, Florida,
The Mitchell Wolfson Jr.
Collection. WFIU-139.

The Pierre

The success of the Sherry-Netherland and the Ritz, the two buildings that introduced high-rise hotel living combined with service associated with legendary names, inspired the construction of several skyscraper apartment hotels by other developers. Construction began in 1927 on two buildings, the first a rather undistinguished looking though lavishly appointed hotel at Park Avenue and Fifty-ninth Street designed by Goldner and Goldner and named after the legendary Delmonico's Restaurant, and, in the following year, on Bien and Prince's Art Deco–style Carlyle Hotel on Madison Avenue and Seventy-sixth Street. The construction of skyscraper apartment hotels culminated between 1929 and 1931 with two more buildings designed virtually simultaneously by Schultze and Weaver, the Pierre and the new Waldorf-Astoria.

The Hotel Pierre (1929–1930; fig. 14) was the dream of Charles Pierre, owner of an eponymous restaurant on Park Avenue patronized by the social elite. Pierre, "whose first name is considered useless by his patrons and friends," was a Corsican immigrant who, ironically, had been brought to New York by Louis Sherry and had later worked for the Ritz-Carlton, the names attached to two rival hotels. To finance his luxurious hotel and catering facility, Pierre created a syndicate of wealthy New Yorkers that included Otto Kahn, Walter Chrysler, and E. F. Hutton. In February 1929 the syndicate leased a large site on the southeast corner of Fifth Avenue and Sixty-first Street. According to the statement made by the syndicate and quoted in most of the city's daily newspapers, the proposed hotel would "create the atmosphere of a private club or residence" rather than that of a typical hotel.[38]

For this commission, Schultze and Weaver combined the form of the skyscraper apartment hotel previously employed at the Sherry-Netherland with grand spaces for fashionable entertaining such as they had planned for the Park Lane. The Pierre is seventy feet shorter than the Sherry-Netherland, but it appears larger since the deep plot permitted a bulkier building. Schultze and Weaver manipulated the zoning requirements to create a dramatic massing. The building has a solid two-story rusticated stone base that, unlike the base of the Sherry-Netherland, has no stores. Although only one block north of the earlier hotel, it was located in an area zoned for residential construction where stores opening onto the street were forbidden. Thus, the public rooms in the base have rectangular and round-arch windows. Above the base, the building is faced in white brick with matching terra-cotta trim. The massing consists of a series of

blocks with setbacks, leading to a tower. At the top, the tower steps back to create a crown with a rooftop restaurant capped by a copper mansard. The bulk of the tower faces Sixty-first Street, with a slender profile fronting on Central Park. The vista created by the soaring towers of the Sherry-Netherland and the Pierre rising above Central Park is one of the iconic images of early 1930s New York (fig. 15).

To Schultze and Weaver, the creation of a modern hotel that retained a traditional feel was more important than strict adherence to any one style of architecture. Thus, at the Pierre, the exterior is vaguely French Renaissance, but the conservative public interiors freely interpret English Georgian design. The successful planning of these public rooms and the related service spaces presented a complex problem that the editor of

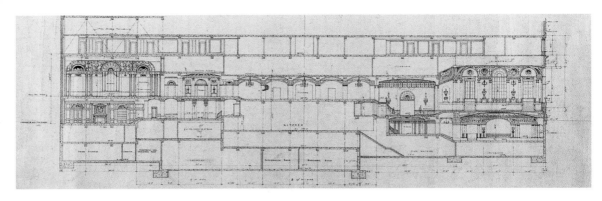

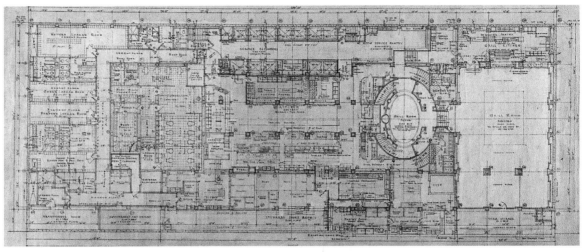

fig. 16
(above, top)
Hotel Pierre, New York,
longitudinal section of the
lower stories, job no. 205,
drawing no. 26, ink on
linen, 29 x 47 ¾ in.
(73.7 x 121.3 cm), 1929.
The Wolfsonian–Florida
International University,
Miami Beach, Florida,
The Mitchell Wolfson Jr.
Collection. WFIU-152.

Architecture felt Schultze and Weaver had solved magnificently, especially since the rooms had to be arranged on a long narrow lot.[39] The architects' mastery of hotel planning is evident in their careful interweaving of the public rooms and related service spaces over several levels and in their designing separate entrances for the restaurants, ballrooms, lobby, apartment suites, and service areas so that those using one of these facilities would not impede those using another (fig. 16). On Fifth Avenue there is a discrete entrance from which a resident gained access to the elevator lobby or to the dining rooms. However, the main entrance for residents was in the center of the Sixty-first Street elevation, sheltered by a large marquee. To the east was the entrance to the hotel lobby with its adjoining lounge, while to the west a door opened onto an oval foyer with double stairs leading down to the dining room and grill room and up to the gallery from which a visitor reached the large and small ballrooms. At the far east end of the Sixty-first Street facade was the service entrance, for employees and deliveries.

Schultze and Weaver incorporated an extensive array of service spaces for the enormous staff employed at the Pierre in the kitchens, laundry, and offices and in service to visitors and permanent residents (fig. 17). In the

fig. 17
(opposite page, bottom)
Hotel Pierre, New York,
plan of kitchen and grill
room floor, job no. 205,
drawing no. 3, ink on
linen, 29 x 47 ¾ in.
(73.7 x 121.3 cm), 1929,
revised 1930. The
Wolfsonian–Florida
International University,
Miami Beach, Florida,
The Mitchell Wolfson Jr.
Collection. WFIU-153.

fig. 18
(right)
Hotel Pierre, New York,
dining room, 1930.
From *Architecture* 63
(January 1931): 27.
Avery Architectural
and Fine Arts Library,
Columbia University,
New York. Photograph
by Richard Averill Smith.

center of the first floor and basement was the kitchen, located between the foyer and lobby and below the ballroom gallery. From there food could be efficiently delivered to the restaurants and ballrooms and to a pair of service elevators rising to the apartment floors. Associated with the kitchen were a host of individual rooms for the preparation of candy, ice cream, pastries, poultry, meat, dairy, fruit, and vegetables, as well as the steward's store room, the scullery, the garbage room, and separate lockers for the elevator and bell boys, porters, cooks, and waiters. In addition, guests could visit the barbers, manicurists, and boot blacks who worked in the basement. On the third floor, Schultze and Weaver provided bedrooms for live-in staff, a sitting room and office for the housekeeper, a dressing room for the maître d'hôtel, a sewing room, a servant's parlor, separate dining and dressing rooms for various levels of employees, and rooms for auditors, bookkeepers, and switchboard operators.

For each of the grand public rooms, Schultze and Weaver adapted a different aspect of the eighteenth-century English Georgian design familiar to the Pierre's wealthy clientele. Walnut Corinthian columns, crystal chandeliers, and Chinese Chippendale chairs decorated the dining room along Fifth Avenue (fig. 18); white oak paneling and a massive pedimented fireplace mantel in the main lounge "present[ed] the quiet richness of a great mansion," while the oval foyer and the main ballroom were decorated with more delicate Adamesque detail.[40] As was typical of hotels of the era, the grill was the most innovative space. Called the Neptune Room, it created the illusion of dining under water, with its ceiling painted vivid blue and its murals depicting marine life.[41]

fig. 19
Lloyd Morgan, *Old Waldorf Superimposed on the New*, c. 1929. From Frank Crowninshield, *The Unofficial Palace of New York: A Tribute to the Waldorf-Astoria* (New York: Hotel Waldorf-Astoria Corp., 1939). The Wolfsonian–Florida International University, Miami Beach, Florida, The Mitchell Wolfson Jr. Collection. 87.1459.2.1.

As at the Sherry-Netherland, Schultze and Weaver gave special attention to the layout of the Pierre's guest rooms, which included single rooms and suites of from two to ten rooms. Contemporary observers were impressed with the large size of the rooms and the expense that had gone into their construction and furnishing. Walls were furred out for recessed bookcases and cabinets, pantries were conveniently placed adjacent to service elevators and halls, and the reproduction Georgian furniture with chintz and damask upholstery was chosen in an effort "to recreate the residential traditions of Fifth Avenue" and "to suggest the private home rather than the ordinary hotel room."[42] So impressed was the *New Yorker*'s critic Duplex that she proclaimed the Hotel Pierre "a millionaires' Elysium."[43]

fig. 20
Outline of the
Waldorf-Astoria Hotel
superimposed on the
power plant and other
buildings on the site,
c. 1929. The
Wolfsonian–Florida
International University,
Miami Beach, Florida,
The Mitchell Wolfson Jr.
Collection. WFIU-154.

Waldorf-Astoria

Almost simultaneous with the commission for the Pierre, Schultze and Weaver were hired to design the new Waldorf-Astoria. The complexity of the Pierre paled in comparison to the demands for the world's largest and tallest hotel, a building with a massive footprint, complex structural requirements, vast service areas, transient and semitransient rooms, apartment suites, facilities for the Junior League and the Canadian Clubs, restaurants, lounges, a multistory ballroom, and function rooms of various sizes. In addition to the physical and design challenges facing Schultze and Weaver was the owner's requirement that the new Waldorf surpass the legendary grandeur and elegance of its predecessor, "a national institution," according to critic Kenneth Murchison, "known the wide world over as the first really great American hotel."[44] Schultze and Weaver succeeded in creating a prestigious entertainment and convention venue and in designing a hotel that became "the pinnacle of luxurious and comfortable living in the most luxury-loving country in the world."[45]

The original Waldorf-Astoria consisted of two adjoining hotels on Fifth Avenue between Thirty-third and Thirty-fourth streets—the Waldorf, which opened in 1893, and the Astoria, completed in 1897 (fig. 19). In 1916 T. Coleman du Pont bought the Waldorf-Astoria, but only after hotelier Lucius Boomer agreed to run it. Du Pont and Boomer retained control until the hotel closed in 1929.[46] At the closing, Boomer retained the rights to the name "Waldorf-Astoria." The idea for a new Waldorf-Astoria is generally credited to Louis Horowitz, chairman of the Thompson-Starrett building firm, who proposed raising the capital for a great new hotel, but only if Boomer would run it and, of course, allow the use of the Waldorf-Astoria name.[47] Although Horowitz may have inspired Boomer to act, it was clear when the closing of the old hotel was announced in December 1928 that Boomer and his backers intended to build a new Waldorf-Astoria.[48] They searched for an appropriate site for more than a year, announcing in March 1929 that the new hotel would rise on the

block bounded by Park and Lexington Avenues and Forty-ninth and Fiftieth streets on land leased from the New York Central Railroad. Planning for and construction of the vast new hotel continued even after the stock market crashed in October 1929. Indeed, incredulous commentators reported that financing had been secured on the very day of the crash. Although this report may not have been precisely true, it added to the aura of inevitability surrounding the construction of the new enterprise.[49]

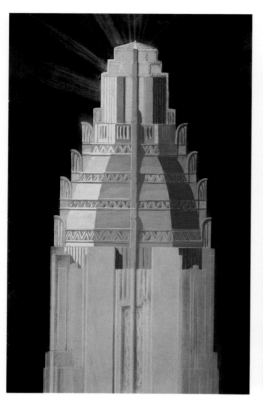

fig. 21
(above)
Waldorf-Astoria Hotel,
New York, final study
of a tower lantern,
presentation drawing
by Lloyd Morgan, color
pastel and tempera on
board, 45 x 29 in.
(114.3 x 73.7 cm), c. 1930.
The Wolfsonian–Florida
International University,
Miami Beach, Florida,
The Mitchell Wolfson Jr.
Collection. WFIU-67.

To build the hotel, the architects first needed to clear the site of a power plant, a YMCA, and other buildings that Schultze had designed a little over a decade earlier while working at Warren and Wetmore (fig. 20). Next, to solve the problem of supporting a monumental building over the New York Central's tracks, they placed 216 concrete footings between the tracks for the steel frame, with lead and asbestos mats to dampen the vibrations caused by passing trains.[50]

Boomer and his architects worked closely, often exchanging multiple letters each day concerning the planning, design, decoration, and furnishing of the building.[51] The architects continuously refined and revised their design concept. In order to conform to the setback requirements of the city's zoning code and to provide all guest rooms with adequate natural light, Schultze and Weaver developed a powerful massing scheme. Four eighteen-story pavilions with wide light courts facing north and south rise from a low base occupying the entire site. The west pavilion, which provides the hotel's main entrance, retains the street wall and general massing of Park Avenue's residential buildings. Above the pavilions, in the center of the block, is a twenty-nine-story slab extending from east to west, designed to resemble a pair of connected towers crowned by freestanding pinnacles with illuminated lanterns which, despite their dramatic form, Schultze insisted "were not built for decorative purposes" but were purely utilitarian, housing elevator machinery

fig. 22
(opposite page)
Waldorf-Astoria Hotel,
New York, view from
the northwest, with
the General Electric
Building to the left and
the Chrysler Building
to the right, c. 1931.
The Wolfsonian–Florida
International University,
Miami Beach, Florida,
The Mitchell Wolfson Jr.
Collection. WFIU-155.
Photograph by Wurts Bros.

fig. 23
(right)
Waldorf-Astoria Hotel,
New York, preliminary
design with Gothic
detail, presentation
drawing by Lloyd Morgan,
view from the northeast,
photograph on
board, 51 x 34 ³/₄ in.
(129.5 x 88.3 cm), 1929.
The Wolfsonian-Florida
International University,
Miami Beach, Florida,
The Mitchell Wolfson Jr.
Collection. WFIU-46.

and water tanks (fig. 21).[52] These soaring features immediately became an important element of the Midtown skyline. Indeed, the impressive mass of the hotel—"dignified" and "overpowering" in Kenneth Murchison's words, especially with its towers complementing the nearby tower of the contemporaneous General Electric Building—is the Waldorf's most important architectural contribution to New York (fig. 22).[53]

The exterior of the Waldorf is relieved by very little ornament, which led Lewis Mumford to bemoan the "dull limestone lower facade which becomes an equally dull brick wall."[54] In their initial scheme, Schultze and Weaver had planned a more ornate Gothic exterior (fig. 23)—as Murchison described it, "a sort of a glorified Woolworth Tower–St. Patrick's effect."[55]

Eventually, however, the overtly Gothic ornament was eliminated.
Instead, Schultze and Weaver adopted a refined Modern Classical style
derived from French sources, now known as "Art Deco," that became
fashionable in New York following the 1925 Exposition Internationale
des Arts Décoratifs et Industriels Moderne in Paris (fig. 24). This
ornamental style is evident in the fins and zigzags of the towers and in
the entrance ensemble with its nickel-silver door frames and screens,
limestone bas-reliefs of female figures symbolizing abundance by sculptor
Charles Keck, and in the winged nickel-silver figure above the central
entrance (fig. 25).

fig. 25
(right)
Waldorf-Astoria Hotel, New York, Park Avenue entrance, c. 1931. The Wolfsonian–Florida International University, Miami Beach, Florida, The Mitchell Wolfson Jr. Collection. WFIU-157.

fig. 26
(top, far right)
Waldorf-Astoria Hotel, New York, Norse Grill, c. 1931. The Wolfsonian–Florida International University, Miami Beach, Florida, The Mitchell Wolfson Jr. Collection. WFIU-158. Photograph by Richard Averill Smith.

fig. 27
(below, right)
Waldorf-Astoria Hotel, New York, barbershop, c. 1931. The Wolfsonian–Florida International University, Miami Beach, Florida, The Mitchell Wolfson Jr. Collection. WFIU-159. Photograph by Richard Averill Smith.

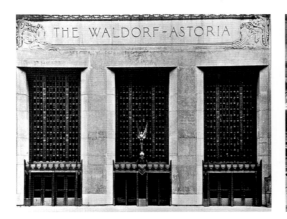

The simple monochromatic exterior contrasts with the lavish, highly ornate interior public rooms, planned as stages for social rituals and the conventions and benefits that attracted an international clientele.[56] These uses were lucrative for the hotel. However, Schultze and Weaver had to carefully segregate the restaurants and nightclub from the ballroom and other function rooms so that a member of the social elite could host a select group at a dinner or a dance "without even knowing that the American Meat Packers may also be disporting themselves under the same roof."[57] Thus, Schultze and Weaver placed the society entertainment venues near Park Avenue. They designated less-fashionable Lexington Avenue for the entrances to the ballroom as well as for a Savarin Restaurant, one of a chain of modestly priced coffee shops owned by the Boomer–du Pont interests; the Norse Grill, an informal restaurant catering to men, with "masculine" Scandinavian-inspired chestnut woodwork (Schultze said it was "done in a Swedish manner") and a mural highlighting all of the golf courses, polo fields, yacht clubs, and other sporting facilities in the New York area (fig. 26); and the vast men's barbershop (fig. 27).[58] The hotel's large lobby was placed in the center of the main floor surrounded by lounges and small shops as a further buffer between these distinct areas of activity.

fig. 28
(right)
Waldorf-Astoria Hotel,
New York, isometric
drawing by Lloyd Morgan,
c. 1930. From Frank
Crowninshield, *The
Unofficial Palace of
New York: A Tribute to
the Waldorf-Astoria*
(New York: Hotel Waldorf-
Astoria Corp., 1939).
The Wolfsonian– Florida
International University,
Miami Beach, Florida,
The Mitchell Wolfson Jr.
Collection. 87.1459.2.1.

fig. 29
(below)
Waldorf-Astoria Hotel,
New York, preliminary
presentation drawing
by Lloyd Morgan for
the main foyer, pastel
and wolfe pencil on
board, 30 x 54 in.
(76.2 x 137.2 cm), 1930.
The Wolfsonian–Florida
International University,
Miami Beach, Florida,
The Mitchell Wolfson Jr.
Collection. WFIU-38.

An isometric drawing of the Waldorf, showing the interior of the hotel.

Below and between the restaurants, ballroom, and other public spaces were the enormous kitchens, storerooms, and other service spaces where hundreds of workers toiled, mostly out of sight, to provide the hotel's clientele with fine food and efficient service (fig. 28).

The circulation through the main public areas off Park Avenue was masterfully calibrated by Schultze and Weaver. The architects placed rooms on various levels connected by staircases and terraces, thus maximizing the dynamism of elegantly dressed guests congregating and flowing through the space. Hotel guests and visitors entered from Park Avenue and ascended a broad stair to the foyer, the hotel's main public reception room (fig. 29). From there, they either continued directly to the elevators and main lobby or turned and climbed one of two low staircases leading onto terraces in front of the main dining rooms—the informal Sert Room to the north, with its Don Quixote mural cycle by popular Spanish artist José Maria Sert, and the more formal neoclassical Empire Room, reminiscent of the Empire Room in the original Waldorf, to the south.

This dynamic arrangement of spaces was heightened by the careful choice of materials—imported marbles, exotic woods, painted murals, elaborate rugs, gilded plaster reliefs, and nickel-silver highlights—and by the use of decorative detail that Schultze noted was in "a simple modernistic" style.[59] The foyer, for example, was ornamented with Modern Classical fluted stone piers, stylized antelopes that leaped across the gilded plaster ceiling, and a frieze decorated with murals by French painter Louis Rigal, featuring stylized figures in scenes representing the Pleasures of the Table, Music, and Dancing. Rigal also designed the foyer's colorful "Wheel of Life" rug (later reproduced in mosaic). Like many of the public spaces in the hotel, the foyer was bathed in diffused indirect light, some reflected from eight elongated silver-leaf urns.[60] Burl walnut elevator cabs with nickel-silver doors led to the Starlight Roof on the eighteenth floor, where a skylight opened on mild evenings, permitting patrons to view the stars through the ceiling grille. Fashionably clad guests in their finery on the nightclub's multiple levels were reflected in gold-hued mirrored walls with tropical foliage painted by Victor White (fig. 30). Originally White had included monkeys, but Boomer strongly objected, fearing that the room would become known as the "monkey house."[61]

To compete with other hotels—including the Pierre, St. Regis, Plaza, and Astor—that provided ballrooms and rooms for weddings, dinners, and other events, Boomer was determined to create the grandest group of function rooms in New York, rooms that would continue the tradition of hospitality established at the old Waldorf. This connection to the earlier hotel was immediately evident in the Silver Gallery on the third floor where Edward Simmons's murals representing the months of the year, salvaged from the Astor Gallery of the old hotel, were installed. The gallery

fig. 30
(right)
Waldorf-Astoria Hotel,
New York, Starlight
Room, c. 1931. The
Wolfsonian–Florida
International University,
Miami Beach, Florida,
The Mitchell Wolfson Jr.
Collection. WFIU-161.
Photograph by
Richard Averill Smith

fig. 31
(opposite page, top)
Waldorf-Astoria Hotel,
New York, Basildon Room,
c. 1933. Library of
Congress, Prints and
Photographs Division.
LC-USZ62-116038.

fig. 32
(opposite page, below)
Waldorf-Astoria Hotel,
New York, main ballroom,
preliminary presentation
drawing by Lloyd Morgan,
pastel and tempera on
board, 34 x 52 ¾ in.
(86.4 x 134 cm), 1929.
The Wolfsonian–Florida
International University,
Miami Beach, Florida,
The Mitchell Wolfson Jr.
Collection. WFIU-88.

led to large and small party and meeting rooms. The most unusual was the Basildon Room, which incorporated ceiling roundels attributed to Angelica Kauffmann and a marble mantel attributed to John Flaxman, all salvaged from the dining room of Basildon Park, an eighteenth-century country house in Berkshire, England. Schultze and Weaver created a new setting for these historic artifacts, even commissioning additional roundels (rather crudely painted), since the Waldorf's room is larger than the room at Basildon (fig. 31).[62] The arrangement of the public function rooms culminated in the three-story-high ballroom spanned by five ninety-foot-long steel trusses (fig. 32). The 265-ton truss over the proscenium arch was at the time the largest and heaviest that had ever been installed in a building. As in the decor on the main floor, the ballroom was a traditional room with an overlay of "restrained modernistic" ornament, highlighted by indirect lighting. The setting served as a backdrop to the social interactions of "gaily dressed people, and the activity of glamorous occasions" that would bring life to the space.[63]

The public rooms were important in establishing the new Waldorf as "the unofficial palace of New York," a social center in the city. Although Boomer and his backers hoped that these rooms would provide substantial income, they only occupied a small percentage of the hotel's floor area. Most of the building was planned with individual rooms and suites for guests. Just as Schultze and Weaver segregated restaurant and nightclub patrons from those frequenting the ballroom, guests were also segregated—transient visitors were housed in rooms on the fourth through eighteenth floors; semitransient visitors, those who stayed for about a month, had rooms on the nineteenth through twenty-seventh floors; and

the towers were reserved for the apartment suites of the permanent and long-term guests. These suites were marketed to the same group sought by the Sherry-Netherland, Park Lane, Pierre, and Ritz—wealthy people who wanted a full-time residence or a pied-à-terre with the comforts of a private house or apartment and the amenities of a hotel.

Boomer and Schultze and Weaver created large, well-furnished rooms with many modern conveniences, such as radio hookups and multiple telephone lines. The one condition that Boomer placed on the designers of the rooms was to avoid a "hotel atmosphere" and to create individually

fig. 33
(right)
Eighteenth-century
French-style living room
of a tower suite, planned
and furnished by Mrs.
Rudy S. Chapman,
Waldorf-Astoria Hotel,
New York, c. 1931. The
Wolfsonian–Florida
International University,
Miami Beach, Florida,
The Mitchell Wolfson Jr.
Collection. WFIU-162.
Photograph by
F. M. Demerest.

fig. 34
(below, right)
Eighteenth-century
English-style living room
of a tower suite, furnished
by Mrs. Charles B. Sabin,
Waldorf-Astoria Hotel,
New York, c. 1931. The
Wolfsonian–Florida
International University,
Miami Beach, Florida,
The Mitchell Wolfson Jr.
Collection. WFIU-163.
Photograph by
Mattie Edwards.

distinct rooms with a homelike environment.[64] "Diversity and individuality
have been sought in the furnishings of every suite," said *New York Times*
critic Walter Rendell Storey, "so that each possesses the atmosphere of a
well-decorated home."[65] To accomplish this, Boomer and his architects
hired thirteen prominent interior decorators from New York, London,
Stockholm, and Paris to furnish the rooms. Most rooms were planned
in either eighteenth-century French or English style, representing a time
when, according to the hotel's publicity, "domestic furnishing attained
acknowledged heights of excellence" (figs. 33, 34).[66] Although the

furnishings and wall coverings reproduced historic pieces, the focus of each suite was an antique marble fireplace mantel purchased in either England or France and authenticated by an expert at the Victoria and Albert Museum or the Musée Carnavalet.[67] Only the large Presidential Suite employed eighteenth-century American Colonial motifs. Once the decorators had planned their rooms, models with every detail were set up for review in a commercial loft or in designers' showrooms so that the architects could be sure that every element contributed to the ensemble.[68]

The homelike atmosphere was augmented by a special nineteenth-floor kitchen where women cooks, the first hired by a major hotel, prepared old-fashioned, American-style, home-cooked meals for permanent residents (fig. 35). Oscar, the hotel's maître d'hôtel, exclaimed, "This kitchen will be for the convenience of those who tire of reading hotel menus and sometimes prefer cabbage and boiled beef to partridge and pheasant."[69] Among many other dishes, the kitchen's menu offered such American fare as "Baked Fish with Creole Sauce as done in Louisiana," "Mutton Pudding (A New England Dish)," and "Chicken Fricassee and Waffles as served in a tavern on the Pittsburgh-Philadelphia Pike."[70]

Boomer and his staff were masterful in their public relations during the planning and construction of the Waldorf, providing periodic news items to maintain public awareness of the new building and generate excitement, culminating in the grand opening of the hotel. New York newspaper articles between 1929 and 1931 chronicled the plan for the Waldorf's private rail siding; designs for a ninety-foot-wide drive that would run through the building and connect Forty-ninth and Fiftieth streets; construction milestones, such as the driving of the first rivet and the start of steel work; orders for the elevators, furniture, telephone and radio systems, lighting, ornamental metalwork, and gold-plated doorknobs; and Herbert Hoover's speech on opening day. *Fortune* was impressed with the shrewd manner in which Boomer kept the Waldorf-Astoria name alive during design and construction, noting how he wrote to patrons of the old hotel asking for advice (and occasionally incorporating suggestions) but, more important, enticing them to become patrons of the great new hotel and commenting on how he had turned Oscar into a major celebrity touring the country.[71]

If the level of publicity on a building's opening is any indication of its success, then the new Waldorf-Astoria was a triumph when it opened its doors on 1 October 1931. Newspapers and popular magazines reported the opening and extolled its amenities, while architecture and furnishing magazines documented and generally praised its designs in many articles, including a series of ninety photographs, drawings, and plans in *Architecture* in November 1931, only a month after the hotel opened. As a result, the hotel succeeded in attracting numerous patrons and major events such as conventions of the National Association of Book Publishers and the American Jersey Cattle Club, and an annual gathering of architects for their Beaux-Arts Ball.

However, the Depression was not a propitious time for the financial health of large hotels. Unable to meet its debt of $5,412,119, the Waldorf-Astoria Corporation declared bankruptcy in 1934. Indeed, all four of Schultze and Weaver's hotels went bankrupt during the first half of the 1930s—the Pierre in 1931, the Sherry-Netherland in 1933, and the Park Lane in 1935. All were reorganized under the bankruptcy laws, with their original management in place. In spite of the fact that the apartment hotel had become an important feature of New York's social world in the few years between the end of the First World War and the onset of the Depression, the financial retrenchment forced on New York's elite and the resulting impossibility of funding large-scale new construction signaled the end of the development of the luxury apartment hotel.

Major changes have been made to Schultze and Weaver's apartment hotels since their opening. Some changes occurred early and were designed by Schultze and Weaver, including the addition of bars when Prohibition ended in 1933. Unfortunately, later changes made by other architects and by new owners were destructive to the hotels' architectural integrity. The public interiors of the Sherry-Netherland have been destroyed, while those at the Pierre have been substantially altered, and those at the Waldorf partially compromised, although several historic interiors have been restored. The Park Lane was demolished in 1965, replaced by a mediocre office tower, although ornamental stonework was salvaged by the Brooklyn Museum. Nonetheless, Schultze and Weaver's skyscraper apartment hotels, once the three tallest hotels in the world, still command attention and admiration. The exterior of the Waldorf-Astoria has been designated a New York City landmark, and the Sherry-Netherland and Pierre are located within a historic district. These buildings created the stage for a new type of urban living by wealthy New Yorkers who were splitting their time between the city and the country. They also provided venues for small-scale private celebrations and large-scale public parties and conventions. While the city has changed all around them, the three surviving hotels continue to serve the city in much the same way that they did when they opened to great fanfare and were considered to be among the most glamorous places in New York City.✧

Acknowledgments

Much of the research for this article was undertaken in the Wolfsonian-FIU's extensive Schultze and Weaver collection and would not have been possible without the extraordinary generosity of the Wolfsonian's curators, librarians, and staff. Special thanks to registration assistant Amy Silverman, who assisted with my research at the museum and located material after I had departed. My research assistant Pilar Davida pursued many leads, Charles Pugh at the British National Trust provided information on Basildon Hall, Jim Blauvelt opened the Waldorf-Astoria's archive, and librarians at Columbia University's Avery Library, the New-York Historical Society, and the New York Public Library graciously assisted with my inquiries. Special thanks to my editor Paris R. Baldacci.

Notes

1. Leonard Schultze, résumé, in "History of Firm," file D-3, Schultze and Weaver collection, The Wolfsonian–Florida International University, Miami Beach, Florida, The Mitchell Wolfson Jr. Collection (hereafter cited as SW); "L. Schultze Dead; Architect Was 73," *New York Times* (26 August 1951): 76.

2. "John M'E. Bowman, Hotel Builder, Dies," *New York Times* (28 October 1931): 12; *National Cyclopaedia of American Biography*, vol. 17 (New York: James T. White, 1920), 10–11.

3. "The Ambassador Hotel," *American Architecture* 119 (22 June 1921): 644–45; see also "Hotel Ambassador, New York," *Architecture and Building* 53 (June 1921): 45–46; "The Ambassador—A Homelike Hotel," *Decorative Furnisher* 40 (June 1921): 59–60; Robert A. M. Stern, Gregory Gilmartin, and Thomas Mellins, *New York 1930: Architecture and Urbanism Between the Two World Wars* (New York: Rizzoli, 1987), 202.

4. "Maj. Weaver Dead; Park Ave. Builder," *New York Times* (2 January 1939): 26; *National Cyclopaedia of American Biography*, vol. 33 (New York: James T. White, 1947), 449–50.

5. "Worldly Known Lloyd Morgan is Praised as Architect-Teacher-Humanitarian," *AIA Journal* 54 (October 1970): 13.

6. "History of Firm: Appendix I," 1922–1926, SW.

7. Kenneth M. Murchison, "The Drawings for the New Waldorf-Astoria," *American Architect* 139 (January 1931): 30. Each partner wrote about hotel design: Leonard Schultze, "The Architecture of the Modern Hotel," *Architectural Forum* 39 (November 1923): 199–204; S. Fullerton Weaver, "Planning the Modern Apartment Hotel," *Architectural Forum* 41 (November 1924): 205–12.

8. For a general discussion of luxury apartment hotels, see Paul Groth, *Living Downtown: The History of Residential Hotels in the United States* (Berkeley and Los Angeles: University of California Press, 1994), 26–55.

9. "Apartment Hotels," *Real Estate Record and Builders Guide* 68 (24 August 1901): 738.

10. Edith Wharton, *Custom of the Country* (New York: Scribner's, 1913), 4.

11. "The Apartment Hotel," *Real Estate Record and Builders Guide* 64 (12 August 1899): 64.

12. "Apartment Hotels in New York," *Architectural Record* 13 (January 1903): 91.

13. Matlock Price, "The Latest Type of American Hotel Apartment," *Arts and Decoration* 21 (September 1924): 41.

14. "Two Notable Houses on Sutton Place, New York," *Architectural Forum* 41 (August 1924): 49.

15. Martin Clary, *Mid-Manhattan* (New York: Forty-second Street Property Owners and Merchants Association, 1929), 81.

16. "Apartment Hotels Worth $300,000,000 Are Held Illegal," *New York Times* (7 October 1926): 1; Stern et al. *New York 1930*, 206–7; Steven Ruttenbaum, *Mansions in the Clouds: The Skyscraper Palazzi of Emery Roth* (New York: Balsam, 1986), 98–100.

17. "Big Leases Pending," *New York Times* (29 April 1922): 28; "Another Big Apartment Hotel to Be Erected on Park Avenue," *New York Times* (10 September 1922): sec. 8, 1.

18. "Big Rush To Finish Apartment Hotels," *Hotel Gazette* 47 (14 February 1923): 10; see also "The New Park Lane," *New York Times* (11 February 1923): sec. 9, 1.

19. Price, "American Hotel Apartment," 41; see also "Park Lane Apartment Hotel To Be Opened in September," *Real Estate Record and Builders Guide* 113 (1 March 1924): 9; "Interior Architecture: An Important Addition to the New Hotel Life of New York City," *American Architect* 126 (25 November 1924): 445–47; Stern et al., *New York 1930*, 207.

20. Weaver, quoted in "Park Av. Changes Made in a Decade," *New York Times* (9 November 1924): sec. 11, 2.

21. Price, "American Hotel Apartment," 41.

22. Weaver, quoted in "Park Av."; "Social Notes," *New York Times* (8 October and 10 October 1924): 19.

23. "World's Tallest Hotel Is Nearing Completion," *Real Estate Record and Builders Guide* 117 (1 May 1926): 11; "The Ritz Tower, New York," *Building and Building Management* 26 (21 June 1926): 47–53; "Ritz Tower Apartment Hotel," *Architecture and Building* 58 (December 1926): 128–29; Ruttenbaum, *Mansions in the Clouds*, 95–113; Stern et al., *New York 1930*, 212–14; New York City Landmarks Preservation Commission, "Ritz Tower Designation Report," prepared by Virginia Kurshan, 2002.

24. Robert A. M. Stern, Gregory Gilmartin, and John Massengale, *New York 1900: Metropolitan Architecture and Urbanism, 1890–1925* (New York: Rizzoli, 1983), 261; "Netherland Hotel Sold by Astor Estate; To Be Made Into Stores and Apartments," *New York Times* (6 December 1924): 1; "May Rebuild Old Hotel in Florida," *New York Times* (21 February 1926): sec. 10, 1.

25. Eli Jacques Kahn did not include the hotel in a monograph on his work, *Eli Jacques Kahn* (New York: Whittlesey House, 1931), nor was his work credited in many contemporary accounts of the hotel's construction. For example, in "$8,500,000 Apartment Hotel to Replace New Netherland," *Real Estate Record and Builders Guide* 117 (26 June 1926), 7, only Schultze and Weaver is credited as architect.

26. "Hotel Netherland Tower Ablaze," *New York Times* (13 April 1927): 1; "38-Story Tower Ablaze At 59th Street Showers Fifth Av. With Flame," *New York Herald-Tribune* (13 April 1927): 1.

27. H. I. Brock, "Color Splashes In the City's Drabness," *New York Times Magazine* (9 October 1927): 8.

28. "New 5th Av. Hotel in Boomer Chain," *New York Times* (8 March 1927): 7.

29. Kenneth Murchison, "Mr. Murchison of New York Says —," *The Architect* 9 (November 1927): 238.

30. Vance A. Koehler, curator at the Moravian Pottery and Tile Works, Doylestown, Pennsylvania, provided information about the tiles.

31. "The Sherry-Netherland," brochure, file B-22, SW.

32. Duplex, "New Apartments," *New Yorker* 3 (28 May 1927), 75.

33. "The Sherry-Netherland," SW.

34. Duplex, "New Apartments."

35. "The Sherry-Netherland," SW.

36. *House and Garden* 51 (June 1927): 41.

37. United States Census, 1930, E. D. 31, 26.

38. Rian James, *Dining In New York* (New York: John Day, 1930), 134; "See Society Trend Back to Fifth Av.," *New York Times* (15 July 1930): 30; "Charles Pierre, Hotel Man, Dead," *New York Times* (9 October 1934): 19; "Gerry Mansion to Give Way to 40-Story Hotel," *New York Herald-Tribune* (9 February 1929): 1; "Pierre Hotel to Rise on Gerry Home Site," *New York Times* (9 February 1929): 5.

39. "The Editor's Diary," *Architecture* 59 (May 1929): 327.

40. Walter Rendell Storey, "Making the Hotel Room More Homelike," *New York Times Magazine* (14 December 1930): 8.

41. The Pierre discussed and/or illustrated in "Hotel Pierre, New York City," *Architecture and Building* 62 (November 1930): 310–11, 319–23; T-Square, "The Skyline," *New Yorker* 6 (20 December 1930): 46; "Hotel Pierre, New York City," *Architecture* 31 (January 1931): 23–32; Stern et al., *New York 1930*, 217.

42. "Hotel Pierre Breaks Down the Efficient Rentable Area Tradition," *Real Estate Record and Builders Guide* 126 (26 July 1930): 8; "The New Hotel Pierre," *Decorative Furnisher* 59 (October 1930): 80; see also "Hotel Pierre," *Architecture and Building*.

43. Duplex, "New Apartments," *New Yorker* 6 (23 August 1930): 50.

44. Murchison, "Drawings for the New Waldorf-Astoria," 28. For the Waldorf-Astoria, see Henry B. Lent, *The Waldorf-Astoria: A Brief Chronicle of a Unique Institution Now Entering Its Fifth Decade* (New York: Waldorf-Astoria Corp., 1934); Frank Crowninshield, ed., *The Unofficial Palace of New York: A Tribute to the Waldorf-Astoria* (New York: Waldorf-Astoria Corp., 1939); Stern et al., *New York 1930*, 223; New York City Landmarks Preservation Commission, "Waldorf-Astoria Hotel Designation Report," prepared by Anthony Robins, 1993.

45. Mary Fanton Roberts, "A New Ideal in City Living," *Arts and Decoration* 35 (October 1931): 50.

46. "Lucius Boomer, 68, Hotel Leader, Dies," *New York Times* (27 June 1947): 22; *National Cyclopaedia of American Biography*, vol. 36 (New York: James T. White, 1950), 289.

47. Lucius Boomer, "The Greatest Household," in Crowninshield, ed., *The Unofficial Palace*, 12–13; Louis J. Horowitz and Boyden Sparkes, *The Towers of New York: The Memoirs of a Master Builder* (New York: Simon & Schuster, 1937), 11–12, 250–51.

48. Several newspaper articles indicated that the Waldorf would be rebuilt; see "Waldorf Is Sold; 50-Story Building to Supplant Hotel," *New York Times* (21 December 1928): 1; "Oscar at Dinner Hints of a Second Waldorf," *New York Times* (22 February 1929): 31.

49. "Arrange Financing for New Waldorf," *New York Times* (3 October 1929): 47; Leonard Schultze, "The Waldorf-Astoria Hotel," *Architecture* 64 (November 1931): 252; "The Editor's Diary," *Architecture* 64 (December 1931): 370.

50. "Waldorf-Astoria," *Architecture and Building* 63 (December 1931): 153.

51. The Wolfsonian's Schultze and Weaver collection includes letters dating from February through April 1931 (file M-1, SW).

52. Leonard Schultze, "The Plan," *Building Investment* 8 (January 1932): 26.

53. Murchison, "Drawings," 33.

54. Lewis Mumford, "The Skyline: Unconscious Architecture," *New Yorker* 7 (23 February 1932): 43.

55. Murchison, "Drawings," 32.

56. The interiors are discussed in Lent, *Waldorf-Astoria*; Francis H. Lenygon, "Furnishing and Decoration," in Crowninshield, ed., *Unofficial Palace*, 33–48.

57. "A Hotel Is Built," *Fortune* 4 (October 1931): 126.

58. Schultze, "The Plan," 27.

59. Ibid.

60. Lester H. Graves, "Planned Lighting in the Waldorf-Astoria Hotel," c. 1930, pamphlet in Waldorf-Astoria file, New-York Historical Society.

61. Schultze, "Waldorf-Astoria Hotel," 295; Boomer to Schultze, 16 February 1931, file M-1, SW.

62. [Basildon Park], *Architectural Review* 68 (September 1930): 114–15; "Old English Ballroom," *New York Times* (8 February 1931): 164; *Basildon Park* (Bromley: National Trust, 2002); additional information from National Trust curator Charles Pugh.

63. "Waldorf-Astoria," *Architecture and Building*, 153; Lenygon, "Furnishing and Decoration," 39.

64. "Furnishing the Waldorf-Astoria," *Progress Bulletin* 3 (April 1931): 2; "A Hotel Is Built," 122.

65. Storey, "Hotel Decoration."

66. "Furnishing the Waldorf-Astoria."

67. Photographs of each mantel are in file W–6B, SW; Lent, *The Waldorf-Astoria*, 76–77.

68. Schultze to Boomer, 5 February 1931, file M-1, SW; "New Waldorf Models its Rooms," *Decorative Furnisher* 59 (March 1931): 53–55.

69. "Women Will Cook in New Waldorf," *New York Times* (25 September 1931): 25.

70. "Home Cooking in The Waldorf-Astoria Menu Suggestions," 1938, Waldorf-Astoria file, New-York Historical Society.

71. "A Hotel Is Built," 60.

Molly W. Berger

The Rich Man's City: Hotels and Mansions of Gilded Age New York

Molly W. Berger is instructor of history in the Department of History at Case Western Reserve University and assistant dean in the College of Arts and Sciences. Dr. Berger is writing *The Modern Hotel in America, 1829–1929*, a cultural history of nineteenth-century American urban luxury hotels that explores technology, democracy, and urban growth. The book is under contract to Johns Hopkins University Press.

On Tuesday, 18 November 1884, the "principal social event" of New York City's season took place, according to the *New York Times*. With three hundred guests witnessing the ceremony and nearly two thousand attending the reception that followed, Miss Caroline Schermerhorn Astor married Mr. Marshall Orme Wilson in the bride's father's expansive art gallery, located at the family residence at 350 Fifth Avenue. The gallery, adorned on this date by "an extraordinary display of floral decorations," served on other occasions as Mrs. Caroline Astor's celebrated ballroom, the capacity of which determined the numeric limit of the "New York Four Hundred," that list of Gilded Age New York's elite society. Before and after the wedding, the city's newspapers described in intricate detail the preparations, gowns, presents, decorations, food, invitation lists, room layouts, procession, wedding trip, and so forth. The gowns worn by the bride, bridesmaids, and bride's mother were all designed by the Parisian couturier Charles Worth. Mrs. Astor wore her diamond tiara and necklace, and, as the *New York Times* described, "the waist of [her] dress was literally covered with diamonds." The bride wore a $75,000 diamond necklace, a gift from her groom, and carried a bouquet of "priceless white orchids, fringed with lilies of the valley."[1] The bridesmaids were "pretty" and the ushers "all well-known society men." Today, one still recognizes many names of those attending: Vanderbilt, Livingston, Whitney, Lorillard, Belmont, Van Rensselaer (figs. 1, 2).[2]

Within less than a decade, being married in an Astor ballroom became a possibility for many New Yorkers, not just those few whose Fifth Avenue addresses and fortunes could accommodate hundreds and even thousands of guests. With the completion of the Waldorf (1891–1893, demolished 1929), Astoria (1895–1897, demolished 1929), Astor (1902–1904, demolished 1967), and St. Regis (1901–1904) hotels, all Astor properties,

Detail of *A Glimpse of the St. Regis Restaurant.* From an advertisement in *Town and Country*, c. 1910 (see fig. 26).

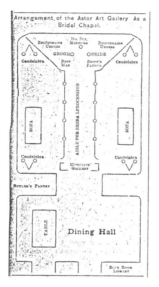

families of comfortable yet relatively more modest means could arrange to have their special celebrations and social events in elegant rooms, decorated in the high style and provided with a level of service that rivaled the infamous excesses of old landed and newer industrial wealth. Thus, as the front pages and society columns compulsively detailed the goings-on of the very richest, other financially successful New Yorkers could participate in similar activities at the city's best hotels. These hotels were a very important dimension of the decades-long building project that began in earnest after 1850 and that, by the end of the twentieth century's second decade, produced the New York City landscape that is familiar to us now.[3] So-called captains of industry imprinted their values and interpretations of industrial society on the city's built environment through their personal residences, office and industrial buildings, corporate towers, cultural institutions, and the hotels that often bore their names. While certainly not alone in these kinds of endeavors, the Astors and the Vanderbilts were the two families who were perhaps the most conspicuous contributors to this project (fig. 3).

This essay will look at the construction of private residences and palace hotels—for the most part those of the Vanderbilts and the Astors—in the period approximately spanning 1880 to the beginning of the First World War, a time during which families with enormous industrial wealth communicated a forceful statement about power, status, and social organization through their architectural projects. The material world that they created served to shape, promote, and reproduce economic and social relationships and the values that underpinned them.[4] These two categories of housing have striking similarities. Indeed, New York's Gilded Age mansions and luxury hotels were, in many ways, the same category of housing, on opposite ends of a continuum that blurred—perhaps in some ways eliminated—analytical boundaries between private and public and between production and consumption. Palatial homes and hotels were the material manifestation of an industrial society that encouraged the transitive quest for social status, comfort, and happiness through ostentatious display and consumption. Within their walls, owners masked the two forms of production that supported the enterprise: the class-defined service work that directly enabled the day-to-day functioning

fig. 3
Henry Janeway
Hardenbergh, Waldorf
Hotel, New York. From
Edward Hungerford,
*The Story of the Waldorf-
Astoria Hotel* (New York:
Putnam's, 1925), 88.

of the houses and hotels, and the industrial production, speculative investments, and severe labor practices that contributed to the production of wealth and exacerbated the disparity of wealth among classes. Luxury hotels became a public venue for extending the very same fruits of industrial society represented by the palace home to the middle classes, whose support was a vital part of the industrial system's success.[5] With their names emblazoned on the doorways and roofs of their hotels, scions of wealth seemed to say, "This, too, can be yours."

While elite private residences have been studied in a number of different ways, there is no scholarship that examines them in concert with the hotels built by the same families during that time. The mansions that went up along upper Fifth Avenue in the 1880s and 1890s had much in common with the luxury hotels that served New York City beginning in the 1830s and continuing through the next fifty or sixty years and beyond. A 1904 article in the *Architectural Record* commending the St. Regis Hotel made this connection explicitly, underscoring its logic when the author stated, "New York has become … the financial centre of the country, the rich man's city, and its precedence as the rich man's city has received full expression in the large number of costly and handsome residences which have recently been erected."[6] With large public rooms on the street level and private rooms above, all elaborately decorated and supported by a parallel network of service rooms, only scale—and the obvious elimination of public services such as railroad ticket counters and stores—distinguished the mansions from the hotels.

Gilded Age mansions have always been the focus of public fascination, and many that survive are protected by the National Register of Historic Places and have been opened for tours by the foundations that preserve them or converted to other uses. The public and commercial status of a palace hotel has kept them classified apart from the mansions. Since their inception, a wide swath of American society has had the occasion to stay or visit. This higher degree of familiarity and access has rendered hotels separate from their private counterparts. This essay seeks to eliminate many of those distinctions. Members of New York society participated in the deprivatization of their lives by issuing invitations numbering in the thousands, leaking details of their events to the local and national press in a way designed to build interest, hiring police to hold back the hordes of onlookers these articles attracted, and even, in at least one example, opening their homes to the public.

Hotels are extremely complicated buildings—materially, socially, and culturally—precisely because they reproduce an elite social order for their clientele through the organization of space. The demand for commercial profits requires that entrepreneurs exploit the comings and goings of the social and financial elite, not only for their business, but also to engage the middle class in similar and very profitable rituals of consumption and theatricality. Thus, a history of wildly elaborate and notorious parties set the stage for the transfer of analogous activities to the new generation of modern luxury hotels, of which the Waldorf-Astoria was only the first.

fig. 5
Isaiah Rogers,
Tremont House,
Boston, 1829.
Warshaw Collection
of Business Americana–
Hotels, Archives Center,
National Museum of
American History,
Behring Center,
Smithsonian Institution.

For example, the Vanderbilt family's "great fancy dress ball" of 26 March 1883, planned to inaugurate Alva Vanderbilt's mansion at Fifth Avenue and Fifty-second Street, was just one illustration of the public being whipped into a frenzy of anticipation and vicarious participation, at least by reading the numerous newspaper articles preceding the event. This was the party that epitomized the social dueling between Caroline Astor and Alva Vanderbilt, and the one where Cornelius Vanderbilt II's wife Alice dressed infamously as "the Electric Light," in a Worth-designed "pale yellow and shell-pink satin dress embroidered with tinsel, gilt and silver thread" accessorized with a diamond-encrusted headdress and battery-lighted torch.[7] Twelve hundred invitations were issued, and on the night of the ball "a squad of Police officers arrived to keep the expected crowd of sightseers in order and direct the movement of drivers and cabmen."[8] Between the revelers, onlookers, police, newspaper reporters, florists, hairdressers, dressmakers, and workmen—some of whom were said to have labored for two months to produce life-size "hobby horses," made of real hides, for one of the several quadrilles—the event engaged the hearts, minds, and hands of literally thousands of New Yorkers (fig. 4). In this way, citizens of the city, the nation, and the world were amply prepared to participate in their own events in the exquisite rooms of the luxury hotel.

Contemporary observers and chroniclers regarded the original Waldorf-Astoria (1893–1897) as a hotel that was different than what had come before. But, in fact, large urban luxury hotels had been a fixture on the American urban landscape since at least the mid-1820s, when Isaiah Rogers, the "father" of American hotels, established the basic architectural program.[9] Thus, a time traveler arriving at Boston's early nineteenth-century Tremont House (1828–1829) would readily recognize the basic features of a modern hotel: ground-floor shops, a distinguished entrance, elaborate lobby, receiving counters and rooms, first-floor dining rooms and bars, and individual rooms and suites arranged along long hallways in the stories above (fig. 5). Less obvious, but equally important, would be the parallel service universe of kitchens, laundries, dormitories, storage areas, and repair shops.

The middle half of the nineteenth century witnessed an incredibly competitive elaboration of the "hotel idea." This was a national phenomenon, well documented by the national and foreign press and mass-circulation periodicals. For example, New York's Fifth Avenue Hotel (1856–1859, demolished 1908), at the intersection of Broadway and Twenty-third and Twenty-fourth streets across from Madison Square, anchored the Ladies'

fig. 6
William Washburn,
Fifth Avenue Hotel,
New York, c. 1859.
Warshaw Collection
of Business
Americana–Hotels,
Archives Center, National
Museum of American
History, Behring Center,
Smithsonian Institution.

Mile and boasted the world's first hotel elevator (fig. 6). It covered more than an acre of land, housed as many as eight hundred guests at a time, and became a center of political, commercial, and social activity. San Francisco's Palace Hotel (1874–1875, demolished 1906) dominated the city's landscape and retained its hold on the title of world's largest hotel for years. More important, it, too, was a significant example of the central role that luxury hotels served for American cities, large and small. Each new luxury hotel did its best to be the largest, most exquisite, or most expensive yet built, even if it was only able to maintain that status for a very short time.

While entrepreneurs, commercial men, and civic leaders trumpeted the hotel's importance and celebrated its excesses, these "monster piles," as they were often referred to in the press, garnered their share of criticism as well. Public remonstrances in newspapers and periodicals warned against the hotel's detrimental effect on women and family life, the inherent danger in the promiscuous mixing between strangers and classes, and, most often, the choice of hotel living by people who could not afford to live this sort of lifestyle if compelled to build and furnish a commensurate house of their own.[10] In an 1859 article describing the Fifth Avenue Hotel, *Harper's Weekly* remarked that "our hotel life is nothing but a sort of barbaric splendor which ruins hotel-keepers, and renders dwellers in hotels infinitely wretched."[11] Thus, this critique was well established long before the Gilded Age's celebrated excesses. In substantial ways, hotel life threatened the American middle-class value system being established in concert with the emerging economic and social structures of an industrializing nation.

An 1873 *New York Times* editorial, entitled "How We Live," made a direct connection between the domestic lifestyle of the post–Civil War industrial elite and that of their children, who chose hotel living precisely because they could not yet afford to conduct such a household of their own:

> This class consist[s] entirely of young people connected with the wealthy of the City, young married couples, whose incomes are quite handsome, but who cannot afford to keep house in the lavish style of their friends and relatives. They demand from the hotels, who find a profit in supplying them, all the extravagant furnishing to be found in private houses, and are willing to pay for this very large sums in the abstract, but nothing, comparatively, to what the same things would cost them if they were themselves the purchasers.[12]

After describing in detail the cost of custom carpets, window coverings, mantels, and ceiling frescoes, the editorial then lashed out again at the hotel-dwellers:

> They have insisted on frescoed ceilings, on gorgeous furniture, on lace curtains, on Aubusson carpets.… They are not satisfied with reps covers or Brussells carpets. No; they must have Cretonne covers and Axminster or Aubusson carpets, with Wilton in the halls and on the staircases. They have bathrooms attached to their bedrooms, dressing rooms, an increased army of waiters to obey their orders, whom they call by electricity.[13]

The newspaper drew a sharp distinction between transient guests, who had every right to expect comfortable and luxurious accommodations, and permanent renters who found themselves castigated for aspiring to a life that was beyond their station. American ideology revered both owner-ship and the single-family home and was offended in multiple ways by those, particularly women, who would give up the sanctity of home and housekeeping in favor of a lifestyle that had not been legitimately earned. Editorial comments such as these forge the link between elite mansions and luxury hotels. Pundits and observers of the time perceived the hotels to be, in this way, a variation of the mansions, albeit one compromised by their place in the commercial and public world.

With the expansion and consolidation of large industrial fortunes, the creation of impressive buildings housing corporate headquarters changed the landscape of the city's commercial centers.[14] Tall buildings such as the Equitable Building (1868–1870), Western Union Building (1872–1875), Tribune Building (1873–1875), New York Times Building (1888–1889), and Pulitzer Building (1889–1890) began the transforma-tion of the city's skyline.[15] Industrialists such as John D. Rockefeller, Collis P. Huntington, and Andrew Carnegie relocated their corporations and families to New York City, further cementing its place as the nation's

fig. 7
George B. Post, residence of Collis P. Huntington, Fifth Avenue and Fifty-seventh Street. From *Munsey's Magazine* 19 (June 1898): 350.

financial capital and contributing to the building boom (fig. 7). Until the advent of the tall office building, hotels had been the tallest buildings in any given city. As they, too, began to soar in height, they contributed to New York's transformation.[16] And a parallel domestic building boom produced the expanse of Gilded Age mansions up Manhattan's spine.

The march of mansions northward on Fifth Avenue was one of several ways that the city's economic and social elite presented themselves to the world. The spectacle of their homes reinforced the social and economic order of the city. The similarities between luxury hotels and the homes of American wealth are found in their material form and their intent. Both were products of industrial society as outlets for expenditure and investment and as sites of technological development and the redefinition of comfort and luxury. As cultural geographer David Harvey observes about capitalist producers, these buildings and the lives of the people who owned them cultivated an interest in excess and intemperance, fueling "imaginary appetites" that contributed to the cycle of wealth production through consumption.[17] In the case of mansions and hotels, the distinction between those who owned and those who merely rented is particularly important in identifying and ordering the players and their contributions to this cycle. Hotels provided an entrée for "regular folks" into an elite world of unlimited appetites, but the power of ownership was never left in doubt as economic dynasties such as the Astors, Vanderbilts, and Belmonts mounted their names in giant letters onto hotel rooftops and etched them into dinnerware.

In 1869 Junius Browne described the long stretch of Fifth Avenue between Washington Square and Fifty-ninth Street as an "unbroken line of brown-stone palaces."

> Block after block, mile upon mile of the same lofty brown-stone, high-stoop, broad-staired fronts wearies the eye…. The stately mansions give the impression that they have all dreamed the same dream of beauty the same night, and in the morning have found it realized; so they frown sternly upon one another, for each has what the other wished, and should have had alone.[18]

In her memoir, *A Backward Glance*, Edith Wharton (1862–1937) described the neighborhood as "this little low-studded rectangular New York, cursed with its universal chocolate-coloured coating of the most hideous stone ever quarried."[19] However, by the 1880s, second- and third-generation Vanderbilts had built seven buildings on Fifth Avenue between Fifty-first and Fifty-eighth streets that punctuated the flow of brownstones. Referring to Cornelius Vanderbilt's new home at

fig. 8
Vanderbilt residences,
Fifth Avenue extending
from Fifty-first to
Fifty-second streets.
The view captures the
spires of St. Patrick's
Cathedral on Fifth Avenue
between Fiftieth and
Fifty-first streets. From
Munsey's Magazine **19**
(June 1898): 349.

Fifty-eighth Street and Fifth Avenue, *Harper's Weekly* declared, "In truth, we have never had in this country an example, in a town house, of architecture so evidently palatial as opposed to domestic."[20] The Triple Palace (640 Fifth Avenue) was the first of these built, a block-long structure on the northwest corner of Fifty-first Street (fig. 8). It was actually home to three Vanderbilt families: the commodore's heir, son William Henry Vanderbilt, and William's two married daughters, Emily Sloane and Margaret Shepard. The father gave the homes to his daughters as gifts. While each residence was separate and private, connecting doors could be thrown open to use the entire structure for formal events.

The house received an inordinate amount of attention from the New York press and was so well known to the public that one historian notes that it was referred to by neither address nor name, but only as "the great house lately built near the cathedral."[21] The *New York Times* reported, "A few Princes and Emperors of the Old World may have more pretentious palaces, but it has been reserved for an American sovereign to eclipse them in the construction of an edifice which, while it contains all that can be desired in architecture and in art, is also replete with everything that contributes to the comfort of a real home."[22] Between six and seven hundred men worked on the mansion during the year and a half it took to build.[23] As was fashionable in both private homes and hotels, every room—and there were fifty-eight of them in William H. Vanderbilt's house alone—had a different themed decor. Rooms included Japanese, Renaissance, Louis XIV, Moorish, and Pompeian styles. Again, the *New York Times* observed, "In all the three houses, there are no two rooms alike in finish or decorations."[24] The first floor included two art galleries, one a two-story room thirty-two by forty-eight feet. Vanderbilt had begun to amass a vast art collection of French contemporary painters as well as old masters.[25] As remarkable as it seems, William Vanderbilt

fig. 9
(above, left)
Richard Morris Hunt,
Fifth Avenue front,
William K. Vanderbilt's
house, Fifth Avenue and
Fifty-second Street.
From John Vredenburgh
Van Pelt, *A Monograph of
the William K. Vanderbilt
House* (self-published
monograph, New York,
1925), pl. 21.

fig. 10
(above, right)
Richard Morris Hunt, detail
of the grand staircase in
William K. Vanderbilt's
house, Fifth Avenue and
Fifty-second Street. From
John Vredenburgh Van
Pelt, *A Monograph of the
William K. Vanderbilt
House* (self-published
monograph, New York,
1925), pl. 13.

opened his two enormous art galleries to the public one day per week, undermining the notion of a private residence. A vast four-story atrium, or grand hall, reached to the roof, with balconies on all four sides. Indeed, one historian noted it "resembled nothing so much as an ornate hotel lobby, all claw-footed chairs, horsehair couches, oriental rugs, marble and gilt."[26]

At the same time that the Triple Palace was under construction, two of William H. Vanderbilt's sons, William Kissam Vanderbilt and Cornelius Vanderbilt II, were also building similarly spectacular homes at 660 Fifth Avenue at Fifty-second Street and at One West Fifty-seventh Street. Architect Richard Morris Hunt designed William K. Vanderbilt's $3 million house after France's Château de Blois (figs. 9–11). Hunt's student, George B. Post, designed Cornelius Vanderbilt II's home (fig. 12). Architectural critic Montgomery Schuyler described the homes for *Harper's Weekly* in 1882, asserting that while the designs had been carried out with "an amplitude of means," nowhere did they degenerate "into profusion or mere ostentation," a curious disclaimer often attached to laudatory descriptions of Gilded Age excess that acknowledged the contemporary cultural critique of industrial capitalism.[27]

Alva Smith Vanderbilt, William K. Vanderbilt's wife (and the future Alva Belmont), used the 1883 opening of 660 Fifth to fight her way into Caroline Astor's social circle. The apocryphal story can be found in nearly every history of the Astors, Vanderbilts, and Gilded Age society. Alva's

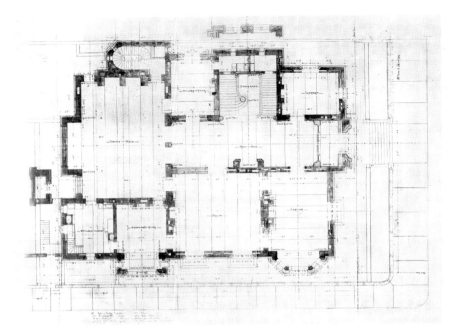

guest list included twelve hundred of New York's "bluest-blooded socialites," everyone except Mrs. Astor and her daughter, Carrie, whose wedding description opened this essay. Alva claimed Mrs. Astor had never called on her. Assuming she would be invited, Carrie had been practicing the star quadrille with her friends for weeks who had costumes designed that were accessorized with electrically lit stars on their foreheads. Not wanting her daughter to be left out, Mrs. Astor, who had been excluding Mrs. Vanderbilt from her infamous New York Four Hundred, finally relented and delivered a calling card to the Vanderbilt home to secure her daughter's place at the ball.[28]

Events such as these received extensive coverage in the daily newspapers and the society journals. For example, the *New York Times* devoted four full columns beginning on the front page to the description of the Vanderbilt ball. Announcements leading up to the events ensured an audience of onlookers, giving the festivities a public character. Despite the seemingly private and exclusive nature of both the residences and the parties (if you consider a guest list of twelve hundred people exclusive), the palace homes functioned very much like public hotels, where there are grand and spacious public foyers that open to the street and more secluded private rooms situated more deeply in the structure. In this case, Fifth Avenue itself served in the same way as the hotel's public entrance and lobby, a place from which the public could not be excluded. The festive awnings, decorative lights, servants in livery, and traffic police were, to an engaged public, scarcely different than what might be witnessed in front of a hotel. And in both venues, private parties retreated to parlors, suites of rooms, or dining rooms where participants could often be seen through lighted windows while remaining protected from direct interaction with those whose attention they courted, even as they disdained the onlookers' company.

The Vanderbilts were, of course, not the only ones to build these incredible homes, although between the various generations and the multitude of town homes and country estates they became the patrons of the period's most recognized architects, among them Charles McKim, Stanford White, Richard Morris Hunt, and George B. Post. In June 1898 *Munsey's Magazine* published an article called "Two Miles of Millionaires." In it, the magazine pictured and described the palatial homes that lined what it called "the backbone of New York from Murray Hill almost to Harlem."[29] The article listed the names of sixty men and women who made up "the two miles of millionaires." They included Russell Sage, Henry Plant, D. O. Mills, Robert Goelet, John Mackay, William T. Astor, Harry Payne Whitney, Andrew Carnegie, George Gould, Charles Yerkes, William C.

fig. 14
McKim, Mead, and White,
ballroom, William C.
Whitney's house, Fifth
Avenue and Sixty-eighth
Street. From *Architects'
and Builders' Magazine* 2,
no. 9 (June 1901): 323.

Whitney, John Jacob Astor, and all the various Vanderbilts and their offspring (figs. 13, 14). Excluded from the list was anyone who lived on one of the cross streets—even John D. Rockefeller, who lived on West Fifty-fourth Street, and whom the article described as "the man who is undoubtedly the richest in New York, and the richest in America, and the richest in the world as to that matter."[30] While *Munsey's* restricted itself to Fifth Avenue addresses, off-the-avenue homes could be as extravagant. Henry Villard's house on Madison Avenue between Fiftieth and Fifty-first streets, for example, included a Saint-Gaudens mantelpiece somewhat smaller in scale than the one the eminent sculptor designed for Cornelius Vanderbilt II's Fifth Avenue third-floor billiard room (now on display at the Metropolitan Museum of Art). Not surprisingly, his parlor was described as "chaste," with "no attempt at ostentation."[31]

Sprinkled among these residences were other kinds of places to live: private men's clubs and hotels. The men's clubs, for the most part equally extravagant, fit easily among the domestic residences. But the hotels were different. During this period, hotels began to rise to unprecedented heights, blurring boundaries in a different way between domestic and commercial architecture (fig. 15). Especially significant was the Waldorf-Astoria at Thirty-fourth Street and Fifth Avenue, the hotel that architecture critics, hotelmen, New Yorkers, and citizens of the world regarded as a landmark. The Waldorf-Astoria was actually two hotels. The Waldorf opened in 1893 and the Astoria in 1897. Upon the Astoria's completion, a large, elegant corridor joined the two, making it the largest hotel in the world. Like his grandfather John Jacob Astor, William Waldorf Astor built the Waldorf on the site of his inherited family home at the corner of Thirty-third Street and Fifth Avenue. His cousin John Jacob Astor IV

fig. 15
(above, left)
*The Up-town Movement:
A Group of Hotels at
Fifty-ninth Street and
Fifth Avenue.* From
*Frank Leslie's Illustrated
Newspaper* 74
(10 March 1892): 101.

fig. 16
(above, right)
Richard Morris Hunt,
John Jacob Astor's house,
Fifth Avenue and Sixty-
fifth Street. From *Harper's
Weekly* (7 April 1894): 317.

lived next door with his mother Caroline, "*The* Mrs. Astor," on the site
at Thirty-fourth Street and Fifth Avenue. Some say that William Waldorf
Astor was a somewhat grumpy man, angry at losing an election to Congress,
and not at all fond of his Aunt Caroline, who some chroniclers claim he
hated. And so he built a thirteen-story skyscraper hotel, reportedly as an
act of vengeance toward "rubbernecking" sightseers who had so disturbed
his life over the years. By erecting a towering commercial building in a
formerly sacrosanct wealthy residential district, Astor reduced the three-
and four-story brownstones to what one historian characterized as "squat
hovels."[32] This, of course, included Aunt Caroline's house. She soon
moved uptown to a Richard Morris Hunt–designed two-family home at
Sixty-fifth Street and Fifth Avenue that she shared with her son John
Jacob Astor IV (fig. 16).

John Jacob Astor IV financed the Astoria, which at sixteen above-ground
floors ranked well among the tall buildings in New York at the time.
With the exception of the American Surety Building, a twenty-story office
tower on lower Broadway, the vast majority of tall buildings were between
nine and fourteen stories. Henry Janeway Hardenbergh (1847–1918),
the Waldorf-Astoria's architect, took pains, however, to distinguish the
new skyscraper hotel from the office towers being built farther to the south.
Hardenbergh differentiated his hotels by treating the German Renaissance
roofline with dormers to evoke a domestic appearance. Montgomery
Schuyler commented, "To set the gabled front of a three-story North
German dwelling bodily above the cornice of a huge nine-story schloss by
way of a dormer was a bold device quite justified by the result"(fig. 17).[33]
The interior was distinctive as well. Hardenbergh emphasized the need
for the hotel to be a place of "amusement." The main feature of amusement at the Waldorf-Astoria was the Palm Garden, or Palm Room, which
stood exposed through glass walls and open doors directly opposite the

fig. 17
(above, left)
Grand stairway, Waldorf
Hotel, New York. From
Decorator and Finisher 22,
no. 5 (August 1893): 174.

fig. 18
(above, right)
Peacock Alley, Waldorf-
Astoria Hotel, New York.
From James Remington
McCarthy, *Peacock Alley,
The Romance of the
Waldorf-Astoria*
(New York: Harper, 1931).

Waldorf's main entrance. The glass walls allowed observers a clear view of New York society, who embraced the Palm Room as their province. Each night, oglers jammed the corridors to watch the fashion parade. Walter T. Stephenson, writing in London's *Pall Mall Magazine*, claimed that "it was perfectly fair to affirm that nearly every adult resident of Manhattan, male or female, excluding the labouring and poorer classes, visited the Waldorf once a week."[34] One historian asserted that on any given day, as many as twenty-five thousand people might move through the corridor known as "Peacock Alley." If a president or prince were staying at the hotel, that number would rise to thirty-five thousand (figs. 18, 19).[35]

The events that opened both the Waldorf and the Astoria were as extravagant as any New York had experienced. The hotel's manager shrewdly ensured the patronage of the city's elite by opening the Waldorf with a society charity ball in support of St. Mary's Free Hospital for Children. The sponsors received more than fifteen hundred guests in the hotel's Marie Antoinette drawing room, a reproduction based on the queen's apartments at Versailles. Mrs. W. K. Vanderbilt (Alva) engaged the New York Symphony Orchestra, which played to one thousand guests seated on one thousand small matching gilt chairs in the hotel ballroom. Fourteen "special" guests gathered in the small private dining room that had been moved from William Waldorf Astor's home and reconstructed in the Waldorf, complete with the family dinnerware and silver service.[36] The Astoria's opening was as spectacular and included a special afternoon

fig. 19
Peacock Alley,
Waldorf-Astoria Hotel,
New York. From *Harper's
Weekly* 44, no. 2256
(17 March 1900): 248–49.

"fairy spectacle and children's dance" held in the ballroom, featuring forty-four little girls aged four to twelve dancing "The Realm of the Rose."[37]

A worried note crept in, however, several days after the Astoria's opening when the *New York Times* reported on the first of a series of orchestra concerts planned for the winter season at the new hotel. The headline lamented, "Society Leaders Present, Boxes Were Filled Early, but the Audience Was of a Mixed Character and Town Toilets Predominated." Despite the presence of society's best in the hotel's ballroom, including Mrs. Astor, the reporter was appalled at the lack of brilliance and fashion.

The reporter observed "the presence of at least fifty women in street dresses, or demi-toilets, with hats and bonnets," who "struck a jarring note, greatly marred the beauty of the scene, and entirely destroyed the desired and hoped-for idea of a brilliant social assemblage." Calling for the establishment of rules "compelling the wearing of evening dress by men and women alike," the reporter was clearly dismayed by the promiscuous mixing of classes that such a public event produced. While box seating to the twelve-concert series cost $350 per seat, a subscription that admitted one to the ballroom could be had for $60, thus expanding the audience.[38] The reporter noted that the event did not compare to such evenings at the opera, the fin-de-siècle site of social contests over box seating between old and new wealth.[39] The comments recognized, if not explicitly or happily, that the hotel was a place where social and cultural events could and would be expanded to include different sets of people.

And so a hotel like the Waldorf—and others that followed—became a curious place. The restaurant achieved a reputation for being one of the places at which society chose to dine. It was said that after seven o'clock, it was impossible to get a table. Peacock Alley became an elaborately decorated set for what cultural historians would interpret as interactive theater. One observer noted in 1903:

> The place is like Port Said as Kipling described it in the phrase that if you stopped long enough there everybody in the world that is worth knowing would eventually happen along. You meet the "magnets" from everywhere in the provinces. You bump into adventurers, pikers, *chevaliers d'industrie*. Money moguls from mule towns are abundant. Senators from the far West are in evidence with wives who still wear big diamond earrings.[40]

The hotel framed an urban ritual characterized by audience participation, broadcast even more widely by society reporters and newspaper commentary. Whether or not we can believe that twenty-five thousand people walked its halls per day, the hotel captured the nation's imagination in a way that allowed many more people not just to read about the high life, but also to experience it.

The Waldorf's maître d'hôtel, known to everyone simply as "Oscar," arranged the balls and dinners, but also advised businesses, alumni groups, national organizations, and "regular" folk on how best to entertain (fig. 20). The hotel's entertainment correspondence describes an array of social events that run the gamut from small weddings with few frills to those with menus engraved by Tiffany's. Oscar responded to explicit directions on replicating and hanging the exact bulldog picture for the Beta Theta Pi reunion while advising groups on how to plan their dances, charity balls, and company banquets in accordance with the highest social standards.[41] Mr. Samuel Blum, whose eponymous company manufactured men's, youth's, boy's, and children's suits, married his daughter off in front of twenty-four guests at $6.00 per plate (in 2003 dollars the equivalent of

$117.21 each).[42] A very small sample of celebrants from the Waldorf-Astoria's 1906 entertainment correspondence book includes the Kenyon Alumni, Kentucky Society, St. Andrew's Society, Sons of the American Revolution, Daughters of Ohio, Barnard College's senior class, Italian Chamber of Commerce, National Board of Fire Underwriters, Lumber Trade Association, and National Association of Stove Manufacturers, a mix of people if ever there was one.

fig. 21
(right)
Machine ironing. From
Jesse Lynch Williams,
"A Great Hotel,"
Scribner's Magazine, **21**
(February 1897): 139.

fig. 22
(right, below)
Clinton and Russell,
the Chinese alcove,
Astor Hotel, New York.
From *Architecture and
Building* **37** (1904): 63.

The hotel was a fluid yet controlled place through which the upper classes moved in parallel with the middle classes. The building's design and customs ensured separate universes. Both groups were served by yet another rigidly hierarchical society of managers, chambermaids, bellboys, waiters, machinists, tradesmen, laundresses, chefs, and dishwashers who lived and worked in that mysterious netherworld known as the "back of the house" (fig. 21).

Other hotels followed in the next ten years that bore the patronage of the Astor family. At Longacre Square, the Hotel Astor and the Knickerbocker (1905–1906) rose to compete with the Times Building, which was completed in 1905. John Jacob Astor had bought the site with a partner in 1803 for $25,000 when it was Medcef Eden's seventy-acre farm.[43]

fig. 23
Maxfield Parrish,
King Cole mural, 1895.
Courtesy of the St. Regis
Hotel, New York.

It was divided in 1890 among third- and fourth-generation Astors. A 1904 *Architecture and Building* article noted that "Longacre Square, or if we follow the modern nomenclature, and take the name that the 'Times' is trying to impose on this plot of ground—'Times Square,' has become one of the busiest parts of the city."[44] The new IRT opened a Times Square station that also had an entrance to the Knickerbocker, marked just as at the Astor Place stop, with a seal incorporating the beaver in reference to the first John Jacob Astor's fur trade.

Architecture and Building mused that the new hotels would eclipse the Waldorf-Astoria. The Astor, in particular, was known for its many themed rooms, including an American Indian grill room, a hunting room, a Pompeian billiard room, an Elizabethan men's lounge, an Italian garden complete with a Mediterranean sky, and a Chinese alcove as well as an East Indian alcove, connected by a Japanese midway. Ballrooms were decorated in Louis XV and Louis XVI styles, and three private dining rooms were designed as yacht cabins (fig. 22).[45] The Knickerbocker, for its part, was "a veritable triumph of Science and Art in every feature of construction and equipment." Its decorations included an Indian battle scene painted by Frederic Remington and a mural of Old King Cole by Maxfield Parrish. Lest anyone not yet know who owned the hotel, King Cole's face was that of John Jacob Astor IV.[46] Today the mural hangs in the bar at the St. Regis (fig. 23).

The St. Regis, designed by Trowbridge and Livingston, was built by John Jacob Astor IV on the corner of Fifth Avenue and Fifty-fifth Street, in the heart of the "Two Miles of Millionaires." At eighteen stories, it rose high above the mansions that surrounded it (fig. 24). The *Architectural Record* observed:

fig. 24
(above, left)
**Trowbridge and
Livingston, St. Regis
Hotel, New York. From**
Architectural Record
(14 April 1906): 552.

fig. 25
(above, right)
**Trowbridge and
Livingston, detail of
main dining room,
St. Regis Hotel, New York.
From** *Architectural Record*
(14 April 1906): 583.

It was not intended to cater to the thousand and one New Yorkers and transient visitors who want a big show for either a good deal or a very little money. It is intended for a class of people, both New Yorkers and transients, who want absolutely the best quality of hotel accommodation and who do not mind paying for it.[47]

The *Architectural Record* recognized the relationship between the hotel and its neighbors and cited objectives to both represent and transcend the standards set by the nearby residences. The architect, owner, and manager of the St. Regis strove for an effect that was domestic, despite the great height, and of the best style, avoiding, they thought, "the sin of decorative excess."[48] The article claimed that "they have made the public rooms rich, handsome and even 'stunning,' but in doing so they have not piled on swollen detail and gaudy colors." And despite the interior style being that of "Louis XV and Louis XVI—as exemplified particularly at Versailles"—the hotel averred, "Nowhere can the charge be made of over ostentation" (fig. 25).[49] The banquet halls, reception rooms, and sitting rooms were decorated with a combination of antique and modern furniture, hangings, accessories, and art objects, all chosen explicitly to "give that spirit of esthetic refinement that is so characteristically present in the home of a man of taste and culture and so necessary to his complete comfort."[50] Acutely aware of the responsibility to create magical surroundings, hotel promotional material described the effect of the ballroom:

> Rich yellow and white Venetian damask hangings relieve the marble, and at a dance or dinner, when the heavy crystal electroliers shed their mellow light and the variegated costumes of the ladies contribute to the ensemble, the effect is most artistic and fairy like.[51]

Advertisements for the hotel featured the restaurant, with its glittering surfaces, elaborate dinner settings, and the bare necks and shoulders of beautifully dressed women in full dinner costume, enticing customers into a world of rarefied social ritual (fig. 26). Despite these boasts, the hotel tread a fine line between distinguishing itself from every other hotel and scaring away customers who might be fearful of exorbitant prices. Advertisements in magazines such as *Town and Country* reassured potential guests that "although the St. Regis Restaurant and its service are acknowledged as the best in America, the charges are no higher than at other first-class Hotels."[52] Single rooms could be had for $3.00 per day.

This essay has, necessarily, only hinted at the complexity of the social and economic relationships that created New York City's built environment and has been able to focus on only a few of the palace homes and hotels

of the Gilded Age. One could easily add the Grand Central grouping of hotels such as the Belmont, Biltmore, and Vanderbilt, and it is embarrassingly egregious to mention only in passing the 1907 Plaza Hotel on Grand Army Plaza between Fifty-eighth and Fifty-ninth streets and Fifth Avenue. These buildings were embedded in political, industrial, economic, and social systems that enabled and created the elaborate architectural projects that characterized the new industrial age. These especially included the proliferating and competitive skyscrapers that created a skyline named and dominated by corporate and industrial power. As important were the vast projects that created an infrastructure for moving people and goods, including the Grand Central and Pennsylvania Stations, the subway, the ports, bridges, road systems, food terminals, communication and energy networks, and vast industrial and manufacturing centers. Palace homes and hotels were the proverbial tip of the iceberg and, as the showiest and perhaps most accessible monuments to industrial society, captured the attention of a fascinated public and served as a lightning rod for public debate on American capitalism's underlying value system.

The first goal of this essay was to make a case for palace hotels and homes as the same kind of building on a continuum of size, development, and ownership. Architecturally, they were similar in design, often drawing from the same architectural influences. Internally, often size was the only distinguishing factor. The same architects and architectural firms designed them, using the same materials, construction techniques, and contractors. Both incorporated commercial-grade technological systems, such as laundry, heating, and plumbing equipment. The arrangement of rooms encoded identical social divisions, those of race, class, and gender. Each was divided into the front of the house and back of the house and all that division implied about the close domestic relations between master and servant. And both were guilty of cannibalizing the world, especially Europe, for exotic materials, entire rooms, decorative items, and *objets d'art*. Moreover, the finest hotels, such as the Waldorf-Astoria, the Plaza, and the St. Regis, established themselves in residential neighborhoods and helped to define those neighborhoods.

The second important point is to recognize that looking at palace homes and palace hotels is another way to look at industrial producers and consumers as a single system. The construction of palace homes was one way that the post–Civil War rich established themselves among the financial and social elite. As the example of Alva Vanderbilt showed, it was not enough to simply have wealth. She used the house—the house as theater— to manipulate her place in New York City's most elite social circle. With their entertainments and other activities, elite families created public spectacles that were at once exclusionary and extended to the public realm. These same wealthy families used hotels such as the Waldorf-Astoria and the St. Regis as venues for charity balls and costume parties, while their young people met there for sorority and fraternity functions and dances and teas. This use accelerated as new wealth permeated the boundaries of elite social circles, thus allowing their inclusion without violating the sensibilities of private society.[53] Edith Wharton captured this perfectly in *The House of Mirth* when the protagonist Lily Bart, in her experience as social secretary to the hotel-living arriviste Mrs. Hatch, "had the odd sense of being behind the social tapestry, on the side where the threads were knotted and the loose ends hung."[54] Just as new wealth could use the palace hotel as a staging area from which to establish themselves, middle-class patrons could indulge their mid-level place in the hierarchy of industrial society by appropriating the luxury hotel as their own palace home. People of less affluence and social standing used the hotel to participate in this same kind of public-private theater, ignoring the disdain of purveyors of middle-class values such as the *New York Times* or *Harper's Weekly* and, indeed, reveling in their ability to socialize in the same places as the elite. However, placing the Astor or Vanderbilt name on top of the hotel reinforced the hierarchy of ownership that extended in a continuum from those who owned the land on which the building stood to those who rented the three-dollar-a-night room.

Of the two building types, the hotel represents the more complex form. Its commercial and transient nature and its undeniable excesses create an undercurrent that is both exciting to people who visit and stay and threatening to those who value ownership over pretense, advocate living according to one's means, and value egalitarian principles. In a single building, luxury hotels can represent the best and worst of industrial society. Often touted as democratic institutions that admit anyone with money to pay, they nonetheless inscribe social inequities among both patrons and workers. Their excesses are as legendary as their comforts, and customers with the least bit of social conscience can never fully enjoy the experience. Yet many hotels become urban monuments that often are dearly beloved by cities and their visitors. The demolition of a private residence is rarely met with the same kind of communal sadness expressed at the destruction of a landmark hotel. Cultural geographer Delores Hayden talks about the life cycle of places as a way to think about how the places come to be. She describes how they are planned, designed, built, inhabited, appropriated, celebrated, despoiled, and discarded and asks us to consider what that process reveals about our social history and cultural identity.[55] Most of the houses I have talked about and many of the hotels have disappeared from the landscape, but their stories can help us to understand what kinds of buildings we value and why.❖

Notes

1. "A Wedding Amid Flowers," *New York Times* (19 November 1884): 5.

2. Ibid.; "Merry Hearts of Gold," newspaper clipping in John Jacob Astor Family Papers, box 3, Manuscripts and Archives, New York Public Library; "Diamonds Amid Roses," newspaper clipping in John Jacob Astor Family Papers, box 3, Manuscripts and Archives, New York Public Library.

3. See David M. Scobey, *Empire City: The Making and Meaning of the New York City Landscape* (Philadelphia: Temple University Press, 2002). While most historians focus on a technologically driven process that began around 1880, Scobey argues successfully for an earlier onset, linked to the institutionalization of the New York City real estate economy.

4. This essay draws on the works of cultural geographers such as Delores Hayden, "Urban Landscape History: The Sense of Place and the Politics of Spaces," in *Understanding Ordinary Landscapes*, ed. Paul Groth and Todd W. Bressi (New Haven, CT: Yale University Press, 1997); David Harvey, *Social Justice and the City* (Baltimore: Johns Hopkins University Press, 1973); Henri Lefebvre, *The Production of Space*, trans. Donald Nicholson-Smith (Oxford: Blackwell, 1991).

5. A similar argument is advanced about world's fairs in Robert Rydell, John E. Findling, and Kimberly D. Pelle, *Fair America, World's Fairs in the United States* (Washington, D.C.: Smithsonian Institution Press, 2000), 8.

6. Arthur C. David, "The St. Regis—The Best Type of Metropolitan Hotel," *Architectural Record* 15 (June 1904): 554.

7. Joanne Olian, "The Gilded Age: The Worth Collection 1860–1918," Museum of the City of New York, www.mcny.org/Collections/costume/worth/worth.htm; "All Society in Costume," *New York Times* (27 March 1883): 1–2.

8. "All Society in Costume"; Edwin G. Burrows and Mike Wallace, *Gotham: A History of New York City to 1898* (New York: Oxford University Press, 1999), 1071–72.

9. *Dictionary of American Biography*, s.v. "Rogers, Isaiah."

10. See Catherine Cocks, *Doing the Town: The Rise of Urban Tourism in the United States, 1850–1915* (Berkeley and Los Angeles: University of California Press, 2001), 97–101. Examples of stories with moral lessons about hotel life include "The Great American Hotel," *Lippincott's Magazine of Popular Literature and Science* 10 (September 1872): 295–302; "Another Glimpse at My Hotel," *Putnam's Monthly* 11 (August 1857): 162–74; "Decline and Fall of Hotel Life," *Harper's Weekly* (2 May 1857): 274; and "Hotel Morals," *Harper's Weekly* (5 September 1857).

11. "The Fifth Avenue Hotel, New York," *Harper's Weekly* (1 October 1859): 634.

12. *New York Times* (22 November 1873): 4.

13. Ibid.

14. See Burrows and Wallace, *Gotham*, 1041–58.

15. Nikolaus Pevsner, *A History of Building Types* (Princeton, NJ: Princeton University Press, 1976), 220. See also Sarah Bradford Landau and Carl W. Condit, *Rise of the New York Skyscraper 1865–1913* (New Haven, CT: Yale University Press, 1996).

16. Landau and Condit, *Rise of the New York Skyscraper*, 15–17.

17. David Harvey, *The Condition of Postmodernity* (Oxford: Basil Blackwell, 1989), 102.

18. Junius Henri Browne, *The Great Metropolis: A Mirror of New York* (1869; repr., New York: Arno Press, 1975), 221–22.

19. Edith Wharton, *A Backward Glance* (New York: Appleton-Century, 1934), 55.

20. "Some New York Palaces," *Harper's Weekly* (7 April 1894): 317.

21. John Tauranac, *Elegant New York: The Builders and the Buildings* (New York: Abbeville Press, 1985), 116. See also *Historic Resource Study, Vanderbilt Mansion National Historic Site* (unpublished paper, 20 September 1999).

22. "The Vanderbilt Palaces," *New York Times* (25 August 1881): 3.

23. Edwin P. Hoyt, *The Vanderbilts and Their Fortunes* (New York: Doubleday, 1962), 234.

24. See also "The Vanderbilt Palaces."

25. For a partial list of art works, see "Vanderbilt's New House," *New York Times* (8 March 1882): 2.

26. Hoyt, *Vanderbilts and Their Fortunes*, 240.

27. "The Vanderbilt Houses," *Harper's Weekly* 26 (21 January 1882): 42.

28. Tauranac, *Elegant New York*, 116; Burrows and Wallace, *Gotham*, 1071–72; "All Society in Costume," *New York Times* (27 March 1883): 1–2.

29. "Two Miles of Millionaires," *Munsey's Magazine* 19 (June 1898): 348.

30. Ibid., 356.

31. Tauranac, *Elegant New York*, 188–220; Robert B. King, *The Vanderbilt Homes* (New York: Rizzoli, 1989), 36.

32. Molly W. Berger, "The Modern Hotel in America, 1829–1929" (Ph.D. diss., Case Western Reserve University, 1997), 286–87; Albert Stevens Crockett, *Peacocks on Parade* (1931; repr., New York: Arno Press, 1976), 42–44.

33. Montgomery Schuyler, "Henry Janeway Hardenbergh," *Architectural Record* 6 (July 1896-June 1897): 364.

34. Walter T. Stephenson, "Hotels and Hotel Life in New York," *Pall Mall Magazine* 31 (September-December 1903): 253.

35. James Remington McCarthy, *Peacock Alley* (New York: Harper, 1931), 61.

36. Edward Hungerford, *The Story of the Waldorf-Astoria* (New York: Putnam's, 1925), 64–65.

37. "Opening of the Astoria," *New York Times* (2 November 1897): 3.

38. "Opening the Ballroom," *New York Times* (13 October 1897): 5.

39. Maureen E. Montgomery, *Displaying Women: Spectacles of Leisure in Edith Wharton's New York* (New York: Routledge, 1998), 30–31.

40. *New Yorker* (February 1903), quoted in McCarthy, *Peacock Alley*, 62–63.

41. The Entertainment Correspondence books of the Waldorf-Astoria are held by the New York Public Library, Manuscript Division. There is a limited finding aid.

42. Waldorf-Astoria Hotel, Entertainment Correspondence, March-December, 1906, A-Z, box 1, Special Collections, Manuscript Division, New York Public Library.

43. Tauranac, *Elegant New York*, 110.

44. "The Hotel Astor," *Architecture and Building* 37 (1904): 50.

45. Ibid., 67. In April 1904, August Belmont II, the IRT's financier, urged naming subway stations after important landmarks, in this case the Times Building, and convinced the city to rename Longacre Square accordingly. Tauranac, *Elegant New York*, 102.

46. Tauranac, *Elegant New York*, 113.

47. David, "The St. Regis," 553–54.

48. Ibid., 576.

49. *The St. Regis Hotel* (New York: St. Regis Hotel Co., 1905), 36.

50. Ibid., 34.

51. Ibid., 33–34.

52. *Town and Country* (12 March 1910): 69.

53. Frederic Cople Jaher, *The Urban Establishment: Upper Strata in Boston, New York, Charleston, Chicago, and Los Angeles* (Urbana: University of Illinois Press, 1982), 275–81.

54. Edith Wharton, *The House of Mirth* (1905; repr., New York: Viking Penguin, 1985), 276.

55. Hayden, *Urban Landscape History*, 111.

Lisa Pfueller Davidson

Early Twentieth-Century Hotel Architects and the Origins of Standardization

Lisa Pfueller Davidson is an architectural historian with the Historic American Buildings Survey / Historic American Engineering Record Division of the National Park Service. She received a doctorate in American studies from George Washington University in Washington, D.C. Her dissertation examined the architectural and cultural evolution of the urban commercial hotel during the early twentieth century.

I n 1922 the British writer G. K. Chesterton observed, "Broadly speaking, there is only one hotel in America. The pattern of it, which is a very rational pattern, is repeated in cities as remote from each other as capitals of European empires."[1] Chesterton (1874–1936), with characteristic paradoxical wit, perceived the underlying "rational pattern" informing current hotel design even as most popular accounts focused on the decorative and technological novelties of each major new urban hotel. Even the more management-oriented hotel journals frequently dwelled on the tension between creating a homelike versus a businesslike environment, with the goal being an elusive balance between the two. This dichotomy pervaded the discussion of hotel development and was part of the larger struggle between narratives of sentimentality and of efficiency in early twentieth-century culture.[2] In spite of rhetoric about preserving a personal atmosphere in the ever-larger urban hotel, efficiency clearly dominated the concerns of architects and managers. Growing out of an early twentieth-century shift toward scientific management, the business-oriented features of hotel architecture prevailed well before they became stylistically obvious in post–Second World War business hotels and motels. Two questions bear investigation. First, what were the sources and form of the rational pattern that Chesterton noticed? And second, how did the concern with efficiency in this period set the stage for standardized hotel architecture? The most prominent hotels of the 1910s and 1920s illustrate the emergence of design formulas that constitute the basis of a remarkably consistent building type. A handful of major architectural firms specializing in hotels—Warren and Wetmore, George B. Post and Sons, Holabird and Roche/Holabird and Root, and Schultze and Weaver—helped usher in design processes for hotels that incorporated the profit-driven concerns of hotel industry

Detail of Statler Hotel postcard, St. Louis, c. 1927 (see fig. 8).

leaders, particularly pioneers of hotel chain management such as E. M. Statler (1863–1928). This melding of early twentieth-century business, architecture, and technology created hotels that were fundamentally modern in their rationalized response to complex functional requirements. The emergence of a standardized logic for hotels helped lead the way toward more sophisticated commercial architecture designed to maximize profits while serving consumers, as well as toward the later mainstream acceptance of a Modernist aesthetic for franchise hotel-chain architecture.

During the early twentieth century, hotel design expressed the architectural transition from Victorian eclecticism to Beaux-Arts classicism, inspired by the academic program of the École des Beaux-Arts in Paris.[3] Beaux-Arts ideals influenced all the major architectural firms specializing in hotel design, both indirectly as the prevailing architectural philosophy of the day and directly through partners trained at the École. Whitney Warren (1864–1943) studied at the École and, with partner Charles Delavan Wetmore (1866–1941), created a large architectural firm specializing in office buildings, railroad stations, and hotels.[4] Leonard Schultze (1877–1951) was a lead designer for Warren and Wetmore during the 1910s and went on to design some of the most prominent hotels of the 1920s under the aegis of his own firm, Schultze and Weaver. George B. Post and Sons, a large and venerable New York firm known for its Beaux-Arts commercial and civic architecture, became a specialist in modern hotels under the leadership of his École-trained sons, William S. Post (1866–1940) and J. Otis Post (1874–1951).[5] Both generations of the Chicago architectural firm of Holabird and Roche/Holabird and Root specialized in hotels, among other commercial and public building types. John Augur Holabird (1886–1945), William Holabird's son, and John Wellborn Root Jr. (1887–1963) joined the firm around 1914 after returning from the École.[6]

One American hotel that Chesterton visited was the New York Biltmore (Warren and Wetmore, 1912–1913), prompting him to wonder "how many national humorists had made the obvious comment of wishing they had built less."[7] Indeed, the Biltmore was one of many immense hotels being built in major American cities. Opened in January 1914 near Grand Central Station, the twenty-seven-story, one-thousand-guest-room Biltmore was one of the growing number of modern skyscraper hotels in New York City, arguably the urban hotel capital of the world. The product of a collaboration between station architects Warren and Wetmore and budding chain hotel entrepreneur John Bowman (1875–1931), the Biltmore also illustrates the role of Beaux-Arts design as an important framework for the modern hotel building type. Although Beaux-Arts training was greatly concerned with the artistic adaptation of neoclassical motifs and forms, it also emphasized the importance of logical circulation and planning for large-scale structures. This combination of historical

fig. 1
Warren and Wetmore,
Biltmore Hotel, New York,
c. 1913. Museum of the
City of New York, Byron
Collection. 93.1.1.5777.

decoration with a rational, hierarchical arrangement of spaces shaped the materials and systems of the early twentieth-century hotel.

Leonard Schultze echoed one of the basic precepts of academic classicism as taught at the École when he wrote in *Architectural Forum* that "the best designed hotels in this country are those which distinctly express in their exteriors the plans of the buildings behind the outer walls."[8] The Biltmore Hotel's exterior composition held true to this ideal (fig. 1). It consisted of a vertically elongated Italian palazzo form containing major public spaces in a five-story block that created the base of the structure. A U-shaped tower shaft containing the guest-room floors rose above. The tower was topped by a row of monumental arches and a decorative cornice, indicating the presence of the formal ballrooms on the upper floors. While this tripartite solution for the problem of adapting historic architectural forms to the modern skyscraper was not unique, it did reflect the state of the art for commercial architecture. According to critic Montgomery Schuyler,

DAPA 25

TYPICAL FLOOR PLAN
OF 4TH, 5TH, 6TH, 7TH, 8TH, 9TH, 10TH, 11TH, 12TH, 14TH & 15TH, FLOORS

fig. 2
**Warren and Wetmore,
Biltmore Hotel, New York,
typical guest-room floor
plan. From *Hotel Monthly*
(January 1914): 45.**

architects could more easily mimic the proportions of a classical column
for hotels because the multifunction interior created opportunities for the
logical division of the facade, unlike the "arbitrary, illogical" divisions
sometimes required in the design of tall office buildings.[9]

Schuyler's detailed discussion of the Biltmore in the trade journal *Brickbuilder* focused entirely on the formal analysis of its exterior composition.
In his concern for the artistic rather than the functional aspects of hotel
design, Schuyler failed to articulate the growing movement in hotel architecture toward formulas and patterns for interior layout based on ideals of
efficiency. The logical and well-established division of commercial hotels
like the Biltmore into lower-level public rooms, guest-room towers, and
an upper-floor ballroom was a familiar pattern starting to be shaped by
more detail-oriented management concerns. *Hotel Monthly* praised the
operating benefits of the Biltmore's regular, square-shaped plan, including
symmetrical layout of corridors with very few turns, easing the circulation
of guests (fig. 2).[10] The U-shaped light well of the guest-room floors
allowed better light and ventilation, creating a large number of desirable
rooms. The arrangement of the lobby and other public spaces on the

ground floor encouraged the unobstructed flow of visitors from the nearby train station and indicated the usefulness of Beaux-Arts *marche*, or attention to the logical circulation of crowds, to hotel design. The Beaux-Arts approach provided a foundation for visual and spatial harmony that later expanded when architects also sought economic efficiency. This shift occurred from the inside out, starting first with the hidden aspects of building design, largely the domain of engineering specialists, and then moving to more visible attributes such as the arrangement and decoration of guest rooms and public spaces.

While hotel architects were versed in the artistic and planning precepts of Beaux-Arts, the large firms considered here also served their fellow corporations in the context of an emerging culture of efficiency. During the early twentieth century, efficiency signified a rational approach to systems and methods that helped bridge the gap between large-scale production and the need for large-scale consumption. Based on engineer Frederick Winslow Taylor's (1856–1915) promotion of a "one best way" for manufacturing methods, Taylorism became synonymous with the belief in efficiency that infused the reform ethos of the Progressive Era. Efficiency did not reflect a spare approach but held that eliminating waste would increase success in nearly any endeavor. The "science" of efficiency became emblematic of the producer side of the growing consumer culture. For hotel architecture, eliminating wasteful design through efficiency became essential to the larger project of encouraging mass consumption of hotel services in the effort to maximize profits. Hotel managers embraced efficiency both to control costs more effectively in the large-scale hotel and to distinguish their new professionalism from haphazard industry practices of the past.[11]

Hotel management first sought to modernize by focusing on new methods of mechanizing guest bookkeeping and tracking supplies, while an understanding of more fundamental operating costs lagged behind. A 1915 *Hotel World* cartoon illustrated construction expenses such as "uneconomical design" and "unnecessary delay" siphoning money away from the hotel (fig. 3). It was no longer enough to hope that an attractive and logical hotel building could be run as a successful business. Hotel architects, in concert with managers and equipment specialists, also needed to create more systematic approaches to efficient hotel architecture; otherwise, the drive for efficient management would be futile. As one business journalist in 1920 noted, "The majority of hotels are a double disappointment—they are neither homelike nor businesslike. A gilt palace run by guesswork is no place even for a millionaire."[12]

WHERE THE OWNER'S MONEY GOES.

The shift in hotel architecture, already well under way with the design of the Biltmore, began with the original grand dame of modern American hotels, the Waldorf-Astoria on Fifth Avenue in New York. Designed by architect Henry J. Hardenbergh (1847–1918) in two stages during the 1890s, the Waldorf-Astoria was the first thousand-room hotel, representing the transition between nineteenth-century "gilt palaces" and twentieth-century commercial hotel architecture (fig. 4). Part of an earlier generation of architects, Hardenbergh became well known for his skill in the aesthetics of apartment and hotel design during the late nineteenth century, but his design for the Waldorf-Astoria lacked the systematic hotel planning of the next generation.[13] In 1925, just a few years before the hotel's demolition, journalist Edward Hungerford declared:

> The Waldorf pioneered, truly. There were few precedents by which its architects and furnishers might be guided. It was a part—and a very difficult part—of their task to establish precedents, to help in that bygone day to win for the house the title of "The mother of the modern hotel." But how perplexing it all was—away back there in 1893. No skilled or experienced efficiency engineer figured so many square feet of space for the kitchen, so many for the laundry, so many for refrigeration—all the rest of it.[14]

Hungerford was clearly influenced by contemporary discourses on progress and thus exaggerated the pioneering role of the Waldorf-Astoria in establishing sophisticated methods for hotel operation. Nonetheless, he was correct in marking the hotel's establishment as a turning point in the development of the industry. While the first-class hotels of the 1890s and earlier, including the Waldorf-Astoria, thrived on a vision of excess and luxury, commercial hotels catering to a broader audience after the turn of the century began to emphasize efficiency in business methods and design as a means of achieving profits and attracting consumers, an increasing challenge as buildings became larger and larger.

Early chains such as Bowman-Biltmore, Hotels Statler, United Hotels, and Boomer-DuPont Properties led the way in embracing modern business methods steeped in the promise of efficiency. Lucius Boomer (1878–1947) assembled several well-known East Coast luxury hotels such as the Waldorf-Astoria and the Bellevue-Stratford in Philadelphia into the Boomer-DuPont chain, but more important, wrote the detailed operational manual *Hotel Management*, first published in 1925. Here Boomer recommended procedures, materials, and accounting methods for every aspect of hotel operation, with the aim of educating hotelkeepers as well as outside investors about the benefits of scientific organization.[15] Boomer also promoted the collective importance of his fellow chain entrepreneurs. Today, major chains such as Hilton, Sheraton, and Ramada dominate the hotel industry, but in 1900 chains owned less than 1 percent of the total number of hotel rooms. By 1930, with the hotel industry expanding dramatically, chains owned 15 percent of all hotel rooms, and their leaders exerted considerable influence on the organizational structure and future of the industry.[16] In this period, hotel chains typically had fewer units than chains of restaurants, cigar stores, or other straightforward sales outlets,

but hotel chain management adapted this business method to a service industry that was far more complex and varied.

As hotel chains developed centralized accounting and purchasing procedures, translating these economies of scale into architectural design occurred more slowly. Many architects and managers railed about the hotel industry's bad financial reputation, caused by inattention to the hidden costs of poorly planned and extravagant structures. Leonard Schultze cautioned:

> The architect must always bear in mind the ultimate cost of the structure. If the appointments and decorations are too expensive and the volume of cubic contents too great, it is sure to prove a financial burden to its operators and ultimately be classed among the failures.... There are others upon which too little money has been spent, which made necessary the omission of many of the essential parts of such a building.[17]

Chains engaged in the construction of multiple hotels led the way toward a more rigorous approach for all aspects of operations, including the planning of new hotels. More precise calculation of construction and potential operating costs became the critical step in hotel planning during the 1910s, particularly when Prohibition removed the economic cushion of liquor profits. On the eve of this major change, John Bowman and the Warren and Wetmore firm applied their prior experience to a more systematic cost analysis for the new Commodore Hotel in New York (1918–1919).

Bowman intended the Commodore, located directly east of Grand Central Station along Forty-second Street, to be more affordable than the Biltmore (fig. 5). A comparison of costs with potential income indicated that 1,750

fig. 6
**Warren and Wetmore,
Commodore Hotel,
New York, typical
guest-room floor plan.
From** *Hotel Monthly*
(January 1921): 38.

rooms would be needed to make a profit; Bowman chose to provide an unprecedented two thousand guest rooms to gain additional profits and publicity. He explained:

> This large number of people includes many who are not used to complete personal service such as the attendance of a valet, and who do not like to be waited upon too much. So the degree of our service which corresponded with the reduced cost as compared with the Biltmore, also corresponded with fair exactness to the desires and business demands of the guests. This great volume as compared with the overhead makes it possible to give say roughly eighty percent of Biltmore service at sixty percent of the prices.[18]

Bowman assumed that his potential clientele for the Commodore was willing, if not eager, to trade elaborate personal service for more affordable accommodations. His decision to create a hotel of extraordinary size was based on the belief that efficient planning and operation would keep service costs from rising proportionally.

High-volume sales covered the overhead costs and allowed lower prices at the Commodore, as did the architects' attention to construction costs. *Hotel World* declared:

> No other hotel in the world offers so much at any price. In the construction of the building the thought has been kept constantly in mind to produce a great hotel that could be operated at a very low cost.... This the architects have been able to accomplish.[19]

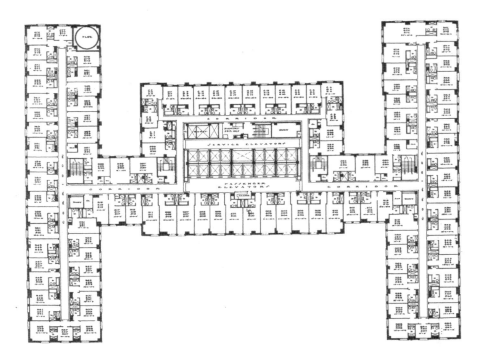

While the trade journal neglected to elaborate on how the architects were responsible for this feat, the plans and descriptions accompanying the article illustrate a number of equipment and layout decisions linked to emerging standardization in hotel architecture, particularly those pioneered by E. M. Statler. Uniform pairs of guest rooms shared bathroom plumbing shafts. One central grouping of passenger and service elevators consolidated space and equipment (fig. 6). Ballrooms were located at the base of the guest-room towers, instead of far from ground level, for ease of access and service. These shifts in the hotel building program indicated the rising influence of efficiency concerns in addition to Beaux-Arts logic. Guests might notice the job specialization of front-office clerks, cashiers, bookkeepers, and other systems designed to serve large numbers efficiently, but the benefits of a rationalized plan remained hidden.

Nearly simultaneous with the Commodore's debut, chain-hotel entrepreneur E. M. Statler opened his first New York hotel, expanding his chain to five properties. The Statler-operated Hotel Pennsylvania (McKim, Mead, and White, 1917–1918), built by the Pennsylvania Railroad across Seventh Avenue from their station, edged out the Commodore as the largest hotel in the world (fig. 7). According to Statler, "its 2,200 rooms give it a big volume of business, and that volume automatically makes a fair and reasonable rate profitable."[20] Statler's casual linkage of volume with profit belied the attention he gave to calculating the relationship between hotel architecture and efficient management. One illustration is the differing character of the interior decoration at the Pennsylvania and the Commodore. *Hotel World* publisher Henry Bohn described the Commodore as "more lighthearted, changeable, ephemeral," while "the average big hotel manager would probably say the Pennsylvania is more 'practical,' of a more durable type."[21] Bohn was comparing, in particular, the lavish greenery, rugs, and marble floor in the Commodore lobby with the columns and decorative glass ceiling in the Pennsylvania lobby. Less expensive and more durable building materials such as terra cotta tiles, terrazzo, cast iron, artificial marble, and stone appeared extensively at the Pennsylvania. Although both these hotels sought to attract a similar middle-class clientele from their respective New York train stations, Bohn suggested that Statler's attention to architectural detail more successfully blended architectural planning decisions and management goals.

Like Pennsylvania Station, the Hotel Pennsylvania was designed by architects McKim, Mead, and White, but Statler had already pioneered a hotel design method with the firm of George B. Post and Sons, particularly architect W. Sydney Wagner (1883–1932). Wagner admired Statler's ability to read blueprints and his encyclopedic knowledge of construction techniques and the latest hotel features. Statler's hands-on approach to hotel development, including visiting the firm's offices in New York and critiquing drawings in progress, earned him the nickname "The Boss"

fig. 7
McKim, Mead, and White,
Statler's Hotel
Pennsylvania, New York,
1919. Museum of the
City of New York, Byron
Collection. 93.1.1.6461.

among the draftsmen. One draftsman, Irving Simon, recalled that "[Statler] could visualize… not only the way the room would look, but where its furniture would be located. He was better than most architects… because he not only could read a drawing but could come to a quick decision as to whether, as represented in the drawing, a room's design was practical."[22] J. Otis Post also acknowledged the contribution of Statler's practical insights on hotel architecture toward "the study of the modern hotel's problems,… [and] the standardization of that which might lead to greater efficiency in hotel operation."[23] Statler's business acumen and keen conceptual grasp was commensurate with that of other self-made entrepreneurs of the time period, especially Henry Ford.

Wagner was newly returned from study at the École when he began working on the Cleveland Statler in 1910. By 1917 Wagner promoted the "Statler Idea" of hotel building in a series of *Architectural Forum* articles. The architect expressed confidence that the details of planning and equipment pioneered at the Statler hotels "point[ed] out the paths by which … the

Hotel Statler
St. Louis

Washington Avenue at Ninth and Saint Charles

Hotel Statler
Boston

Park Square at Arlington Street

final solution of the problems involved in the planning of the great modern American hotel will be reached."[24] Wagner's invocation echoed the Tayloristic vision of "one best way." In addition he urged simplification and standardization of the parts of the hotel to "avoid ultimate chaos as a result of this ever increasing complexity."

fig. 8
(opposite page, top)
George B. Post and Sons,
Statler Hotel, St. Louis,
postcard, c. 1927.
Author's collection.

fig. 9
(opposite page, bottom)
George B. Post and Sons,
Statler Hotel, Boston,
postcard, c. 1927.
Author's collection.

fig. 10
(below)
Statler Hotels luggage
sticker, c. 1928.
Author's collection.

Often presented as a Henry Ford–like figure and passionate devotee of scientific management, Statler's successful marketing of his persona and affordable comfort supported a steady expansion of the chain. A third Hotel Statler built in Detroit (George B. Post and Sons, 1914–1915) initially offered 800 rooms, then another 200 rooms less than a year later. A St. Louis Statler (George B. Post and Sons, 1916–1917) opened in November 1917 with 650 rooms (fig. 8).[25] After the Hotel Pennsylvania, the chain added a new Buffalo hotel with 1,100 rooms (George B. Post and Sons, 1922–1923) and a Boston hotel (George B. Post and Sons, 1926–1927) with 1,300 rooms (fig. 9). W. Sydney Wagner commented on the emergence of a distinctive Statler hotel design:

> Now this similarity in style, together with a studied similarity in the forms and arrangements of the public rooms, corridors, and guest rooms, has given to these hotels a striking family resemblance. The guest arriving at one, after having stopped at another, is immediately impressed with the fact that he is again in a Statler Hotel. There is, in addition to a definite advertising value, a good deal of sound psychology in this principle of intentional similarity.[26]

In this instance the family resemblance of the Statler hotels began with their exterior motifs and decoration, even as each hotel responded to a uniquely shaped site (fig. 10).

TYPICAL FLOOR, HOTEL STATLER-CLEVELAND.

**fig. 11
(above, left)
George B. Post and Sons,
Statler Hotel, Cleveland,
typical guest-room floor
plan. From *Hotel Monthly*
(January 1913): 61.**

**fig. 12
(above, right)
*Details of Standard Tub
and Shower Bath Rooms*
for Statler Hotels. From
Architectural Forum
(November 1923): 217.**

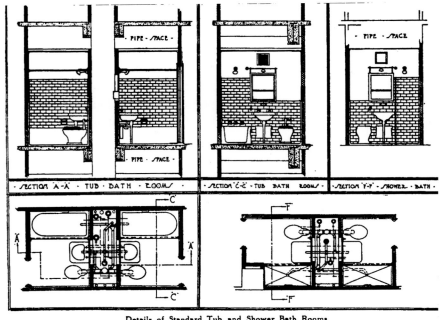

Details of Standard Tub and Shower Bath Rooms
Geo. B. Post & Sons, Architects

The "Statler Idea" in hotel architecture did not create the nearly identical structures identified with standardized chain hotels today, but emphasized a methodical approach to planning, starting with the steel frame and extending to the location of guest bathrooms, kitchens, and other key hotel features (fig. 11). While the placement of steel columns typically dictated the arrangement of guest room floors, "like a poor tailor fitting a suit of clothes," Wagner noted of the Statler hotels:

> This process was reversed. The rooms and bathrooms were planned in standardized double units to conform to requirements of service, and the spacings of the structural steel columns were then so planned as to become part and servant of this standard arrangement. This may have involved the use of a few additional pounds of steel. But what was the resulting gain?[27]

By making the functional plan primary to hotel design, rather than the least expensive arrangement of the structural steel frame, the Statler hotels claimed long-term benefits in efficient operation. Another telling incident was the complete redesign of the steelwork for the Boston Statler to take advantage of newly advanced standards issued by the American Steel Institute. The lighter steel frame allowed for the regular size and placement of rows of guest rooms while saving approximately one thousand tons of expensive structural material.[28]

The Statler chain was first famous for its slogan of "A Room and a Bath for a Dollar and Half" to promote a popular amenity at a time when shared bathrooms were common, even in some luxury hotels. At Statler

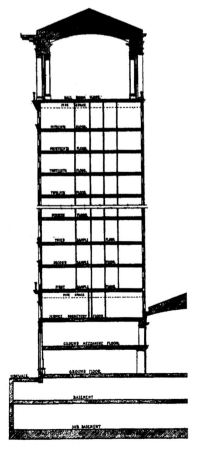

fig. 13
George B. Post and Sons,
Statler Hotel, St. Louis,
section drawing. From
Architectural Forum
(December 1917): 165.

hotels, as at the Commodore, bathrooms were arranged in pairs to share a plumbing shaft that could be easily accessed for repairs (fig. 12). Limiting the room type and size created a regular, more cost-efficient floor plan that offset the expense of individual bathrooms. In addition, the space saved by not having public restrooms on each floor allowed Statler to have more rentable rooms. This deceptively simple concept, known to some architects as the "Statler plumbing shaft," seems to have been introduced by Statler in Buffalo at his first hotel (Esenwein and Johnson, 1907) and then widely applied by George B. Post and Sons and other hotel architects such as Warren and Wetmore. Statler commented in an interview that even though the Commodore adopted his paired bath arrangement, smaller areas allotted to the pipe rooms at the rival hotel meant that later plumbing renovations were much more expensive than similar work at the Hotel Pennsylvania.[29]

The division of hotels into related functional zones in the lower floors, towers, and upper floors, and the efficient flow between these zones, was becoming more precise and organized. At the Statler hotels the service and passenger elevators were grouped in one area to share mechanical equipment and to provide better service than staff elevators tucked away in distant corners of the hotel. The Commodore's elevators had a similar arrangement, in contrast to the multiple elevator locations in the Biltmore. Statler also pioneered separate sample-room floors to keep spaces dedicated to traveling salesmen away from regular guest rooms; previously, sample rooms filled irregular spaces on all guest-room floors. Each guest-room floor could then be standardized according to its purpose, while sample-room floors created a buffer between the staff dormitory and regular guest-room floors (fig. 13).[30] Although the chain had only seven properties at the time of Statler's death in 1928, a tiny grouping compared to later hotel chains, attention to his methods made these hotels widely influential.

In addition to their profitable collaboration with Statler, George B. Post and Sons led the way in developing hotel architecture based on precise cost accounting. Accountant Edward Horwath, whose firm became prominent specialists in hotel accounting during the 1910s, helped Post analyze his commercial structures with modern cost-accounting principles and later determine the cost per square foot of hotel room units.[31] The ability to make this type of calculation proved essential to the planning of a new hotel. By the 1920s a new, systematic approach to controlling costs through efficiency emerged as a key factor in hotel design, beyond the usual vague concerns with construction budgets. From this foundation, the Post firm became known for careful attention to the details of hotel management:

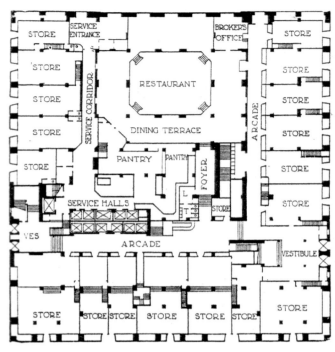

fig. 14
(above, left)
United Hotels Company
advertisement. From
Hotel Monthly **(March**
1925): 113. Courtesy of the
Cornell University Library.

fig. 15
(above, right)
George B. Post and Sons,
Roosevelt Hotel, New
York, ground-floor plan.
From *Architectural Forum*
(December 1929): 678

It was up to [the architects]… to have the structure not alone a thing of beauty, but essentially a thing of use; to have maximum earning qualities…. Few architects have mastered the details of hotel design and construction to these ends; but George B. Post and Sons have gone about it the right way. They have made a careful study of hotel requirements…, they have listened carefully to their clients as to the actual needs, and have produced near perfect hotel structures.[32]

The firm's expertise in hotel design attracted more major commissions, most notably the structures designed for another important early chain, the United Hotels Company. Founded in 1910 by lawyer Frank Dudley, this chain was one of the largest in the country by 1926.[33] Functioning as a holding company, United Hotels acquired existing hotels and built new ones. Many early properties were located in smaller cities, but by the 1920s the chain also included large new hotels designed by George B. Post and Sons in New York (the Roosevelt, 1924, 1,100 rooms), and Seattle (the Olympic, 1924, 600 rooms). Although United hotels were over-whelmingly concentrated in the Northeast, construction of the Olympic allowed the company to advertise "The United Hotels Trail—across the continent a mighty chain of service!" (fig. 14).

Like Post and Sons' calculation of architectural costs, the United chain sought to quantify information for decisions once dependent on vague traditions. When choosing a new location, United looked for growing areas with diversified economies and year-round business, using data from traffic surveys, questionnaires, and local business statistics to determine whether to locate in that place and to calculate how large the new hotel should be. Dudley emphasized this methodical approach as a means to bring the "hotel business into modern business practice."[34]

Eliminating wasted and therefore unprofitable space from the hotel plan was key to establishing modern business practice for hotels. United Hotels Managing Director Horace Leland Wiggins wrote in *Architectural Forum* that "a basic test of the efficiency of a hotel plan from the standpoint of profitable operation is the amount of cubic footage it contains in comparison with the number of guests the building will accommodate."[35] A stricter accounting of profitable cubic footage encouraged development of the typical ground floor for income-earning potential. According to J. Otis Post, his firm's design for United Hotels' Hotel Roosevelt established the importance of ground-floor retail space, at least in dense urban areas such as New York or Chicago (fig. 15).[36] At United's Olympic, Buffalo and Boston Statlers, and numerous other Post and Sons hotels built during the 1920s, the lobby shifted from the ground floor to a raised first floor. Having rentable retail space on the ground level proved so desirable in New York that the old Waldorf-Astoria, the Biltmore, and the Astor (Clinton and Russell, 1904) all engaged in expensive remodeling to incorporate this new layout.[37] Another example was the new Palmer House (Holabird and Roche, 1924–1926) in Chicago. While the old Palmer House featured the nineteenth-century arrangement with the main entrance opening directly into the lobby, the raised first-floor Great Hall of the new hotel formed the very center of the building plan and was accessible only after walking along one of the ground-floor shopping arcades or up a staircase from the Monroe Street entrance (fig. 16).

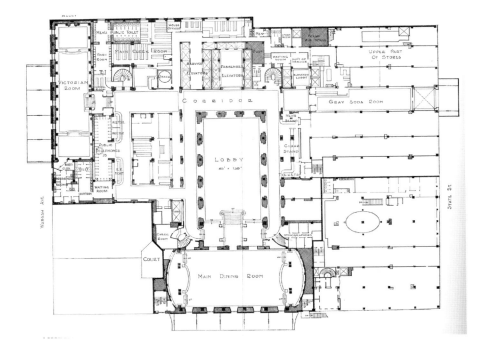

fig. 17
(right)
Holabird and Roche,
Hotel Schroeder,
Milwaukee. From
Randolph Williams
Sexton, *American
Apartment Houses,
Hotels, and Apartment
Hotels of Today* (New
York: Architectural Book
Publishing, 1929), 177.
Courtesy of the Cornell
University Library.

fig. 18
(far right)
Holabird and Roche,
Palmer House, Chicago,
construction view
showing the old and
new hotels. From *Hotel
World* (7 May 1925): 15.
Courtesy of the Cornell
University Library.

As this important semipublic space now focused inward, the realities of
large-scale real estate development and mixed-use hotel needs took precedence over the public monumentality of the institution.

During the 1920s Holabird and Roche designed progressively larger and
more modern hotels, including the new Palmer House (2,268 rooms) and
the Stevens Hotel (1925–1927, 3,000 rooms), each the largest hotel in
the world when built. Frank Long, chief draftsman and lead designer on
many of the firm's hotel projects, readily acknowledged the contribution
of his hotel manager clients, as well as other industry leaders:

> Holabird and Root have much reason to thank such hotel operators as
> Mr. E. J. Stevens … for who they have built, and many others thru
> who they have gained ideas and a measure of insight into the business….
> Such decisions can be made jointly by experienced architects and
> experienced operators. It is worth much to these men to know the
> opinions of Mr. Statler and other operators on many questions, to
> know what Post and other architects of standing have done.[38]

Holabird and Roche's technical prowess and flexible attitude toward style
perfectly matched the business goals of their hotel clients. The firm's
contribution to the development of American architecture, like that of
their commercial peers, is often couched in terms of engineering, not
aesthetic, skill.

Although the hotels designed by Holabird and Roche do not exhibit the
frank machine aesthetic associated with avant-garde Modernism, they
share an embrace of sophisticated engineering and modern materials.
By the 1920s the firm's designs typically featured boxy forms and flat,

fig. 19
(above, left)
Holabird and Roche,
Palmer House, Chicago.
From *Hotel Monthly*
(October 1927): 31.
Courtesy of the Cornell
University Library.

fig. 20
(above, right)
Holabird and Roche/
Holabird and Root,
Stevens Hotel, Chicago,
construction view. From
Hotel Monthly **(March**
1926): 35. Courtesy of the
Cornell University Library.

stylized exterior decoration enclosing a complex interior layout (fig. 17). Perhaps most challenging was the structural system for the new Palmer House, which needed to be configured to allow the hotel to operate during its reconstruction (fig. 18). By scheduling the demolition of the 1872 building in stages and grouping the major spaces (lobby, ballroom, kitchen) into one section of the new building, service continued at a remarkably uninterrupted pace while a replacement hotel rose on the same site.[39] The new State Street frontage, with five stories of retail shops underneath three twenty-story towers of guest rooms, required a simple gridlike structural system attached to the complex framing of the larger spaces in the center section. The division between the two sections reads awkwardly from the exterior, but Holabird and Roche's structural scheme aided the construction process and prioritized the hotel's interior functional requirements (fig. 19). Although indebted to Beaux-Arts ideals, Holabird and Roche's emphasis on function over exterior composition suggests the growing prominence of a pragmatic approach to creating businesslike hotel architecture.

Holabird and Roche embraced rational design of the structural system and plan as the key to efficient hotel architecture. Long emphasized the need to balance good design and sufficient investment with careful cost control:

> The cost must be held down because fixed charges work all the time, good seasons or bad. Poorly arranged front offices cost as much to build as well arranged ones, and so with the back door and other parts of the hotel. Many hotels that have failed could have been saved by the judicious expenditure of a little more money.[40]

For example, the added expense of arranging ballrooms to host conventions had become essential to profitable hotel operation. To group the public spaces on the lower levels and better facilitate the movement of large crowds, hotel ballrooms more frequently appeared on the mezzanine level starting around 1920, as already shown at the Commodore. Accommodating this change in architectural program within the increasing size of their 1920s hotels created additional structural challenges. As construction was under way on the Stevens, a Holabird and Roche structural engineer noted how the shifting location of a hotel's public rooms enhanced the importance of engineering to the entire design process:

> In years gone by the large and special rooms of hotels were placed on the upper floors, or had open courts above them, and the problems of the structural engineer were comparatively simple. It was found, however, that these rooms must be placed on the lower floors in order to prevent interruption in the normal operation and service of the hotel. The problems of the structural engineer are thus greatly complicated, and it was necessary in the case of the Stevens Hotel for him to work with the architects from the beginning (fig. 20).[41]

In larger hotels, upper-floor ballrooms caused an inconvenient strain on elevators and other services, while rising expenses, combined with more extensive public rooms, precluded the use of open courts above large interiors. Instead, hotel engineers designed massive trusses to support the weight of many floors over uninterrupted interior ballroom space, while staying mindful of the impact of construction costs on future profits. Like the raised interior lobby and uniform guest-room floors, new patterns in operation for hotel ballrooms and banquet halls reshaped hotel architecture according to ideals of efficiency.

In spite of the growing sophistication of hotel engineering and functional design formulas, the overwhelming impression upon experiencing a hotel of this era was the lavish interior decoration inspired by a variety of historical motifs and periods. During the 1920s Schultze and Weaver emerged as one of the premier hotel design firms, largely because of its ability to combine experience regarding the functional requirements of hotels with fashionable decorative schemes. The firm's work was featured prominently in the lead article of *Architectural Forum*'s December 1929 hotel theme issue.[42] Among its many hotel designs were the Biltmore Hotels in Los Angeles (1922–1923), Atlanta (1923–1924), and Coral Gables, Florida (1925) for Bowman, and several major New York hotels, including the new Waldorf-Astoria (1929–1931), the Lexington (1928–1929, for United Hotels; fig. 21), the Pierre (1929–1930), and the Sherry-Netherland (with Buchman and Kahn, 1927). *Architectural Forum* cautioned, however, that it would be incorrect to mistake the stylized approach to historical motifs

fig. 21
Schultze and Weaver,
Hotel Lexington, New
York, rendering by
Chester B. Price. From
Architectural Forum
(December 1929): 587.
Courtesy of the Hagley
Museum and Library.

found at the new Waldorf-Astoria and other Schultze and Weaver hotels as more than surface laid over the already established structural modernism of the hotel.

Notwithstanding the validity of *Architectural Forum*'s assessment, the decoration of hotels had shifted toward a relatively simplified approach in concert with the development of efficient structural changes. On this subject Leonard Schultze wrote:

> [The architect] has no right to indulge his fancy in over-decoration, or in the use of more expensive materials for decoration than may be deemed essential—necessary to make the building a safe commercial investment. Hotels are planned and erected, except in a few and rare cases, with the primary idea of making money; in addition they are expected to supply the needs of the public, and at the same time afford the greatest number of conveniences possible.[43]

Like other aspects of hotel design, decoration required a more systematic accounting of the relationship among cost, upkeep, and economic benefit. As one *Hotel World* writer noted:

> Today, the decorating and furnishing of a hotel is an art and a science. An art in that it depends upon handicraft, judgment and selection; a science because the rules governing most of its elements have been resolved into exact known quantities…. Durability should not altogether be overlooked for the artistic effect of a hotel, but the man decorating and furnishing a hotel who will today go further to imitate the home ideas and home arrangements into his hostelry will be the talked of man of today.[44]

The interest in creating a homelike atmosphere represents both a backlash against the lavish hotels of a previous generation and a concern about the inefficiency of extravagant decor. In this instance, striving for the comfort of homelike surroundings while in a corporate hotel is presented as an efficient business decision, again illustrating the dominance of efficiency over sentimentality as a cultural theme.

Conventional wisdom also held that public tastes had shifted to more subdued decorative styles, most notably the ubiquitous Colonial Revival. Wagner, when discussing his firm's use of Italian Renaissance and Georgian Revival motifs for the Statler chain, seemed confident that "the old idea of what the public wanted, as expressed in the original decorative scheme of the Waldorf-Astoria, and resulting in that noisy, but luckily short lived 'red and gold period,' was a fallacious one;… The public is capable of appreciating our best efforts in decoration."[45] Henry Hoskins of Holabird and Root also declared that "with the development of a more democratic taste the desire for regal expenditure and lavishness has diminished to a large extent in favor of simplicity and refinement."[46]

Even with the waning of the "red and gold period," interior decoration for hotel public rooms remained a focal point for display, whether done in Italian, French, English, Art Deco, or hybrid motifs. The lobby of the Los Angeles Biltmore was a tour de force of Mediterranean Revival decoration (fig. 22). In contrast, the typical guest room featured simple wood furniture and other

fig. 23
(above)
**Schultze and Weaver,
Biltmore Hotel,
Los Angeles, view of
guest room.** From
Architectural Forum
(November 1923): 253.
Courtesy of the Hagley
Museum and Library.

fig. 24
(opposite page, top)
**Holabird and Roche,
Palmer House, view of
Great Hall (lobby).** From
Hotel Monthly (October
1927): 30. Courtesy of the
Cornell University Library.

fig. 25
(opposite page, bottom)
**Holabird and Roche,
Palmer House, view of
guest room.** From *Hotel
Monthly* (October 1927):
61. Courtesy of the
Cornell University Library.

contemporary appointments (fig. 23). At the new Palmer House, Holabird and Roche used a modified French Neoclassical style for many of the hotel's public rooms, most notably an ornate plaster ceiling in the main lobby (fig. 24). Again the guest-room decor tended toward Colonial Revival domestic design. The "typical" bedroom at the Palmer House had early American–inspired wood furniture, chosen because of its "ability to create a homey, comfortable atmosphere" (fig. 25).[47]

Like the configuration of the hotel plan around the guest-room unit, guest rooms were the initial focus of simplification in hotel interior decoration. Hotel furniture company Berkey and Gay noted the trend toward standardization in guest-room furniture and the advantages of a professional and systematic approach:

> One of the recently built large hotels, in equipping something over 1,000 bedrooms, used three special designs throughout, all entirely different, yet in keeping with the general scheme of decoration. Another of over 600 rooms kept to one design and finish for all…. But in each case keeping to one design or motive [sic] throughout … means less cost to start with and less maintenance afterward.[48]

Interior design firms and furniture companies specializing in the cost-effective and appropriate decor for large commercial hotels aided the shift toward simpler room appointments. Starting with the Cleveland

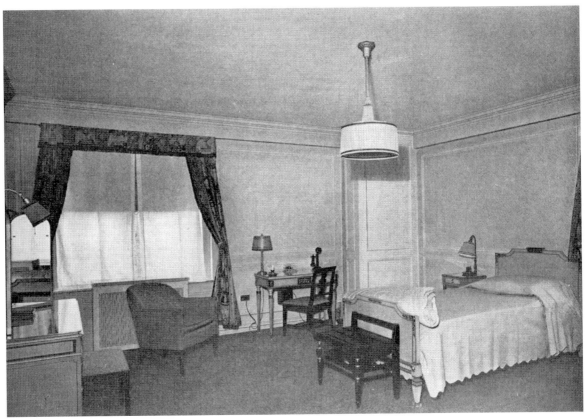

Statler, Rorimer-Brooks Studios worked as the interior designer for all of the chain's hotels. The designers developed a systematic approach to hotel room decor for the Statler hotels that employed a complementary palette of colors and appointments, allowing for easy repair of the rooms and their furnishings.[49] Lyman W. Cleveland, consulting decorator for United Hotels, recommended colorful yet tasteful wallpaper for guest rooms based on the premise that this approach made the room appear warmer and cozier and allowed easier maintenance than paint.[50] A 1925 trade journal article welcomed the "trend to colonial simplicity" for hotel interior design:

> During recent years America has witnessed a marked trend toward simplicity in its homes and hotels.... From the ornate hotel that was developed 150 years ago in Europe, and which came to the United States with all its European detail, America is turning to the simple hotel that is an outgrowth of the inns and taverns of colonial days.[51]

By invoking an imagined colonial past and exaggerating past European influences, less ornate hotel decor was couched in convenient patriotic terms. Comparing the massive commercial hotel of the 1920s to the colonial inn seems a bit far-fetched, particularly given the discussion of United's thousand-room Roosevelt Hotel as an "outstanding example" of this trend. However, the relatively simple Colonial Revival decoration of the Roosevelt was considered indicative of new tastes and the practical benefits of simpler designs for both cost savings and easier maintenance.

Architectural rhetoric surrounding the rise of modernistic architectural styles in the late 1920s emphasized "greater consideration to refinement, to good lines and proportions, and the elimination of unwarranted and illogical ornament and decoration. Structure and construction materials serve as the foundation from which the design is developed."[52] The commercial requirements of hotel design, however, had already created a modern building type based on these principles. Architect Parker Morse Hooper praised hotel specialists for their "years of conscientious study and thought to the problem [of hotel design]," resulting in the most advanced type of commercial structure.[53] In the "Hotel and Apartment Hotel" chapter for the 1952 publication *Forms and Functions of Twentieth-Century Architecture*, John Wellborn Root declared that "the commercial hotel ... fulfills just as important a function in our present-day metropolitan civilization as does that other characteristic twentieth-century structural type, the skyscraper office building."[54] Attention to balancing the economics and aesthetics of hotel design characterized the work of Schultze and Weaver, George B. Post and Sons, Holabird and Roche/Holabird and Root, and Warren and Wetmore. These architects were instrumental in reshaping the urban hotel, previously idealized as an overgrown inn or

fig. 26
Holabird and Root,
Statler Hotel,
Washington, D.C., c. 1943.
Library of Congress,
Prints and Photographs
Division, Theodor
Horydczak Collection.
LC-H814-T-2545-012-B.

criticized as a "gilt palace run by guesswork," into a representation of modern business culture in the United States.

In spite of the ideals of efficiency, the varied services and massive spaces of the modern commercial hotel generated enormous overhead and operating expenses. The immediate economic contraction of the Great Depression severely affected service industries like the hotel business. In 1931 Edward Romine of Horwath and Horwath cautioned his hotel clients that "each manager must work out his own salvation … and many a manager has learned to his sorrow that he cannot give de luxe service at popular prices."[55] By one estimate, in the early 1930s approximately 70 percent of the hotels in the United States were in some form of receivership or financial difficulty. The beginning of the Second World War finally accelerated economic recovery, but lack of trained help and continually deferred maintenance made the importance of economical architecture and efficient operation all the more apparent. In addition, the pervasive impact of the automobile on American travel and commercial architecture made the motel formidable new competition for the older urban hotel.[56]

Postwar motel and hotel chain structures, while often responding to a new roadside location and pattern of travel, still were indebted to the idea of efficient buildings refined by hotel architects during the 1910s and 1920s. With the continued growth of corporate chains, the earlier efforts to standardize and simplify hotel design came to full realization, aided by the Modernist postwar architectural climate. The work of Holabird and Root (later Holabird, Root, and Burgee) provides a direct connection between these two eras. Root saw his firm's prewar Hotel Roosevelt and the Washington Statler (1941–1943) as illustrations of the continual progression of hotel architecture.[57] In consultation with architect and engineer William Tabler, Holabird and Root built the Washington Statler and the Los Angeles Statler Center (1950–1951) using frankly Modernist exterior forms and interior furnishings (fig. 26). As a consultant for the Statler Corporation and then Hilton Hotels, Tabler embarked on a long career as a hotel design specialist, focusing on cost-accounting formulas and guest-room plans for contemporary building practices reminiscent of earlier hotel architects.[58] By the 1950s and 1960s, standardized motels and hotels offered design and construction savings while promoting the chain's corporate identity with easily identifiable structures.[59]

Furthermore, the recognition of efficiency as the driving force behind commercial architectural types made acceptance of a Modernist aesthetic possible, or at the very least more palatable to the American public. The gradual move toward emphasizing the businesslike aspects of commercial architecture paved the way for equating standardized franchise architecture with efficiency and value. While émigré European Modernists such as Walter Gropius and Mies van der Rohe taught a radical new design vocabulary to young architects, their impact would have been considerably muted if not for the corporate embrace of the International Style. Removed from its political context, Modernism became the latest manifestation of efficiency in commercial architecture, particularly for everyday structures such as chain hotels and motels. Today the reemergence of historical pastiche in commercial design has brought hotel decoration full circle, although the underlying principles of measuring architectural costs to ensure profits remain consistent. Regardless of the aesthetic differences among twentieth-century hotels, these structures share a continuity of form and a fundamental relationship with consumer culture that make them essential to a fuller and more nuanced understanding of American architecture.❖

Notes

1. Gilbert Keith Chesterton, *What I Saw in America* (London: Hodder & Stoughton, 1922), 27.

2. See Martha Banta, *Taylored Lives: Narrative Productions in the Age of Taylor, Veblen, and Ford* (Chicago: University of Chicago Press, 1993); and Cecelia Tichi, *Shifting Gears: Technology, Literature, Culture in Modernist America* (Chapel Hill: University of North Carolina Press, 1987).

3. See Arthur Drexler, ed., *The Architecture of the École des Beaux-Arts* (New York: Museum of Modern Art, 1977).

4. Robert A. M. Stern, Gregory Gilmartin, and John Montague Massengale, *New York 1900: Metropolitan Architecture and Urbanism, 1890–1915* (New York: Rizzoli, 1983), 272.

5. Diana Balmori, "George B. Post: The Process of Design and the New American Architectural Office (1868–1913)," *Journal of the Society of Architectural Historians* 46, no. 4 (December 1987): 352.

6. Robert Bruegmann, *Holabird and Roche, Holabird and Root: An Illustrated Catalog of Works*, vol. 1 (New York: Garland, 1991), xiii, xv. William Holabird died in 1923. After Martin Roche's death in 1927, the firm was reorganized as Holabird and Root. Outside of Chicago, important hotel commissions included the Morton in Grand Rapids, the Read in Chattanooga, the Schroeder in Milwaukee, the Muehlebach in Kansas City, and the Nicollet in Minneapolis. See also Robert Bruegmann, *The Architects and the City: Holabird and Roche of Chicago, 1880–1918* (Chicago: University of Chicago Press, 1997).

7. Chesterton, *What I Saw in America*, 29.

8. Leonard Schultze, "The Architecture of the Modern Hotel," *Architectural Forum* 39, no. 5 (November 1923): 202.

9. Montgomery Schuyler, "Distinctive American Architecture: The Biltmore Hotel, New York City," *Brickbuilder* 23, no. 1 (January 1914): 37–40.

10. See "The Biltmore, New York's Newest Hotel Creation," *Hotel Monthly* 22, no. 250 (January 1914): 44–52; and "New York's Last Word in Hotel Creation," *Hotel Monthly* 22, no. 256 (July 1914): 44–82.

11. On Taylorism, in addition to Banta and Tichi's cultural readings, see Samuel Haber, *Efficiency and Uplift: Scientific Management in the Progressive Era, 1890–1920* (Chicago: University of Chicago Press, 1964); David Montgomery, *Workers' Control in America* (Cambridge: Cambridge University Press, 1979); Angel Kwolek-Folland, *Engendering Business: Men and Women in the Corporate Office, 1870–1930* (Baltimore: Johns Hopkins University Press, 1994); and Robert Kanigel, *The One Best Way: Frederick Winslow Taylor and the Enigma of Efficiency* (New York: Viking, 1997).

12. Edward Earle Purinton, "Master Workshops of America: The Largest Hotel in the World," *The Independent* (8–20 May 1920): 202.

13. On Hardenbergh, see Montgomery Schuyler, "Henry Janeway Hardenbergh," *Architectural Record* 6, no. 3 (January-March 1897): 335–75.

14. Edward Hungerford, *The Story of the Waldorf-Astoria* (New York: Knickerbocker Press, 1925), 92.

15. Lucius M. Boomer, *Hotel Management: Principles and Practice* (New York: Harper & Bros., 1925), 1–2. Revised editions were published in 1931 and 1938.

16. Paul L. Ingram, *The Rise of Hotel Chains in the United States, 1896–1980* (New York: Garland, 1996), 3.

17. Schultze, "Architecture of the Modern Hotel," 202.

18. John Bowman, "How We Find What Will Sell Best," *Hotel Management* 3, no. 4 (April 1923): 204–05.

19. "Hotel Commodore, New York City Now Heads Bowman Chain of Caravansaries," *Hotel World* 88, no. 5 (1 February 1919): 27.

20. "Mammoth Pennsylvania, New York City, To Open in Formal Way Tonight," *Hotel World* 88, no. 4 (25 January 1919): 7.

21. Henry J. Bohn, "New York's Two Newest—How Do They Compare?" *Hotel World* 88, no. 11 (15 March 1919): 8.

22. Mrs. E. M. Statler with H. Hatch, "The Statler Story," unpublished manuscript, c. 1950, 262, Ellsworth Milton and Alice Statler papers, no. 3879. Division of Rare and Manuscript Collections, Cornell University Library, Ithaca, NY.

23. J. Otis Post, "Efficient Planning for Economical Operation," *Architectural Forum* 61, no. 6 (December 1929): 677.

24. W. Sydney Wagner, "The Statler Idea in Hotel Planning and Equipment: I. Introduction," *Architectural Forum* 27, no. 5 (November 1917): 115.

25. "Statler Hotels Enlargement," *Hotel World* 81, no. 17 (23 October 1915): 19; "Statler Hotels Perennial Source of News: Completion of Annexes New Building for Cleveland and Detroit Houses Will Give Total of 2,450 Guest Rooms," *Hotel Monthly* 23, no. 272 (November 1915): 88; "Fourth Hotel Statler Is Located in St. Louis," *Hotel Monthly* 26, no. 299 (February 1918): 43.

26. Wagner, "The Statler Idea," 118.

27. W. Sydney Wagner, "The Statler Idea in Hotel Planning and Equipment: The Development of the Typical Floor Plan," *Architectural Forum* 27, no. 6 (December 1917): 167.

28. Statler, "The Statler Story," 264–65.

29. Walter Tittle, "A Host to Millions: E. M. Statler, Who Created a New Style in Hotels," *World's Work* 55, no. 1 (November 1927): 76–81.

30. Wagner, "The Statler Idea" (December 1917), 168–69.

31. Balmori, "George B. Post," 353.

32. "Fourth Hotel Statler is Located in St. Louis," 41–42.

33. "Mr. Dudley's Heart-to-Heart Talk," *Hotel Monthly* 34, no. 405 (December 1926): 59. In combination with its small-town hotel subsidiary, American Hotels, United operated forty-eight hotels in 1926.

34. Frank A. Dudley, "Sizing Up a Town's Buying Power," *Hotel Management* 6, no. 5 (November 1924): 292–94.

35. Horace Leland Wiggins, "Service and Administration Requirements," *Architectural Forum* 39, no. 5 (November 1923): 242.

36. Post, "Efficient Planning," 667–701.

37. Arthur Tappan North, *The Hotel Building: The Influence of Construction on Investment Value and Profitable Operation* (1928), 12.

38. Frank B. Long, "Is Your Hotel Wisely Planned?" *Hotel Monthly* 38, no. 450 (September 1930): 31.

39. "Chicago's New Palmer House to Cost $20,000,000," *Hotel Monthly* 32, no. 373 (April 1924): 39. Richard Neutra, soon to become one of America's preeminent Modernists, worked as a draftsman for Holabird and Roche on the Palmer House shortly after immigrating from Germany. He eagerly documented the construction of its structural system in his book *Wie Baut Amerika?* (Stuggart: J. Hoffmann, 1927).

40. Long, "Is Your Hotel Wisely Planned?" 31.

41. Benjamin B. Shapiro, "Structural Design of the Stevens Hotel," *Architectural Forum* 48, no. 2 (August 1927): 103.

42. See Parker Morse Hooper, "The New Hotel," *Architectural Forum* 61, no. 6 (December 1929): 583–666.

43. Schultze, "Architecture of the Modern Hotel," 204.

44. Aaron B. Dikeman, "Art of Hotel Furnishing: A Comparison of Old and New Tastes and Ideas—Harmonizing Furnishings and Decorations," *Hotel World* 80, no. 18 (1 May 1915): 37.

45. Wagner, "The Statler Idea" (November 1917), 118.

46. Henry J. B. Hoskins, "Hotel Decorations and Furnishings," *Architectural Forum* 61, no. 6 (December 1929): 706.

47. "Chicago's New Palmer House, 2268 Rooms," 61.

48. Berkey and Gay Furniture Co., "In the Furniture World: The Old and the New Way of Hotel Furnishing," *Hotel World* 80, no. 18 (1 May 1915): 31–32.

49. See Leslie A. Pina, *Louis Rorimer: A Man of Style* (Kent, OH: Kent State University Press, 1990).

50. P. A. Young, "The Hotel Business and Its Problems: Room Furnishings in Hotels," *American Greeter* 20, no. 4 (February 1928): 17–18.

51. Charles G. Muller, "The Trend to Colonial Simplicity," *Hotel Management* 8, no. 3 (September 1925): 165.

52. Randolph Williams Sexton, *American Apartment Houses, Hotels, and Apartment Hotels of Today* (New York: Architectural Book Publishing, 1929), 7.

53. Hooper, "The New Hotel," 583.

54. John Wellborn Root, "Hotels and Apartment Hotels," in *Forms and Functions of Twentieth-Century Architecture*, ed. Talbot Hamlin (New York: Columbia University Press, 1952), 107.

55. Edward C. Romine, "56 Ways to Cut Costs," *Hotel Monthly* 39, no. 464 (November 1931): 60.

56. Robert J. Kennedy, "Reconstruction Hotel Corporation," *Hotel Monthly* 40, no. 475 (October 1932): 49; Horwath and Horwath, *Hotel Operations in 1941* (1942), 13. For the changes brought by the motel and automobile travel, see American Institute of Architects, *The Hotel Building* (New York: American Hotel Association, 1947).

57. Root, "Hotels and Apartment Hotels," 96–130.

58. Annabel Jane Wharton, *Building the Cold War: Hilton International Hotels and Modern Architecture* (Chicago: University of Chicago Press, 2001), 176–84. Wharton aptly describes the connection between prewar and postwar commercial hotels as the shift from Fordism to a related consumer phenomena, McDonaldization. For Tabler's later work, see "The New Big-City Hotel," *Architectural Record* 138, no. 1 (July 1965): 142–50.

59. See John A. Jakle, Keith A. Sculle, and Jefferson S. Rogers, *The Motel in America* (Baltimore: Johns Hopkins University Press, 1996), esp. chap. 5, "The Rise of Place-Product-Packaging," 120–49.

Reiko Hillyer

The New South in the Ancient City: Flagler's St. Augustine Hotels and Sectional Reconciliation

Reiko Hillyer is a doctoral candidate in United States history at Columbia University. Her dissertation examines tourism to the South in the New South period. She is currently a scholar-in-residence at Lewis and Clark College in Portland, Oregon. Her teaching and research interests include the history of the American South and the social history of the built environment.

In the late 1880s Henry M. Field (1822–1907), a northern clergyman and editor, was advised by his doctor to spend time in Florida. In 1890 Field wrote of himself and his fellow Yankee sojourners to St. Augustine: "We do not feel that we are strangers here.... We are still at home, in the same country, under the same flag, and among those who are our countrymen and brothers." Describing the Civil War as a family quarrel whose resolution brought its participants closer together, Field wrote, "The great Civil War, which covered our land with mourning and woe, accomplished in four years what could have not been accomplished for us in a hundred years of peace." The war "removed the one great bar to a perfect union"—slavery, a "bar" between fellow white Americans—"and made us know each other as never before." Unlike European nations whose language and cultural barriers prevented "free communion" with one other, Americans from the former Union and former Confederacy could not long be hateful rivals because they shared, according to Field, "the same race and speech, passing to and fro, from city to city."[1] As the northern clergyman suggested, this "passing to and fro"—in particular, white northerners' travels to the South in the years following Reconstruction—went hand in hand with sectional reconciliation, because it allowed white Americans to repair the putative brotherhood that had been soured by the issue of slavery. To stimulate tourism, this sense of white brotherhood was secured by erasing Florida's participation in the sectional conflict.[2]

The economic and social relations that characterized the New South did not just develop in cotton mills and coal mines, but in the parlors and piazzas of the South's grand resort hotels. Much can be said—and has been said—about the ways in which the Gilded Age hotels of Florida, particularly of St. Augustine, tapped into nineteenth-century northerners' fascination with the exotic. Scholars have discussed the grand resorts of

Bird's-eye view of the Alcazar Hotel from the Ponce de Leon, St. Augustine, postcard (detail), before 1902 (see fig. 15).

fig. 1
Panorama of Henry
Flagler's St. Augustine
hotels, the Ponce de Leon,
Cordova, and the Alcazar,
photographic print, c. 1910.
Published by the Harris
Co. Library of Congress,
Prints and Photographs
Division. PAN US GEOG–
Florida no. 6.

St. Augustine's Flagler era as architectural marvels notable for their stylistic and technological innovation, have examined them as quintessential manifestations of Gilded Age luxury, and have identified them with the birth of modern Florida's tourist economy.[3] But only when the exoticism and opulence of St. Augustine's Spanish Renaissance Revival hotels are examined in the context of the sectional tension that characterized the decades following the Civil War can we begin to understand their political significance.

In St. Augustine, Henry Flagler's (1830–1913) Spanish Renaissance Revival hotels cast in concrete the city's claim to Spanish heritage, untainted by reminders of sectional friction in the recent past (fig. 1). Once northern visitors and investors could enjoy the opportunities for health and wealth promised by Florida's climate and untouched bounty without the bother of dwelling on unresolved political problems, the industrial and commercial development of Florida could commence. As a *New York Times* reporter in Florida proposed in 1873, if southerners and northerners could "amicably work out their material advantages," then "social ethics and political theories [would] take care of themselves."[4]

The prospect of reconciliation between North and South raised the question of how northern travelers and their southern hosts would confront the recent troublesome past, but of course, the former enemies did so selectively. As historian Nina Silber writes, "Forgetfulness, not memory, appears to be the dominant theme in the reunion culture."[5] This forgetfulness took various forms: late nineteenth-century tourists and travel writers sentimentalized southern plantation life, and guide-books in the late nineteenth century portrayed Gettysburg as "the Mecca of American Reconciliation," muting the complex political issues that led to the Civil War in the first place.[6] Boosters promoted southern cities such as Jacksonville and Atlanta as tabulae rasae that embraced northern-style bustle, cosmopolitanism, and modernity. As one of the earliest southern destinations to attract northern tourists after the Civil War, St. Augustine, Florida, had the task of fashioning a relationship to its southern past and putting forward a history that appealed to northern visitors. In contrast to

B-51. THE OLD GAMBLE MANSION, ELLENTON, FLA., NEAR BRADENTON.

fig. 2
(above, left)
Advertisement of slave sale, Leon County, Florida, 1842. Courtesy of the Florida Photographic Collection, Reference Collection, Florida State Archives.

fig. 3
(above, right)
Old Gamble Mansion, Ellenton, Florida, postcard, n.d. Courtesy of the Florida Photographic Collection, Postcard Collection, Florida State Archives. The printed note on the reverse states that "Mr. Gamble built this colonial mansion on his sugar plantation, then comprising about three thousand acres, furnishing employment to three hundred slaves."

Jacksonville, whose leading newspaper asserted, "Blessed are the people that has no history,"[7] St. Augustine depended heavily on its history as the nation's oldest city to attract tourists. Founded in 1565 and known as "the Ancient City," St. Augustine had Spanish origins that allowed it to mute its southern heritage and create an iconography that was at once exotic and uncontroversial. By ignoring St. Augustine's Confederate past and dramatizing its Spanish past, travel writers, preservationists, northern developers, town boosters, and hotel architects expunged the history that was politically contentious, portrayed white Floridians as the descendants of nation-builders, and, by casting St. Augustine as the birthplace of the United States, claimed a heritage of patriotism rather than one of treason.

By the late nineteenth century Florida had a history as a plantation state, and it also had a history of rewriting that history. In the decades following American acquisition in 1821, restless and hopeful planters migrated from older southern states to middle and east Florida, forcing their slaves to clear land for large-scale cotton plantations (fig. 2).[8] Simultaneously, smaller farmers migrated to Florida from the same southern states in the hopes of escaping planter-dominated counties and achieving economic independence. As historian Edward Baptist argues, the result was fierce conflict between newly settling planters and small farmers over land and political power. But as sectional disputes over the future of slavery came to a crisis in the 1850s, middle Florida's ruling class, still wounded by local political defeats and increasingly anxious about external threats to slavery, traced their origins to old Virginia, depicted their southern past as stable and static, and "redrew their particular corner of a very new South as one that was 'Old,' unchanged from the past and unchanging in present and future."[9] Some of these Florida elites also reached into the more distant past and began to show interest in, and even identify with, the Spanish dons of colonial conquest. But the predominant historical narrative of these planters, recent arrivals with a tenuous hold on their plantation economy, was that their newly hewn fiefdoms were simply grafted intact from a mystical old Virginia (fig. 3).[10] The myth that Henry Flagler awoke a virginal Florida is a revealing variation of the history disseminated by Florida's elites a few decades earlier. Promoters of Florida in the decades after the Civil War went one step further in rewriting Florida's history by deleting Floridian planters' claims to an epic "Old South" past altogether, replacing the "Old South" with "Old Spain." Just as antebellum Florida planters had created an "Old South" heritage to erase recent conflict between themselves and yeomen farmers, Florida publicists created "Old Spain" to erase conflict between northerners and southerners. If Florida was Spanish rather than ex-Confederate, Henry Flagler, like a modern-day Ponce de Leon, would be a "discoverer" rather than a carpetbagger. When a journalist referred to Flagler as an "industrial conquistador,"[11] he knew it would be taken as a compliment.

Florida's claim to an "Old South" tradition may have been ambiguous, but its participation in the Confederacy was not (fig. 4). In December 1860 Governor Madison Perry urged immediate secession, arguing, "If we wait for [an act of northern aggression] our fate will be that of the whites in Santo Domingo."[12] The state convention in January 1861 voted overwhelmingly for secession, and Florida became the third state, after South Carolina and Mississippi, to secede from the Union (fig. 5). In the years immediately after the Civil War, federal officers visiting the South during Reconstruction remarked that the feeling toward Union men and northern immigrants in Georgia, South Carolina, and Florida was "unmistakably bitter" and that "no northern resident could remain there unless he courted the favor of the influential." John W. Ricks, the federal Collector of Customs in Florida, reported that "the general impression among the people was that they had been overcome but not conquered."[13] In 1866 an article in the *St. Augustine Examiner* emphatically denied that there were "outrages from secessionists … reported here," but within several months the same newspaper expressed panic about the "Southern Radicals" who threatened to establish a "dominant class" from the black population and warned its black readers that the object

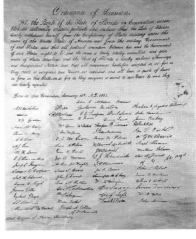

THE DIS-UNITED STATES.
OR THE SOUTHERN CONFEDERACY

fig. 4
Currier and Ives, *The Dis-United States. Or the Southern Confederacy*, lithograph on wove paper, 10 ³/₅ x 16 in. (27 x 41 cm), 1861. Library of Congress, Rare Book and Special Collections Division, Stern Collection. LC-USZ62-92048. Florida, second from the left, is portrayed as a state inhabited by pirates.

fig. 5
(above, right) Florida Ordinance of Secession, 1861. Courtesy of the Florida Photographic Collection, Reference Collection, Florida State Archives.

of "wicked and designing" Republican political associations was to "cheat and deceive, to entrap and lead astray the simple and unsuspecting."[14] Throughout the late 1860s the Ku Klux Klan terrorized black officeholders and landowners in Florida.[15] Though northern journalists writing in *Harper's Weekly* were hopeful that "disorder [was] passing away," as late as 1873 they observed that Florida was "ravaged by a violent rebellion, by a long reign of Ku-Klux outrages, and a resolute persistence on the part of the Democracy to ruin the reputation and the prosperity of the State. Nowhere were the acts of the Democratic associations more infamous or more bloody than Florida."[16]

The areas of north and east Florida that had been settled and cultivated by the Reconstruction period remained undeveloped by northern standards. Northern observers attributed the state's backwardness to the shiftlessness and sectional bitterness of its people. In 1876 a *New York Times* reporter calling for a railroad into Florida that would "triumph over climate, locality, custom, and race" attributed the railroad's slow arrival to the local population's lack of "life and bustle." The reporter claimed that instead of welcoming a railroad that would "obliterate the differences that exist on either side of the Mason and Dixon's line,… moss grows on their brick walls" and "spiders spin cobwebs in their counting-houses."[17] In the 1870s northern visitors complained of "swarms of Negroes" and railroads that were "poorly built and kept, the rails loose and broken, with no regard paid to the time-table."[18] Particular venom was directed at "ignorant and degraded 'crackers,'" who "stare, yawn,… apparently contented, [and go] to their comfortless homes, their rude fare, and dense ignorance."[19] In 1873 *Harper's Weekly* maintained that Florida was "suited for cultivation as a resort … but for its ceaseless political disturbances it might already have won immigration." In a Darwinian assessment of Florida's natives, *Harper's* hoped that "the indolent population will pass off, and the sooner the better."[20] Repeatedly, northern reporters threatened that Floridians'

No. 5. Residence of Prof. & Mrs. H. B. Stowe, with Family Group.

fig. 6
Harriet Beecher Stowe and her family outside their winter home in Mandarin, Florida, c. 1868–1890. Courtesy of the Florida Photographic Collection, Stereograph Collection, Florida State Archives.

imbecility and intolerance would drive away potential investment and reduce the state to a perpetual wasteland. Only openness to northern "brains and capital," such observers warned, would allow the state to achieve commercial greatness. If northern projects were welcomed, then "Florida will probably be more truly a land of flowers in 1983 than when Ponce de Leon named it, about four hundred years ago."[21]

Tourism in the New South depended on northerners abandoning their perception that the South was backward, barbarous, lawless, and disloyal. In what historian C. Vann Woodward has called the South's "pathetic eagerness for northern approval,"[22] Florida boosters attempted to find ways of luring northern visitors and investors and assuring such northerners that they would find comfort, opportunity, and order in their state. The *Florida Times-Union* claimed in 1882 that Florida was "giving up insular sectionalism" and that "the Old South is a thing of the past as a political entity."[23] Noting the symbiotic relationship between northern visitors and northern investment, the *Times-Union* contended that visitors to Florida "should be courteously received, and should be made to feel that the social attractions and moral worth of our people are in accord with the eternal fitness of things."[24] One editorial even claimed that "the way to save the country" was to "have Northerners and Southerners fall in love with each other and marry, ending all sectional ill-feeling."[25] Boosters writing in the journal the *Semi-Tropical*, a Jacksonville periodical edited by former Reconstruction governor Harrison Reed, emphasized the alleged law-abiding character of Florida, comparing Florida favorably to other southern and western states. One writer promised that in Florida "the rowdy element and hoodlum nuisance is unknown," and "the colored people are generally industrious.... We have no strikes, no riots, no communists."[26] In the aftermath of the Great Railroad Strike of 1877

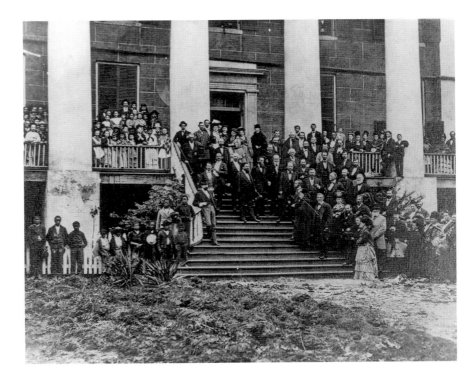

fig. 7
Governor Marcellus L. Stearns greeting Harriet Beecher Stowe at the Capitol, Tallahassee, Florida, 1874. Courtesy of the Florida Photographic Collection, Reference Collection, Florida State Archives.

that had rocked the North and Midwest just several months earlier, the alleged absence of strikes and communists had particular resonance for northern elites fearful of class warfare. Florida promoters knew very well that the image of social stability and worker docility was essential to attract both genteel tourists and savvy investors from the North.

The Florida press enthusiastically publicized examples of "northern approval." Harriet Beecher Stowe (1811–1896), a quintessential Yankee with a vacation home in Florida, was a favorite advocate of Florida's merits (fig. 6). After Stowe's visit to the state capital in 1874, the *Florida Weekly Press* printed her accolades of Florida's "friendly and hospitable attentions." Stowe reported that in a significant gesture of sectional reconciliation

> we were assembled on the State-house steps of Tallahassee, Northerners and Southerners, and a photographer took a picture of the group as a representation of the South receiving the North and giving the right hand of fellowship [fig. 7]. Let it stand for a memorial…. Why should we not be friends?

Stowe wrote optimistically, "The interest of every new settler in Florida must henceforth be that of every old settler: we are helpers of one another." Perhaps recognizing the link between sectional friendship and northern tourism, Stowe ended with the postscript: "We are happy to hear that a movement has been set on foot for a large and elegant hotel for winter boarders in Tallahassee."[27]

ST. FRANCIS STREET—ST. AUGUSTINE

fig. 8
(above, left)
**St. Francis Street,
St. Augustine, 1887.**
Courtesy of the Florida
Photographic Collection,
General Collection,
Florida State Archives.

fig. 9
(above, right)
**Bridge Street,
St. Augustine, promo-
tional photograph,
c. 1860–1879.**
Courtesy of the Florida
Photographic Collection,
General Collection,
Florida State Archives.

To attract northern tourists, boosters had to hail the South not only as progressive, but also as picturesque. St. Augustine's colonial Spanish heritage provided a ready-made set of images and associations that allowed Florida to portray itself as an enchanting destination that embodied the chivalry and romance of a defeated colonial Spain. As a result, Florida would become less the subject of political suspicion and cultural disdain and more a desirable mecca for winter visitors from the North.

Americans from outside Florida had begun to visit St. Augustine as a health resort in the antebellum years, but poor transportation facilities rendered it the destination of only the most desperate and adventurous. However, in the 1870s, as the South in general became more accessible by steam and rail and as the burgeoning industrial economy in the North produced a Gilded Age elite, St. Augustine became an increasingly enticing tourist destination as part of a steamer tour down the St. Johns River. In these decades, tours to St. Augustine were still largely motivated by health concerns; doctors advised their respiratory patients that the temperate climate and balmy breezes would work miracles on their ailments. Other visitors simply wanted to escape the stresses of urban life and were lured by the Ancient City's promise of quaintness and slow pace. During the 1870s and 1880s a growing volume of travel literature and promotional photography celebrated St. Augustine's attractions and homogenized its imagery.[28] Most of this promotional material was subsidized by railroad, steamship, and hotel companies that stood to profit from increased tourism to Florida.

St. Augustine's stagnancy was contemptible to those restless for economic development, but this very stagnancy provided a picturesque escape for northern travelers. One trope that emerges in the travel literature is the representation of the city as "slumbering through the centuries."[29] First, the image of sleepiness and stasis was a way of characterizing St. Augustine's inhabitants. Abbie Brooks (Sylvia Sunshine) observed:

fig. 10
View of St. Augustine from
Fort Marion, promotional
photograph, c. 1880s.
Courtesy of the Florida
Photographic Collection,
General Collection,
Florida State Archives.
Photograph by
Stanley Morrow.

Most of the old inhabitants ... apparently live and grow old, ripen and die, with as little effort toward great designs or grand projects as the sweet potato on the hull. Many of them live seventy or eighty years, are born and die in the same house without forming any foreign attachments or associations—the machinery of their human frames not being moved with as much rapidity here as North.[30]

Second, such lethargy was not the exclusive domain of human beings; travel writers attributed a slumbering quality to the physical landscape itself. Margaret Deland wrote, for example: "A date palm, leaning across a fence that is gray with lichen, looks down into the silent street, which seems in the blaze of sunshine to be sunk in sleep," and "gardens sleep beyond these high walls."[31] She described St. Augustine as a town in quaint disrepair:

> The windows have been boarded up, for sill and sash have long since vanished, so readily does wood crumble in the hot, wet shadows; but even these shutters have warped and broken, so that the passer-by can peer into the dusky room within. Its hard earthen floor is spotted with dim, white mould; there is no furniture except some empty shelves upon the wall.[32]

The souvenir and promotional images of St. Augustine affirmed these picturesque descriptions of ancient narrow streets in an effort to cater to northern tourists' romantic interests and hunger to escape the hurly-burly of northern industrial life (figs. 8, 9). Alice Brown, a tourist, was most likely thinking about her own "caged" life in Philadelphia when she observed joyfully that in St. Augustine "the air was vocal with the song of the mocking birds as they flew about among the branches of the trees and they were the first we had ever seen flying around enjoying life and

not shut up in a cage as in our northern cities."[33] Photographers knew there was a market for images—either as advertisements or as souvenirs—that suggested timelessness and rusticity, an antidote to the chaos of northern cities. Photographs of St. Augustine promised an environment that was simple, romantic, and soothing (fig. 10).

In contrast, when boosters described Jacksonville as an attractive tourist destination, they called upon the typical New South lexicon, using the language of "enterprise," "energy," "creative power," "growth," and "rapid-thinking." One such Jacksonville booster looked scornfully at St. Augustine, a potential rival, and charged its citizens with never having been "wide awake." Unlike Jacksonvillians, St. Augustinians were "stupidly inert," and "with folded hands now await the advent of northern strangers with capital, to work out salvation for them. Wouldn't a little more self-effort hoist them nearer the kingdom? In Jacksonville we have more energy and life."[34]

What Jacksonvillians saw as "stupidly inert," St. Augustine boosters hoped tourists would consider charming. But this image of "slumbering" does more than just connote a lack of enterprise. Portraying St. Augustine as "asleep" allowed it to stand outside of history, untouched by recent events, untroubled by politics, timeless. If St. Augustine was, as one Florida journalist wrote, "emphatically the Rip Van Winkle of our cities,"[35] it could not be considered part of the Confederacy; Rip Van Winkles do not make good rebels. But St. Augustinians did not sleep through the Civil War. Contrary to assertions that the Ancient City had been taking a nap for two centuries,[36] by the time of Lincoln's election, secessionist Democrats, supported by the majority of Florida's newspapers, dominated the state. Lincoln's election inspired St. Augustinians to raise homemade "secession flags" above their homes, and the local newspaper warned those opposed to secession to leave the state. On 10 January 1861, St. Augustine's representatives to the Florida state convention joined their counterparts from other areas of Florida and voted for secession.[37] Hearing word of federal troops approaching St. Augustine in the spring of 1862, hundreds of St. Augustinians fled the city. Local women loyal to the Confederacy cut down a flagpole so that it would not be used to support the Stars and Stripes.[38] Though writers like Deland and Brooks depicted St. Augustine's dilapidated landscape as insulated from external events, the town's very decay was more accurately a modern phenomenon—the result of the ravages and economic dislocations caused by the recent Civil War rather than evidence of St. Augustine's insulation from it.[39]

St. Augustine—and, by extension, Florida—indirectly claimed to have slept through (and thus was unaccountable for) the rest of the South's controversial past by simply truncating the chronology of its history. In almost every guidebook that included a "brief history" of Florida, the authors devoted a disproportionate number of pages or paragraphs to

fig. 11
Franklin W. Smith,
Villa Zorayda,
St. Augustine, postcard,
c. 1910s. Courtesy of
the Florida Photographic
Collection, Florida
Artistic Series Postcard
Collection, Florida
State Archives.

Spain's occupation of Florida and then abruptly ended their chronology with 1821, the year the United States officially acquired Florida territory, or 1845, the year Florida became a state. The years from 1845 to the present were not a part of Florida's history. The *Rambler*, for example, one of the first among many post–Civil War guidebooks subsidized by railroad and steamship companies, devoted fifty-six pages to the fifty-five years from 1513 to 1568, and all of two pages to the 253 years between 1568 and 1821.[40] Only two or three guidebooks out of dozens actually mentioned the Civil War, and then in a passing and passive manner: "During the late war between the North and South, [Florida] changed hands several times,"[41] or, "The bloody Seminole war raged from 1835 to 1842. Florida was admitted into the Union as a State in 1845. During the Civil war several battles were fought within the State. The population, which was in 1830 only 34,739, numbers now 350,000."[42] This trend persisted as late as the 1930s, when a 1935 guidebook entitled *Romantic and Historic Florida* noted that for most of its history

> the greater portion of the country remained an untamed wilderness, a vast morass populated by the implacable Seminoles and Creeks.... Indian warfare, raids and massacres, lack of transportation, the character of the country and its evil reputation as a white man's grave all militated against its settlement and development ... until one man dreamed a dream.[43]

This "one man" was Henry Flagler, former Rockefeller partner and Standard Oil baron turned railroad and hotel magnate. It is true that much of the Florida peninsula was undeveloped until entrepreneurs such as Flagler and Henry Plant (1819–1899) extended railroads and constructed hotels throughout the state during the 1880s and 1890s.[44] But more significantly, because the state was depicted as an ancient battleground of rival European empires and Indian tribes until Flagler's arrival, Florida could be "historic" and yet outside of politics.

Villa Zorayda, St. Augustine, Fla.

The construction of Flagler's Spanish Renaissance Revival hotels in
St. Augustine in the 1880s—the Ponce de Leon, the Alcazar, and the
Cordova[45]—enshrined the town's claim to an uninterrupted Spanish
heritage. Flagler expressed his determination to transform quaint St.
Augustine into the "Winter Newport" after a visit to the town in the
winter of 1885.[46] He was encouraged and aided by influential St. Augustine
civic leader Dr. Andrew Anderson, owner of a large citrus estate and
future mayor, who helped rally local support for Flagler's venture. While
Anderson acted as Flagler's agent in St. Augustine, Flagler sought out
architects Thomas Hastings (1860–1929) and John Carrère (1858–1911),
former students of the École des Beaux-Arts in Paris and former employees
of the prestigious New York firm McKim, Mead, and White. In part
inspired by the Villa Zorayda (fig. 11; 1883–1884), an exotic, concrete
Moorish mansion designed and built by Boston transplant Franklin W.
Smith, Flagler informed his architects that he wanted his first hotel to be

> a palace, with towers, courts, fountains, loggias and cool retreats, to be
> set amid appropriate surroundings, in design to embody the beauties of
> Spanish architecture, with decoration suggestive of the history of Florida
> and St. Augustine, and every detail … befitting to its position here in the
> city, whose patent came three centuries ago from the sovereign of the
> proudest dominion of the globe.[47]

fig. 13
(above, left)
Carrère and Hastings,
Alcazar Hotel,
St. Augustine,
promotional photograph,
1891. Courtesy of the
Florida Photographic
Collection, General
Collection, Florida
State Archives.

fig. 14
(above, right)
Franklin W. Smith, Cordova
Hotel, St. Augustine,
promotional photograph,
c. 1890s. Courtesy of
the Florida Photographic
Collection, General
Collection, Florida State
Archives. Photograph by
Pierre Havens.

Flagler's concerns were in part simply practical, and in part simply aesthetic; a concrete palace would be less likely to burn to the ground than would a wooden hotel, and a Spanish style would indeed recall the town's distant heritage. But the hotels' designs also provided a symbolic manifestation of the New South ideology in the Ancient City (figs. 12–14).

Construction began on the Ponce de Leon in 1885. No doubt stirred by the sight of hundreds of workers pouring concrete, planting trees, widening streets, and filling creeks, contemporary guidebook writers turned to the Rip Van Winkle imagery once again: "[St. Augustine] has awoke from her sleep of three centuries…. Change is written upon every feature. Old and crumbling walls are giving way to more portentous structures."[48] The Ponce de Leon and Cordova both opened in January 1888. The Alcazar opened nearly a year later, in December 1888. Flagler's own promotional material, with text attributed to architects Carrère and Hastings, perpetuated the image of St. Augustine as moribund until blessed with Flagler's Midas touch. In a booklet entitled *Florida, The American Riviera; St. Augustine, The Winter Newport*, Carrère and Hastings asserted that until recent years the town appeared to "have sunk under the enchanter's wand into almost eternal sleep." The denizens of the town experienced "no excitement" and engaged in "no events" until, with the arrival of Flagler and his hotels, "the scene changes, the enchanter's wand has been uplifted, and every count in the above indictment has been reversed."[49] Flagler's Spanish Renaissance Revival hotels completed the stage-set for the historical narrative that St. Augustine had been asleep since the last Spanish occupation and thus ensured St. Augustine's identity as a "Spanish" city rather than a southern one.

In their colors, materials, lavishness, scale, and expense, these hotels were unprecedented in Florida. Their style was actually an eclectic mix of Spanish, Italian, and Moorish styles, but overall they recalled the estates and defenses of sixteenth-century Spain. These hotels were consistent with architecture in northern and midwestern cities that catered to the

fig. 15
(above)
Bird's-eye view of the
Cordova and Alcazar
hotels from the Ponce
de Leon, St. Augustine,
postcard, before 1902.
Courtesy of the Florida
Photographic Collection,
Postcard Collection,
Florida State Archives.

Gilded Age elite in their fantastical decorative exaggeration, exoticism, and material excess. They featured lush and manicured courtyards, fountains ornamented with mosaics and carved dolphins and lions' heads, arched loggias, and tennis courts. The interiors showcased marble fireplaces, oak paneling, allegorical murals, Tiffany windows, and elegant furniture and chandeliers. But more significantly for St. Augustine as a whole, the three hotels and their grounds were a coherent complex (fig. 15) that more resembled the planned, predictable City Beautiful landscapes that would soon dominate northern cities than the crooked local streets with which the hotels allegedly harmonized (fig. 16).[50]

As would the Renaissance classicism of Chicago's World's Columbian Exposition several years later, the Spanish Renaissance Revival hotels of St. Augustine offered a visual expression of American cultural progress.

Stairway and Roman Arch, Fort Marion, St. Augustine, Fla.

fig. 16
(opposite page,
bottom left)
View of St. Augustine
from the Florida House,
promotional photograph,
n.d. Courtesy of the
Florida Photographic
Collection, General
Collection, Florida State
Archives. Photograph by
Charles Seaver.

fig. 17
(opposite page,
bottom right)
Stairway and Roman
arch, Fort Marion,
St. Augustine, postcard,
n.d. Courtesy of the
Florida Photographic
Collection, Postcard
Collection, Florida
State Archives.

fig. 18
(right)
Edward Bierstadt,
*From the Watch Tower
of Fort Marion*. From
*Sunlight Pictures:
St. Augustine* (New York:
Artotype, 1891),
pl. 49. Courtesy of
the St. Augustine
Historical Society.

One requisite activity for tourists was a visit to the seventeenth-century Spanish fort—known alternately as the Castillo de San Marcos and Fort Marion—with its massive moss-covered walls and gloomy passageways (fig. 17). In recounting the history of the fort, guidebooks and tour guides emphasized the horrible and the barbaric, romancing visitors with tales of Spanish torture chambers and rotting skeletons chained to the walls of the clammy vaults below.[51] From 1875 to 1878, Fort Marion held captive Indians from the western plains, and Richard H. Pratt (future founder of the Carlisle Indian School) assumed custody and aimed to "civilize" them. Again in the 1880s, 497 Apache Indians were held in Fort Marion. Both groups of Indians became popular tourist attractions during their imprisonment. Visitors witnessed the Indians performing military drills and war dances and purchased curios that the captive Indians had created for sale.[52] With the help of guidebook explanations, the fort came to be associated with the earlier phases of America's cultural past—Spanish and Indian barbarism. And then, just as visitors to Chicago's "White City" would later return from the Midway Plaisance—the Barnumesque section of the world's fair that displayed "anthropological" exhibits of Indians, Chinese people, and African villagers—St. Augustine's tourists could turn from the "hoary ramparts of the ancient fort" back toward the panorama of the city, where the elaborate, soaring, bright red towers of the Ponce de Leon and Alcazar asserted only the glory and artistic sophistication of Spanish culture and the benefits of luxurious consumption (fig. 18).[53] Once again, the city's Confederate and Civil War past was omitted from guidebook tracts about Fort Marion; contemporary descriptions of the fort did not mention that it had been held

fig. 19
(above, left)
Federal artillery
inside Fort Marion,
St. Augustine,
c. 1862–1865. Library
of Congress, Civil War
Photographs.
LC-DIG-cwpb-03320 and
LC-DIG-cwpb-03321.
Photograph by
Sam A. Cooley.

fig. 20
(above, right)
Carrère and Hastings,
Ponce de Leon Hotel,
St. Augustine, with
George Maynard's murals
on the rotunda, promo-
tional photograph,
Detroit Publishing Co.,
1891. Courtesy of the
Florida Photographic
Collection, Reference
Collection, Florida
State Archives.

by Union forces from 1862 to 1865 (fig. 19). The arrangement of
St. Augustine's physical landscape and the uniformly scripted explanations
of its sights taught visitors that Flagler's grand hotels represented the
pinnacle in a narrative of progress from barbarism to civilization.

The murals and paintings in the Ponce de Leon's interior echoed this
same historical narrative (fig. 20). The ceiling of the Ponce de Leon's
rotunda swirled with painted personifications of the phases of Spanish
exploration by George Maynard (1843–1923): "Adventure," "Discovery,"
"Conquest," and "Civilization." Though clearly referring to the particular
history of Spanish Florida, these figures were becoming stock characters
in the general celebration of American progress. Maynard supplied similar
figures in a mural in the southwest pavilion of the Library of Congress.[54]
His murals in the Ponce de Leon dining room detailed the same historical
narrative that guidebooks articulated: images that represented the indige-
nous Indian population, the landing of the Spanish, Menendez's massacre
of the French, and the transfer of Florida to the United States.[55] Like the
guidebook histories, the murals' depictions of Florida's history do not
include images of plantations or of sectional strife.

Even as they boasted the most modern amenities—electric lighting,
gleaming kitchen appliances, first-class cuisine, the latest furnishings, and
linens from smart northern establishments—the Flagler hotels were
described as though they were just as historically significant as structures
from the actual periods of Spanish dominion. An admiring journalist
commented that the hotels "look like they had always been there," and
Carrère and Hastings remarked that the Casa Monica (later the Cordova)
"would be at home in any of the old cities of Spain, like those huge castles

fig. 21
*Greetings from
St. Augustine*, postcard,
c. 1911. Courtesy of the
Florida Photographic
Collection, Reference
Collection, Florida
State Archives.

fig. 22
(below, left)
Florida House,
St. Augustine, stereo-
graph, c. 1870s.
Courtesy of the Florida
Photographic Collection,
Stereograph Collection,
Florida State Archives.

fig. 23
(below, right)
Magnolia House Hotel,
St. Augustine, stereo-
graph, n.d. Courtesy of
the Florida Photographic
Collection, Stereograph
Collection, Florida
State Archives.

which dominated neighborhoods in feudal times." [56] Even Charles Reynolds, a St. Augustine native and guidebook author persnickety enough to question the genuineness of some of the town's most storied tourist attractions, blurred the past and present when he enthused, "As the bastions and watchtowers of Fort Marion were significant of the military prowess of the sixteenth-century Spain—the Spain of Philip II and Menendez—so this new structure, the Hotel Ponce de Leon, should in the beauty and harmony of its parts, furnish a token of that other Spain, the mother of artists and architects and cunning craftsmen." [57] No doubt because of their beauty but also because of their illusion of authenticity, Flagler's St. Augustine hotels became tourist destinations in their own right, must-see sights on a par with true relics like the city gates (fig. 21). The hotels' architectural styles reinforced the town's continuity from its Spanish past and lent an air of historic value to buildings that were brand new.

Flagler's grand hotels diverged from the relatively vernacular and unspec-tacular hotels that preceded them. St. Augustine's accommodations had consisted of rooms in the homes of local residents, boardinghouses, and several large hotels, such as the Magnolia House (c. 1848), the St. Augustine Hotel (1867), and the Florida House (c. 1848). [58] Contrary to the claims that Flagler's hotels were consistent with the preexisting local landscape, most of the hotels and lodging houses in the pre-Flagler era were decidedly

fig. 24
(above, left)
**Magnolia House Hotel,
St. Augustine, after
renovation, postcard,
c. 1910s.** Courtesy of the
Florida Photographic
Collection, General
Collection, Florida
State Archives.

fig. 25
(above, right)
**McGuire and McDonald,
Hotel San Marco,
St. Augustine, promo-
tional photograph,
c. 1882–1887.**
Courtesy of the Florida
Photographic Collection,
Reference Collection,
Florida State Archives.
Photograph by
Stanley Morrow.

fig. 26
(right)
**Grand Hotel, Catskill
Mountains, New York.
c. 1884–1891.** Library
of Congress, Prints and
Photographs Division.
LC-USZ62-30429.
Photograph by
Joseph John Kirkbride.

un-Spanish: simple, wooden, shuttered, two- or three-story affairs with exterior porches to provide shady outdoor comfort in the humid weather. The older hotels' overall effect was more Greek Revival than Spanish Renaissance Revival (figs. 22, 23). In 1885 one St. Augustine guidebook described the Magnolia House as the "most Southern-like hotel in St. Augustine."[59] Occasionally early hoteliers added balconies, verandas, and mansard or gabled roofs to keep pace with fashionable trends set in northern resorts, but these features were rarely, if ever, Spanish. When the Magnolia Hotel underwent renovation around 1901, the hotelier borrowed from the Queen Anne and shingle styles that were modish in the North (fig. 24). Even many of the names of the pre-Flagler hotels—the Magnolia, the Planters Hotel, the Sunnyside—suggest that they were built in an era when St. Augustine's business people saw little need to conjure images of Old Spain to attract visitors.

The construction of the Hotel San Marco in 1884 was, in some respects, a transitional moment in St. Augustine's hotel architecture. Its name alone suggests a shift to Spanish imagery. The San Marco, designed by the firm of McGuire and McDonald, was built on a much more monumental scale than its predecessors and offered its guests greater amenities and entertainments (fig. 25). Carrère and Hastings later mocked its Queen Anne style as so out of place in St. Augustine's Spanish atmosphere as to suggest "that Queen Anne has gone staring mad and has attired herself like a dude on Easter Day."[60] But examined in the context of the New South, it is significant that the San Marco's style, however out of place, was almost an exact replica of the Grand Hotel in the Catskills (fig. 26). Whatever its stylistic merit, the fact that the San Marco so precisely recalled the northern resorts with which most of St. Augustine's guests would be familiar suggests that a movement was under way to remake the city according to the tastes and expectations of northern visitors.[61]

The grand resorts of the Flagler era also marked a departure from the purely quaint and picturesque image of St. Augustine. To attract the high society of the North, Florida's town leaders agreed that "life [in Florida] must be made luxurious."[62] Just over a decade before the opening of the Flagler hotels, Elizabeth Stuart Phelps had described St. Augustine as a "queer little town" populated with soulless natives who cared nothing for a "high standard of culture." Bishop sardonically asked St. Augustinians: "Why be a king when you can be a peddler?"[63] But the Flagler hotels were settings for kings; peddlers were no longer welcome. Though St. Augustine remained "historic," it was also "awakened to new life" and "up-to-date."[64] The Ancient City was fast becoming the Winter Newport, offering opulence and order, spectacle and security.

This kind of grandeur attracted northerners eager to escape the pandemonium and soot of northern cities and anxious about the potential for social disorder in southern ones. Whereas tourists to St. Augustine before Flagler's resorts might have little choice but to wander through narrow streets with guidebook in hand and not much else to do but watch "little darkies … turning somersaults, tumbling about in a bag-race … or, as occurred here last week, climbing a greased pole and chasing greased pigs,"[65] winter visitors to Flagler's grand resorts entered a much more controlled, genteel, and self-contained setting. Entry pavilions and guarded gatehouses assured guests that they were in an exclusive, extraordinary, protected environment (fig. 27). Pinkerton detectives watched the hotel grounds closely for predatory types.[66] Guests attended hotel-sponsored formal balls, concerts, and card parties and were invited to visit the artists' studios that Flagler had built on the premises of the Ponce de Leon. The Alcazar housed its own shopping arcade, spa, exercise gym, and therapeutic baths. In 1876 Elizabeth Stuart Phelps had complained that St. Augustine was so backward that visitors waited expectantly for

fig. 27
Carrère and Hastings,
Ponce de Leon Hotel,
St. Augustine, postcard,
n.d. Courtesy of the
Florida Photographic
Collection, Postcard
Collection, Florida
State Archives.

schooners to arrive with necessities, such as lemons, sugar, ice, and even hominy; a decade later, in an effort to render his hotel complex more self-sufficient, Flagler had purchased a nearby farm to deliver fresh produce to his guests' dining tables. Generally, the tourists were insulated from the hotel workers, who, according to historian Thomas Graham, "were not permitted to appear on hotel grounds except on prescribed paths while coming or going from work."[67] Luggage magically appeared in hotel rooms as workers remained concealed in cellars, freight elevators, and crowded quarters behind the hotels. Aside from contexts of hotel service, guests interacted with hotel workers only in controlled situations, such as watching workers participate in cakewalk contests or baseball games staged for guests. Flagler's managers imported most workers from northern resorts rather than hiring locals, perhaps helping to guarantee northern guests familiar and predictable service. Overall, the grand resorts of the Flagler era were self-contained, highly regulated worlds that shielded guests from the relative decrepitude of the local surroundings and the poverty of many of its inhabitants (fig. 28).

Beyond the controlled environments of their loggias and dining halls, the hotels also both signaled and mandated more decorum and social order in the rest of the city. In the decades immediately after the construction of Flagler's grand resorts, city boosters became increasingly vigilant about enforcing bourgeois manners in St. Augustine. The town's new image as a Winter Newport had to be upheld, unmarred by the idiosyncrasies and roughness of the pre-Flagler era. Anna Marcotte, founder and editor of St. Augustine's *Tatler*, was particularly vocal about galvanizing her fellow

fig. 28
Carrère and Hastings,
courtyard of the Ponce de
Leon Hotel, St. Augustine,
postcard, 1898.
Courtesy of the Florida
Photographic Collection,
Postcard Collection,
Florida State Archives.

citizens to maintain the city's appeal. A civic leader in St. Augustine whose status as northern transplant and wife of a Union veteran made her particularly attuned to the needs of northern visitors, Marcotte warned her readers that "the world moves, and every day people grow more luxurious in their tastes and desires. What was a luxury ten years ago has become a necessity today."[68] Her pages repeatedly called for cleaner streets, free from hack stands, roaming pigs, weeds, mud, and banana peels, because, she pointed out, "frequenters of resorts want to wear white, dainty hats, pretty gowns, and this cannot be done with comfort on streets as dirty as these."[69] Marcotte expressed the boosters' impulse to screen out lower-class activities and behavior when she asked rhetorically, "What is to be the future of St. Augustine … Shall this be Newport or Coney Island?"[70] Perhaps in response to the plea for order in the city, arrests for foul language, vagrancy, and disorderly behavior nearly doubled in the 1880s and 1890s.[71] Not coincidentally, in that same decade, the Florida legislature instituted the poll tax and enacted segregation laws. Florida's tourist economy, much like other industries throughout the South, depended on a disenfranchised and controlled labor force, in this case, to accommodate the tastes of northern tourists.

In 1901 the editors of the *St. Augustine Record*, another boosterish newspaper devoted to improving the town "morally, mentally and materially,"[72] also argued that the local government needed to codify genteel standards of behavior. Observing the potential for unsavory encounters between locals and elite tourists in the central plaza, the authors distinguished between "loafing" and "lounging." The *Record* wanted the plaza to be an environment

fig. 29
(top, right)
Edward Bierstadt, *From the West Tower of the Ponce de Leon*, artotype. From *Sunlight Pictures: Saint Augustine* (New York: Artotype, 1891), pl. 23. Courtesy of The Wolfsonian–Florida International University, Miami Beach, Florida, The Mitchell Wolfson Jr. Collection. XB1991.273.

fig. 30
(bottom, right)
Street in St. Augustine, stereograph, n.d. Courtesy of the Florida Photographic Collection, Stereograph Collection, Florida State Archives. Photograph by George Barker.

that encouraged "human nature in its most amiable character," a spot agreeable to respectable tourists, "the aged and infirm … young maids and their lovers."[73] In swift response to the *Record*'s call, the St. Augustine City Council passed an ordinance to "suppress the loafing nuisance," outlawing sitting on the fences around the plaza, expectorating, and using foul language.[74] The motley assemblage of local, working-class men in a public plaza had grown incompatible with the interests of wealthy tourists and the city leaders who depended on their patronage. One week after the "loafing nuisance" ordinance was passed, it was amended to include the walls and fences of the Alcazar and Ponce de Leon grounds.[75]

A so-called aristocratic air was advertised and enhanced through the publicity photographs of Flagler's grand hotels, many of which were taken by the professional photographer Edward Bierstadt (1824–1906; fig. 29). Bierstadt emphasized the monumental grandeur of the hotels and created the impression that the palatial hotels represented the character

fig. 31
(above, left)
Charlotte Street,
St. Augustine, n.d.
Courtesy of the Florida
Photographic Collection,
General Collection,
Florida State Archives.
Photograph by
Charles Seaver.

fig. 32
(above, right)
Edward Bierstadt, *The
Ponce de Leon. From the
West*, artotype. From
*Sunlight Pictures: Saint
Augustine* (New York:
Artotype, 1891), pl. 6.
Courtesy of The
Wolfsonian—Florida
International University,
Miami Beach, Florida,
The Mitchell Wolfson Jr.
Collection. XB1991.273.

of the rest of the city. The wide boulevards and manicured gardens showcased in these photographs stood in sharp contrast to the narrow, crumbling streets populated with lolling locals (figs. 30, 31). One reporter claimed that upon entering the roof garden of the Ponce de Leon, "beneath us humanity is pygmified, and the heretofore great buildings of the city are awed into insignificance."[76] In Bierstadt's photographs, humanity was "pygmified" indeed; people are either minuscule or entirely absent from his images (fig. 32). Although the absence of people may simply result from his practical concern that moving figures would be a blur, the effect was to assure visitors that the town was fashionable, orderly, and safe. Gone were the days when northern visitors were forced to endure discomfort in dilapidated cottages, eating indigestible cornbread, surrounded by "tawny urchins."[77] Bierstadt's photographs supported Anna Marcotte's claim that in St. Augustine, "the absence of fakirs, of shows with dreadful monstrosities, hand organs, beggars, performing bears, and nuisances of like ilk, are all blessings, not disguised, but very plainly seen and appreciated."[78]

As grand expressions of commercial wealth and comfort, the Flagler hotels legitimated St. Augustine's new relationship to northern investors. Echoing typical New South booster rhetoric, commentators interpreted the hotels and the transportation infrastructures that made them accessible as testaments to the magic touch of northern capital. Flagler's own promotional literature asserted as much when it declared that the hotels represented the new "aggressive spirit of enterprise": "Northern astuteness has measured the possibilities of the place, and Northern capital has made them available."[79] As his contemporaries, the Morgans, Rockefellers, and Mellons, gained control of railways elsewhere in the South, by 1889 Flagler had purchased, consolidated, and standardized the Jacksonville, St. Augustine, and Halifax River Railroad, the Palatka Railroad, and the

St. Johns Railroad. Observers' reactions reaffirmed the New South creed. Julia Tuttle, a Florida transplant from Cleveland, whose memoir *Twelve Years Constant Residence in Florida* encouraged fellow northerners to invest or settle in her adopted state, hailed the reach of Flagler's "iron bands," which bound "the ripened sheaf of barbarism for the harvest of civilization."[80] Celebrating the rapid development of Florida by capitalists like Flagler, the editor of the *Florida Times-Union* went so far as to argue that "there is a national need for the millionaire." Far from being a robber baron or a carpetbagger, Flagler was

> like a mule in that he does the work impossible to every other thing we know.... Can the Government or the average man build our roads, drain our swamps, maintain universities and endow hospitals as the millionaires are doing?... Shall we not think of these things when the street loafer is calling us slaves and worse?[81]

The speedy and efficient railroad journeys, rewarded by the highly ornamental Spanish Renaissance Revival architecture of the Flagler hotels, justified northern investment in St. Augustine and its increasing dependence on a northern tourist economy.

Flagler's supporters further validated his enterprises by describing him as a philanthropist rather than an entrepreneur. Henry Field, who dedicated his book on his journeys south to Flagler, compared the monumental beauty of Flagler's hotels to churches and cathedrals and asserted that these hotel ventures were acts of public service. "Whether it will pay in the common sense, does not enter into his calculations," Field wrote, "any more than it does into the mind of one who gives himself a costly library or gallery of paintings." The loyal Field even cast Flagler as a great democrat: "The best of it all is that his beautiful creation is for the public good. Palaces abroad are for kings and princes. This American palace is open to all—a place of rest and health, as well as of luxury and enjoyment: and he who has placed it within reach of his countrymen, is a public benefactor."[82]

It is no coincidence that Carrère and Hastings, architects of the Ponce de Leon and the Alcazar, would a decade later be pioneers of the City Beautiful movement. City Beautiful architects and planners in northern cities would argue that a more attractive, coherent, impressive urban environment would call forth a surge of civic loyalty from the urban populace. If traditions could not be summoned from the city's own heritage, grand classical architecture would be a symbolic substitute. Indeed, the Spanish Renaissance Revival architecture of the hotels served such a purpose: it inspired loyalty to Flagler's economic project while evoking historic associations that made this radical economic development seem natural and inevitable. As Field said, the hotels' architecture appeared antithetical to commercialism but in fact commemorated enterprise and consumption.

Celebration of Ponce de Leon
Ponce de Leon at the City Gate.
St. Augustine, Fla.

fig. 34
Ponce de Leon
Celebration, promotional
photograph, c. 1910.
Festivals and Events
Photographic Collection,
St. Augustine Historical
Society. Photograph by
W. J. Harris.

With evidence of St. Augustine's Spanish heritage—however fabricated or recently built—firmly secured in the physical environment, the stage was set for civic and business leaders to create ritualized pageants that reinforced this heritage. St. Augustine boosters deployed the town's Spanish past to attract tourists by creating the Ponce de Leon Celebration, a spectacle reenacting the landing of Ponce de Leon, strategically scheduled in April to extend the tourist season (fig. 33). As Robert Torchia has shown in *A Florida Legacy: Ponce de Leon in Florida*, travel writers and historians were not always enamored of Ponce de Leon. In the early nineteenth century he was cast as a pathetic Pollyanna, deluded and overly ambitious at best, aging and bumbling at worst. Only in the 1870s, Torchia shows, when Floridians turned more heartily to tourism to stimulate the state's economy, did Ponce de Leon become fixed in Florida iconography as a heroic, visionary, even prophetic trailblazer, the symbol of the adventure and romance that Florida offered its visitors (fig. 34).[83] But the creation of the Ponce de Leon Celebration by local boosters and businessmen in 1885 and its institutionalization in the early 1900s was more than a marketing ploy. Like the Spanish Renaissance Revival hotels and guidebook histories, the celebration aided the project of sectional reconciliation because it presented an uninterrupted continuity between the age of Spanish explorers and the age of tourism (fig. 35).

fig. 35
Ponce de Leon
Celebration, promotional
photograph, c. 1910.
Festivals and Events
Photographic Collection,
St. Augustine Historical
Society. Photograph by
W. J. Harris.

The *St. Augustine Record*'s souvenir booklet of 1907 made a direct link between "the warriors of centuries ago" and their "descendants" who portrayed them in costume. The *Record* suggested that the luxury resorts of the Flagler era were the realization of Ponce de Leon's dreams and the culmination of Florida's destiny as a tourist paradise. The booklet proclaimed in 1907, "Turning from the visions of the past, the eyes of the spectators encounter the magnificent palace hotels, which have made the Ancient City the most famous resort in the world,"[84] and in 1909, "The grandeur of the past harmonizes with the luxury and magnificence of the present."[85] Northern developers such as Flagler and his architects contributed to this narrative in their own promotional material. They made a direct connection between Spanish cavaliers and contemporary entrepreneurs when they asserted that "the day-dreams of the sixteenth century have become the realizations of the nineteenth," and they charac-terized the local population as having "no participation in the active schemes of life" until the arrival of northern investors and visionaries.[86] There was no space in such a narrative for slaveholders and secessionists— only romantic Spanish explorers, sleepy but picturesque locals, and northern saviors, the perfect cast of characters for a New South drama. The choreography of the Ponce de Leon Celebration reinforced this notion, as the "Change of Flags" segment of the festival—which took place at the fort that Union forces had occupied during the Civil War—included Spanish, French, English, and American flags, but not a Confederate flag. This was especially striking in an era during which there was a mounting interest in symbols of the "Lost Cause" in other former Confederate states. Though a souvenir booklet declared that "the past blends harmoniously with the present," this "blending" was more a blurring of specific episodes into a heroic mythology that leapfrogged the political conflicts of the nineteenth century and culminated with Flagler's grand hotels. Indeed, the celebration was, as the *St. Augustine Record* put it without a trace of irony, "history clothed in the most attractive guise."[87]

Newspaper editor A. K. McClure expressed the spirit of the New South when he wrote in 1886: "The [civil] war now belongs to the memories of more than twenty years ago; its warriors of blue and gray are rapidly passing to join the great majority that has gone before, and a new generation is fast filling the places of the men of that generation that fought the most heroic battles of history. The victories of peace are now to become their chaplets, and the surplus capital and industry of the North will soon be inseparably interwoven with the New South." The aim of southern "redeemers" and their northern allies was "to hasten the complete restoration of fraternal and business intercourse between the North and South, and thereby enlarge the prosperity of both."[88] Elsewhere in the South, northern and southern elites shook hands and extracted cheap raw materials and hired cheap labor. Tourism to St. Augustine's grand resorts fostered both fraternal and business intercourse by reassuring the former warriors of blue and gray that the past that had led to the Civil War had not actually happened. But, ultimately, the "victories of peace" were leisure, consumption, commerce, and selective memory, erasing evidence of slavery, the sectional conflict, and the failure of Reconstruction. ❖

Notes

1. Henry M. Field, *Bright Skies and Dark Shadows* (New York: Scribner's, 1890), 84.

2. I am using C. Vann Woodward's definition of the "New South." Though the term began as a propagandistic slogan wielded by business-oriented southern leaders and their northern allies in the decades after Reconstruction, historians have come to use "New South" to describe both a time period (roughly 1877–1913) and a particular shift in the southern economy toward industrialization. In the New South, the fate of the southern economy was in the hands of northern capitalists—"empire builders"—who, with the help of a new entrepreneurial leadership class in the South, exploited the South's raw materials and cheap labor and maintained control of the region's profits. As a result, the South became a "colony" of the North and grew increasingly poor and underdeveloped in comparison to the North. This period is also distinguished by the rise of Jim Crow legislation, racist violence, and federal acceptance of the same. C. Vann Woodward, *Origins of the New South, 1877–1913* (Baton Rouge: Louisiana State University Press, 1951).

3. Susan Braden, *The Architecture of Leisure: The Florida Resort Hotels of Henry Flagler and Henry Plant* (Gainesville: University Press of Florida, 2002); Rafael Agapito Crespo, "Florida's First Renaissance Revival" (Ph.D. diss., Harvard University, 1987); Thomas Graham, *The Awakening of St. Augustine: The Anderson Family and the Oldest City, 1821–1924* (St. Augustine, FL: St. Augustine Historical Society, 1978).

4. "Florida. Its Rapid Political and Agricultural Improvements," *New York Times* (20 October 1873): 5.

5. Nina Silber, *The Romance of Reunion: Northerners and the South, 1865–1900* (Chapel Hill: University of North Carolina Press, 1993), 4.

6. Quoted in David W. Blight, *Race and Reunion: The Civil War in American Memory* (Cambridge, MA: Harvard University Press, 2001), 199.

7. "The Southern Question," *Florida Times-Union* (14 December 1881).

8. See Charlton Tebeau, *A History of Florida* (Coral Gables, FL: University of Miami Press, 1971), 182: "The center of cotton planting and the concentration of slaves was in the region between the Apalachicola and Suwanee Rivers in Gadsden, Jefferson, Leon, and Madison counties. After 1845 cotton growing expanded into nearby counties in East Florida, and Alachua and Marion became known as plantation counties."

9. Edward Baptist, *Creating an Old South: Middle Florida's Plantation Frontier before the Civil War* (Chapel Hill: University of North Carolina Press, 2002), 251.

10. Ibid., chap. 9.

11. Edwin Lefevre, "Flagler and Florida," *Everybody's Magazine* 12 (January-June 1910): 168. Italics in original.

12. *Tallahassee Floridian and Journal*, 1 December 1860, cited in Baptist, *Creating an Old South*, 270. By "the fate of whites in Santo Domingo," the author was referring to the Haitian Revolution, a slave rebellion of the 1790s that lasted more than a decade, resulted in the independence of Haiti from colonial rule, and created the first republic governed by people of African descent.

13. "Testimony Before Reconstruction Committee," *Harper's Weekly* (31 March 1866): 206.

14. *St. Augustine Examiner* (16 November 1866); *St. Augustine Examiner* (4 May 1867).

15. Eric Foner, *Reconstruction: America's Unfinished Revolution, 1863–1877* (New York: Harper & Row, 1988), 426, 429, 431, 433, 435, 439.

16. "Florida's Debt," *Harper's Weekly* (26 July 1873): 643.

17. "To Florida in Winter. Comforts and Discomforts of the Trip," *New York Times* (27 January 1871): 2.

18. "Experiences in Florida," *New York Times* (14 December 1876): 6.

19. "Leaves of Travel, A Journey to Florida III," *New York Times* (14 February 1875): 2.

20. "Florida's Debt," *Harper's Weekly* (26 July 1873): 643.

21. "In the Orange Groves. Some of the Disappointments of Florida Scenery," *New York Times* (19 April 1883): 4.

22. C. Vann Woodward, *Origins of the New South*, 3rd ed. (Baton Rouge: Louisiana State University Press, 1997), 150.

23. "Dying Sectionalism," *Florida Times-Union* (7 January 1882).

24. "Florida's Opportunity," *Florida Times-Union* (1 October 1882).

25. "The Way to Save the Country," *Florida Times-Union* (2 February 1882).

26. "Notes, Queries, and Comments," *Semi-Tropical* 3, no. 10 (October 1877): 633–34.

27. "Harriet Beecher Stowe on West Florida," *Florida Weekly Press* (23 May 1874).

28. Influential early guidebooks and travel literature include Harriet Beecher Stowe, *Palmetto Leaves* (Boston: J. R. Osgood, 1873); Sidney Lanier, *Florida: Its Scenery, Climate, and History* (Philadelphia: Lippincott, 1875); and George Barbour, *Florida for Tourists, Invalids and Settlers* (Gainesville: University of Florida Press, 1882).

29. *St. Johns County Illustrated, Pictorial Edition of the St. Augustine Evening Record*, c. 1908, 5.

30. Abbie Brooks, *Petals Plucked from Sunny Climes*, facsimile reproduction of the 1880 edition, introduction and index by Richard A. Martin (Gainesville: University Press of Florida, 1976), 162–63.

31. Margaret Deland, *Florida Days* (Boston: Little, Brown, 1889), 64–65, 67.

32. Ibid., 70.

33. Alice Brown, "Florida in 1870 and 30 Years Later," unpublished manuscript, Biographical Folder, St. Augustine Historical Society, 2.

34. W. O. Ruggles, "Saratoga-Jacksonville," *Semi-Tropical* 2, no. 4 (April 1876): 221.

35. *Florida Daily Times* (8 December 1881).

36. See, for example, "Our City," *St. Augustine Examiner* (29 September 1866): "The old town went to sleep about two centuries ago and one mistook the sleep for death, but that turns out to be all a mistake; she was only taking a nap.... [W]e see spasmodic signs that this rather long doze is approaching an end."

37. Graham, *Awakening of St. Augustine*, 89–90.

38. Letter from Commander Rodgers (who received the town's surrender), 12 March 1862. Reprinted in William W. Dewhurst, *The History of St. Augustine, Florida* (New York: Putnam's, 1885), 176.

39. Graham, *Awakening of St. Augustine*, 133. Only an English visitor seemed to be willing to attribute St. Augustine's decomposing quality to the ravages of the Civil War rather than its mere antiquity: "[The inhabitants of St. Augustine], possessing no money, but heaps of confederate bonds are, in many instances, literally penniless." The "English visitor" paralleled the citizens' "listless apathy" to the same "hopeless feeling ... hanging over most of the Southern cities. They are crushed, broken, ruined, and humiliated, if a people so proud can ever realize that sentiment." *St. Augustine, Florida. Sketches of Its History, Objects of Interest, and Advantages as a Resort for Health and Recreation. By an English Visitor* (New York: Putnam's, 1869), 40–41.

40. *Rambler, Guide to Florida*, facsimile reproduction of the 1875 edition, introduction by Rembert W. Patrick (Gainesville: University of Florida Press, 1964).

41. W. M. A. Pringle, *A Guide to the Land of Flowers, with a Tour through Florida* (Charleston, SC: Parry, Cooke, 1878), 91.

42. *Florida* (New York: Wittenman, c. 1885), 2.

43. A. Hyatt Verrill, *Romantic and Historic Florida* (New York: Dodd, Mead, 1935), 66.

44. For detailed studies of Henry Morrison Flagler and his enterprises in Florida, see Edward Akin, *Flagler: Rockefeller Partner and Florida Baron* (Kent, OH: Kent State University Press, 1988; Gainesville: University Press of Florida, 1992); David Leon Chandler, *Henry Flagler* (New York: Macmillan, 1986); Sidney Walter Martin, *Florida's Flagler* (Athens: University of Georgia Press, 1949); George Pettengill Jr., *The Story of the Florida Railroads, 1834–1903* (Boston: Railway and Locomotive Historical Society, 1952); and Graham, *Awakening of St. Augustine*.

45. The Cordova Hotel was originally called the Casa Monica and was built and owned by Boston transplant Franklin W. Smith, but because of financial difficulties, Smith sold to Flagler, who renamed it the Cordova. Graham, *Awakening of St. Augustine*, 176.

46. Ibid., 168.

47. Quoted in Crespo, "Florida's First Spanish Renaissance Revival," 109.

48. Walter E. Knibloe, *Schneur's Illustrated Guide and History of St. Augustine, Florida* (St. Augustine, FL: Schneur, 1885), 20.

49. Carrère and Hastings, *Florida, The American Riviera; St. Augustine, the Winter Newport. The Ponce de Leon, the Alcazar, the Casa Monica* (New York: Gillis Bros. & Turnure, Art Age Press, 1887), 10.

50. For the City Beautiful movement, see William H. Wilson, *The City Beautiful Movement* (Baltimore: Johns Hopkins University Press, 1989); Robert Fogelsong, *Planning the Capitalist City: The Colonial Era to the 1920s* (Princeton, NJ: Princeton University Press, 1986); Daniel Bluestone, *Constructing Chicago* (New Haven, CT: Yale University Press, 1991).

51. E. H. Reynolds, *The Standard Guide to St. Augustine and Fort Marion, Season 1885–1886* (St. Augustine, FL: Reynolds, 1890), 51; Brooks, *Petals Plucked from Sunny Climes*, 184.

52. Robert Perkinson, "'Within San Marco's Gloomy Walls': Performance and Cultural Exchange around the Indian Prison at Fort Marion, 1875–1878" (unpublished paper, Yale University, 2002).

53. Carrère and Hastings, *Florida, The American Riviera*, 12. For an analysis of America's world's fairs as expressions of American progress and imperialism, see Robert Rydell, *All the World's a Fair: Visions of Empire at American International Expositions, 1976–1916* (Chicago: University of Chicago Press, 1984).

54. Braden, *Architecture of Leisure*, 166–68.

55. Ibid., 171–72.

56. Lefevre, "Flagler and Florida,"178; Carrère and Hastings, *Florida, The American Riviera*, 41.

57. Charles B. Reynolds, *The Standard Guide to St. Augustine* (St. Augustine, FL: Reynolds, 1890), 26.

58. Braden, *Architecture of Leisure*, 142. Rafael Crespo dates the St. Augustine Hotel to 1869. Crespo, *Florida's First Spanish Renaissance Revival*, 65.

59. Wanton S. Webb, *Webb's Historical, Industrial and Biographical Florida. Part I* (New York: Webb, 1885), 198.

60. Carrère and Hastings, *Florida, The American Riviera*, 22.

61. Catskills resorts, developed in the late nineteenth century, originally aimed to attract the same elite urbanites in summer as did Flagler's Florida resorts in winter. By the 1920s many of these elite resorts began to serve a Jewish clientele, so that by the 1940s the southern Catskills came to be known as the "Borscht Belt." See Architectural League of New York, *Resorts of the Catskills* (New York: St. Martin's, 1979).

62. "City Improvements," *Florida Times-Union* (4 December 1881).

63. Elizabeth Stuart Phelps, "Confession of St. Augustine," *Atlantic Monthly* 37, no. 220 (February 1876): 129–30.

64. *St. Augustine, St. Johns County Illustrated*, pictorial edition of the *St. Augustine Evening Record*, (c. 1908): 5.

65. "Florida: St. Augustine, A Venerable City," *New York Times* (5 April 1873): 4.

66. Graham, *Awakening of St. Augustine*, 201.

67. Ibid., 201.

68. *Tatler* 7, no. 3 (27 January 1898): 1.

69. *Tatler* 16, no. 2 (12 January 1907): 1.

70. *Tatler* 7, no. 3 (27 January 1898): 1.

71. St. Augustine Municipal Court Records, books 35–37, 1858–1895. St. Augustine Historical Society.

72. "Confidential," *St. Augustine Record* (23 December 1901).

73. "Loafing vs. Lounging," *St. Augustine Evening Record* (30 December 1901).

74. "Council To Suppress Loafing Nuisance. Record's Suggestions are Heeded. Ordinance Introduced to Prevent Lounging on Fences near the Plaza," *St. Augustine Evening Record* (9 January 1902).

75. "Be Clean," *St. Augustine Record* (16 January 1902).

76. "Ponce de Leon," *Florida Times-Union* (16 January 1888).

77. "Leaves of Travel," *New York Times* (14 February 1875): 2.

78. *St. Augustine News* (1 February 1891). A fakir is a peddler or a street hawker.

79. Carrère and Hastings, *Florida, The American Riviera*, 4.

80. L. R. Tuttle, *Twelve Years Constant Residence in Florida. With Some Relevant Remarks regarding the state as it now appears to a pioneer of '74* (Louisville, KY: Press of the Courier-Journal Job Printing Co., 1885), 17.

81. Editorial, *Florida Times-Union* (17 June 1899).

82. Field, *Bright Skies and Dark Shadows*, 4, 49–51.

83. Robert W. Torchia, *A Florida Legacy: Ponce de Leon in Florida* (Jacksonville, FL: Cummer Museum of Art and Gardens, 1998).

84. *St. Augustine Record's Special Souvenir Edition, Ponce de Leon Celebration*, 1907, 1.

85. *St. Augustine Record's Special Souvenir Edition, Ponce de Leon Celebration*, 1909, 3.

86. Carrère and Hastings, *Florida, The American Riviera*, 8–10.

87. *St. Augustine Record's Special Souvenir Edition, Ponce de Leon Celebration*, 1907, 1.

88. A. K. McClure, *The South: Its Industrial, Financial and Political Condition* (Philadelphia: Lippincott, 1886), introduction.

United Slates

Myra B. Young Armstead

Revisiting Hotels and Other Lodgings: American Tourist Spaces through the Lens of Black Pleasure-Travelers, 1880–1950

Myra B. Young Armstead is professor of history at Bard College, where she chairs her department and cochairs the American studies program. Her primary research and teaching interests are in nineteenth-century American social history with a focus on United States urban history and African American history. She has published *"Lord, Please Don't Take Me in August": African Americans in Newport and Saratoga Springs, 1870–1930* (1999) and *Mighty Change, Tall Within: Black Identity in the Hudson Valley* (2003).

Technology and social history converged in the late nineteenth century when the introduction of the handheld camera and the emergence of a black tourist class in the United States coincided. But these two developments shared more than a moment in history. The camera could be used to provide visual confirmation of prescribed social relations and ideals. Black tourists at mainstream vacation spots implicitly defied prevailing expectations for tourist spaces during an era of officially sanctioned racial segregation. Black bodies recorded unwittingly on film enjoying popular tourist destinations inherently reflected the black belief that African Americans, as consumers, were entitled to occupy such places despite white hostility. Moreover, the small black middle and upper classes that could claim leisure time and leisure spaces also enlisted photography and other print media in deliberate fashion. By documenting their own tourist experiences and holiday venues into the early twentieth-century era of continuing racial separation, African Americans created visual texts that asserted their respectability and rightful place within the ranks of "good" society.

Losing Ground in Mainstream Venues

The pleasure-traveling public of black Americans in the late nineteenth century, like its white counterpart, consisted of the most economically privileged segment of the African American population. This elite group amounted to roughly 10 percent of the black population and included professionals—doctors, lawyers, professors, writers, publishers, clergymen, politicians, judges, political office holders—as well as successful independent entrepreneurs. These "aristocrats of color" were linked nationally through a network of black fraternities, sororities, fraternal lodges, and social clubs.[1] This group expanded to some extent in the early twentieth century as the

Waiters at the United States Hotel dining room (detail), Saratoga Springs, New York, c. 1890s (see fig. 2).

fig. 1
Two black men strolling on Broadway, Saratoga Springs, New York, opposite the United States Hotel, c. 1907. The Bolster Collection at the Saratoga Springs History Museum. Photograph by Jesse Sumner Wooley.

popularity of the automobile made less-expensive short, day, or weekend excursions accessible to a middle stratum of blacks—civil service workers, porters, social workers, and the like.

After the Civil War, blacks who could afford to patronize resort hotels and other new vacation spots joined a new class of wealthy Americans created by nineteenth-century industrialization. Thus, many upper-class African Americans enjoyed the celebrated playgrounds of the nation's monied whites. A set of black vacationers from all points in the country summered in late nineteenth- and early twentieth-century northeastern resorts like Newport in Rhode Island, Saratoga Springs in New York, Atlantic City, Cape May, and Sea Isle on the Jersey shore, and Sag Harbor on Long Island. Further south, Silcott Springs in Virginia and Harpers Ferry in West Virginia attracted others. In the Midwest, African Americans vacationed at Bois Blanc Island, a northern Michigan retreat near Mackinaw Island.[2]

An early twentieth-century photograph of Broadway, the major thoroughfare of Saratoga Springs, includes two well-dressed black gentlemen promenading along with white visitors, confirming the presence of African Americans at this spa (fig. 1). Yet the placement of the figures in the picture attests to the mounting tide of white opposition to black commingling with whites that typified the infamous segregationist era of race relations following Reconstruction. By emphasizing the vanishing point from several different lines, the photographer underscores the expansive, boulevard-like quality of the street rather than the two black figures, just right of center in the foreground. The image was taken roughly a decade after the 1896 *Plessy v. Ferguson* Supreme Court decision legally authorizing racial segregation as national practice. Racial proscriptions against blacks were already spiraling after the Supreme Court's declaration in 1883 of the unconstitutionality of the Civil Rights Act of 1875, which had sought to make hotels and other such facilities accessible to African Americans. After *Plessy*, these proscriptions proliferated by law and custom all over the country. Black vacationers, regardless of status, increasingly found accommodations at mainstream travel destinations closed to them entirely, separated from those offered to whites by time (blacks were served on different days or at different hours) or offered to them in distinct locations. So, for example, it was not unusual that from the 1880s until it was destroyed in 1926, blacks could use the round yellow wood pavilion on Pablo Beach, Coney Island, Florida, on Mondays only. Similarly, in 1882, Detroit's Kirkwood Hotel denied rooms to the Fisk Jubilee Singers as a matter of policy. The manager told a local newspaper that African American guests were harmful to his business.[3]

By the early twentieth century the so-called Jim Crow system of segregation was firmly established and affected both public and private vacation facilities. In 1916, for example, the commissioners of the State Reservation at Saratoga Springs announced their decision to install separate black and white bathhouses in the park and to limit the former "as the number of colored people applying for treatment is not over one per cent of the aggregate number of both races at present."[4] The commissioners capitulated to the discomfort and vigorous opposition expressed among the white public regarding any existing practice of blacks occupying the same pleasure spaces as whites. The very next year, W. E. B. Du Bois (1868–1963) observed that the issue of "ever-recurring race discrimination" generally made it "a puzzling query as to what to do with vacations," whether traveling to national or regional popular resorts, major cities, or remote getaways.[5] Even Booker T. Washington (1856–1915), the Great Accommodationist who urged blacks to accept segregation patiently while he personally enjoyed the facilities at "a first-class, midtown hotel" whenever he visited New York City, experienced in the last four years of his life the bite of Jim Crow while traveling there. He became embroiled in a strange scandal in 1911 when a white carpenter and his "wife" accused him of trying to break into their house in the Tenderloin District and of accosting the woman verbally in a sexually suggestive manner. After that incident, Washington found his access to the stylish Hotel Manhattan suddenly withdrawn. His appeal to the hotel owner fell on deaf ears, and he never again enjoyed comparable facilities in that city. One year before he died, Washington was reduced to sending the maître d' of the McAlpin Hotel in New York a copy of his latest book and promising to eat his meals in his room, not the hotel dining room, if permitted to stay there. He received no reply to this request.[6] Apparently, one alleged misstep by this prominent, "exceptional" Race Man was sufficient to cast him into the same heap as other African Americans regarding certain travel amenities.

This pattern of discrimination continued after the First World War into the Depression and the Second World War era. Indeed, flouting the rules of segregation in recreation and leisure, however innocently, could be dangerous for African Americans and lead to physical reprisals from angry whites.[7] Wendell Dabney, an African American newspaper editor, explained the situation that black visitors to Cincinnati faced in the 1920s:

> Hotels, restaurants, eating and drinking places, almost universally are closed to all people in whom the least tincture of colored blood can be detected. The Bartenders' Union has passed a resolution forbidding its members to wait on a colored person, and they live up to it.... At the Stinton Hotel,... the colored man is not welcome even to standing room in the lobby. No matter how prominent he is, if he desires to see a white man on one of the upper floors he must take the freight elevator, or the lower compartment of the elevator, the "Jim Crow" compartment, we may call it.[8]

Similarly, in the 1930s, black vacationers in Ocean City, New Jersey, faced bathing restrictions, according to one contemporary sociological study.[9] Ironically, even within African American ghettos of major northern cities, blacks were not permitted in certain hotels: the Jim Crow system kept the famed Hotel Theresa, a Harlem landmark, a segregated establishment closed to African Americans until 1940. Not until after then did it become celebrated for its clientele of popular black entertainers like Lena Horne and Duke Ellington. As late as 1943, after conducting an informal survey of 105 northeastern travel establishments, black journalist George S. Schuyler complained, "Many colored families have motored all across the United States without being able to secure overnight accommodations at a single tourist camp or hotel." He concluded from his investigation that blacks would have an easier time traveling abroad than in the United States.[10]

As the momentum toward Jim Crow hardened into a racialized caste system during the late nineteenth century and the first decades of the twentieth century, it was mainly left to African American proprietors to provide hotels and boardinghouses for black tourists and travelers. For instance, in the last quarter of the nineteenth century, the Banneker Hotel in Cape May, New Jersey, catered to an all-black traveling clientele. Cincinnati's Dumas House hosted black guests at least through 1894.[11] For several decades after 1910, Ella Holmes operated her Holmes Cottage for summering blacks on Walworth Street in Saratoga Springs. Reporting on a trip to Chicago in 1921, Du Bois wrote favorably of the Vincennes Hotel: "I stayed at the Vincennes. Around me were ghosts of white folks

fig. 2
Waiters at the United
States Hotel dining room,
Saratoga Springs,
New York, lantern slide of
original photograph,
c. 1900. Collection of
Brookside Museum,
Saratoga County
Historical Society.
Photograph by
Jesse Sumner Wooley.

who used to live at this beautiful, quiet, and exclusive hotel. Now Negroes own it and it is still beautiful and quiet but, thank heaven, neither exclusive nor dear. Every Negro in the United States ought to take a trip to Chicago, just to stop at the Vincennes with his family." [12]

An equally acceptable alternative to black-owned operations in mainstream resorts and pleasure capitals were white-owned establishments in major cities catering to an exclusively black clientele. In the early twentieth century, Cincinnati's Old St. Clair Hotel, patronized by wealthy whites, was converted by its white owner into a first-class hotel for blacks and renamed the Hotel Sterling.[13] Only places like the Sterling and the Gordon hotels in Cincinnati hosted leading members of the national black community, Du Bois and Marcus Garvey (1887–1940) among them. Despite their prominence, these luminaries could not find accommodations in hotels with white customers. White business adventurers apparently capitalized on this situation, as did their black counterparts, and exploited profitably the special need among blacks for travel amenities produced by the Jim Crow system. Whether black or white owned, places like the Sterling, Gordon, Banneker, Holmes Cottage, and the Vincennes functioned as insular leisure residences within hostile vacation environments.

As Jim Crow solidified, black tourists were rendered invisible in white representations of mainstream resorts. Instead, the visual record shows blacks mainly as servants and helpers for whites. Thus, images of black waiters standing attentively at their posts in the dining room of Saratoga's United States Hotel (fig. 2) and a black nursemaid watching the children

fig. 3
A nursemaid in Saratoga Springs watches her charges, c. 1910. The Bolster Collection at the Saratoga Springs History Museum.

under her care in that spa's Congress Park (fig. 3) confirmed the preferred racial order. They replaced the peripheral notice of black vacationers at popular white tourist venues, shown in the photo of two black men strolling on Broadway opposite the hotel (see fig. 1). These images raise questions about whether the dignified carriage and presentation of African Americans within resort settings inhered in them as independent users of such spaces, as it does for the two black men promenading on Broadway, who appear to be taking in the sights for their own enjoyment. Instead, the meticulous dress and bearing of the waiters, seen against the backdrop of the impressive dining room interior, ironically underscore the privilege of the invisible white hotel patrons. The neatness of the maid's attire similarly reflects the propriety of her white employer and her employer's children. Even assuming that the waiters and maid in the photographs chose to project a public image of self-respect in these poses, the point is that the camera permitted such an impression within the context of servanthood, but not consumption.

Framing Respectability in All-Black Venues

Besides seizing the initiative to develop black-serving leisure spaces in established resorts and metropolitan centers, African Americans developed their own all-black tourist venues. Through their photographic inventory of these places, they revealed a self-assessment that countered prevailing notions of them as "a race" and as individuals. Major examples of venues for the black elite include Oak Bluffs on Martha's Vineyard, Massachusetts, Highland Beach in Anne Arundel County, Maryland, and Idlewild in northern Michigan. But there were certainly smaller, more localized versions of the more celebrated spots—American Beach in Florida, for instance.[14]

Technically, Oak Bluffs was never frequented exclusively by African Americans. Rather, at a time when mainstream vacation havens strictly observed an exclusionary policy toward blacks, Oak Bluffs evolved as the sole town on Martha's Vineyard that tolerated a noticeable black community of both permanent residents and summer visitors. The town initially developed as a Methodist summer camp meeting and revival center in the antebellum period of the nineteenth century. Eventually, the religious atmosphere faded and made way for more varied secular pursuits, and blacks came to the town as both year-round small business operators and service workers profiting from the burgeoning leisure industry. Around the turn of the twentieth century, Charles Shearer (1854–1934), who had first arrived with his family to start his own laundry operation for white summer residents, transformed his facility into a guesthouse, including tennis courts, catering to African Americans. One of the daughters of this former Boston hotel maître d' had recognized the need for suitable accommodations for black visitors there. Mrs. Anthony Smith operated another "deluxe" black-run Oak Bluffs inn for African Americans in the first part of the twentieth century. After Reverend Oscar Dennison established a black church mission in Oak Bluffs, his presence and congregation helped solidify and anchor the year-round African American population. This church, another indication of the town's relative openness toward blacks in an unfriendly age, spurred an increase in black summer tourists from nearby cities. In time, certain streets and neighborhoods in Oak Bluffs were firmly established as black summer enclaves. By the end of the Second World War, the resort was firmly established among blacks as a beachfront haven and as a special spot where one could rub shoulders with "certain prominent personalities" from around the nation.[15]

Black visitors to Oak Bluffs documented their experiences visually through photography as a record of their travel and status among that class of Americans who could participate in leisure activities. Take, for example, the well-dressed group of black tourists shown formally posing some time at the turn of the last century outside of Thayer Cottage, an Oak Bluffs rooming house on the religious campground there, despite the fact that

fig. 4
Group outside Thayer
Cottage, Oak Bluffs,
Martha's Vineyard,
Massachusetts, c. 1890.
Martha's Vineyard
Historical Society.

the campground did not generally welcome African Americans during this era (fig. 4).[16] Although we no longer know the identity of the tourists, the photograph itself is a document of many things: not only their presence at the vacation site, but also, as the quality of their stylish yet modest clothing suggests, their ability to afford such a vacation and their embrace of contemporary standards of middle-class self-restraint. The photograph captures the sitters as a group participating in one of the rituals of tourism as discussed by photo historian Michel Frizot: the "official" pose beside a landmark whereby the subjects stake their claim upon or association with that site. Furthermore, the cottage in the photograph displays a bourgeois mix of historicist elements typical of the period. These African American tourists, in other words, decidedly linked themselves, in dress and location, to mainstream tastes.

Around the same time that Oak Bluffs was establishing itself as a summer retreat for African Americans, a similar resort was developing further south in the Chesapeake Bay region. Denied access to a Maryland vacation stop, Frederick Douglass's son, Charles (1844–1920), bought a nearby beachfront parcel of land, which he and his wife established after 1893 as a seaside haven for family and friends who also purchased land in the area. At first called Arundel-on-the-Bay, the place was later renamed Highland Beach. This leisure set was limited to a tight circle of Washington, D.C.–based, high-ranking black elites. In 1922 it was incorporated as the first black town in Maryland.[17]

Highland Beach vacationers claimed mainstream middle-class values (figs. 5–7). In these images the subjects are distributed evenly within the frame to convey a sense of balance and order in their lives, even as they "relax." The photo encases them in activities—croquet, possibly picnicking, bathing—that all fell neatly within the list of acceptable and/or fashionable pastimes at the turn of the twentieth century. Croquet, in particular, reached a peak of popularity in the United States in the late nineteenth century as a French import via England, and the American middle and upper classes associated it with the leisure life of the wealthy in Britain. As a sport practiced by mixed sexes, croquet was rather unique for the time, so the presence of men and women together at play did not challenge social convention (fig. 5). Croquet and picnics are manifestations of human activity on lawns or in backyards, both of which were pacifications of the wilderness. The vegetation and trees are dwarfed by the human imprint on both scenes and therefore associate black vacationers with the cultivation of the wild or with domesticity—a core value of the age. Thus, the

fig. 5
(above, left)
Patrons at croquet,
Highland Beach,
Maryland, c. 1898.
Gregoria Fraser Goins
Papers, Moorland-
Spingarn Research Center,
Howard University.

fig. 6
(above, center)
Picnickers under a
swing, Highland Beach,
Maryland, 1899.
Gregoria Fraser Goins
Papers, Moorland-
Spingarn Research Center,
Howard University.

fig. 7
(above, right)
Swimmers, Highland
Beach, Maryland.
Gregoria Fraser Goins
Papers, Moorland-
Spingarn Research Center,
Howard University.

potentially overwhelming tree seen towering over the picnicking group is harnessed by the swing and the bench beneath it and by the placement of women on both (fig. 6). As the swing was a favorite prop in mainstream photographic poses of women during this period, the young black woman sitting on the tree swing visually anchors the shot and embodies its intent. The parasols and swimwear donned by the female bathers define them as respectable bathers of the late Victorian period (fig. 7). The men in both images announce their vigilance and honor, almost as sentries among the women, by the rigidity of their stances. One holds a lady's handbag and parasol (see fig. 6), putting aside any apprehensions for more gentlemanly concerns, and the other has graciously lowered himself behind the woman seated on the swing, holding on to one of the ropes. A single male among the women, seen at the left near the shoreline (see fig. 7), stands at attention like some sort of watchman, clutching a thick, clublike stick. Thus, the men in both images advertise their readiness to guard and protect womankind. As a trio, these Highland Beach photographs scream African American conformity to prevailing social and cultural norms.[18]

In the Midwest, Idlewild emerged in the early twentieth century as the foremost black summer spot—a place like Highland Beach where African American vacationers evinced bourgeois values. Founded in 1912 on 2,700 acres of overcut timberland in Lake County, Michigan, the resort drew patrons like Dr. Daniel Hale Williams (1858–1931), a heart surgeon, founder of Chicago's Provident Hospital, and an influential man in contemporary medicine, who was also one of the largest property owners at Idlewild. Williams built Oakmere, a summer cottage, and created a park of the same name across the street. Eventually, the Oakmere Hotel was established near the park. The exterior architecture of the Oakmere displayed the simplicity and rusticity increasingly prized among rural vacationers in the 1910s and 1920s as a reflection of the burgeoning camping movement (fig. 8). His modest but "modern" bungalow is "made luxurious with electricity and Oriental rugs" (fig. 9).[19] The limited furnishings—a stark departure from the overstuffed homes of the late Victorian period—may reflect the extent to which "bareness and restraint

fig. 8
(right)
Oakmere Hotel, Idlewild,
Michigan. State Archives
of Michigan.

fig. 9
(below, right)
Daniel Hale Williams in
his parlor, Idlewild,
Michigan. Daniel Hale
Williams Papers,
Moorland-Spingarn
Research Center,
Howard University.

[were] slowly being accepted by the middle class" in the years after 1900.[20] Williams, at the picture's center, is defined as an educated man by the instructional materials that surround him—books, papers, and even a human skull. By his neat attire, his unsmiling face, his preoccupation with reading, and his unpretentious house furnishings, Williams projects sobriety and seriousness even as he relaxes in his retreat. Through the camera, Williams conveys the message that although vacationing, he remains a staid and thoughtful individual, unwilling to sacrifice a commitment to work—a perennial virtue among Americans of his class—for play. Williams also sold land to his wealthy friends, thereby virtually creating an enclave of like minds and tastes. That taste is evident in the interior of an Idlewild hotel dining room, where order and modesty are projected through the camera lens (fig. 10).[21]

fig. 10
(above, left)
Idlewild dining room
interior, c. 1920,
thought to be at the Club
El-Morocco. State
Archives of Michigan.

fig. 11
(above, right)
Gass Point, Idlewild,
Michigan. State Archives
of Michigan.

Claiming the Landscape

As real estate speculators, Idlewild's founders understood well that middle-class blacks hungered for land, places where they would be assured a welcome, and spaces they could claim. These speculators divided the terrain into plots and sold them to African Americans as summer vacation retreats from the sweltering cities of Chicago, Detroit, Indianapolis, and Cleveland. Eventually, scenic views at the resort were named after prominent black landowners. Gass Point, for example, was named for Charlie Gass, who sold plots at Idlewild while employed as a shoeshine man at the Pantlind Hotel in downtown Grand Rapids, Michigan (fig. 11). Similarly, in the 1920s, Dr. Williams purchased a large plot and named it the Daniel Hale Williams Subdivision.[22]

The importance of such gestures cannot be overstated. The practice of naming views and sites has a long history in the commodification of the landscape. As historian Dona Brown has shown, "The naming of unnamed places and things was crucial to making the region scenic: The more named things, the more places for tourists to visit, and the more orderly and differentiated the landscape became."[23] Equally as significant was the fact that the landscape had been named for a black man. Historically and ideologically dispossessed men like Gass could claim a bit of the American landscape for themselves. Understood this way, the sweeping view of Gass Point pictorially proclaims that everything in the horizontal and vertical range of vision belongs to African Americans.

Embracing the Pastoral

From the visual record, it is evident that black Americans shared the same passion for the pastoral that typified mainstream domestic travelers in the period studied here. During the late nineteenth and early twentieth centuries, Americans sought rustic retreats and encounters with nature as antidotes to what were perceived as the unhealthful, stultifying, and corrupting aspects of modernization—congested residential arrangements, aesthetically and intellectually uninspiring vistas, and the escalating pace of work. As part of this national drift, African Americans with the means,

fig. 12
(top)
Idlewild Lake, Idlewild,
Michigan. State Archives of
Michigan.

fig. 13
(bottom)
The bridge to Idlewild
Island, Idlewild, Michigan.
State Archives of Michigan.

time, and inclination opted to remove themselves from cities to beaches, country getaways, and wild spaces to enjoy the restorative qualities associated with these settings.

In their vacation selections and photographic record of them, African Americans participated in a national critique of industrial life and urbanization. One black school principal, who decided in 1917 "to leave the city for absolute rest" by vacationing on the homestead of another African American family in rural Georgia, reported: "Every day was

fig. 14
(above, left)
**Boathouse at Highland
Beach, Maryland, c. 1929.**
Gregoria Fraser Goins
Papers, Moorland-
Spingarn Research Center,
Howard University.

fig. 15
(above, right)
**Porch at Highland Beach,
Maryland, 1929.**
Gregoria Fraser Goins
Papers, Moorland-
Spingarn Research Center,
Howard University.

back to nature,… a long ways from the railroad."[24] Du Bois's rapturous description of Idlewild in 1921, bordering on poetry, must be appreciated in this same sense. He wrote, "For sheer physical beauty—for sheen of water and golden air, for nobleness of tree and flower of shrub, for shining river and song of bird and the low, moving whisper of sun, moon and star; it is the beautifulest stretch I have seen for twenty years."[25]

At Idlewild, the absence, or near absence, of any humans in these photographs celebrates the virtues of nature. A serene Lake Idlewild balances the expanse of the sky, offset only by a few tall trees (fig. 12). And in the photo of the approach to Idlewild, the lake dominates the foreground, but this time a lone individual runs toward the island across a quaint wooden bridge, away from the viewer, in a hurried escape from the mainland and all the complications it implies (fig. 13).

Photographs also celebrated country life at Highland Beach. A group of three women, including one who appears to be elderly, have been captured by the camera taking a moment to admire the water and the pristine, bucolic shore in the distance (fig. 14). A country porch, filled with empty rattan furniture, beckons any who may approach to slow down and quite literally sit a spell (fig. 15). The low camera angle sweeps the viewer fully across the porch toward the vanishing point, in the center of the shot, an open door revealing yet another unfilled seat awaiting a weary occupant. Household wicker furnishings connoted for late nineteenth- and early twentieth-century Americans the more leisurely pace of undeveloped, preindustrial societies, perhaps because of their Asian origin. Significantly, in order to preserve its rustic character, Highland Beach did not permit commercial development, and this continues to be true today; the retreat now claims about sixty homes.

De-Racializing Space
The security offered by black-owned resorts, especially those in rural areas, joined with a general belief in nature's benefits in the minds of blacks to invest these particular spaces with special health-inducing powers during the Jim Crow era. In black-owned rustic spaces, there was the tranquility that came from having escaped the rhythms of a work routine. But there was also the serenity that came from having escaped the protocols of

systematic and systemic racial discrimination. Du Bois expressed this sentiment by contrasting mainstream resorts or tourist centers at which blacks were permitted with certain limitations—places like Atlantic City, New York City, and even Oak Bluffs—with Idlewild, a resort created specifically for African Americans: "Not for one moment in fine joy of life, absolute freedom from the desperate cruelty of the color line and for the wooing of the great silence which is Peace and deep Contentment—not for one little minute can they rival or catch the bounding pulse of Idlewild."[26]

For African American tourists, then, black-owned resorts represented a return to a primeval nature, but a completely de-racialized nature that therefore exuded healing, humanizing qualities in a singular and utopian way. So when African Americans viewed photographs of black-owned country resorts, they could infuse these places with a curative power bearing a distinctly "race"-free character. In the country, blacks would not only be healed of the detrimental effects of city life, they would also experience a soothing balm for the wounds of life under segregation. Highland Beach's decision to ban commercial development should be understood in this light as well.

Affirming Citizenship

African American tourists believed in the ideology of the American landscape and its nationalistic association with the frontier where the "American Character"—vigorous, youthful, pure—is formed and regenerated. Black-owned tourist venues granted African Americans the rights of land ownership that historically were tied to conceptions of American citizenship and the right to vote. Historian Marguerite S. Shaffer has described how in the early twentieth century "tourism solidified into a popular leisure activity" that helped shape a national identity for all Americans. As early as the 1830s the act of surveying the American landscape developed, both

fig. 17
Map of lots in Idlewild,
Michigan, 1919.
Ben C. Wilson Collection,
Africana Studies
Program, Western
Michigan University.

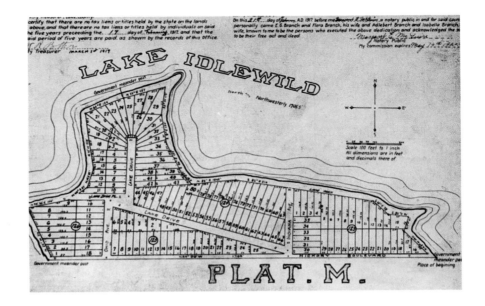

in prescriptive guidebooks and in touring practices, into a patriotic exercise.
Traversing representative locations across state and regional topographies,
the American tourist encountered and reconstructed a narrative history
that included Native American villages, colonial settlements, Revolutionary
battlefields, and sites of agricultural innovation and industrial development.[27]
As travelers, African Americans participated in the celebration of the
nation with which they identified. In an especially telling photograph,
summer visitors to Idlewild in the 1920s pose in front of the clubhouse
next to an American flag (fig. 16). Quietly, unselfconsciously, and yet
defiantly, the shot proclaims the full citizenship of African Americans at a
time of severe compromise of their civil rights.

Marketing Black Tourist Spaces

As the advertising industry exploded in the first three decades of the
twentieth century, African Americans exploited formal ways of publicizing
safe travel options among themselves. Black resorts like Idlewild and
American Beach in Florida were marketed through real estate corporations
and publicity media of all sorts—photographs, brochures, guidebooks,
and newspapers, to name a few. The printing and circulation of maps, for
example, helped to sell Idlewild land merely by giving tangible, physical
substance to African American dreams (fig. 17). Taking advantage of
new marketing technology, Idlewild boosters even provided a twenty-
three-minute silent promotional film to advertise the developing resort's
amenities.[28] In the mid-1920s, Frank B. Butler (1885–1973), a real estate
broker, grocer, and civic leader, formed a corporation to develop the
seaside resort that would bear his name. The founder of Butler Beach in
St. Augustine, Florida, presents a thoroughly professional image of
himself and his real estate company, which specialized in vacation properties,
in a photograph from about 1925 (fig. 18).[29] He stands alert and trim

fig. 18
(right)
Frank Butler at the front counter of Butler Realty offering African Americans beachfront property in St. Augustine, Florida, c. 1925. Courtesy of Florida State Archives.

fig. 19
(below, right)
Mack Wilson's pavilion, c. 1927. From the Eartha M. M. White Collection, Carpenter Library, University of North Florida, Jacksonville, Florida. This facility was the first recreational spot on Manhattan Beach in northeastern Florida operating twenty-four hours a day to offer lodging, food, and entertainment to an all-black clientele.

in the back of the frame amid an orderly layout that exudes efficiency, a picture of the consummate businessman ready to serve. In this image, which probably accompanied advertising text in black newspapers and magazines, the modest office is furnished with wicker seating and table, suggesting the unhurried, charming idylls in store for the happy purchasers of the lots featured in what appears to be a large map on the left wall.

Mack Wilson, who ran a sort of one-stop operation "providing entertainment, dining, lodging, and bathing facilities" for African American seaside vacationers on Florida's Manhattan Beach, was hardly shy about announcing his services (fig. 19). A c. 1927 photograph of his establishment illustrates

Cottages at Venice and Highland Beach, Md. 1930

fig. 20
Postcard of summer cottages, Highland Beach, Maryland, 1930. Gregoria Fraser Goins Papers, Moorland-Spingarn Research Center, Howard University.

how he used the exterior walls as a billboard, proclaiming messages to ocean bathers and beach denizens in apparently hand-painted block letters to say "Mack Wilson Café Open Night and Day." The garishness and abundance of his signage was in keeping with the spirit of the Roaring Twenties, a decade of heightened mass marketing. Notably, there is one professionally printed poster—for Orange Crush soda. The market for this carbonated drink, invented in 1916, had expanded greatly, most likely because of aggressive advertising.

Postcards provided another advertising medium for all-black resorts. The publication of postal cards by private outfits was not permitted in the United States until 1898. Then it was not until the First World War that American postcard printing technology caught up with German competitors—at the time barred from the U.S. market because of the war. Rushing into the vacuum, American postcard manufacturers experienced a boom in the decade following the Great War, when the view card, as opposed to the greeting postcard and the historic-site postcard, enjoyed great popularity. A view card for Highland Beach advertises examples of the simple, rustic structures and waterside plots (upper right quadrant) available to black patrons of this retreat (fig. 20). The blank edging forming a perimeter for the four photos marks the card as a "white-border" postcard of the type produced between 1916 and 1930; the handwritten script on the lower right-hand corner of this particular view card supplies a date—1930.

fig. 21
(right)
Cover of the *Negro Motorist Green-Book* (New York: Green, 1940). General Research and Reference Division, Schomburg Center for Research in Black Culture, the New York Public Library, Astor, Lenox, and Tilden Foundations.

fig. 22
(far right)
The *Negro Motorist Green-Book* (New York: Green, 1938), 21. General Research and Reference Division, Schomburg Center for Research in Black Culture, the New York Public Library, Astor, Lenox, and Tilden Foundations.

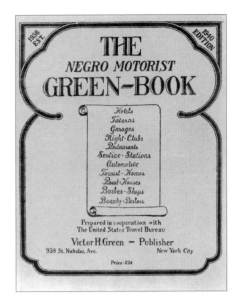

Historian Lizabeth Cohen's work on American consumption offers compelling insights that may be applied to the marketing of black tourist spaces during the 1930s and into the postwar era. Probably the most consulted source of information for black travelers, the *Negro Motorist Green-Book* (later known as the *Negro Traveler's Green-Book*), did not appear until 1936, but continued publication through 1967, when the achievements of the civil rights movement and desegregation rendered its information less compelling. Victor H. Green, the guide's editor, explained the need for his publication: "The idea of 'The Green Book' is to compile facts and information connected with motoring, which the Negro Motorist can use and depend upon."[30] Green was savvy about the growing use of the automobile by vacationing Americans. He enlisted the help of readers and black businesses in his effort to produce a state-by-state national roster of "hotels, road houses, taverns, night clubs, tourist homes, trailer parks and camps, restaurants, garages, service stations, summer resorts, barber shops, beauty parlors, dance halls, [and] theatres"[31] that were open and hospitable to black travelers (figs. 21, 22). By 1940 the *Green-Book* included listings for forty-three states (excluding the South) and Washington, D.C., entries for New York City apart from New York State, and a section labeled "Southward," consisting of accommodations below the Mason-Dixon line.[32]

The comprehensiveness of the volumes and the diligence with which Green pursued this goal suggests that he, along with his advertisers and subscribers, approached the issue of black travel consumption as a nationalistic enterprise. To Cohen, American-made consumer items were symbols of the nation, so that acquiring them was a way of fulfilling citizenship. When vacation trips across the American countryside are similarly seen as politicized consumer items, African Americans who "purchased" cross-country holidays enhanced their status as Americans. This view was especially prevalent during the 1930s and 1940s, when the Depression and Second World War turned consumption into a patriotic act. This attitude would explain Green's solicitations for additional, geographically diverse listings from his readers—not that this request was unrelated to his concern for the publication's sales, but by building a list of vacation outlets he facilitated African American citizenship in a political and social sense. Blacks could belong more fully to their country by participating in the growing national preoccupation with motoring for pleasure.[33]

Augmenting the utility of Cohen's argument, the federal Works Progress Administration turned its attention in 1935 toward the production of national travel guides, the American Guide series. The Roosevelt administration showed an unprecedented sensitivity to the needs of African Americans, publishing its own *Directory of Negro Hotels and Guest Houses in the United States* through the National Park Service in 1939.[34]

Trade associations of black entrepreneurs in resort centers also promoted their facilities in patriotic terms during this period. In the summer of 1945, for example, an all-black business organization called the Atlantic City Board of Trade produced a substantial illustrated brochure advertising an assortment of black-owned amenities at the famous beach resort. The brochure text reveals the extent to which both the convention committee and its black consumer base were invested in projecting an optimistic Americanism. Aware of the stakes of a hard-fought war in which intolerance toward another group (Jews) was a major component, the board anticipated American victory and its aftermath, a future in which all people, including African Americans, might "live in freedom." Identifying themselves as full-fledged American "citizens," the board members offered to assist other "citizens" at a time of national crisis: "Atlantic City is today serving thousands of returning veterans ... [and] many tired and war torn workers.... Our citizens are happy to add this very vital contribution [leisure] to these deserving folk and to offer its good health-giving and recreational facilities toward a bigger and better post-war period."[35] It is notable that the text never explicitly mentions African Americans; it does not contain a single use of the word "Negro" or "colored people"—the polite reference to blacks at the time. Rather, the authors prefer the more oblique allusion to "our people"—the referent for which is supplied by portraits of apparently African American board members displaying an appropriate combination of seriousness, rectitude, and friendliness in their expressions (fig. 23). Atlantic City black business people preferred to look beyond the history of discrimination in the travel industry (from which they benefited as sellers in a sheltered market) and promote their activity to all Americans as a patriotic service to veterans, their families, and exhausted war-industry laborers. Thus, to invest in an Atlantic City holiday was to contribute to the welfare of the national public.

WILLIAM A. DART

ARCHIE RICE

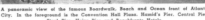

A panoramic view of the famous Boardwalk, Beach and Ocean front of Atlantic City. In the foreground is the Convention Hall Plaza. Hamid's Pier. Central Pier. Steel Pier. Heinz Pier and Beachfronts Hotels.

DR. L. D. WRIGHT

C. J. NEWSOME

fig. 23
(right)
Atlantic City Board of Trade brochure, 1945. Moorland-Spingarn Research Center, Howard University.

fig. 24
(below, right)
Atlantic City Board of Trade brochure, 1945. Moorland-Spingarn Research Center, Howard University.

fig. 25
(below)
Advertising brochure issued by the Idlewild, Michigan, Chamber of Commerce, c. 1950, as illustrated in Ronald J. Stephens, *Images of America, Idlewild: The Black Eden of Michigan* (Charleston, SC: Arcadia, 2001), 68. Phil Giles Enterprises, Idlewild Chamber of Commerce. Courtesy of Ronald J. Stephens.

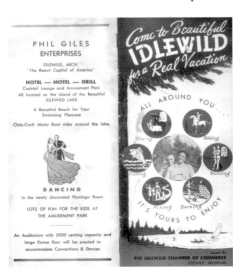

There was more at work in the catchy cover of the same brochure (fig. 24). Three fetching young women appear in bathing suits to welcome readers to their city. Here, the Board of Trade reflected its appreciation for the power of sex to sell anything to anybody. Moreover, the board may have taken a lesson from Hollywood, which in the 1940s invested heavily in movie posters and pin-up ads featuring leggy, beautiful women to advertise movies. Like the film studios, the Board of Trade hoped to sell entertainment. And just as the studios used "fair-skinned and smiling" white girls for their promotions, these black businessmen were selective in employing only light-complexioned African American women with amiable expressions for their ad.[36]

Cohen argues that American consumption after the Second World War became politicized, as the purchase of goods to meet individual goals came to be associated with national prosperity through the support of free enterprise during the cold war. This type of thinking permeated American society and is key to understanding the message conveyed by a brochure advertising Idlewild, the Michigan summer retreat (fig. 25). Appearing

fig. 26
Edward Mitchell Bannister at Battery Park, Newport, Rhode Island, painting the U.S.S. *Richmond* and Newport harbor, c. 1887. The Newport Historical Society. P39. Photograph by Jonas Bergner.

around 1950, the pamphlet was published by the Idlewild Chamber of Commerce. The left panel promotes a major Idlewild operation, Phil Giles Enterprises. The activities symbolically surrounding the happy couple at the heart of the right panel fall well within the range of "wholesome," "traditional," and "family"-based pursuits so prized during the 1950s. The hiking circle on the lower left corner of this right panel underscores the point by depicting the ideal family of four—mother, father, son, and daughter. The use of the circle motif itself in fact connotes perfection and completion. Implicit in this pictorial communication, then, is first the idea that an Idlewild experience allowed a vacationer to support an American business. Moreover, the text of the brochure, which includes the phrase "all around you … it's yours to enjoy," gives African Americans a sense of ownership and pride in the leisure spaces that they had carved out for themselves.[37]

Conclusion

Like Edward Mitchell Bannister (1828–1901), the painter photographed at the Newport, Rhode Island, harbor (fig. 26), privileged African American tourists between 1880 and 1950 achieved a communion with the national landscape unheralded in the history of black people in the United States. The significance of this image of a black artist taking a prospect—that is, creating a landscape—cannot be overemphasized. Barred from mainstream hotels, African Americans constructed alternatives—their own hotels, country cottages, and beachside resorts—or supported white-owned hospitality establishments that welcomed them. There, they maintained contemporary standards of decorum in their bearing and accoutrements. There, they purchased land, and named it in honor of themselves. There, they traversed the terrain with intent—finding respite in the face of modernity and emotional, spiritual, and intellectual restoration as human beings in the face of Jim Crow. There, they affirmed themselves as members of the American body politic. Through the necessity of all-black resorts, black tourists reconfigured domestic vacation travel such that they, too, became part of the history, literature, and art associated with the commercialization of the American landscape.✧

Acknowledgments
I wish to thank Kirsten Buick at the University of New Mexico and Julia Rosenbaum at Bard College for their early reviews of this essay and express my deepest gratitude to Donna Wells and Joellen ElBashir of Moorland-Spingarn Research Center for their assistance in securing vital images.

Notes
1. E. Franklin Frazier, *Black Bourgeoisie* (New York: Collier, 1957), 31–76; Bart Landry, *The New Black Middle Class* (Berkeley and Los Angeles: University of California Press, 1987), 18–36; Willard B. Gatewood, *Aristocrats of Color: The Black Elite 1880–1920* (Bloomington: Indiana University Press, 1990), 210–46.

2. Gatewood, *Aristocrats of Color*, 3–4, 12, 19, 41–42, 110, 124–25, 200–1; Myra B. Young Armstead, *"Lord, Please Don't Take Me in August": African Americans in Newport and Saratoga Springs, 1870–1930* (Urbana: University of Illinois Press, 1999), 18; David M. Katzman, *Before the Ghetto: Black Detroit in the Nineteenth Century* (Urbana: University of Illinois Press, 1973), 124, 128, 141, 154, 158–59, 161, 176, 200; Armstead, "The History of Blacks in Resort Towns: Newport, Rhode Island and Saratoga Springs, New York 1870–1930" (Ph.D. diss., University of Chicago, 1987), 18.

3. Katzman, *Before the Ghetto*, 94–95.

4. *Seventh Annual Report of the Commissioners of the State Reservation at Saratoga Springs 1916* (Albany, NY: Lyon, 1916), 23.

5. *Crisis* 14 (August 1917): 169.

6. Louis R. Harlan, *Booker T. Washington: The Wizard of Tuskegee, 1901–1915* (New York: Oxford University Press, 1986), 379–404.

7. William M. Tuttle Jr., *Race Riot: Chicago in the Red Summer of 1919* (Urbana: University of Illinois Press, 1970).

8. Wendell P. Dabney, *Cincinnati's Colored Citizens: Historical, Sociological and Biographical* (Cincinnati: Dabney, 1926), 75.

9. J. Ellis Voss, "Summer Resort: An Ecological Analysis of a Satellite Community," (Ph.D. diss., University of Pennsylvania, 1941), 39.

10. George S. Schuyler, "Vacation Daze," *Common Ground* 3, no. 3 (Spring 1943): 41–42, 44; quotation on 41.

11. Gatewood, *Aristocrats of Color*, 75; Armstead, *"Lord, Please Don't Take Me in August,"* 74; Dabney, *Cincinnati's Colored Citizens*, 129–32.

12. *Crisis* 22 (August 1921): 158.

13. Dabney, *Cincinnati's Colored Citizens*, 194; *The Negro World* (7 June 1924): 5.

14. Gatewood, *Aristocrats of Color*, 201–2; Armstead, *"Lord, Please Don't Take Me in August,"* 18–19; Lawrence Otis Graham, *Our Kind of People: Inside America's Black Upper Class* (New York: HarperCollins, 1999), 151–81.

15. Adelaide M. Cromwell, "The History of Oak Bluffs as a Popular Resort for Blacks," *Dukes County Intelligencer* 26, no. 1 (August 1984): 3–8; Graham, *Our Kind of People*, 156–58.

16. Cromwell, "History of Oak Bluffs," 52; see also Jacqueline L. Holland, "The African-American Presence on Martha's Vineyard," *Dukes County Intelligencer* Special Edition (October 1997): 7–10; Michel Frizot, "Rituals and Customs: Photographs as Memories," in *A New History of Photography*, ed. Michel Frizot (Cologne: Könemann, 1998), 750, 748; Bobbie Kalman, *Historic Communities: The Victorian Home* (New York: Crabtree, 1997), 6–7.

17. Gatewood, *Aristocrats of Color*, 37, 43–45, 55, 58, 59, 66, 101,137, 180, 201; Graham, *Our Kind of People*, 178–79; "Highland Beach, Maryland," www.mdmunicipal.org/cities/index.cfm?townname=HighlandBeach&page=home (accessed 12 July 2003).

18. See Virginia Scott Jenkins, *The Lawn: A History of an American Obsession* (Washington, D.C.: Smithsonian Institution Press, 1994); James Charlton and William Thompson, *Croquet: The Complete Guide to History, Strategy, Rules, and Records* (New York: Turtle Press, 1977); and Michael Colmer, *Bathing Beauties: The Amazing History of Female Swimwear* (London: Sphere, 1977). Regarding American insistence on mediating their encounters with nature, see Peter J. Schmitt, *Back to Nature: The Arcadian Myth in Urban America* (Baltimore: Johns Hopkins University Press, 1990), 20–32; James L. Machor, *Pastoral Cities: Urban Ideals and the Symbolic Landscape of America* (Madison: University of Wisconsin Press, 1987), 121–210; and Roderick Nash, *Wilderness and the American Mind* (New Haven, CT: Yale University Press, 1967), 44–66.

19. Lewis Walker and Ben C. Wilson, *Black Eden: The Idlewild Community* (East Lansing: Michigan State University Press, 2002), xiii, 6–28, 39–41, quotation on 41; Edwin DeMerritte, "The Emergence of the Camping Movement," *Camping Magazine* (June 1929).

20. William Seale, *The Tasteful Interlude: American Interiors through the Camera's Eye, 1860–1917* (New York: Praeger, 1975), 170.

21. See also Cindy S. Aron, *Working at Play: A History of Vacations in the United States* (New York: Oxford University Press, 2001).

22. Walker and Wilson, *Black Eden*, xi–xii, 1–13, 23–26, 30–39.

23. Dona Brown, *Inventing New England: Regional Tourism in the Nineteenth Century* (Washington, D.C.: Smithsonian Institution Press, 1995), 63.

24. H. H. Thweatt, "The Best Summer I Ever Spent," *Crisis* 14 (August 1917): 169–71.

25. W. E. B. Du Bois, "Hopkinsville, Chicago, and Idlewild," *Crisis* 22 (August 1921): 159.

26. Ibid., 160.

27. Marguerite S. Shaffer, *See America First: Tourism and National Identity, 1880–1940* (Washington, D.C.: Smithsonian Institution Press, 2000), 170, 202–20. For the rise of domestic tourism in the late 1820s and early 1830s, see also Brown, *Inventing New England*, and Eric Purchase, *Out of Nowhere: Disaster and Tourism in the White Mountains* (Baltimore: Johns Hopkins University Press, 1999).

28. Walker and Wilson, *Black Eden*, 47–48.

29. Marcia Dean Phelts, *An American Beach for African Americans* (Gainesville: University Press of Florida, 1997), 9–13.

30. See Lizabeth Cohen, *A Consumer's Republic: The Politics of Mass Consumption in Postwar America* (New York: Knopf, 2003); *The Negro Motorist Green-Book* (New York: Green & Smith, 1937), n.p. (introduction).

31. *The Negro Motorist Green-Book* (New York: Green, 1938), n.p. (front cover).

32. *The Negro Motorist Green-Book* (New York: Green, 1940), passim.

33. Cohen, *Consumer's Republic*; *Negro Motorist Green-Book, 1937*; *Negro Motorist Green-Book, 1938*; *Negro Motorist Green-Book, 1940*.

34. United States Department of the Interior National Park Service, *United States Travel Bureau Directory of Negro Hotels and Guest Houses in the United States*, 1939, Moorland-Spingarn Research Center, Howard University, Washington, D.C. (hereafter Moorland-Spingarn); Shaffer, *See America First*, 202–20; *Negro Motorist Green-Book, 1940*, 4, 26–27, 31. On the Roosevelt administration's progressive racial policies, see, for example, Nancy Joan Weiss, *Farewell to the Party of Lincoln: Black Politics in the Age of F.D.R.* (Princeton, NJ: Princeton University Press, 1983).

35. Atlantic City Board of Trade Brochure, 1945, Moorland-Spingarn.

36. Ibid. See also Tom Reichert, *The Erotic History of Advertising* (Amherst, NY: Prometheus Books, 2003); Joshua James Curtis and Ann Rutherford, *Sunkissed: Swimwear and the Hollywood Beauty, 1930–1950* (Portland, OR: Collector's Press, 2003).

37. Ronald J. Stephens, *Idlewild: The Black Eden of Michigan* (Chicago: Arcadia, 2001); Walker and Wilson, *Black Eden*, 63.

A. K. Sandoval-Strausz and Daniel Levinson Wilk

Princes and Maids of the City Hotel: The Cultural Politics of Commercial Hospitality in America

A. K. Sandoval-Strausz is assistant professor of history at the University of New Mexico with research and teaching interests in urban history, cultural landscape studies, and legal history. He received his Ph.D. from the University of Chicago and is currently at work on a book tentatively entitled *Hotel: An American History*, under contract to Yale University Press.

Daniel Levinson Wilk is a Ph.D. candidate in American history at Duke University specializing in the business, labor, and cultural history of the service sector in urban America. His dissertation examines how New York City's apartment houses and hotels evolved from the traditions of servitude into a modern service sector.

A hotel is in essence a hospitality machine. Since the invention of the hotel in America more than two hundred years ago, its basic function has been to provide travelers with shelter, accommodation, food, refreshment, and related services and goods. Our households usually supply these amenities, but when we travel we must obtain them by other means—hence the familiar phrase "home away from home." Historically, hotels have also taken on many other functions, serving as business exchanges, centers of sociability, places of public assembly and deliberation, decorative showcases, political headquarters, sites of technological innovation, vacation spots, and permanent residences. At base, though, the business of hotels has been the business of commercial hospitality.

Hotel hospitality depended upon large numbers of workers to tend to the needs and wants of numerous guests (fig. 1). As a result, hotels gradually developed exceptionally sophisticated methods of structuring work, with the largest establishments employing hundreds of people in some of the most labor-intensive operations in the United States. But these new modes of employee management came at the cost of increasing friction between hotel workers and the guests they served. This article examines the role and representations of two of the most storied of these workers: hotel clerks and chambermaids. In the nineteenth century popular resentment toward clerks and maids reflected widespread discomfort over the transformation of hospitality. After about 1900, however, changes in personnel management and cultural production led to less caricatured and more favorable public images of hotel workers. Exploring this aspect

Detail of *The Lobby and Office of the United States Hotel in Saratoga*, wood engraving with modern handcoloring, 1876 (see fig. 1).

fig. 1
Artist unknown,
*The Lobby and Office
of the United States
Hotel in Saratoga*,
wood engraving with
modern handcoloring
(signed in the block,
Hyde). From *Frank Leslie's
Illustrated Newspaper*,
2 September 1876. The
Old Print Shop, New York.

of American culture reveals the early history and ongoing development of a service economy in the United States and offers a look at the relationship between the internal workings and external perceptions of one of the most familiar institutions on the national landscape.

Hotelkeeping was an extremely competitive trade in the nineteenth century. The success or failure of a hotel depended entirely upon its keeper's ability to attract paying guests, provide them with comfortable accommodations, and persuade them to return in the future—and, of course, to advise their friends and associates to do the same. Any manager who failed to do this would be driven out of business in a matter of weeks, since a hotel required constant infusions of cash for hiring employees, purchasing food and drink, and paying rent, and guest receipts were its only source of income. Adding to the hotelkeeper's worries was the fact of competition: in all but the smallest cities, a number of hotels vied for patronage. The historical record is replete with evidence of how precarious the hotel proprietor's situation could be. City directories document the high turnover in management: two or three different people were often listed as the keepers of a given hotel over the course of several years, and the names of the hotels often changed as new proprietors reopened establishments on new terms at the same address. In an uncertain economic environment, hotelkeepers were constantly preoccupied with every aspect of their establishments' operation.[1]

fig. 2
(below, left)
C. S. Reinhart, *Our Centennial: The Rush for Rooms at the Philadelphia Hotels*, woodcut cover illustration. From *Harper's Weekly*, 27 May 1876. University of New Mexico Libraries. The hotel clerk is pictured wearing a characteristically flashy suit.

fig. 3
(below, right)
[First name unknown] Abbey, *Shoddy English Rebuked*. From *Harper's Weekly*, 21 February 1874. University of New Mexico Libraries. The clerk assigns the gentleman and his female companion separate rooms a discreet distance apart to allay any suspicion of immoral intentions.

The hotel clerk was a vital part of this operation. He was the first line of contact with guests, since it was he who greeted them as they arrived at the front desk, had them sign the hotel register, assigned them rooms and gave out keys, anticipated their needs and responded to their requests, and, when the time came for them to depart, collected their money and bade them farewell (fig. 2). Given the importance of cordial customer relations in establishing a hotel's reputation, logic would dictate that every hotel clerk should have been at least competent and personable, if not outright charming.[2]

Yet the hotel clerk was an extremely unpopular figure. In nineteenth-century American fiction, journalism, travel writing, cartoons, and folklore, he was the constant subject of complaints, the butt of jokes, the stock character in any number of stories and anecdotes. Some attacks, like one in the trade publication the *Hotel Mail* calling clerks "depraved" and "vulgar," revealed little about what precisely was the matter.[3] Far more common were complaints that hotel clerks were arrogant and unhelpful. The popular author Henry Hooper referred to the hotel clerk as "the supercilious embodiment of Philistinism," and a traveling salesman noted that an encounter with a clerk was a useful corrective "whenever I feel that I need taking down a peg or two, and that I am getting too big for my clothes."[4] In *Roughing It*, Mark Twain (Samuel Clemens, 1835–1910) characterized the species by writing about the "nice American hotel clerk who was crusty and disobliging, and didn't know anything about the time tables, or the railroad routes—or—anything—and was proud of it."[5] And an aggrieved contributor to *Harper's Weekly* asserted in 1857:

SHODDY ENGLISH REBUKED.
TRAVELER (*registering*). "John Smith and Lady."
HOTEL CLERK. "All right, Sir. Put you in 115, the Lady in 94."
TRAVELER. "But the Lady's my Wife."
HOTEL CLERK. "Then why didn't you say so?"

The hotel clerk devotes his life to trying to look as if he was in the office entirely by accident. He hands you your key as if he was in a dream, and rarely condescends to answer any question that you may address to him. He spends his days like his master, reading the paper, picking his teeth, and indulging occasionally in a little light conversation with some particular friend who is staying in the house, and who you may be sure has the best room in it.[6]

Other observers alleged that hotel clerks constantly ridiculed and intimidated guests. One commentator recalled that the hotel clerk was "feared by the general public" and was "the one being in existence before whom the free-born American quailed."[7] A willingness to casually insult patrons underlay the punch line in an 1874 cartoon in which a hotel clerk seems to imply that a guest's female companion is a prostitute (fig. 3). But the most comprehensive defamation of hotel clerks came from the pen of William Dean Howells (1837–1920), whose satirical and semiautobiographical 1872 novel *Their Wedding Journey* included the following passage:

It was with a sudden sinking of the heart that Basil beheld presiding over the register the conventional American hotel clerk. He was young, he had a neat mustache and well-brushed hair; jeweled studs sparkled in his shirt-front, and rings on his white hands; a gentle disdain of the travelling public breathed from his person.... He did not lift his haughty head to look at the way-farer who meekly wrote his name in the register; he did not answer him when he begged for a cool room; he turned to the board on which the keys hung, and, plucking one from it, slid it towards Basil on the marble counter.... When I reflect that this was a type of the hotel clerk throughout the United States, that behind unnumbered registers at this moment he is snubbing travellers into the dust, and that they are suffering and perpetuating him, I am lost in wonder at the national meekness.

Further examples of the same sentiment could be referenced practically ad infinitum.[8]

What are we to make of this? It is difficult to believe that hotel clerks could really have been as indifferent and hostile as these depictions suggest. Hotelkeepers, perennially nervous about maintaining the favor of the public, surely would not have hesitated to remove rude clerks from their payrolls, and it would not have been difficult to replace them, since American cities were home to a growing middle class that taught its sons the importance of good manners and refined etiquette.[9] The popular image of the hotel clerk thus poses something of a historical puzzle. To solve it, we need to broaden our understanding of hotel labor by looking at another key employee: the chambermaid.

fig. 4
F. Opper, *The Growing Field of Woman's Work. A Short Look Ahead*, color lithograph, 1891. Library of Congress, Prints and Photographs Division, American Political Prints Collection. LC-USZC2-1218.
The ironic caricatures show how closely Americans identified the occupation of hotel clerk (like physician, juror, etc.) with men.

The hotel chambermaid was in some ways the opposite number of the clerk (fig. 4). He was highly visible, occupying a prominent spot at the hotel entrance. She, by contrast, was invisible, since she worked in the guests' bedrooms, the most private and intimate spaces in the hotel. But it was precisely the chambermaid's invisibility and proximity that aroused the most hostility. What people most feared from chambermaids sprang from what they could not see them doing. The more conventional of these anxieties was that chambermaids would steal guests' belongings while they were away from their rooms. Eliza Leslie, the author of a series of widely read etiquette books, illustrated this popular suspicion when she noted in an 1853 edition that many patrons were "afraid to trust the chambermaid alone, lest she should steal something."[10]

More revealing than public concern about theft, though, were fears that centered on more primal, personal, bodily concerns—in particular, the threat of uncleanliness and contagion. These fears were epitomized by a sensationalistic 1884 pamphlet entitled "Horrors of Hotel Life," whose anonymous author explained:

> Arriving at a hotel, travel-stained and weary, the guest is shown at once to his chamber, where he may either sleep or dress. Whichever he does he is confronted at once with dangers and dirt, not apparent to the eye, indeed, but a thousand times the worse for being concealed under apparent cleanliness.... The guest finds certain indispensable things in his room. Things he must use. Things that will come in contact with certain parts of his body.

The pamphlet continued with a litany of stomach-turning scenarios involving unclean bodies and unpleasant personal habits, confronting readers with extremely graphic accounts of spitting, oozing, probing, and wiping. Chambermaids were accused of such practices as utilizing towels as cleaning rags, reusing dirty dishes and soiled linens without washing them, and availing themselves of dinner napkins in place of sanitary napkins. Both sets of anxieties about chambermaids thus involved a fear of trespass or invasion—in one case, of the guest's room, and in the other, of the guest's body.[11]

This brings us back to the historical puzzle noted earlier. If hotel clerks really were so rude, why were they not being disciplined or fired? And why did chambermaids inspire such antipathy at a time when many Americans employed servants in their own homes? Part of the answer is that hotel employees were not, in fact, uniformly rude or felonious or unhygienic. The images surrounding them were simply stereotypical or formulaic. But this begs another question: why were so many people, including talented and perceptive literary figures, willing to believe, or at least repeat and reinforce, these ungenerous portrayals of hotel workers?

The key to answering these questions is the recognition that the ideas in question were neither categorical nor random—they followed a coherent cultural logic. They did not, to begin with, reflect a wholesale dislike of all hotel personnel: hotelkeepers were well-respected figures, the most successful of whom were celebrated in the press and public discourse; indeed, the common expression "he can keep a hotel" was understood to denote an exceptionally talented and resourceful person.[12] Nor were complaints about clerks and chambermaids simply examples of indiscriminate grousing. They in fact shared a fairly limited conceptual vocabulary of familiar imagery, one that was deployed so consistently as to elevate it to the level of popular folklore. It is precisely the folkloric quality of the animus against these hotel employees that most strongly suggests an identifiable cultural tension.

fig. 5
Louis Dalrymple,
Sizing Each Other Up,
india ink over pencil
with scraping out
on bristol board,
8 3/10 x 5 9/10 in.
(21.3 x 15.2 cm), 1891.
Library of Congress,
Prints and Photographs
Division, Swann
Collection.
LC-USZ62-133843.

Popular accounts of hotel clerks were laden with references to status. The most common image was that of clerks living beyond their means. Critics constantly mocked them for their outré taste in clothing and alleged attraction to expensive jewelry. "The clerk is generally an appalling example of the extent to which dress may be carried," noted *Harper's Weekly* in 1857. "His waistcoat is of radiant velvet with perhaps gold buttons, and he wears diamond shirt-studs, and diamond sleeve-links that, if he came by them honestly, must have cost him a couple of years' salary"(fig. 5).[13] Other observers made much of an apparent fondness for the diamond stickpin, an accessory that became practically synonymous with the clerking fraternity.[14] The other set of metaphors most regularly applied to hotel clerks placed them in the role of petty tyrants from an effete European aristocracy. One writer referred to the clerk as "a haughty and unapproachable despot," and another described him as one who "sits enthroned, at a considerable elevation."[15]

Within the cultural context of nineteenth-century America, the intended meaning was clear: clerks were unacceptably climbing above their proper station in life. Scoffing at clerks' fashion sense emphasized the disparity between their limited incomes and their social aspirations: the wealthy were entitled to dress themselves extravagantly, but when others did so, they invited ridicule. Taunts of aristocracy conveyed the same idea in a more metaphorical fashion. In a republic dedicated to the ideal of formal equality, to say that a person was playing the aristocrat was to suggest that he was pretending to a status that he did not deserve, thereby rendering himself as ridiculous and out of place as an Old World autocrat. It is worth noting that similar accusations of frivolous dressing and aristocratic pretensions were hurled at black Americans at times when their aspirations made white people uneasy.[16]

The folklore regarding chambermaids was admittedly very different. Rather than using figurative imagery to poke fun at the clerk's self-importance and delusions of grandeur, it directly and literally called attention to the maid's impecuniousness, abject social status, and exploitative working conditions. The belief that chambermaids were in the habit of filching valuables from guests' rooms suggested that they were so poor as to be reduced to stealing from the very people they were supposed to be serving. Accusations of slapdash cleaning and personal uncleanliness—strongly gendered ideas patterned on traditional suspicions about the leaky bodies of women—likewise indicated poverty and the dirt and grime that accompanied it. Notably, though, these images also seemed to suggest a degree of sympathy for the maids' pitiable personal circumstances. Even the author who described them as having "low moral status, little or no education, small means, demoralizing habits of both physical and mental nastiness, and vile associations" allowed that they were "scarcely to be blamed for much that seems to be their fault," since they were chronically overworked and underpaid. The clerk's detractors, by contrast, displayed no such empathy.[17]

Given these important structural and semiotic differences, what does it mean to say that these folkloric traditions are related? While at first glance they might seem to involve contrary lines of criticism, a closer examination reveals that both were responses to a single underlying cultural phenomenon: the transformation of hospitality. Anxieties about clerks and chambermaids arose precisely because longstanding traditions of household hospitality were being replaced by a new, institutional mode of hospitality embodied in the rise of the hotel as an architectural and social form.

Hospitality is the name given to an array of rituals for dealing with strangers. While hospitality exists in all cultures and takes innumerable forms, its function is always essentially the same: to incorporate outsiders into a community on a temporary basis. Upon arrival, a stranger has an uncertain status. He or she may be a danger to the community or a benefit to it, but either way is ignorant of its social norms and cannot be trusted to behave appropriately. Through a rite of hospitality, the stranger enters into an intermediate status between outsider and insider by being assigned to a host and taking on the role of guest. In the host-guest relationship, a community member serves as the link between the community and the outsider. The host is answerable for the welfare of the guest and responsible for his or her behavior, while the guest agrees to accept the host's authority and abide by his rules. Hospitality thus serves to manage the potential dangers of encounters among strangers, protecting the community from disruption and the visitor from harm.[18]

In the Western world, hospitality was traditionally modeled on the patriarchal household. As far back as classical antiquity, the master of the house, who held authority over domestic subordinates including his wife, children, servants, and slaves, also accommodated travelers as part of his fatherly role. In the medieval period, hospitality was an important part of the personalistic ties of duty and obligation on which feudalism was based, and as a result it was regarded as an essential social protocol. In the late Middle Ages, the gradual development of market economies fostered new forms of hospitality offered on a commercial basis. These changes did not, however, alter the domestic character of hospitality, which was still provided on a personal scale, in relatively small spaces that were tended by an actual or fictive family.[19] In British North America, the innkeeper-patriarch was assigned the role of both guardian and sentry. He was not only responsible for sheltering the visitor and his or her possessions, but was also expected to play a disciplinary role by notifying authorities of the arrival of any and all outsiders. The visitor was thus temporarily integrated into the social order of the local community as part of a household, an arrangement that was analogous to the figurative assignation of apprentices and slaves to the families of their masters. This ideological construct worked very well in the colonial and early national periods because travelers were relatively few and were accommodated in homelike environments: taverns were small enough to be monitored directly by their keepers, as were the large number of homes that regularly took in boarders and served as a vital private auxiliary to a community's public houses.

As hotels gradually replaced taverns as the standard form of American public house—as establishments of ten or twenty rooms gave way to those with hundreds—they brought with them a new form of hospitality, an array of distinctive protocols for accommodating travelers. This new order of hospitality was characterized first and foremost by the replacement of a household model of hospitality with an institutional model. In place of a tavern that was kept by a proprietor, comprised members of the family, and offered personalized attendance, the new hospitality was characterized by a hotel that was operated by a professional manager, employed a large number of wage workers, and provided systematized service. This transition was driven by the sheer scale of hotels, which were far too large and their guests far too numerous to be overseen personally by a single proprietor. In 1852, for example, the *Daily True Democrat* reported that in Cleveland, then a city of only about seventeen thousand inhabitants, a hotelkeeper had "entertained 457 strangers at the American House" over the course of only four days.[20] Under such conditions, it made sense that the household became unsuitable as an organizing metaphor for the proper reception of outsiders. This did not, however, portend a total abandonment of the household: its functions were retained, but in a subdivided or disaggregated form, offered piecemeal rather than as part of a familial whole. The increasing number and scale of hotels over the course of the nineteenth century required ever-larger numbers of clerks, and indeed the available census data indicate that the number of employees in this profession was growing more than three times faster than the population.[21] In this sense, the host-guest relationship was being reshaped in much the same way as the master-servant relationship: the rise of the factory system of manufacturing moved production out of the household, subdividing and contracting it out according to the demands of a new economic rationality. Both relational pairs exemplified how the logic of the market was restructuring centuries-old arrangements of labor, architectural space, and human geography.

Understood in this historical context, the antipathy directed at hotel clerks can be seen as the result of the discrepancy between their level of authority and their social standing as traditionally defined. The clerk's power operated only within the hotel lobby, but within that realm it was not inconsiderable. He exercised a sort of temporary dominance over guests because he had discretion over whether to assign them a better or worse bedchamber and whether to give them the room right away or find some pretext to make them stand and wait for it. The clerk also effectively possessed the power to sit in judgment over guests' social status, since his attentiveness, demeanor, and courteous or indifferent service reflected his estimation of whether they were people of consequence who required the white glove treatment or ordinary folk who did not. Despite their authority, though, hotel clerks were still young, propertyless hirelings, and many people refused to recognize them as acceptable substitutes for absent patriarchs. This represented something of a cultural hangover, one that afflicted people who were used to the household as a governing social metaphor and were willing to accept the authority of an actual head of household, but for whom being ordered around by a mere wage worker, a person with no property or standing, violated their sense of proper social order. Thus, when critics called attention to the clerk's foppish preoccupation with clothing and jewelry, they sought to put him back in his place by attributing to him a thoroughly unpatriarchal effeminacy. By the same token, the satisfaction of turning the tables on a hotel clerk provided the humor in an 1862 cartoon that also served political ends (fig. 6).

Mistrust of chambermaids also followed the cultural logic of nostalgia for the household because it was precisely the lack of a domestic connection between maid and guest that was troublesome. Many hotel patrons surely had servants of their own, and because they were incorporated into a household, they were easier to trust. Likewise, the household model of hospitality meant that servants were responsible to, and supervised by, the master of the establishment. But in the transition from household to institutional hospitality, guests were apparently unprepared for the replacement of the patriarch's domestic dependents with wage laborers who existed outside household bonds of deference and discipline yet had the kind of constant access to intimate spaces that normally required familial or quasi-familial trust. In hotels, the disconnectedness of guests and workers tended to generate a form of alienation in both. Even as hotels became people's temporary homes away from home, hotel hospitality often failed to reproduce the proper level of domesticity that Americans associated primarily with the *sanctum sanctorum* of their own households.[22]

Nostalgia notwithstanding, as the decades passed it became increasingly obvious that the institutional hospitality of the hotel was becoming the dominant mode of accommodating travelers in the United States. Americans were building ever-larger hotels and staying in them in ever-greater numbers, voting with their bricks, feet, and money in favor of the new order of hospitality. Hotels promised their guests a great deal, and in most respects they did a good job of serving the needs of their clientele. Yet the persistence of unflattering folklore about hotel workers reveals the ongoing unease that people felt about the declining influence of the household as an all-purpose structuring metaphor for human relationships beyond the home. To be sure, the glorification of traditional public houses and their domestic hospitality involved a great deal of historical amnesia: in their eighteenth-century heyday, taverns had elicited far harsher invective for their dirt, bedbugs, bad food, uneven service, and constant overcharging than was ever directed at hotels for their impersonality. Clearly, the sense that something had been lost persisted beyond the close of the nineteenth century.

Antipathy toward clerks and chambermaids never completely died away, though it did eventually mellow. In the twentieth century, and especially in the 1920s and 1930s, portrayals of clerks and chambermaids grew in number and variety, expanded into new media, and found greater circulation. For example, hotels could confidently promote new services through the familiar—and now comfortable—tableau of the interaction

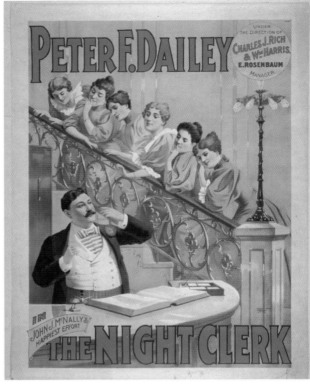

fig. 7
(above, left)
Artist unknown, *"I'm So Glad I Telephoned First,"* serigraph, 22 x 14 in. (55.9 x 35.6 cm), c. 1932. The Wolfsonian–Florida International University, Miami Beach, Florida. Purchased, Curatorial Discretionary Fund. 2004.5.1

fig. 8
(above, right)
Artist unknown, *Peter F. Dailey in John J. McNally's happiest effort, The Night Clerk,* color lithograph, 39 $^2/_5$ x 29 $^2/_5$ in. (101 x 76 cm), 1895. Library of Congress, Prints and Photographs Division, Theatrical Poster Collection. LC-USZ6-416. The poster anticipates a common twentieth-century theme: the desk clerk as object of romance.

between the front desk clerk and guests (fig. 7). Friendly, jocular, helpful, and competent hotel employees joined the old stereotypes (fig. 8). This can be explained in part by the simple passage of time; after a hundred years of hotel life, Americans had slowly adjusted to the scale of hotels and modern capitalism in general. But three specific developments pushed this process along. In the early twentieth century, hotel managers began to measure and monitor the quality of customer service more carefully, leading to improvements in training. Meanwhile, a new generation of writers came to depend on hotels more than ever for leisure activities, professional contacts, and permanent housing. Finally, movies brought clerks and chambermaids before the public eye in a more appealing mode than any that had come before.

In the early twentieth century, hotels increased in both number and size as the nation's burgeoning cities supported ever-greater transient populations. The largest establishments had thousands of rooms and were sometimes organized into regional and national chains. The industry's growth led in turn to heightened competition for guests to fill the increasing supply of hotel rooms. It also accelerated a process that had developed more gradually through the nineteenth century—the decline of personal relationships between hotelkeepers and their employees and guests. Hotel housekeepers had long supervised maids on behalf of the manager, and hotel clerks had already assumed many of the proprietor's

fig. 9
(above)
3rd Annual Convention of Ill. State Hotel Clerks Association, Decatur, Ill., 6 Aug. 1910. Library of Congress, Prints and Photographs Division, Panoramic Photographs Collection.

fig. 10
(below)
Alfred Joseph Frueh, *Man: Is Mr. Pinfield Stopping Here?* India ink over pencil with scraping out on bristol board, 11 x 14 ³/₁₀ in. (28.2 x 36.6 cm). From *Good Morning*, 1 May 1920. Library of Congress, Prints and Photographs Division, Swann Collection. LC-USZ62-94637.

public roles, but the industry's expansion in the early twentieth century brought this devolution of authority to a crisis point with respect to the alienation of guests. In hotels with thousands of employees, who would take personal responsibility for the comfort and happiness of customers? As the chasm between rich and poor deepened, how would bejeweled ladies and chambermaids learn to trust each other? When clerks, always members of a cliquish cultural fraternity, formalized these associations through regional and national professional societies, did they risk further alienating the public they served (fig. 9)? Managers, workers, and guests worried about the mechanics of this problem in the everyday provision of services and pondered it on an existential level: "A big hotel," opined a 1923 editorial in the *New York Evening Post*, "can be one of the loneliest places in the world."[23]

In response, hotel managers increasingly emphasized the proper training and monitoring of clerks, chambermaids, and other employees. Soon after the turn of the century, trade journals first published articles stressing the importance of clerks in selling rooms to short- and long-term guests. The trade press acknowledged the "haughty and disagreeable air" attributed to clerks and promoted an actively polite, dignified, and tactful manner as a way of countering the negative expectations of guests and boosting revenues (fig. 10).[24] Some articles advised paying a premium for clerks who knew how to size up potential customers, acknowledge their humble status, and defer to guests. "He's a wise clerk," wrote one editor, "who can always tell which is the owner of the car and which the chauffeur."[25] Other contributors sought to improve the working conditions

of chambermaids and thereby undermine stereotypes. Mary E. Palmer, a hotel housekeeper herself, derided "snobs" who claimed that chambermaids had no morality.[26] She was echoed by other writers who asserted that lax standards were not inherent to chambermaids, but rather stemmed from managers who did not urge supervisors to treat maids kindly, promote camaraderie in the ranks, and lead by setting a good example.[27]

fig. 11
*Hotel Clerk, Dover,
Delaware,* July 1938.
Library of Congress,
Prints and Photographs
Division, FSA/OWI
Collection.
LC-USF34-008524-D.
Photograph by
John Vachon.

This growing conversation about labor management led to organizational changes. The Statler chain set the pace for the industry by promoting innovative practices in hiring, training, and supervision. For example, Statler hotels lined service corridors with placards offering general instructions and motivational slogans like "There can't be 'CLASS' in this hotel without a courteous gracious attitude on the part of every one toward every one." Other hoteliers stressed a more personal touch in labor management or tinkered with strategies of welfare capitalism—health benefits, stock options, free classes, paid vacation time, and employee representation plans—that began to appear before the First World War and blossomed in the 1920s.[28]

In the case of chambermaids, the greatest improvements were made over the objections of managers. As part of a movement to protect the rights of women workers, the National Consumers' League and allied organizations publicized the conditions under which many hotel maids labored—seven-day weeks, poor pay, abysmal food and housing, harsh supervision, and sexual danger. Exposés about women's labor persuaded state legislatures to limit their working hours; once the Supreme Court ruled such laws constitutional, hotel managers in many states were forced to reduce the workdays of chambermaids and other female employees to ten hours.[29] In the 1920s, in response to these legislative defeats and to stave off labor radicalism, hoteliers began to phase out the most oppressive aspect of chambermaids' jobs: maids were no longer required to live on-site like house servants, subject to the constant demands and surveillance of managers regardless of official hours of work. The number of household servants also declined during these years, and many who stayed in domestic service moved out of their masters' and mistresses' houses. This transition was a critical one in the history of service. Under the pressure of workers, government, business competition, and muckrakers' appeals to the conscience of the consuming public, old traditions of servitude began to wither away. In their place grew a service sector that popular culture began to portray with fewer misgivings (fig. 11).[30]

It is admittedly difficult to measure how these changes affected the quality of service provided by hotel clerks and chambermaids or how improved service may have affected their popular image. It is nonetheless reasonable to assume—as did many hotel managers at the time—that improved working conditions attracted better workers, encouraged them to excel in their jobs, and led them to stay on for longer tenures. Such changes would in turn lead to better service in the real world and therefore more favorable representations in popular culture.

But other factors may have played an equally significant role in changing perceptions of workers. Over time, hotels had become increasingly intertwined with the lives of America's cultural producers. Writers, artists, and performers of earlier years had certainly possessed extensive knowledge of commercial hospitality. By 1900, however, decades spent sniffing out stories in hotel bars and making homes in upstairs suites had made hotels a prominent feature of the nation's material and creative consciousness. William Dean Howells and Mark Twain, fascinated by the rapid pace of social change, portrayed hotel workers as novel, quirky, and often annoying ambassadors of modernity.[31] Theodore Dreiser (1871–1945) pursued this idea even further in *Sister Carrie, Jennie Gerhardt,* and *An American Tragedy,* three novels that place hotels and hotel workers—Jennie the chambermaid, Clyde the bellhop—at the center of the narrative and present them as accomplices and victims of a complex and sinister modern world.[32]

As cynicism gave way to celebration in the 1920s, however, a new generation of writers reached a level of total immersion in hotel life and increasingly produced very different portrayals of hotels. The reporters, columnists, critics, and authors of the Algonquin Round Table—who met daily for lengthy lunches (with Dorothy Parker coming down to the dining hall from her room upstairs)—offer the best-known example of this phenomenon, but they were not alone. From F. Scott and Zelda Fitzgerald's drunken honeymoon antics at the Biltmore and the Commodore to Dashiell Hammett's serial nonpayment of bills at the hotels where he lived and wrote, the folklore of the interwar literary scene vividly illustrates how accustomed twentieth-century writers were to the hotel milieu.[33]

Writers' familiarity with hotel life usually did not translate into novels that centered on hotel employees. For every Jennie Gerhardt, a thousand clerks and chambermaids went about their work unsung. The narcissism of the 1920s ensured that hotel workers in literature would usually play as underdeveloped straight men and women to the alcohol-fueled hijinks of the main characters. In Anita Loos's (1888–1981) 1925 satire *Gentlemen Prefer Blondes,* Lorelei Lee and her friend Dorothy pursue adventure and rich men through America and Europe with the help of a string of service workers, including "quite an intellectual hotel clerk." In a sequel, *But Gentlemen Marry Brunettes,* headwaiter George (an artful misspelling of Georges, the name of the real-life Algonquin's headwaiter) seats Lorelei in a position to meet the members of the Round Table. Dorothy becomes "more and more a chum to the elevator boy" at the Algonquin and gives away her red satin dress and all her imitation jewelry to a chambermaid. The minor characters and the protagonists help each other along, reinforcing a class distinction but also demonstrating bonds of reciprocity and patronage that could form without re-creating the constrictions of servitude.[34]

The Great Gatsby also appeared in 1925. F. Scott Fitzgerald (1896–1940) took a darker tone than Loos in describing the Jazz Age, and it carried through to his portrayals of hotel workers. In the first scandal of Tom and Daisy Buchanan's marriage, a drunken crash rips the front wheel off Tom's car and breaks the arm of the girl sitting beside him—a chambermaid borrowed from the Santa Barbara Hotel. At the climax of the novel, the protagonists "all talked at once to a baffled clerk" at the Plaza Hotel "and thought, or pretended to think, that we were being very funny." They then ride upstairs to the final confrontation between Gatsby and Tom.[35] In the novels and short fiction of Loos and Fitzgerald, as well as Dorothy Parker, John Dos Passos, and many other writers of the 1920s, hotel employees play witness, accomplice, and innocent bystander to the protagonists' comedies and tragedies.[36] In the nineteenth century the relative cultural novelty of hotel workers led to a superficial presentation of their place that mainly expressed writers' anxieties, but by the twentieth century the assumption was that for good or ill, service workers had become minor but inescapable partners to the nation's urbanites (fig. 12).

The ubiquity of service employees had its greatest creative expression in the movies, which provided a large and heterogeneous audience.[37] Film, the premier mass medium of the early twentieth century, fundamentally changed the nature of Americans' engagement with popular culture and, in a subsidiary sense, with representations of hotel clerks and chambermaids. The immense popularity of movies meant that millions of people who had never personally encountered a hotel clerk or maid were provided with an image of what they were like. Between 1920 and 1929, hotel clerks and chambermaids appeared as credited roles in twelve movies, all silent but the Marx Brothers' classic *The Cocoanuts* (Paramount, 1929). Then came an explosion in the 1930s: 151 movies with clerks and 25 with chambermaids in credited roles.[38] In the Depression decade, every Hollywood production company made movies that sent their characters into hotels. In westerns, detective and gangster movies, slapstick, melodrama, and musicals, lead actors and actresses checked in with desk clerks and met chambermaids in their rooms or passed them in the halls. At a time when epidemic economic privation fostered frequent portrayals both of the super-rich (by way of escapism) and the hard-up (with whom audiences could identify), a hotel's mixture of wealthy guests and struggling employees made it the perfect film setting. Warner Brothers, the studio whose movies were most sympathetic to working-class underdogs, had by far the most films with chambermaids. Metro-Goldwyn-Mayer, the wealthiest, classiest production company, made *Grand Hotel, Dinner at Eight, Ninotchka,* and other memorable hotel movies, which it lavished with big budgets and the best talent: director Ernst Lubitsch; actors William Powell and the Barrymore brothers; actresses Greta Garbo, Joan Crawford, and Myrna Loy; and art director Cedric Gibbons.[39]

If movies in the 1930s presented clerks and chambermaids in greater number, they also communicated images with greater clarity and detail than the media of previous decades, particularly as the advent of talkies in the late 1920s added sound to the visual grandeur, wide-angle shots, and close-ups of the silent cinema. In a scene from *The Great Ziegfeld* (MGM, 1936), a tuxedoed clerk stands formally behind the desk before rows of pigeonholes. The register rotates on a lazy susan, and next to it a grate rises from the desk with a metal sign marked "Accounts," behind which the cashier usually sits (though not now). The clerk and the two men sorting mail behind him convey the same feeling as the immaculately white pigeonholes and the metal grate: efficiency, propriety, and a touch of glamour. In the next shot, the bellhops carrying Ziegfeld's bags match the plush furniture and potted plants they walk past—all are part of the scene. The clerks, bellhops, costumes, and sets all convey the luxury and excitement of a hotel without articulating it in dialogue. In a rather different mode, the first scene of *Ninotchka* (MGM, 1939) shows three Soviet diplomats marveling over an expensive Paris hotel. One by one, they take a quick look at the lobby, but we see more of their facial expressions than the room itself. Then they stand outside and debate checking into the hotel.

> *Kopalski:* They tell me when you ring once, the valet comes. When you ring twice, you get a waiter. And do you know what happens when you ring three times? A maid comes in! A French maid!
> *Iranoff:* Comrades, if we ring nine times—Let's go!

Though we can see the amazed, bemused look on their faces, it is their voices and dialogue that communicate their objects of desire: luxury, lavish service, and a French maid for each.

The ability to convey ideas in dialogue or with images at the back of the scene gave Hollywood new ways to approach the portrayal of clerks and chambermaids. Still, the most common method was to give workers no more than a few nondescript lines or leave them entirely mute, mere adornments, incidental to the plot. The scene from *The Great Ziegfeld* described above is typical. *Gold Diggers of 1935* (Warner Brothers, 1935) puts a clever twist on the usual anonymity of hotel workers in a sequence of short action shots depicting the varieties of work at a seaside resort hotel. The sequence gives no individual or collective sense of character to the workers, and the demands of cinematic choreography preclude an authentic depiction of work. An entire team of chambermaids is seen pulling sheets off beds in a billowing display, rather than the more realistic

fig. 13
Film still, *Broadway Melody* (Metro-Goldwyn-Mayer, 1929), Margaret Herrick Library. Courtesy of the Academy of Motion Picture Arts and Sciences.

but less dramatic sight of one woman working alone, going methodically from room to room. And despite a clever commentary on kickbacks—bell captains demand payment from bellhops, headwaiters from waiters, and housekeepers from chambermaids—the movie gives little detail about the work of clerks and maids, even by way of stereotype.

On occasion, hotel workers threw off such underdeveloped roles and managed to exchange a few lines with a protagonist or engender a plot twist that gave them some characterization. The old negative stereotypes lived on in the arrogant clerk who enrages Lionel Barrymore in *Grand Hotel* (MGM, 1932) and a sassy chambermaid in *The Broadway Melody* (MGM, 1929; fig. 13):

> *Hank:* Leave us plenty of towels, too.
> *Maid:* I did, and I counted them.
> *Hank:* How high can you count?

But the most important innovation of the movies of the 1930s was the way they increasingly characterized hotel employees as valuable accomplices to the films' protagonists. Though these workers usually remained subordinate to their customers in terms of class, status, and manners, movies began to portray them volunteering help and companionship as much from a sense of friendship or public service as from their economic and occupational position. This was especially true when clerks' and chambermaids' actions went beyond their job descriptions. Hotel workers played the role of informant, passing on gossip gleaned from overheard conversations in *The Great Ziegfeld* and *Ninotchka*. In *Top Hat* (RKO, 1935), a

desk clerk gives Ginger Rogers the impression that Fred Astaire—the man who is staying in the room above her and has been wooing her—is married (fig. 14). Rogers storms out of the hotel, and when Astaire goes to her room, he only realizes what has happened when he sees the chambermaids throwing away the flowers he sent. Interactions with hotel workers also gave lead characters an opportunity to prove their sophistication though conversational ability, innate fairness, big tips, and even posture. In *Swing Time* (RKO, 1936), Fred Astaire leans against the lobby desk at an alarming angle, his dialogue with the clerk and the positioning of his body marking him as the drollest man in the room.

Though usually confined to the roles of movie extra and accomplice, hotel clerks occasionally stepped forward as romantic leads. In contrast with nineteenth-century condemnations of clerks who tried to rise above their proper place, movies like *The Cocoanuts* and *Gold Diggers of 1935* commented favorably on their aspirations for love and economic success. Unlike the haughty clerks of yore, the clerks in these movies are the victims of snobs, surrounded by guests who look down on men who are striving to get somewhere in the world. Notably, however, we rarely see these upwardly mobile clerks performing their duties. In *The Cocoanuts*, for example, the clerk-protagonist is never seen on the job, and another clerk, played by Zeppo Marx, receives only one command over the course of the entire movie from hotel manager Hammer, played by Groucho: "Go upstairs and count the rooms. I think the third floor is missing." In both films, upwardly mobile clerks have good hearts and honest ambitions, but their clerking is only a way station in life and the content

of their labor is largely unimportant to the plot. They are bland variations on a larger Hollywood theme of young men attaining the careers and marrying the girls of their dreams.

A similar theme applied to female protagonists in the movies of the era. Women worked in certain occupations—secretary, stenographer, actress, or department store clerk—and found husbands through their jobs, making the actual content and purpose of that labor essentially moot. Chambermaids were surprisingly absent from this narrative tradition. They walked quietly down halls, said a few caustic words (like the maid in *The Broadway Melody*), or picked up flowers discarded by the protagonists (*Top Hat*). During the 1930s films like *Blonde Crazy* (Warner Brothers, 1931) occasionally placed hotel chambermaids in sexual or romantic situations, but they usually remained silent and asexual, even further in the background than clerks. For screenwriters and directors, cleaning hotel rooms was not a plausible road to upward mobility. Hollywood more frequently used hotel stenographers as protagonists and the objects of male affection, most famously in *Gold Diggers of 1935* and *Grand Hotel*. The greater use of stenographers as love interests suggests that writers and directors still saw chambermaids as too servile, downtrodden, and invisible to serve a similar role.

Most screenwriters, directors, actors, and other movie industry figures learned about desk clerks and chambermaids firsthand as hotel guests (fig. 15). Throughout the 1930s the promise of big money drew New York writers away from their hotel haunts and out to Hollywood to write scripts; George S. Kaufman (1889–1961), screenwriter of *The Cocoanuts* and founding member of the Algonquin Round Table, was only one prominent example. (Vicki Baum, author of the novel that was made into the play and movie *Grand Hotel*, was something of an exception in that she actually took jobs as a chambermaid in Berlin hotels in search of inspiration for her work.) Though desk clerks and chambermaids usually remained incidental in fiction as in the lives of authors, they generally appeared in a favorable light. This was a dramatic departure from the unremittingly negative images of the nineteenth century.[40]

As popular images of hotel employees improved, so did the conditions of their employment in the real world. In the mid-1930s a real-life chambermaid joined the ranks of movie characters in the public eye, pushing the reality of hotel work to the fore. In March 1937 Elsie Parrish won her appeal to the United States Supreme Court in the case of *West Coast Hotel v. Parrish*. The court ruled that a Washington State minimum wage law was constitutional and ordered that Parrish be paid $216.19, the

fig. 16
Peter Radin, *Occupations Relating to Household Arts*, color silkscreen poster created for the Ohio Federal Art Project, WPA, 1938. Library of Congress, Prints and Photographs Division, WPA Poster Collection. LC-USF34-026408-D.

amount by which her wages had fallen short of the legal limit. Because the case also overturned earlier decisions invalidating state regulation of wages, it immediately transformed U.S. labor law and helped usher in a new era of legislation that protected American workers.[41] Other hotel employees turned to labor unions to capitalize on this judicial revolution, and together they improved wages, benefits, and safety measures and increased the dignity of their jobs. While hotel work may have been perceived as an extension of the "household arts" (fig. 16)—labor that was least likely to be unionized—unions empowered workers to break through gendered constructions that limited wage protection. It took the AFL-affiliated Hotel Trades Council several years to consolidate its influence with the industry, but by 1945 it had persuaded the Waldorf-Astoria, the last holdout among the major New York hotels, to sign a contract that included a basic wage scale, regular raises, paid vacations, and holidays.[42]

By coincidence, in that same year MGM used the Waldorf-Astoria to develop its own ideas about hotels to their logical conclusion by releasing *Week-end at the Waldorf*, a remake of *Grand Hotel* and an extended homage to (or advertisement for) the hotel. In the movie, the Waldorf's desk clerk is more polite than the clerk at the Grand Hotel, and the chambermaid's cart serves as a vehicle to bring the war correspondent and the movie star together. The early postwar years thus marked something of a high point for big-city hotels. In the movies, hotels provided glamour, intrigue, and a steady source of workers to be used as witnesses, accomplices, and objects of romance; and in reality, business boomed and highly trained, well-paid hotel workers helped guests realize their movie-stoked fantasies of metropolitan sophistication.

Hospitality, labor, and culture have interacted in complex ways in America. In the nineteenth century the rise of the hotel, with its innovative arrangement of workers and configuration of space, was accompanied by widespread unease about the transition from household to institutional hospitality. This unease was manifested in a popular folklore with apparently contradictory criticisms of hotel clerks and chambermaids that revealed underlying anxieties about the market-driven alienation of traditional relations between host and guest. In the twentieth century the confluence of new management practices and modes of cultural production led to improvement in the public image of hotel employees. Rather than encouraging resentment of arrogant clerks or spreading fears of thieving maids, authors and screenwriters portrayed hotel workers as commonplace, usually unthreatening, often helpful in matters of business or love, and, in certain circumstances, appropriate as objects for romance. Cultural producers altered customary ways of seeing, and in so doing taught Americans to feel comfortable in hotels—sometimes by ignoring hotel workers, sometimes by engaging with them, but always in ways that allowed people to appear and feel more suave, gallant, debonair, and urbane than they ever had before. These changes in popular culture made hotel workers increasingly important as participants in, and determinants of, people's actual or virtual experience of hotels.

The precise nature of the relationship between changes in popular images of hotel workers and improvements in the actual conditions under which they labored is a particularly difficult issue. It would be hard to prove that the plight of Jennie Gerhardt or Joan Blondell's performance in *Blonde Crazy* swayed opinions about minimum wage legislation or contract negotiations. While novels and movies might have persuaded guests to treat workers more cordially, tip better, or refrain from crossing picket lines, documenting this kind of influence is usually impossible. Still, when hotel employees won legal and union battles, they did so in a cultural context that rested on the assimilation of popular images by a vast network of workers, managers, lawyers, judges, politicians, and bureaucrats. And so it may have been more than coincidence that improvements in the reality of hotel work followed upon the burnishing of hotel workers' public image.

The image and reality of hotel labor continue to change in the early twenty-first century. Most recently, actress Jennifer Lopez (b. 1970) used her public persona as a strong, successful woman to invest the story of the Cinderella chambermaid with new meaning. *Maid in Manhattan* (2002), shot on location at the Waldorf-Astoria, recapitulates some of the accusations of the nineteenth century—maids eavesdrop, appropriate guests' property, and imbue the hotel with their sexuality— but completely reverses their moral content. Lopez's character struggles with the ethical implications of her desires and actions, but the film unequivocally portrays her and her fellow chambermaids as working-class heroines and agents of social justice. Moreover, although the dashing and wealthy gentleman wins the maid's heart and carries her away, it is clear that she does not need to be saved: she remains an independent woman who can take care of herself. Lopez's performance completes a shift in popular culture more than a century in the making, bringing sympathy and human scale to the public image of hotel workers. Less obvious to the casual viewer is the debt *Maid in Manhattan* owes to the labor movement. The portrait of work in the movie reflects ongoing improvements in the conditions of real-life hotel work brought about by the Hotel Employees and Restaurant Employees International Union (HERE). Over the past decade, organized labor has responded to the restructuring of the American economy by devoting unprecedented efforts to unionizing immigrant service workers, and it is a sign of the times that HERE has been one of the most dynamic and successful unions of recent years. As life imitates art imitating life, Hollywood may continue to repay that debt by fostering public goodwill toward the hotel workers of today.✧

Notes

1. See New York City directories for 1855–1860, New-York Historical Society, and bankruptcies listed in the R. G. Dun ledgers, Baker Library, Harvard University, especially Sidney Sea (Chicago, 1860–1871), Jas Barker (New Haven, CT, 1870–1877), and Norman W. Rood (New Haven, CT, 1878–1881).

2. Hotel clerks seem to have been exclusively male; we have not yet encountered mention of a female clerk, though we continue to search.

3. Quoted in Jefferson Williamson, *The American Hotel* (New York: Knopf, 1930), 173.

4. Henry Hooper, *The Lost Model* (Philadelphia: Lippincott, 1874), 381; Williamson, *American Hotel*, 174.

5. Mark Twain, *Roughing It* (Hartford, CT: American, 1872), 268.

6. *Harper's Weekly* (18 April 1857): 242.

7. *Harper's New Monthly Magazine* 71, no. 426 (November 1885): 969.

8. William Dean Howells, *Their Wedding Journey* (Boston: J. R. Osgood, 1872), 98. See also Mary Clemmer, *His Two Wives* (New York: Hurd & Houghton, 1875), 317; Lillie Devereux, *Fettered for Life* (New York: Sheldon, 1874), 35.

9. On the American middle class, see Mary P. Ryan, *Cradle of the Middle Class: The Family in Oneida County, New York, 1790–1865* (Cambridge: Cambridge University Press, 1981); Stuart M. Blumin, *The Emergence of the Middle Class: Social Experience in the American City, 1760–1900* (Cambridge: Cambridge University Press, 1989).

10. Eliza Leslie, *The Behavior Book: A Guide for Ladies by Miss Leslie* (Philadelphia: W. P. Hazard, 1855), 106.

11. Anonymous, *Horrors of Hotel Life* (New York: Connelly & Curtis, 1884). See also anonymous, but attributed to James F. Grady, "Abuses; or, About Hotels" (Chicago: Self-published, 1879).

12. Ohio Historical Records Survey Project, *Historic Sites of Cleveland: Hotels and Taverns* (Columbus, OH: OHRSP, 1942), 382.

13. *Harper's Weekly* (18 April 1857): 242.

14. Williamson, *American Hotel*, 171–3.

15. Quoted in ibid., 175; Alexander Mackay, *Travels in the United States in 1846–47* (Philadelphia: Lea & Blanchard, 1849), 1:24.

16. Richard Bushman, *The Refinement of America: Persons, Houses, Cities* (New York: Knopf, 1992), 434–40.

17. Anonymous, *Horrors of Hotel Life*, 8.

18. Julian Pitt-Rivers, "The Law of Hospitality," in *The Fate of Shechem, or, The Politics of Sex: Essays in the Anthropology of the Mediterranean* (Cambridge: Cambridge University Press, 1977), 94–99.

19. Felicity Heal, *Hospitality in Early Modern England* (Oxford: Oxford University Press, 1990), chaps. 1 and 2.

20. OHRSP, *Historic Sites of Cleveland*, 23.

21. *Ninth Census, Vol. 1: Statistics of the Population of the United States* (Washington, D.C.: USGPO, 1872), "Table of the Population" and table XXIX; *Statistics of the Population of the United States at the Tenth Census* (Washington, D.C.: USGPO, 1883), tables XVI and XXII.

22. House servants were also accused of dishonesty and uncleanliness, illustrating a similar species of cultural discomfort with wage relations inside a household. See David M. Katzman, *Seven Days a Week: Women and Domestic Service in Industrializing America* (New York: Oxford University Press, 1978).

23. Reprinted in "Wants 'Old-Time Hospitality' in Hotels of Today," *Monthly Messenger of the New York State Hotel Association* (January 1923): 9.

24. Frank E. Jago, "The Clerk in New York," *Hotel World* (7 July 1906): 42–44.

25. *Hotel Monthly* (August 1911): 33.

26. Mary E. Palmer, "Hotel Housekeeping," *Hotel World* (3 August 1907): 10–12.

27. Jago, "Clerk in New York."

28. Ellsworth Milton and Alice Statler papers, no. 4303, boxes 4 and 5, Division of Rare and Manuscript Collections, Cornell University Library, Ithaca, New York.

29. Louise de Koven Bowen, *The Girl Employed in Hotels and Restaurants* (Chicago: Juvenile Protective Association of Chicago, 1912); Mary W. Dewson, *The Unstandardized Industry: Hotels* (New York: National Consumers' League, 1921); *Behind the Scenes in a Hotel* (New York: Consumers' League of New York, 1922); Herbert H. Lehman, *Message of the Governor Recommending Legislation Providing for One Day of Rest for Hotel and Restaurant Workers* (Albany, NY: J. B. Lyon, 1937).

30. Katzman, *Seven Days a Week*; Elizabeth Clark-Lewis, *Living In, Living Out: African American Domestics in Washington, D.C., 1910–1940* (Washington, D.C.: Smithsonian Institution, 1994).

31. Kenneth S. Lynn, *William Dean Howells: An American Life* (New York: Harcourt Brace Jovanovich, 1970), 5–7, 136.

32. Theodore Dreiser, *Sister Carrie* (New York: Doubleday, Page, 1900); Dreiser, *An American Tragedy* (New York: Boni & Liveright, 1925); Dreiser, *Jennie Gerhardt* (New York: Simon & Schuster, [1926] 1935); Bill Brown, *The Material Unconscious: American Amusement, Stephen Crane and the Economies of Play* (Cambridge, MA: Harvard University Press, 1996).

33. Marion Meade, *Dorothy Parker: What Fresh Hell Is This?* (New York: Penguin, 1989), 73–77; Matthew J. Bruccoli, *Some Sort of Epic Grandeur: The Life of F. Scott Fitzgerald* (New York: Harcourt Brace Jovanovich, 1981), 137; Diane Johnson, *Dashiell Hammett: A Life* (New York: Random House, 1983), 107–108.

34. Anita Loos, *Gentlemen Prefer Blondes; and, But Gentlemen Marry Brunettes* (1925, 1928; repr., New York: Penguin, 1998), 84, 138–45, 190, 193.

35. F. Scott Fitzgerald, *The Great Gatsby* (New York: Scribner's, 1925), 78, 126.

36. John Dos Passos, *Manhattan Transfer* (New York: Harper & Bros., 1925).

37. Robert Sklar, *Movie-Made America: A Cultural History of American Movies* (New York: Random House, 1975); Garth Jowett, *Film: The Democratic Art* (Boston: Little, Brown, 1976); Richard Butsch, "American Movie Audiences of the 1930s," *International Labor and Working-Class History* 59 (Spring 2001): 106–20.

38. *AFI Catalog*, http://afi.chadwyck.com (accessed 15 September 2003).

39. Neal Gabler, *An Empire of Their Own: How the Jews Invented Hollywood* (New York: Doubleday, 1988), 187–236; Christina Kathleen Wilson, "Cedric Gibbons and Metro-Goldwyn-Mayer: The Art of Motion Picture Set Design" (Ph.D. diss., University of Virginia, 1998).

40. Scott Meredith, *George S. Kaufman and His Friends* (Garden City, NY: Doubleday, 1974); "'Grand Hotel' Film," *New York Times* (27 March 1932): sec. 8, p. 5.

41. William E. Leuchtenberg, "The Case of the Wenatchee Chambermaid," in *The Supreme Court Reborn: The Constitutional Revolution in the Age of Roosevelt* (New York: Oxford University Press, 1995), 163–79.

42. Matthew Josephson, *Union House, Union Bar: The History of the Hotel and Restaurant Employees and Bartenders International Union, AFL-CIO* (New York: Random House, 1956); "AFL Wins Waldorf Poll," *New York Times* (18 December 1945): 21.

HOTEL TRAYMORE
ATLANTIC CITY

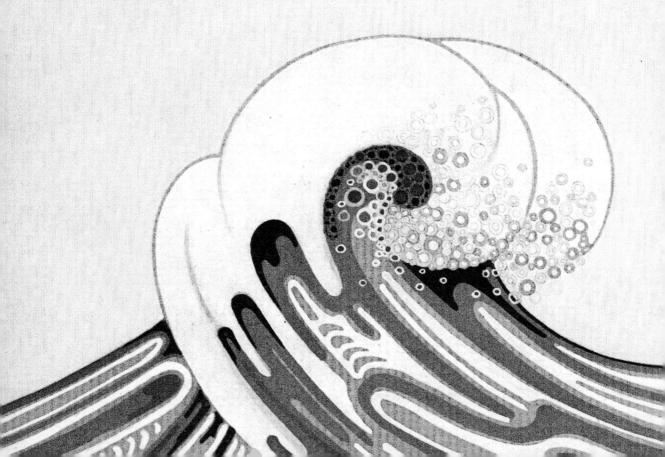

George E. Thomas and Susan Nigra Snyder

William Price's Traymore Hotel: Modernity in the Mass Resort

George E. Thomas and Susan Nigra Snyder are partners in CivicVisions, LP, and together teach collaborative design studios that focus on contemporary life at the Graduate School of Fine Arts at the University of Pennsylvania. Thomas has a Ph.D. in art history from the University of Pennsylvania and has taught in the urban studies, historic preservation, and architecture programs since 1978. He is widely published on nineteenth- and twentieth-century American architecture, with special interest in Frank Furness and William L. Price. Snyder is a registered architect with a degree from the University of Pennsylvania and has taught in the architecture and urban design departments for more than twenty years. She has published several articles on the forces of consumption in contemporary urban life. Together, they are developing a strategic vision for an arts district in Las Vegas.

Modernity, broadly defined, is the all-encompassing transformation of institutions and patterns of social behavior characteristic of post-feudal Europe, but social theorist Anthony Giddens equates it more specifically with the era that began with the industrialized world. In his formulation, modernity as a post-traditional order encompasses social practices that have moved decisively away from the local forms and stable precepts of the agricultural and feudal age. Modern life is shaped by influences beyond local place, by mediated experiences, by the reflexive appropriation of knowledge, and by a plurality of choices resulting in fast-paced change, global connections, and new social forms. In the modern world, identity is not inherited, but rather consists of the narrative each individual constructs to give meaning to life.[1] The conditions of affluence and leisure in early twentieth-century Philadelphia made possible the construction of a modern life for a broad cross section of its populace. As Philadelphians' primary resort destination, Atlantic City, New Jersey, mixed traditional and modern and elite and mass hotels with hundreds of boardinghouses, providing the newly affluent class the opportunity to exercise choices in their leisure life that enabled them to explore multiple narratives of self-identity.[2]

In the twentieth century, the resort hotel, theme park, and shopping mall mark the intersection of innovative design and modern identity, just as the factory and train station expressed the emerging forces of the industrial age. These building types are the creations of a culture increasingly defined by consumption.[3] The modern resort, unencumbered by the constraints

All architectural and interior design and furnishings by Price and McLanahan, except where noted.

Detail of menu cover, Submarine Grill, Traymore Hotel, Atlantic City, New Jersey, 1915 (see fig. 21).

fig. 1
Traymore Hotel,
Atlantic City, New Jersey,
view from Steel Pier, 1915.
Price and McLanahan
Archive, courtesy of
George E. Thomas.

of everyday life, is a place where inventive design both reveals and shapes contemporary life and thus projects an exceptionally vivid expression of a fluid American culture. Post–Second World War fantasy hotels—Morris Lapidus's Fontainebleau (1952–1954) and Eden Roc (1954–1955) in Miami Beach, Michael Graves's richly ornamented Swan and Dolphin hotels (1989–1990) at Walt Disney World, HKS Inc.'s brilliantly colored Atlantis in the Bahamas (1997–1998), and casino hotels such as New York New York (1997) or the Bellagio (1998) in Las Vegas—are part of a trajectory of modernity rooted in Will Price's early twentieth-century Blenheim and Traymore hotels in Atlantic City. The Traymore's innovative design and unabashed embrace of theatrical consumerism, in particular, influenced two generations of resort hotel design, and, despite its 1972 demolition, it remains the cultural icon of Atlantic City. This essay creates a critical framework for understanding resort hotels, from Price's Atlantic City hotels to the present (fig. 1).

The White Family and the Blenheim Hotel

At the end of the nineteenth century, Atlantic City was the nation's most popular seaside resort, serving a diverse clientele drawn from an eastern region spanning New York to Washington, D.C.[4] Created by the Pennsylvania Railroad in the mid-nineteenth century, it grew in fifty years to accommodate dozens of beachfront hotels and nearly seven hundred boardinghouses that together were capable of housing more than twenty thousand guests. Atlantic City became a national summer, later year-round, attraction because of its wide beaches and the cooling influence of the Atlantic Ocean. With the framing element of the Boardwalk and the encouragement of one-dollar round-trip train tickets from Philadelphia (that cost less than a cab ride to Philadelphia's Fairmount Park), pier builders brought amusement rides to the Boardwalk's retail promenade, in turn stimulating the construction of ever-larger hotels. By the twentieth century, all these elements transformed the resort into a "city by the sea."

fig. 2
Blenheim Hotel,
Atlantic City, New Jersey,
view from the beach,
postcard, c. 1930.
Price and McLanahan
Archive, courtesy of
George E. Thomas.

Josiah and Daniel White, owners of the Marlborough-Blenheim and the Traymore hotels, respectively, were members of one of the extraordinary Quaker industrialist families that had shaped the Philadelphia economy in the nineteenth century.[5] The Whites capitalized on the new rhythms of the industrial age that distinguished modern life from the seasonal rhythms of agriculture and in turn made it possible to extend the resort season from the summer to the entire year. With the Marlborough Hotel in 1902, Josiah White (c. 1860–c. 1930) pioneered the modern steel-framed, year-round resort hotel in Atlantic City. Along with other Quaker businessmen, the Whites brought urban expectations and values to Atlantic City with such festivals as the Easter Parade (beginning in the 1870s) and, later, the Miss America pageant (1921). Their Atlantic City became the model of the mass American resort of the twentieth century.

White's architect for his new hotel, to be called the Marlborough Hotel, was fellow Quaker William L. Price (1861–1916), practicing as William L. Price and Brother and after 1903 as Price and McLanahan. He was trained in 1879–1880 in the office of the lusty proto-modernist Frank Furness (1839–1912), a few years after Louis Sullivan (1856–1924) left the same office for Chicago. When he received the Marlborough commission, Price had already designed the château-style Kenilworth Inn (1891) in the Great Smoky Mountains as a part of the development of George W. Vanderbilt's Biltmore estate in Asheville, North Carolina.[6] Recalling the Kenilworth, with its high roofs and châteauesque massing, the Marlborough was set back from the beach by an extensive lawn, connected to the Boardwalk by a narrow bridge. Notable features were the eight-sided fireplace that made the lobby inviting in the winter and the vast dining room that centered on a huge leaded-glass dome capable of seating several hundred diners at a time. At the Marlborough, the guest enjoyed the seclusion of a suburban house along with the comforts of a grand urban hotel in the extraordinary setting of the Boardwalk and the endlessly changing ocean.

fig. 3
Blenheim Hotel,
Atlantic City, New Jersey,
ornamental terra cotta.
Photograph by
George E. Thomas, 1976.

Four years later, Price designed the "Blenheim Annex" for Josiah White using reinforced concrete, a new material that had been reserved largely for industrial purposes. Concrete was strong, fireproof and soundproof, and remarkably inexpensive—50 percent less than conventional high-rise fireproof steel construction (fig. 2).[7] Despite its still-experimental status, it offered enormous opportunities for a hotel. When a strike made steel deliveries uncertain, the owner and architect took the bold step of building in concrete. With the construction of the Blenheim, monumental, fireproof buildings became the norm for first-class hotels along the Boardwalk. Despite modern construction techniques, most of Atlantic City's later hotels were designed in historic styles, as in the case of the French-styled Dennis (1905) and the Breakers (1909), or Georgian variants of English Renaissance design used for the Shelbourne (1926), Chalfonte (1904), and Haddon Hall (1924).[8] The Blenheim, by contrast, caught the nascent spirit of the new century. In a 1906 lecture that Price gave to the Toronto Association of Architects entitled "Modern Architecture," he described his new building's style as "Atlantic City, period of 1906."[9] Instead of overlaying historical details on boring, rectangular blocks in the manner of the other Boardwalk hotels, Price sculpted a plastic mass emblematic of its concrete construction while giving the building extraordinary visual identity.[10] Ornamented with gigantic green-glazed terra-cotta sea creatures—crabs, sea horses, and lobsters—it had the freshness of a modern experiment that celebrated the seashore as a special place (fig. 3).

The Blenheim was sited in a new way as well. Price emphasized its urban setting—unlike the Marlborough's suburban lawn—by linking it to the Boardwalk with an open hemicycle of shops. The engagement of the hotel and the pedestrian way became the model for the next generation of Atlantic City beachfront hotels, anticipating the relationship of Las Vegas's late 1990s casino hotels with the Strip.

fig. 4
Blenheim Hotel (left), and
Traymore Hotel (right),
Atlantic City, New Jersey,
view from the beach,
detail of postcard,
pre-1914. Courtesy of
Architectural Archives,
University of
Pennsylvania.

The Traymore Hotel

Will Price's second Atlantic City masterpiece, the Traymore Hotel, had its beginnings after the Civil War. At the end of the century, it was acquired by Daniel White (c. 1853–1935), cousin and competitor of Josiah White.[11] Price's first Atlantic City project had been a lobby and dining room for the Traymore Hotel in 1898.[12] The Blenheim's completion in the spring of 1906 transformed the Atlantic City hotel market. A successful hotel could no longer ride on its operator's reputation or its European name and historic style. Recognizing the risk to his business, Daniel White immediately commissioned Will Price to improve the Traymore.

Unlike the Marlborough and Blenheim sites, where no earlier buildings existed to affect the design, the Traymore site was encumbered by a Victorian frame hotel that was supposed to remain in service. There was enough space to add a fireproof, winterized urban tower of ten rooms per floor between the old hotel and the Boardwalk. Price conceived a new lobby entered directly from the Boardwalk, surmounted by seven stories of rooms and crowned by a spectacular domed Sky-Room with balconies overlooking the beach and the Boardwalk (fig. 4). The Traymore's Sky-Room rivaled the 1890s amusement ride called the "Revolving Observation Tower," a steel tower with a rising, revolving platform that stood across the Boardwalk. With the new addition, the Traymore could compete with the Marlborough-Blenheim, though its frame rear wing always made it less desirable.

In 1912 Daniel White commissioned Price and McLanahan to replace the old frame wing that remained behind the 1906 tower. That project was stalled by the economic downturn of 1912–1913. Early in 1914, with the world drifting toward war, White made a remarkable offer to his architects. If they would provide the design and the management for the construction of a new hotel and find the financing that had eluded him, he would turn over the hotel site, name, and good will in exchange for preferred stock in a new corporation.[13] The architects would be free to push their imaginations, limited only by their capacity to finance the project.

By late spring, Price and McLanahan and their lawyer were shopping for financing and negotiating with contractors. With the international situation deteriorating by the hour, the mortgages and building contracts were signed late in the evening of 27 June 1914, the night before the First World War exploded on the Continent, ending most construction projects. Two months later, after the Labor Day holiday, the demolition of the old Traymore set off the race for builders to finish its six hundred rooms and seventeen stories in time for the following prime season, little more than

fig. 5
Newell Convers Wyeth,
Sea Fantasy, sketch for
Submarine Grill mural,
Traymore Hotel, Atlantic
City, New Jersey, oil on
canvas, 24 x 77 in.
(61 x 196 cm), 1915.
Collection of
Philip N. Price.

nine months ahead. In the winter of 1915, with the hotel rising above its massive base, Price offered the job of decorating the special public rooms to two of Philadelphia's best-known artists, George Harding (1882–1959) and N. C. Wyeth (1882–1945). They would later be known as members of the Brandywine School. Wyeth, though younger, was already famous for his illustrations for the Scribner's series of adventure books. His retelling of Price's ideas for the project made clear Price's goal of meeting the modern world head-on:

> His ringing, insistent keynote was *modernity, modernity!* A beseeching appeal to us to face our modern spirit and customs unflinchingly, and to cease thinking that unless a building resembles the Parthenon, or a mural decoration resembles Angelo or Donatello, that it is "rotten." That we *must* recognize that our life today, from the frenzied circus-ridden antics of Billy Sunday, to the spendthrifts and money gluttons who patronize hotels of a resort, are *realities....* That to paint, sculpt, or design classically is merely to be true to your era.

Wyeth rose to the challenge:

> And, now I have an opportunity. A gorgeous underground café; stark in its simplicity; a great black marble dancing space dropped below level, upon which are coral-colored tables and chairs; huge pillars, four of them supporting a glass ceiling which is in reality a lake filled with Japanese goldfish! From the dance floor one gazes at the sky through the water and the flashing goldfish. The great flat walls and pillars are to be painted in blues, emeralds and whites, interpreting the feel of the deep sea! Such a chance! Mermaids, flying fish, seaweed, spume and glittering bubbles, rising, rising like champagne in a glass!... The huge [tenth-floor] banquet room is another matter: 65 x 80 feet, fountains, huge glass globes with goldfish magnified as big as shad! Illuminated jets of water running like gold and jewels, Chinese rugs of pumpkin yellow and jet black pillars![14]

Wyeth's oil sketch today resides with the Price family and attests to the jewel-like colors that brought the spaces to life (fig. 5).

fig. 6
Traymore Hotel, Atlantic
City, New Jersey, view
from the Marlborough
Hotel across Park Place,
postcard, pre-1920.
Price and McLanahan
Archive, courtesy of
George E. Thomas.

In late May construction was far enough along for Wyeth and Harding to begin their work, and as the opening day in late June drew near, Wyeth once again wrote to his brother, "Babe":

> The Hotel itself is attracting nationwide attention on account of its size, cost, completeness and numerous *features*, the most talked about being the "submarine café." With the room only half done, *7000* people visited it on Sunday….
>
> We are spending every hour our energy will stand to finish by Friday, midnight. Saturday, a banquet for 400 hotel managers from the principal hotels east of Chicago will be given in this room. A remarkable advertisement![15]

The hotel opened to international acclaim. The nation's principal architectural journal, the *Architectural Forum*, headlined its lead story "America's Greatest Seaside Hotel" and praised the Traymore as the first architecturally significant resort hotel in Atlantic City.[16]

Toward an Extroverted Architecture

In part, it was the site that made the Traymore (fig. 6). For most of its length, the Boardwalk runs east-west and is intersected by dead-end streets that provide access to the long sides of hotels. Close proximity blocked oblique views and made it necessary to concentrate ornament and detail at the Boardwalk end. The exception to this condition is a double bend that occurs in the neighborhood of Price's hotels, marking the point where the original beachfront expanded in the 1870s and 1880s to provide a larger oceanfront for the lucky owners of this key section of beach. Not coincidentally, the largest hotels and piers would be built in this zone. The site also benefited from the open space provided by Brighton Park, a gift to the city in 1879 by Hamilton F. Disston (the son of Philadelphia saw manufacturer Henry Disston) and George F. Lee,

fig. 7
Traymore Hotel,
Atlantic City, New Jersey,
photogravure of lost
perspective showing
original color scheme,
Grant M. Simon,
renderer, 1915.
Price and McLanahan
Archive, courtesy of
George E. Thomas.

owner of the Hotel Brighton. Park Place, as it was also known, occupied an entire city block and prevented another major hotel from being constructed between the Marlborough-Blenheim to the west and the Traymore to the east, ensuring that the Traymore would be visible along its entire length. With this site, Price had the opportunity for architectural expression in the entire building composition, not just the Boardwalk facade.

In his design of the rear wing of the Blenheim, Price substituted vertical registers of bays crowned by projecting horizontal balconies for the familiar Beaux-Arts organizing system of pilasters and cornices. He returned to this strategy for the first wing of the Traymore. The size of the addition suggested an extension of this strategy, but with two significant changes of emphasis. First, by creating secondary wings that were progressively longer the further they were from the ocean, Price could ensure ocean views for most of the rooms of the west facade. This design created a reverse perspective from the Boardwalk that enlivened the optical experience of the hotel, as the shorter front wing appeared to be the same size as the longer rear wings. Second, Price realized that the entire length of the hotel's silhouette had to become the great icon, leading him to compose a rippling and nearly symmetrical silhouette that rose to great dome-capped towers—234 feet above the beach at their highest points—where the central wings projected from the building's long spine.[17]

The large-scale articulation of the bays and balconies together with the even more massive scale of the wings and the rippling skyline became the enduring iconic image of the Atlantic City beachfront. The hotel's cluster of twelve- and eighteen-story towers loomed above the one- and two-story shops of the Boardwalk, not unlike the way European cathedrals rise

fig. 8
(right)
Traymore Hotel,
Atlantic City, New Jersey,
view of south tower.
Photograph by
George E. Thomas, 1972.

fig. 9
(far right)
Raymond Hood,
American Radiator
Building, New York, 1923.
Photograph by
George E. Thomas, 1975.

above their surrounding markets. The color scheme of the hotel added to the effect. Instead of turn-of-the-century monochrome, Price used the yellow of the beach sand for the bricks of the walls and balcony fronts, the gold of the sun for the immense domes, and the blue of the sky and dappled light and dark greens and blues of the water for the pier caps and ornamental tile panels of the walls (fig. 7). Historical, it was not. The center towers anticipated the setback tops of 1920s New York skyscrapers and the famous New York skyline they created (figs. 8, 9). By that time, the Traymore drawings had been exhibited across Europe, introducing the hotel to the world at large. At the moment of its creation there was nothing like it in the world.

Interior: Modern Meets Ocean

The interior was shaped with the same eye to showmanship as the exterior. Price wove the principal themes—the seashore and the new architectural expression—into each major space. Though Price himself did not drive a car, he designed the building to accommodate the new means of travel that was sweeping through all strata of Philadelphia (and American) society.[18] Arriving and departing guests could drive directly to the door and park across the street in a lot, and later in a garage, owned by the hotel. Entrance into the lower foyer introduced the oceanic color scheme, with the light green and white alabaster stairway rising to the main lobby. Flanked by tapering marble pylons and framed by a curving marble railing, the stairway initiated the contemporary shapes that were repeated throughout the interior and exterior (fig. 10). The stairs reached the main floor at the front desk. After checking in, hotel guests entered through the dark doors of the elevator bank. Instead of the usual enclosed cab, windows in the rear wall provided views down the beach and the Boardwalk.

fig. 10
(right)
Traymore Hotel,
Atlantic City, New Jersey,
main stair, 1915.
Price and McLanahan
Archive, courtesy of
George E. Thomas.

fig. 11
(below)
Traymore Hotel,
Atlantic City, New Jersey,
first-floor plan, 1915.
Price and McLanahan
Archive, courtesy of
George E. Thomas.

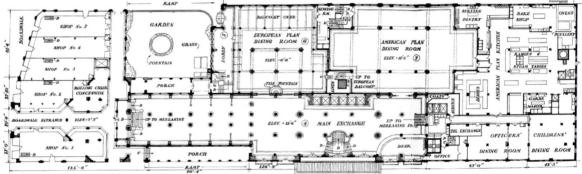

Anticipating John Portman's (b. 1924) glass elevators plying hotel atriums of the 1970s, the Traymore architects made a service event a celebration of the seaside location. Thus, Price's design created an architectural expression from the immediate context of place, not from historical references, and in contrast to neighboring hotels made its competitors look old by comparison.

The hotel's other principal entrance, the Boardwalk portal, gave access to the double attraction of the beach and the Boardwalk. From the central corridor, the route to the beach passed through a vast and airy lobby, lighted by immense windows with French doors in the center that opened onto a side porch. The lobby terminated in a flight of sea-green marble stairs that ascended a half level into the multistoried Music Room or descended half a flight to the main route to the Boardwalk and the beach beyond (fig. 11). This lower route passed across an interior arcade that provided all-weather access to five shops that were built at the Boardwalk's end.

The eastern shop housed M. E. Blatt's luxury jewelry and accessories store, while day-to-day needs were met by a drugstore on the opposite side of the vast arched portal. With a rolling-chair concession, three more clothing and beachwear shops, and a barbershop and newsstand at street level, guests' immediate and luxury needs could be met entirely within the hotel. Beyond the hotel, the Boardwalk was a retail wonderland with three miles of shops.

Mediating between the Boardwalk and the main lobby was the Music Room. It continued the light- and dark-green marbles of the lobby in an architectural vocabulary that was avowedly modern. In its midst stood four of the original structural columns of the 1906 tower, cut off and adapted into flaring two-story-high torchères clad in light green and white alabaster, illuminating the space (fig. 12). The rich mixture of sculptural, streamlined pilasters, glistening tile panels bearing the hotel's lighthouse insignia on the major piers, and hand-hammered, streamlined iron railings anticipated the aesthetic character of the 1920s. In the center of the room was one of the fountains that Wyeth referred to, which pumped goldfish from a floor-level pond into a water-filled glass globe where they were magnified to the size of shad. The Music Room opened out onto solaria and open-roof decks, with industrial-pipe railings that gave something of the feeling of being aboard a ship.

In their cool hues, soaring spaces, and generally modern tones, the great lobbies and Music Room acted as foils to the dining and grill rooms. As in most hotels of the period, there were two principal dining rooms: the dark oak-paneled, European-plan dining room and the marble-paneled and mirrored American-plan dining room. The columns of the European-plan room supported balconies and terminated with cast-plaster figures of medieval monks clad in flowing robes, creating a calculatedly hierarchical

fig. 14
Traymore Hotel,
Atlantic City, New Jersey,
Submarine Grill.
From Edward Hoak
and Willis Church, eds.,
*Masterpieces of
Architecture in the
United States* (New York:
Scribner's, 1930).

space that represented Price's view of European culture (fig. 13). The larger American-plan room brought everyone into the principal space and multiplied them as a crowd of thousands in the mirrored walls to emphasize the number of guests. Price used architectural expression to differentiate the two dining experiences.

The jewel of the hotel, the Submarine Grill, was located on the street level below the main lobby. Intended to attract the youthful dance crowd, it developed its architectural cues accordingly. The construction shifted from the column-and-beam of conventional reinforced concrete to a new form, the so-called mushroom column and flat-plate construction that merged column and slab in a flaring capital.[19] These giant columns carried girders that supported a plate glass–bottomed fish pond as the ceiling of the room, giving the illusion of being under water—an apt representation of Jules Verne's (1828–1905) voyage of the Nautilus in the 1870 science-fiction adventure *20,000 Leagues Under the Sea* (fig. 14). With a black marble dance floor, coral-clad columns, and walls dematerialized into images of mermaids and sea foam by N. C. Wyeth and George Harding, it was a remarkable experience that hyped the great draw of the resort: the ocean.

From the Submarine Grill in the basement to the domed rooms at the top, each public space evoked different experiences. The tenth-floor banquet hall was given a Treasure Island theme in images by N. C. Wyeth, derived from his by then famous Scribner's illustrations.

Another grill room, decorated by George Harding in an exotic fusion of Persians and peacocks, paid homage to the *Thousand and One Arabian Nights*. Price's themed rooms went beyond name and symbolic decoration to create an all-enveloping experience, from illusionistic murals to architectural details. By evoking imaginary worlds where the exotic is an outgrowth of the modern, the building anticipated the disjunctive juxtapositions of contemporary life. Price's enthusiasm for the new had created a twentieth-century masterpiece.

Modern Philadelphia

The 1906 Traymore addition, while connecting the hotel to the Boardwalk, did little to alter its character. This situation changed in 1914, when Price, his partner M. Hawley McLanahan (1865–1929), and their manager Joseph Mott reinvented the hotel to reflect the new forces of contemporary life that were radically reshaping Philadelphia. By the turn of the twentieth century, the cumulative effects of Philadelphia's industrial strength resulted in the doubling of salaries of the regional workforce, from production-line workers to managers, in concert with a reduction of the workweek, increasing leisure time.[20]

These innovations had the unintended but remarkable effect of shifting Philadelphia from a culture driven by work to one driven by consumption. In a work culture, individuals define themselves by their jobs. By contrast, in a consumption culture, work is at best instrumental to achieving the goods and experiences that bring self-fulfillment.[21] Industrial capitalism in Philadelphia produced per-capita wealth that made it one of the wealthiest cities in the world at the end of the nineteenth century.[22] With affordable mass-produced housing and furnishings, cheap rail transportation, and resorts that catered to the general population, the city's workers could construct a life centered on the increasing opportunities offered by the nascent consumption culture.[23] The freedom to choose from ever-expanding options allowed individuals to actualize their self-identity in many ways. By the end of the nineteenth century, Philadelphians were moving away from choices established by tradition and into the increasingly self-constructed world of modernity.[24] The Traymore was the architectural expression of these transformations.

The change to a consumption culture was shaped, too, by local media. Philadelphia was the home of leisure lifestyle publications such as the *Saturday Evening Post, Ladies' Home Journal*, and *House and Garden*, as well as the nation's premier advertising company, N. W. Ayer and Sons.[25] With national accounts including Hires Root Beer and Steinway pianos, the Ayer agency linked the rational and emotional impulses of personal self-expression with product acquisition, while simultaneously demonstrating the value of trade names and slogans. These forces were manifested in patterns that cut across all strata of American society. Jazz, Joe College

fig. 15
(right)
Traymore Hotel insignia, ink on cartridge paper, c. 1906. Price and McLanahan Archive, courtesy of George E. Thomas.

fig. 16
(far right)
Traymore Hotel insignia, ink and gouache on cartridge paper, 1915, Price and McLanahan Archive, courtesy of George E. Thomas.

and Betty Coed, and the flapper girl were new social forms that expressed modern lifestyle and cultural freedoms that could compete with old elite values. Simultaneously, the automobile introduced physical freedom for the working classes, reflected in the garages that appeared behind row houses and the parking lots built adjacent to the larger Philadelphia mills.

On the eve of the First World War, a new generation saw the possibility of constructing self-identity not from inherited social position, from ethnic or religious origins, or even necessarily from achievement, but rather from personal choices that gave material form to a particular narrative of self.[26] The totality of change cutting across society was evident to Edith Wharton (1862–1937), who reported in 1915, "What a woman was criticized for doing yesterday, she is ridiculed for not doing today."[27] In a post-traditional world, change was the new constant, and standards were upended. In the same year that the Traymore opened, Wharton was marveling at the end of a culture based on fixed tradition.

Branding the Traymore

With the N. W. Ayer agency in Philadelphia developing such iconic images as the boy in the yellow rain slicker for the National Biscuit Company's Uneeda Biscuit, it was a short step for Price to conceive of a symbol that would capture the essence of the modern Traymore. The hotel had long used an oil painting of the Absecon Lighthouse hanging in the lobby to represent its coastal setting. When Daniel White owned the hotel, Price's office created an engraved letterhead of the lighthouse surrounded by an oval of sea creatures (fig. 15). In their role as owners, Price and his team further abstracted the lighthouse image to a few bold planes of color—grayed greens and strong ultramarine blues—which they strongly outlined in black, inspired by contemporary advertising art, to give it a modern feel (fig. 16). With stylized waves lapping at its base, the lighthouse aptly conveyed the setting and ambience of Atlantic City and accordingly became the emblem of the resort's great hotel.

fig. 17
(above)
**Blenheim Hotel,
Atlantic City, New Jersey,
lobby, 1906. Price and
McLanahan Archive, cour-
tesy of George E. Thomas.**

fig. 18
(above, right)
**Dining room chair,
Traymore Hotel, Atlantic
City, New Jersey, 1915.
Courtesy of Robert Venturi
and Denise Scott-Brown.
Photograph by Julie
Marquart for VSBA.**

As Frank Lloyd Wright (1869–1959) would later do at Tokyo's Imperial Hotel (1915), Price's office took total charge of every element of the design. For the public spaces, the firm designed furniture that comple-mented the innovative architecture and contrasted with the historically derived furnishings found at neighboring hotels, including their Blenheim Hotel of eight years before (fig. 17). The dining room chairs were stream-lined versions of Thomas Chippendale's exotic Chinese designs—here brilliantly polychromed in Chinese red, with fish ornaments placed in the center of the back splats, further reinforcing the hotel's marine theme (fig. 18). Bold geometric fabrics enlivened lobby sofas and chairs, and the slender legs of the pier tables in the lobbies anticipated the slim lines of post–First World War flapper girls who would later serve as ornaments themselves (fig. 19). For the Submarine Grill, the architects chose Thonet's light and moveable furniture. Where other contemporary hotels were oppressively dark, elephantine, and masculine, the Traymore designers embraced sparkling color and nearly feminine delicacy.

The hotel silver and dish service brought the all-encompassing modern scheme to the table. Late nineteenth-century silver had become progres-sively more baroque, as silversmiths created objects of enormous complexity that mirrored the "more is more" culture denigrated by Thorstein Veblen's (1857–1929) aphorism "the pecuniary canons of taste." Price's team targeted tableware for radical simplification. For the dining service, the designers created plates of a tan hue not unlike the sand color of the exterior, with bright blue and green accents—the colors of the building trim—and marked with the hotel's lighthouse logo. Silver-plate place settings were slender and tapered, with no extraneous ornament; only the hotel's name was engraved on the back to indicate the source. The hotel's silver serving bowls were sleek, almost industrial, their only decorative flourishes being flared, fluted rims. The new accoutrement

fig. 19
(right)
Traymore Hotel,
Atlantic City, New Jersey,
lobby showing furniture,
1915. Price and McLanahan
Archive, courtesy of
George E. Thomas.

fig. 20
(below, left)
Cocktail shaker,
Submarine Grill,
Traymore Hotel, 1915.
Courtesy of Architectural
Archives, University
of Pennsylvania.

fig. 21
(below, right)
Menu cover, Submarine
Grill, Traymore Hotel,
1915. Courtesy of
Architectural Archives,
University of
Pennsylvania.

of sophisticated entertainment, the cocktail shaker, was given the form of a tapered graduate, with indented rings that exactly corresponded to shots, making it possible to "mass produce" martinis (fig. 20). The shakers, like the plates, were accented with the lighthouse logo. Even the menu covers were similarly styled with clean, assertively modern designs evoking the contemporary world (fig. 21).

HOTEL TRAYMORE
ATLANTIC CITY

Clients for Modern Design

Even as Price was inventing a modern vocabulary for the
contemporary world, Philadelphia's elite were turning
toward historicism in their houses and office buildings.
This shift forced Price to find a new clientele for his
original architecture in the leisure culture of Atlantic
City and the industrial culture of the Midwest.[28] In 1911
Price designed a modern residence for auto-parts magnate Frank Wheeler in the Indianapolis suburbs. While
the Wheeler house was being built, Wheeler's neighbors
and codevelopers of the Indianapolis Motor Speedway,
James Allison (who also commissioned Price for his
house) and Carl Fisher, pooled resources to purchase
half of Miami Beach. There they intended to create a
resort that would appeal to their automobile customers
who shared the luxury of leisure time and enjoyed the
freedom of the automobile. Once again, they engaged
Price and McLanahan to design the attractions that
would promote their South Florida land investment. The First World War
delayed their project, and by the time construction resumed in 1918,
Price had died. Led by Price's chief associate, Ralph B. Bencker
(1883–1961), the firm designed Star Island and its causeway, gates,
monumental water tower, and several mansions, as well as the Alton
Beach, Lincoln, and Aquarium Apartments elsewhere on the island.[29]
All of these projects shared the streamlined forms that characterized the
Traymore and Wheeler's mansion. The firm of Price and McLanahan
also made the preliminary designs for the Flamingo Hotel at Fifteenth
Street, on Biscayne Bay (fig. 22). Its Florida identity was obvious in the
palette: brilliant orange for the giant citrus-colored dome that crowned its
central tower and the flamingo-pink detailing, that, according to period
postcards, brightened the facade. In contrast with the traditional Mediterranean styles that characterized Coral Gables on the mainland—largely
influenced by another Philadelphian, Phineas Paist (1875–1937)—Price
and McLanahan's Miami Beach buildings brought a modern aesthetic to
South Florida before the influential 1925 Paris Exposition Internationale
des Arts Décoratifs et Industriels Modernes, which is commonly credited
as introducing Art Deco to the general public. Serving a nouveau riche
clientele, the streamlined style remained vital into the 1950s.

Learning from Consumption

Modern life poses new questions about meaning and how it is communicated.
Anthropologist Mary Douglas, writing about consumption, theorizes that
the value of goods and experiences lies not in their use but rather in the
meaning they communicate about who we are and what we value.[30]
Even something as simple as a cup of coffee is more than a good-tasting

fig. 23
Earl Horter, Traymore
Roof Plaza, ink on
cartridge paper,
16 x 10 ½ in.,
(41 x 27 cm), c. 1922.
Courtesy of Architectural
Archives, University
of Pennsylvania.

beverage or morning pick-me-up. A cup of coffee from Dunkin' Donuts, Starbucks, or the local coffee shop can become a means of communicating identity. In short, consumption decisions describe the culture of the moment and speak to those who can read the nuances. Douglas further theorizes that the selection of goods and experiences operates simultaneously as an affirmation of self-image and as a hostile positioning against other groups who would make other choices. Thus, these kinds of consumption decisions can be used either to make connections or to establish barriers between people.

Consumption is about culture, social relations, and power. Douglas's seminal essay "In Defense of Shopping" frames four different cultural types representing twentieth-century life that function in a four-way pattern of selective opposition. In her framework, *hierarchical* values exemplify those who identify with the existing tradition and whose conservative tastes are generally in opposition to those of the *individualistic* caste. The individualistic group might choose a more aestheticized mode that battles with the hierarchical over questions of new versus old. Anti-hierarchical *enclavists* value their group over the individual and are more likely opposed to the solitary *isolate*, who in turn values a "withdrawn," hence nonenclavist, mode.[31]

The selection of resorts has always been a marker of identity. In the Traymore's time, old hierarchical elites might have chosen Bar Harbor, while enclavist Will Price moved to his own commune at Rose Valley, outside of Philadelphia, and vacationed with numerous friends. Isolates might have taken to the Maine woods, but for the artsy, modern individualist there would have been few urbane resort choices. Atlantic City attracted an audience spanning the entire range, from working class to middle class as well as the wealthier set, but primarily presented itself in the guise of the hierarchical group with hotels that celebrated European

or early American historical forms. In this setting, the Traymore, by contrast, was a stage for the individualistic group, typified by the new cocktail set. That target market is evident in a remarkable set of drawings for a 1920s ad campaign for the hotel by N. W. Ayer's artist Earl Horter (1880–1940).[32] Horter's sketches show a stylish crowd of short-skirted flappers and tuxedoed gents posing in various spaces of the hotel (fig. 23). Derived from John Held Jr.'s well-known Jazz Age figures, they mark the hotel as a center of contemporary modern life.

fig. 24
Easter Parade,
Atlantic City, New Jersey,
postcard, c. 1910.
Price and McLanahan
Archive, courtesy of
George E. Thomas.

Beyond the stylistic expression of the Traymore and its setting on the
Atlantic City Boardwalk, the perspective from the prevailing urban systems
of the era brings another dimension to understanding the significance of
Price's work. After the great suburbanizing phase of the late nineteenth
and early twentieth centuries, the initial period of metropolitan growth
manifested itself in the sudden explosion of soaring apartment and office
blocks. While shops, hotels, and apartment buildings existed in Atlantic
City, its pre-1905 density and scale were commensurate with the size of
small-town America, already artifacts of an earlier day. Price's design for
the Blenheim, with its curved forecourt of shops, and the Traymore, with
its new twelve-story front rising behind its screen of shops, began the
transformation of the Boardwalk into a fanciful urban leisure experience,
anticipating the soaring metropolitan city of the 1920s.

Later Atlantic City hotels continued this metropolitan theme, building at
the density of the modern city along the Boardwalk with highly identifiable,
historical architectural styles as their cultural markers. The Boardwalk's
mixture of uses and vertical stacking of functions made it a city of shopping,
entertainment, spectacle, and leisure where a pleasure-centered life could
be played out. In Atlantic City, the railroad delivered passengers not to a
job but to a vacation. Instead of offices, there were hotel rooms; instead
of city parks, there were the beach and Atlantic Ocean. Photographs from
this era consistently show the Boardwalk so dense with people that they
could scarcely move (fig. 24). Atlantic City was the modern metropolis
transformed into a leisure experience where people delighted in being
part of the new aestheticized lifestyle.

Price's organization of his landmark hotels paralleled the model of the
metropolitan-era urban system, merging elements that we recognize as
the beginning of the modern resort hotel. Unlike the neighboring

fig. 25
Skyline, Atlantic City,
New Jersey (detail).
From left to right, the
Shelbourne, Dennis,
and Blenheim hotels.
Photograph by
George E. Thomas, 1975.

traditional Boardwalk hotels, which provided only conventional hotel functions for guests and depended upon the seaside setting to present the rest of the experience, the Traymore supplied the entire resort experience, replicating in many ways the metropolitan urban system. The hotel encompassed lodging, shopping, dining, dancing, salt-water bathing, and other activities in a variety of themed settings. Though Price may have been partly motivated by the knowledge that a captive audience would increase revenue, it seems likely that he was also inspired by the desire to reflect the modern, youth-inspired lifestyle—a resort experience that no other Atlantic City venue offered.

While the Traymore expressed its own unique identity, it also was an active participant in its urban setting. The screen of shops shielded hotel guests from the Boardwalk, but at the same time created the commercial realm that was accessible from both the Boardwalk and the hotel interior. Here, crowds from all walks of life and paying hotel guests could mix. Price's embrace of commercial uses connected his hotels to the exploding commerce of the contemporary city and provided a social bridge to mass audiences.

When the Traymore was being designed, social culture defined by ancestral tradition prevailed in the Philadelphia region. This traditional world, deriving its architectural identity from Eurocentric antecedents, could be seen in the Dennis and Shelbourne hotels that stood just to the west of the Blenheim (fig. 25). Here, the past was honored as a way of perpetuating a hierarchical social order that restricted entry to those born or married into the group. In addition to the few elites who visited the resort, the larger audiences for these destinations in Atlantic City were those seeking an escape from their routine world by living the fantasy of the affluent life as a leisure break. As the embodiment of the modern narrative, the Traymore broke with tradition and created a new world. Here was modernity in architectural expression—materials, structural systems, and lighting—and in the hotel's decorative arts—murals, furniture, and silver. Looking like giant sand castles ornamented with colorful sea creatures, Price's Blenheim and Traymore stood in stark contrast to the neighboring conventional hotels, where a privileged cultural education and a Grand Tour were prerequisites to understanding the coded meaning of the architectural expression.

fig. 26
Morris Lapidus,
Eden Roc Hotel (left)
and Fontainebleau Hotel
(right), Miami Beach.
Photograph by
George E. Thomas, 2001.

Price's design was fundamentally modern. He understood the necessity of reflexively reinventing the architectural narrative as the context changed. If modernity presents a clean slate on which to compose a narrative of self-identity that gives meaning to life, keeping the narrative going and connected to the external world is a condition of modern life.[33] It also implied, by its connection to and acceptance of the contemporary world, a strategy of cultural accessibility rather than cultural control that extended its reach to a wider audience and continues to underpin the model for mass resorts today.

Miami Modern

Morris Lapidus's (1902–2001) work in Miami Beach adhered to the resort-hotel model that Price pioneered in Atlantic City. The Fontainebleau and Eden Roc were luxury resort hotels that sold the dreams of the 1950s (fig. 26). Lapidus understood his audience: "The guests want to find a new experience—forget the office, the house, the kids, the bills. People wanted fun, excitement, and all of this against a background that was colorful, unexpected."[34] He achieved this ambience by choreographing the experience from the entrance sequence and visual perspectives to create a deep threshold that delivered the visitor to an opulent theatrical setting in a secluded garden.[35] These unconnected beachfront resort hotels might seem to have little in common with Price's celebration of the early twentieth-century urban fabric. Circumstances had changed. By mid-century the dominant system of urban life was no longer the

fig. 27
Morris Lapidus,
Eden Roc Hotel,
Miami Beach, pool.
Morris Lapidus Collection,
Syracuse University
Library, Special
Collections Research
Center. Photograph by
Liddle and Kohn, Miami.

dense, mixed-use form, but rather was a suburban landscape of separated uses and low density made possible by the automobile and expressed in recreation through swimming pools, golf, tennis, and the country club.

Lapidus, like Price, was designing a heightened and transformed experience of the prevailing model of contemporary life—in his case, suburbia. Hence, the Fontainebleau and Eden Roc can be interpreted as what life could be if it were lived entirely at the country club—isolated exclusivity, tropical gardens, swimming, poolside dining, dinner and dancing in formal attire every evening—a Technicolor Douglas Sirk movie life removed from the urban congestion, bustle, and masses of the central city (fig. 27). Just as Price revved up the urban experience before the First World War, Lapidus's post–Second World War resort hotels exaggerated the familiar suburban landscape and turned it into a dream escape. In contrast to the earlier model of small Miami Beach Art Deco hotels, which, while stylishly designed, still worked as traditional hotels on a continuous street, Lapidus condensed the suburban system into a resort hotel and in the process made Miami Beach a contemporary resort.

At their core, Lapidus's hotels were little more than International Modern lofts, overlaid with a commercially derived architectural vocabulary that was intended to be accessible to mass audiences. Just as Price's colorful sea creatures and sandcastles proclaimed that his hotels weren't about traditional European-derived culture, Lapidus's baroque mixture of ornament, decoration, and what he called "cheeseholes" and "woggles" glamorized the rigid Cartesian order of the minimalist, gridded, abstract International Style and knowingly tweaked classical forms with a sense of humor and visual delight. The result was pure theater. Describing the sources of his Miami hotels, Lapidus says:

> I was creating the style that was neither period nor modern…. But what
> direction was I seeking? What was the central theme? Whose tastes was I
> trying to satisfy? What were the tastes of the vast majority of affluent
> Americans? Were Americans accepting … Gropius and Breuer and Mies
> van der Rohe? The answer was an emphatic "no!" So where was I to
> seek that certain style which would satisfy the guests and represent for
> them their dream of tropical opulence and glittering luxury? I finally
> realized that American taste was being influenced by the greatest mass
> media of entertainment of that time, the movies.[36]

Lapidus understood that cultural power was centered in the commercial
world and media, not in ideologically driven design.

Like Price, Lapidus was an American original who reveled in contemporary
life. With his early work in commercial design, he not only understood
how people lived and what they liked, he embraced it as the foundation
of his designs, in counter-distinction to the prevailing culture of the
architecture profession, critics, and the academy that used their designs
as a moral critique of contemporary life patterns.[37] If in Atlantic City the
Blenheim and Traymore define the cultural tension as the traditional
hierarchical way of life being overtaken by modernity and mass culture,
then in Miami Beach this same battle was expressed in the tension
between elite establishment architecture and the commercial world.

Learning from Price, Lapidus, and Las Vegas
The model created by Price's Blenheim and Traymore and continued in
Lapidus's Miami Beach hotels endures in the resort hotels of the Las
Vegas Strip. The Strip is today's closest collective experience to Atlantic
City's Boardwalk of a century ago. But there are some important differ-
ences. Casinos, not the Atlantic Ocean, are the draw in the Las Vegas
resort hotels. The core model that endures distills the realities of the
contemporary world into the architectural experience of the mass resort.

Las Vegas is remarkable in that it has reinvented itself a few times over in
less than fifty years to keep pace with the changing contemporary landscape.
When Fremont Street was the destination in 1950s downtown Las Vegas,
the street glittered with dazzling lights, signs, movement, and color—a
hyped Main Street. When the automobile culture began to dominate in
the 1950s and 1960s, the action moved to the highway and resulted in
the iconic roadside-sign era of the Strip, a paved paradise that expressed
the same suburban fantasy that Lapidus developed in Miami Beach. The
Strip continued to evolve in the next decades by filling in open space with
additional hotel towers, parking garages, and expanded amenities. Gradually,
the automobile shared the Strip with pedestrians, and the Las Vegas experience turned full circle to resemble the Boardwalk.[38]

fig. 28
Las Vegas Strip,
Excalibur Hotel and
Casino (left), New York
New York Hotel and
Casino (right).
Photograph by Matt
Wargo, funded by a
grant to Susan Nigra
Snyder and Steve Izenour,
University of
Pennsylvania Research
Foundation, 1999.

By the late 1990s the Bellagio, Venetian (1999), and Aladdin (2000) had joined Caesar's Palace (1978, with later additions) to combine shopping and casino–resort hotel destinations. The Excalibur (1990) and Luxor (1993) were joined by New York New York, Paris Las Vegas (1997), and Treasure Island (1999) as themed resort hotels (fig. 28). The Strip expresses today's hybrid urban form. It combines six lanes of traffic and five shopping malls—hallmarks of the suburban automobile landscape—all in close proximity and connected by sidewalks. Themed performances provide sidewalk entertainment for pedestrians. Between 1970 and 2003 the high-rise hotels associated with the street-level action added more than 95,000 rooms to the existing 15,208, creating an urban density that is an exaggerated fantasy of contemporary American life.[39] Just as Price's Traymore depended on the forms and patterns of the industry that shaped its time, the Las Vegas Strip hotels reflect the forces of the media age.

Like the early twentieth-century Boardwalk, the Strip depends upon the collective consumption of place by masses of people to be effective, but it does so in a way that reflects the pulse and complexity of life at the beginning of the twenty-first century. As a result, the contemporary Las Vegas resort hotel differs from Price's resort-hotel model of a century earlier. To be sure, they share general organizational principles: shopping as an entrance threshold from the public way, themed dining and entertainment, and high-rise blocks of rooms.[40] What is different, however, is the reversal of the context against which Price struggled. The shock of the Blenheim and Traymore was that their modern architectural identity, accessible to a mass audience, was in opposition to a traditional elite culture. Price influenced the resort-hotel typology with his metropolitan model but, as the Boardwalk developed, most hotels continued to represent the dominant identity of the era, traditional culture. The work of Morris Lapidus in Miami Beach celebrated the commercial-media world as the vital culture, but it was still in opposition to high architecture that was set apart from actual life. By contrast, a century after Price and nearly a half-century after Lapidus, the norm in Las Vegas is a commercial and media-driven context.[41]

What Price started in Atlantic City, and what he alone stood for, echoes throughout every casino–resort hotel along the three-mile Strip. If the Traymore were on the Strip today, it would fit right in, though it would lose its singularity.

The trajectory begun by the Traymore in Atlantic City in 1915 has defined a new concept for architecture and urban space in Las Vegas nearly one hundred years later. The Traymore was important as architecture that synthesized contextual symbols, new materials, multiple uses, and access to mass and elite audiences and urban systems into a single form that enabled the Boardwalk to hold its own against the scale of the Atlantic Ocean. Compared to the Traymore's powerful presence on the Boardwalk, the hotel towers on the Strip are set back and declare little presence. Instead, they are eclipsed by the street experience of scenographic symbols— the New York skyline, the Eiffel Tower, the Great Pyramid, a Venetian palace, a Swiss lakeside village, a medieval castle, and spectacle entertainment such as Treasure Island pirates, erupting volcanoes, and choreographed fountain displays (fig. 29). Each hotel is embellished with signs that combine neon, sculpture, and high-definition video displays in all-enveloping color and movement. Morris Lapidus's mid-century hotel designs may have introduced the influence of movies and theatrical

fig. 30
James' Original Deluxe
Salt Water Taffy,
4 $\frac{1}{2}$ x 9 $\frac{1}{2}$ in.
(11.4 x 24 cm), © 1957,
manufactured in 2003.
Courtesy of James' Candy
Company, Atlantic City,
New Jersey.

experience to the architectural world, but on the Las Vegas Strip, architecture has become the experience, not just a setting for it.[42]

Modern Fantasy

The seed of the modern resort hotel took root in the Traymore and persists in mid-century Miami Beach and present-day Las Vegas. Resorts are still conceived as leisure destinations that provide a respite from work and everyday life. As a fantasy experience, it is not a utopian future but rather a thinly veiled exaggeration of what already exists. The resort needs to keep pace with life, indeed anticipate the future, in order to remain magical and more compelling than home. Ironically, despite its new casinos, Atlantic City has never surpassed the excitement of its first metropolitan phase. In fact, the Traymore, demolished in 1972, is still depicted at the center of the beachfront on the boxes of saltwater taffy sold today (fig. 30)! The Traymore remains the icon of the quintessential Atlantic City experience, circa 1915, regardless of whether that experience endures or not. Alternatively, if the resort can remain intact long enough, it can become a retro experience that uses nostalgia to simulate a fantasy of living in a past era while simultaneously being connected to the buzz of the contemporary world, as Cape May became in the 1970s or South Beach in the 1980s.

What is modern about the hotels of Price, Lapidus, and the Las Vegas Strip? By today's criteria, the Traymore and the Lapidus hotels were traditional buildings. Lapidus could never have imagined the Las Vegas hotels, clad in coated synthetic foam and decorated with ever-changing virtual images, just as Price could never have imagined the Miami Beach resort hotels. These resorts were driven by the pulse of their time, not by style, theory, or ideology. Each invented an architectural identity from the contemporary critical issues and underlying forces, unencumbered by tradition or dominant hegemonies. Just as industrial Philadelphia provided

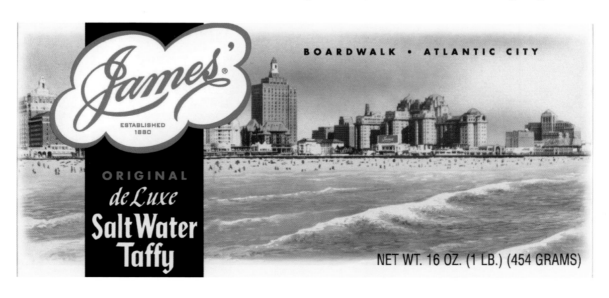

the context for Price and the suburban world unleashed Lapidus, we can read the forces of today's media and leisure age in the resort hotels of Las Vegas. Price, Lapidus, and the unnamed teams that created today's Las Vegas all understood that the seeds of modernity are always in the present and that mass resorts function by providing the experience of a fantasy escape into a thinly veiled reality of the contemporary world. It takes a disregard for conventional paradigms to see the contemporary world with fresh eyes. To be modern is to live the poetry of the present.[43] ✧

Notes

1. Anthony Giddens, *Modernity and Self-Identity: Self and Society in the Late Modern Age* (Palo Alto, CA: Stanford University Press, 1991).

2. For background on Philadelphia in 1900, see George E. Thomas, *William L. Price: Arts and Crafts to Modern Design* (New York: Princeton Architectural Press, 2000), 1–30.

3. Lauren Langman, "Neon Cages: Shopping for Subjectivity," in *Lifestyle Shopping: The Subject of Consumption*, ed. Rob Shields (New York: Routledge, 1992), 40–82.

4. Atlantic City has been the subject of several studies, the most scholarly being Charles Funnell, *By the Beautiful Sea: The Rise and High Times of That Great American Resort, Atlantic City* (New York: Knopf, 1975).

5. In the 1820s, to fuel their factories in Philadelphia, the first Josiah White built the Lehigh Canal, making the vital link between coal and manufacturing that would shape the nineteenth-century city.

6. Funnell, *By the Beautiful Sea*, 226–27.

7. In the early twentieth century, engineers at the University of Pennsylvania's Towne School of Engineering developed material standards for reinforced concrete as part of the testing program of the American Society for Testing and Materials. This program grew out of the industrial standardization process initiated in Philadelphia by William Sellers half a century earlier.

8. For an overview of the next decade of design, see R. W. Sexton, *American Apartment Houses, Hotels, and Apartment Hotels of Today* (New York: Architectural Book Publishing, 1929).

9. William L. Price, "Modern Architecture," originally given as a lecture to the Ontario Association of Architects, January 1907, in Thomas, *William L. Price*, 334–46.

10. William L. Price, "The Possibilities of Concrete Construction from the Standpoints of Utility and Art," *American Architect and Building News* 89, no. 1579 (31 March 1906): 119–20.

11. Charles Harris Whitaker, "The Hotel Traymore: Price and McLanahan Architects," *Masterpieces of Architecture in the United States*, ed. Edward Hoak and Willis Church (New York: Scribner's, 1930), 167–79.

12. Newspaper documentation of work is listed in Thomas, "Chronology of Works and Projects," *William L. Price*, 347–55

13. L. Stauffer Oliver, *The Beach Is a Hard Seat: An Autobiography* (Philadelphia: Dorrance, 1965), 6–8.

14. Betsy Wyeth, ed. *The Wyeths by N. C. Wyeth: The Intimate Correspondence of N. C. Wyeth, 1901–1945* (Boston: Gambit, 1971), 482–84.

15. Ibid., 487.

16. John J. Klaber, "America's Greatest Seaside Hotel: The Traymore, Atlantic City, New Jersey," *Architectural Forum* 127 (November 1917): 119–28.

17. The shifting scale of perception and design is treated in Robert Venturi, Denise Scott Brown, and Steven Izenour, *Learning from Las Vegas*, (Cambridge, MA: MIT Press, 1972). The Traymore's complicated massing and surface is aimed at the pedestrian on the boulevard rather than automobile traffic; ironically it is thus like the scenographic intensity of the current hotels of the Las Vegas Strip, which are again aimed at pedestrians, while signs at their rear face the interstate to the west.

18. By 1925, 20 to 25 percent of Philadelphians owned a car, according to data from the Keystone Auto Club Archives, Philadelphia.

19. For a history of reinforced concrete construction in the early twentieth century, see Carl Condit, *American Building Art: The Twentieth Century* (New York: Oxford University Press, 1961), 151ff.

20. See John MacFarlane, *Manufacturing in Philadelphia: 1683–1912* (Philadelphia: Commercial Museum, 1912). The impact on the city's working population is described in Frank H. Taylor, *The City of Philadelphia as it Appears in 1893* (Philadelphia: George Harris & Sons, 1893). For the efficiency movement, see Robert Kanigel, *The One Best Way: Frederick Winslow Taylor and the Enigma of Efficiency* (New York: Viking, 1997).

21. Zygmunt Bauman, *Freedom* (Minneapolis: University of Minnesota Press, 1988), 71–88.

22. Data are largely deduced from Taylor, *The City of Philadelphia*.

23. Ibid.

24. It was significant that by the end of the nineteenth century in Philadelphia a consumption-centered culture extended beyond the elites and encompassed the mass middle class.

25. Ralph M. Hower, *The History of an Advertising Agency: N. W. Ayer & Son at Work* (Cambridge, MA: Harvard University Press, 1939) provides a history of the nation's preeminent advertising company of the early twentieth century.

26. Giddens, *Modernity and Self-Identity*.

27. Quoted in Claudia Roth Pierpont, "Cries and Whispers–Edith Wharton," *New Yorker* (2 April 2001): 66.

28. It would be interesting to study the relationship between centers of modern industry and contemporary design. The Philadelphia of Frank Furness, Will Price, and George Howe; the Chicago of Furness's pupil Louis Sullivan and his student Frank Lloyd Wright; the Glasgow of Charles McIntosh; and the Berlin of Berlage all share industrialization as a cultural touchstone. In the leisure age, the resort industry is a logical parallel.

29. Beginning in 1924, Bencker became the chief designer for the Streamline Moderne automat restaurants of the Horn & Hardart Company, ubiquitous along the East Coast from New York to Washington, D.C.

30. Mary Douglas and Baron Isherwood, *The World of Goods: Towards an Anthropology of Consumption* (New York: Routledge, 1996), 36–92.

31. Mary Douglas, "In Defense of Shopping," in *The Shopping Experience*, ed. Pasi Falk and Colin Campbell (London: Sage, 1997), 15–19.

32. It was fitting that Horter was the artist for the Ayer team. Horter collected modern art, filling his Delancey Street townhouse with Picassos, paintings and collages by Georges Braque, Marcel Duchamp's *Nude Descending a Staircase No. 1*, and other important works. Horter also formed collections of African art and Native American artifacts. Innis Shoemaker, *Mad for Modernism: Earl Horter and His Collection* (Philadelphia: Philadelphia Museum of Art, 1999).

33. Giddens, *Modernity and Self-Identity*, 52–55.

34. Martina Düttman and Fiederike Schneider, eds., *Morris Lapidus: The Architect of the American Dream* (Boston: Birkhauser Verlag, 1992), 101–102.

35. Ibid., 7.

36. Ibid., 113–14.

37. See Tom Wolfe's discussion of "Cultureburg" in *The Painted Word* (New York: Farrar, Straus and Giroux, 1975), 27–28 and 68–70, and his essay "The Building That Isn't There," *New York Times* (12 & 13 October 2003).

38. Obvious influences on the evolution of the Las Vegas Strip and its resort hotels include Disneyland (1955) and Walt Disney World (1971) for the development of the theme-park, family-friendly typology and fantasy architecture, and the West Edmonton Mall (1981–1985) for its juxtaposition of disjunctive geographical places, time periods, and range of activities extending beyond shopping, all coexisting within a mall typology large enough to describe a separate world.

39. For the number of rooms on the Strip in 1970, see David Schwartz, "Paradise Misplaced: The Xanadu Hotel-Casino," a virtual exhibit on the Web site of the Gaming Studies Research Center, University of Nevada, Las Vegas, http://gaming.univ.edu/Xanadu/spendchart.jpg. The 2003 estimate (73 percent of 130,482 rooms in metropolitan Las Vegas) is based on statistics reported by the Las Vegas Convention and Visitors Authority, in *Metropolitan Las Vegas Tourism Statistics*, 2003

40. Although typologically shopping is similar in both places, there is a vast difference in the role of late twentieth-century shopping. The mall differs from urban stores because it combines the practices of leisure and shopping into a themed experience separate from its context. William Kowinski in *The Malling of America* calls the mall "a house of magic," but none that he visited could have rivaled the Bellagio's Galleria fantasy of high-design shops, the Venetian's Italian streetscape and its canal and gondolas, the Aladdin's desert bazaar, or Caesar's Palace's Roman plazas. All have shops that can be found in almost any city; the experience of the fantasy mall in Las Vegas is enough like home to be recognizable, but it is shopping on steroids.

41. Within this context the new Bellagio and Palm, although thoroughly commercial, set themselves apart as elite against the mass commercial culture of the other hotels.

42. B. Joseph Pine II and James H. Gilmore, *The Experience Economy: Work Is Theatre and Every Business a Stage* (Boston: Harvard Business School Press, 1999).

43. "The poetry of the present" is an expression used by Albert Kelsey, a student of Frank Furness, and recalls the values of Walt Whitman. Will Price knew Whitman's literary executor, Horace Traubel.

Alice T. Friedman

Merchandising Miami Beach: Morris Lapidus and the Architecture of Abundance

Alice T. Friedman is professor of art, chair of the art department, and codirector of the architecture program at Wellesley College. Her publications include *House and Household in Elizabethan England: Wollaton Hall and the Willoughby Family* (1989) and *Women and the Making of the Modern House: A Social and Architectural History* (1998), as well as numerous articles on women's history, gender, and domestic architecture. She has been the recipient of a number of grants and awards, including research fellowships from the National Endowment for the Humanities, the Bunting Institute, the Guggenheim Foundation, and The Wolfsonian–Florida International University.

Ridiculed for his unapologetic populism, but later celebrated as the "architect of the American dream," Morris Lapidus (1902–2001) remains a controversial figure in the history of American architecture.[1] Nevertheless, when his work is viewed in the context of recent reassessments of mid-twentieth century design and culture, Lapidus emerges as a pivotal figure. He not only placed his distinctive stamp on the modern American resort hotel, one of the period's most significant building types, but also created highly successful new forms of tourist accommodation and entertainment in a period of increasing leisure and prosperity.[2]

Throughout the 1950s, Lapidus, who had spent the first twenty years of his career as a successful designer of retail shops and other commercial spaces, was the most sought-after hotel architect in Miami Beach, a city that was experiencing unprecedented growth and change. For an ever-expanding audience of seasonal visitors and new residents, many of whom were Jews of Eastern European descent, Lapidus created a vivid experience, and a powerful image, of contemporary glamour and luxury. Thanks in large part to their commercial success and to wide exposure in the media, his hotels, which combined the design strategies of merchandising with those of elite architectural practice, became synonymous with the pleasures and dangers of American consumerism and popular entertainment in the period following the Second World War.[3]

First as a consultant and associate designer with primary responsibility for hotel interiors and later as principal architect, Lapidus created strikingly original designs for no fewer than eight new hotels in seven years. They included the Sans Souci (1949, with Roy France); the Nautilus

Henry Hohauser, Morris Lapidus, and Melvin Grossman, Algiers Hotel, Miami Beach, night view (detail), 1952 (see fig. 26).

(1950, with Albert Anis); the Biltmore Terrace (1951, with Albert Anis); the Algiers (1952, with Melvin Grossman; Henry Hohauser, architect of record); and the DiLido (1953, with Melvin Grossman). The hotels for which he is best known—the Fontainebleau (1952–1954), the Eden Roc (1954–1955), and the Americana (1955–1956) in Bal Harbour were the culmination of this series.[4] These projects ushered in a new era of postwar development and set the standard for modern resort hotels in Miami Beach for half a century (fig. 1).[5]

Lapidus's success stemmed, in large part, from his ability to appeal to the disparate and sometimes conflicting desires of his audience. His hotels combined elements of sleek modern architecture and the latest forms of new technology (air conditioning, automobile access and parking, in-room telephones, and luxurious bathrooms) with romantic imagery and motifs drawn from history and from exotic, faraway places. Though disdained by critics and by the architectural press, Lapidus's Miami Beach hotels —like a handful of well-publicized and critically acclaimed American resorts built in these years by such architects as Edward Durell Stone (1902–1978) and Skidmore, Owings, and Merrill—were glamorous enclaves of wealth and luxury that remained separate from, but nonetheless intimately connected to, the cultures, landscapes, and/or urban contexts surrounding them.[6] Unlike his contemporaries, however, Lapidus fully embraced the challenge of creating fantasy experiences that permitted guests to escape, however fleetingly, from the everyday. While other hotels might include

fig. 2
Morris Lapidus, Eden Roc
Hotel beachfront and
pool deck, Miami Beach.
Photograph by
Ezra Stoller © Esto.

touches of local craftsmanship, period-revival details, or exotic decor in lobbies, lounges, restaurants, and supper clubs (such as the Beverly Hilton's Trader Vic's and the Sheraton's Kon Tiki), Lapidus's resorts were designed as all-encompassing worlds of make-believe, offered up with exuberance and good humor, but free of self-conscious irony or clearly defined boundaries separating reality from fantasy or business from entertainment.[7] In Lapidus's hotels, entertainment was the business at hand.

Like Walt Disney and other producers of popular entertainment in the period, Lapidus recognized that artificiality and fantasy, though scorned as self-indulgent "kitsch" by many contemporary commentators, offered welcome diversion to world-weary cold war consumers. Thus, he embraced one of the fundamental lessons of Hollywood and Madison Avenue: that glamour could be conferred on anyone who sought it out, thanks to the magical power of material things and a willingness to believe in oneself playing a role. He celebrated American abundance, prosperity, and progress, without seeming to worry much about whether his architecture or the pleasurable feelings that it stimulated were good or bad for his clients.[8]

Adapting Art Deco precedents—which included freestanding blocks with narrow street frontages, picturesque silhouettes, vibrant figural ornament, ample hotel lobbies, and outdoor terraces—to postwar practices and expectations, Lapidus expanded the scale and spaciousness of his buildings, placing them on high podiums and creating elaborate entrance sequences that ushered visitors into a world apart. Thus, his hotels began to look more and more like huge ocean liners (fig. 2), complete with smooth, white walls, bold horizontal balconies, strip windows, and tall pylons that

recalled massive ships' funnels. Moreover, with their theatrical Hollywood decor, lavish appointments, and grand staircases, they offered patrons the opportunity to take an ocean voyage on dry land, with all of the amenities of a vacation cruise. Hotel guests could lounge by the pool, play cards, shop in fashionable boutiques, eat in elegant restaurants and chic brasseries, and dance the night away—all within the protective confines of the hotel and its grounds. Cut off from the street, and with limited views to the outside world, the hotel guests themselves became the main event in these spaces, with every detail of their fashionable clothing, and every activity, staged, framed, lighted, and viewed from optimized vantage points.

Having spent the first part of his career creating fashionable interiors and shop fronts for Ross-Frankel Inc., a leading retail firm in New York, and later (from 1945) in private practice, Lapidus was confident about how his approach to hotel design would fare in the consumer-driven world of the 1950s:

> I was convinced that just as a store had to be designed to make people want to buy what the merchant had to sell, so a hotel had something to sell also. What was that something? A home away from home? Absolutely not! Who wants a homey feeling on a vacation? The guests want to find a new experience—forget the office, the house, the kids, the bills. Anything but that good old homey feeling that the old hotels used to sell with a comfortable bed, a nice rocker on the veranda, a good solid nourishing meal. Not on your life! We were coming out of the war and the postwar period. People wanted fun, excitement, and all of it against a background that was colorful, unexpected; in short, the visual excitement that made people want to buy—in this case, to buy the tropic luxury of a wonderful vacation of fun in the sun. A sense of freedom from the humdrum lives the guests had. A feeling of getting away from it all.[9]

Trained in architecture at Columbia University in the early 1920s, following undergraduate study at New York University (where he received his first exposure to amateur theater and set design, which would remain a lifelong passion), Lapidus certainly knew how to assemble the elements of a project that would suggest glamour and luxury to a broad audience. Throughout this period, architecture students in the United States and Europe were taught to replicate a broad range of historical styles, basing their designs on approved models according to the system of the École des Beaux-Arts. What mattered most was skill in drawing, at which Lapidus excelled, and an ability to create lively ornamental devices derived from freely interpreted Renaissance and Baroque precedents. Lapidus began his career with Warren and Wetmore, one of a handful of large, established practices (including Schultze and Weaver and Holabird and Roche, to name just two) that gave shape and expression to the civic monuments and public institutions of the period. These offices molded the tastes of a generation, using historical references, grand scale, and rich ornament to establish the hallmarks of power and the visual codes of wealth and status. Moreover, the large projects that these offices undertook, and the complexity of drawings and details that were required, provided employment opportunities for many young architects of Lapidus's generation.

The Beaux-Arts style could be adapted easily to a shorthand, popular form. Thus, window dressers, set designers, and interior decorators, from Elsie de Wolfe in the 1910s to William Pahlmann in the 1940s, created luxurious, period-style stage sets for their clients, using antique and reproduction furniture, patterned fabrics, and light-reflecting materials such as gilt and mirrors to set the tone. Often the specific historical styles mattered less than the overall impression of luxury in an environment rich in narrative associations. Thanks to the movies and to popular magazines, these devices quickly entered the visual lexicon of popular culture, and by the 1930s and 1940s had formed a well-worn code for opulence, glamour, and leisure.

Lapidus turned his attention to this mode at a very early point in his career, and it is not surprising, therefore, that he had vivid memories of the decor of the recently built Palmer House Hotel in Chicago (Holabird and Roche, 1927), where he stayed for an extended period of time as a young architect. In 1929, his employer, Ross-Frankel, was commissioned to install a new shop on the ground floor of the hotel for Mangel's, a firm specializing in women's clothing; Lapidus lived on site while he oversaw construction. He described the experience in his memoir, *An Architecture of Joy*:

> When I arrived in Chicago, I went directly to the Palmer House, which was to be my home for the next few months while I supervised the final installation. No expenses had been spared in the design and construction of what was then America's most luxurious hotel. Cast bronze, fine woods, and an abundance of beautiful marbles were used to achieve an elegance in the interiors, hitherto found only in the most luxurious European hostelries. The magnificence of the Palmer House was my first experience as a guest in a fine hotel. Much of what I have used in my hotels years later was inspired by the opulence and luxury that surrounded me during my stay at the then glamorous Palmer House.[10]

Though Lapidus had confronted many similar buildings on the drawing board, nothing could adequately prepare him for the real thing. A self-described "ghetto youth" from New York's Lower East Side, he, like many of his contemporaries, received his first taste of luxury by staying in a hotel.[11]

fig. 3
Times Square, New York,
looking south at night,
1933. Library of Congress,
Prints and Photographs
Division, Gottscho-
Schleisner Collection.
LC-G612-T01-19590.

This experience also introduced him to the complex program of amenities and services that had by then become standard in large, urban hotels. Over the course of the previous half-century, many such establishments had expanded considerably, occupying monumental structures that were both more public and more ornate then ever before.[12] No longer viewed primarily as elegant homes-away-from-home, these new hotels were geared to the tastes of a broad audience, both local and transient, who used them as sites for entertainment, dining, shopping, family celebrations, and community gatherings—to say nothing of such informal activities as window-shopping, strolling, visiting with friends, or popping in to buy a newspaper or a pack of cigarettes at the hotel newsstand.[13] The range of activities and wide choice of spaces, both in the public and back-of-house service areas, reflected the increasing diversity and complexity of urban society in the 1920s and 1930s.

Lapidus was not given the opportunity to design a hotel of his own until many years after this formative experience. He remained an employee of Ross-Frankel until 1945, building scores of shops nationwide and, in the process, refining a set of sophisticated merchandising and display techniques that were to become the staples of his mature style. As a retail designer, Lapidus enjoyed considerable professional success, and he played a significant role in fashioning the American commercial aesthetic in the critical period between 1929 and 1949.[14] With their bright lights, expansive windows, and bold signage, his store designs captured the glamour and excitement of the modern city. Some of his best-known work, documented by Samuel H. Gottscho, one of the leading commercial photographers of the period, stood at the very heart of the new American metropolis, in or near Times Square, an ever-changing environment of light and action (fig. 3).

But Lapidus also traveled and worked in cities and small towns across the United States, modernizing the face of Main Street and helping to create new markets for the merchandise offered up by hundreds of shops and retail outlets.

Many of Lapidus's early projects, such as the Parisian Bootery and the Theresa Pharmacy (both 1929), Swank Jewelry (1931), and the Seagram Bar (1936) in the Chrysler Building (fig. 4), incorporated the fashionable details of the popular Art Deco style. Streamlined forms, attenuated details in chrome and silver leaf, and blocks of bold color dominated these works. Like the pavilions at the 1925 Paris Exposition des Arts Décoratifs et Industriels Modernes, the event that helped to codify and disseminate the style to an international audience, Lapidus's projects created an atmosphere of sophisticated elegance in which art and commerce merged effortlessly.[15] In his shops, large display windows highlighted artfully arranged goods; these lively set pieces substituted for the ornamental relief panels that were the hallmark of the style. As at the Paris pavilions—many of which were sponsored by large department stores—merchandise, applied ornament, and elegant architecture combined to create a stage set that easily accommodated the movements of potential customers. This new approach was easily translated into the contemporary commercial and public realm, and many young American architects, including Lapidus,

fig. 5
Morris Lapidus,
Mangel's, 130 East
Flagler Street,
Miami, 1937. Library
of Congress, Prints
and Photographs
Division, Gottscho-
Schleisner Collection.
LC-G612-T01-41702.

eagerly adopted the elements of the style for offices, movie theaters, nightclubs, and other fashionable venues.

At the Seagram Bar, for example, Lapidus used a striking pattern of lighted circular openings, each of which framed the dark silhouette of a bottle, to create a focal point at the back of the space; this ornamental wall drew people in and defined their movements. With dramatic overhead lighting, a curving counter, and a pictorial mural on the sidewall, the bar was an airy, modern gathering place in which salesmen and clients could conduct business in an atmosphere that suggested entertainment and pleasure rather than the harsh realities of commerce. Lapidus was not wedded to this one mode, however: in the corporate offices of the firm, he used Tudor Revival detailing, complete with linenfold paneling and crowned horses' heads, to create an image of an English baronial hall that symbolized (in his view at least, and that of his client) the company's stability and lineage.[16]

The range of his sources is impressive. Throughout his career, Lapidus acknowledged the influence of German Modernism, for example, noting in particular the importance of projects by the architect Erich Mendelsohn, whose monumental department stores combined large expanses of glass with dramatic lighting to create a vivid image of modern progress. Moreover, in German magazines like *Die Gebrauchsgrafik*, he discovered striking examples of graphic design and lettering.[17] His best-known works, such as Doubleday (1934) and Postman's (1935) in New York City, Mangel's in Miami (1937; fig. 5), or Barton's Candy in Times Square (1948), demonstrate the success with which he drew upon these European sources. Distinctive graphics and dramatic lighting created strong visual identities for these shops, and their lively window displays were enhanced by deep recesses in the storefronts that allowed shoppers to penetrate the facade and view products from all sides.[18]

Lapidus regarded his commercial work as a form of popular entertainment and advertising, calculated to appeal to passersby:

> Once I began studying what made people tick when they went shopping, I began to formulate other principles of design that would help the sales volume of my clients. I studied the effectiveness of the pulling power of storefronts. I concluded immediately that window-shopping was one of the foremost pastimes of Mr. and Mrs. America. Main Street, U.S.A., is, and has always been, the best show in town. Show windows, I reasoned, acted like circus barkers in front of a sideshow tent. They were out there twenty-four hours a day with the same type of appeal as the barker's spiel.[19]

Many changes in American culture helped to shape this view of shopping as a popular pastime, and Lapidus, as a commercial architect, was in a position to observe these developments from close range. One of the most valuable lessons he learned concerned the critical role played by women. Although the retail field was clearly dominated by men (as store owners, executives, supervisors, and product salesmen), it was shaped and evaluated, in large part, by women, who constituted a majority among shoppers and retail sales workers.[20] As denizens of department stores and downtown shopping districts, as avid readers of fashion and home decorating magazines, and as frequent moviegoers, young working women influenced not only the choice of products that were manufactured, but also the ways in which they were sold and displayed. With their penchant for dramatic scenarios and movie-star glamour, this generation of American shoppers preferred to "discover" new products in fantasy settings that highlighted the magical experiences of seeking and finding, yearning and self-transformation.[21]

fig. 6
Robert Law Weed,
Beach Theatre lobby and
stairs, Miami Beach, 1940.
Library of Congress,
Prints and Photographs
Division, Gottscho-
Schleisner Collection.
LC-G612-T01-39564.

The emergence of American consumer culture during this period was accelerated by changes in patterns of urban leisure as well.[22] Not only were men and women in cities increasingly spending their free time in each others' company rather than in homosocial groups, but they occupied themselves in very different ways than their parents had done in previous decades—going out at night, gathering in public places, and seeking out novelty rather than traditional pastimes and entertainments. At amusement parks like Coney Island, in theaters and restaurants, and on ordinary city streets, young audiences discovered exotic architecture, bright colors, electric lights, and a diverse array of other visual entertainments. Moreover, as walkers, browsers, and shoppers, they found (and created) a host of new opportunities to enjoy the pleasures of the material world, both as a form of individual recreation and as a collective activity.

Theatricality and spectacle thus gained new currency in American culture, sharpening the visual skills of consumers and focusing new attention on individuals, their appearance, and the things with which they surrounded themselves. Public buildings were expected to incorporate a variety of staging devices: grand staircases, long vistas, choreographed circulation, and controlled lighting were novel foregrounds for products and people. Popular audiences, made up predominately of women, flocked to the movies in droves, emulating the fashions and scenarios they discovered there. They paraded up and down the grand staircases of Radio City Music Hall and in their local movie theaters (fig. 6); they watched films, read magazines and romance novels, window-shopped, and became experts in the complex language of fashionable products, styles, and gestures.[23] Main Street may not have been the Rue de la Paix, and the

fig. 7
(above, top)
Luggage, manufacturer
unknown, Newark,
New Jersey, wood veneer,
metal, thread, silk, c. 1937.
The Wolfsonian–Florida
International University,
Miami Beach, Florida,
The Mitchell Wolfson Jr.
Collection. xx1990.161
and xx1990.162.
Photograph by Silvia Ros.

fig. 8
(above, bottom)
Advertisement for Queen
Mary Special Perfume,
"Nineteen Thirty-Six,"
by John Wanamaker, 1936.
From *Harper's Bazaar*,
June 1936. The Wolfsonian–
Florida International
University, Miami Beach,
Florida, The Mitchell
Wolfson Jr. Collection.
XC1994.4371.

neighborhood theater was clearly not the Paris Opéra, but the thrill of new commercial and entertainment spaces transported audiences to faraway places.

Throughout the 1920s and 1930s, American companies and advertising agencies contributed to the creation of a broad-based consumer culture in which seeking, discovering, and owning possessions conferred new identities on consumers. In this world, *glamour*, a term that gained currency in these years, was a quality to be cultivated. Thanks to the allure of things and their magical ability to transform, it was something that anyone could acquire.[24] The ornamental patterns of Art Deco lent themselves perfectly to this fashionable enterprise, giving rise to a host of newly designed consumer items, from jewel-like lipstick cases and vibrant fabrics to glamorous luggage sets (fig. 7) and fragrances named after ocean liners (fig. 8). During the Depression years in particular, these objects lifted consumers out of the world of everyday experience and gave them back a new sense of hope and discovery.[25]

By 1939, when New York hosted the World's Fair, this heady cocktail of artistry, commerce, and popular amusement was exerting a strong—and to some, disquieting— effect on American culture and consciousness.[26] Lapidus himself played only a small role in the fair, designing (with Morris Sanders) a display for the Distilled Spirits Institute in the Food Building. Although his own professional contributions were not of great consequence, it is evident that what he saw around him influenced the direction of his work. The fair showcased a new monumentality in contemporary American architecture, suggesting a streamlined yet solid and imposing alternative to European Modernism. Moreover, its monuments—such as Wallace K. Harrison's dramatic Trylon and Perisphere (figs. 9, 10), which served as the "theme building" for the fair, and other structures, such as the General Electric Pavilion of Voorhees, Walker, Smith, and Foley (fig. 11), the Glass Pavilion by Skidmore, Owings, and Merrill, or Albert Kahn's enormous Ford and General Motors Buildings—communicated the image of American prosperity and optimism about the "World of Tomorrow" through an abstract architectural language, enhanced by colored murals, figural sculpture, bold signage, and streamlined ornament. Recalling the glamorous appearance of trains, ocean liners, cars, and household appliances, this architecture conveyed its message of progress to a broad audience.

fig. 9
(above, left)
Hugh Ferris, *Construction of the Trylon and Perisphere*, lithograph, 19 ³/₄ x 26 ³/₄ in. (50.2 x 66.9 cm), c. 1938. The Wolfsonian–Florida International University, Miami Beach, Florida, The Mitchell Wolfson Jr. Collection. TD1993.12.1. Photograph by Bruce White.

fig. 10
(above, right)
Base of Trylon and Perisphere, night view, New York World's Fair, 1939. Library of Congress, Prints and Photographs Division, Gottscho-Schleisner Collection. LC-G613-T01-35145.

fig. 11
(right)
Voorhees, Walker, Smith, and Foley, General Electric Pavilion, night view, New York World's Fair, 1939. Library of Congress, Prints and Photographs Division, Gottscho-Schleisner Collection. LC-G613-T01-35350.

fig. 12
Donald Deskey,
"Amusements" section
title page, photographic
collage. From *Official
Souvenir Book, New York
World's Fair 1939*, ed.
Frank Monaghan (New
York: Exposition, 1939).
The Wolfsonian– Florida
International University,
Miami Beach, Florida,
The Mitchell Wolfson Jr.
Collection. 86.2.25.

Indeed, the fair as a whole was pitched to popular, rather than elite, tastes. Exhibits such as the "Road of Tomorrow" by Walter Dorwin Teague or "Futurama" by Norman Bel Geddes revealed how thoroughly enmeshed leisure, entertainment, and consumer culture had become. Even in the main exhibit halls, the fair had the quality of an amusement park, offering visitors rides, shows, exotic restaurants, and musical revues. The large "Amusement Zone" itself was like a sideshow, with such attractions as Billy Rose's Aquacade, "Amazons in No Man's Land," and the "Arctic Girl's Tomb of Ice" all featuring scantily clad women and raucous performances (fig. 12). Like Lapidus's "circus barkers," these events drew in passersby with seductive images and the promise of new discoveries.

Though the event is noteworthy for the presence of buildings by such Modernist masters as Lucio Costa, Oscar Niemeyer, and Alvar Aalto, the overall impression is not one of sophisticated modernity. Instead, what is most striking is the disparate and aesthetically conservative quality of the visual landscape that greeted visitors. A number of surviving images suggest this quality, but it is perhaps most readily apparent in the frequently photographed Constitution Mall, where the abstract shapes of Harrison's theme building formed a backdrop for the overscaled realism of figures representing George Washington by James Earle Fraser and

fig. 13
(right)
Leo Friedlander,
The Four Freedoms,
Constitution Mall,
New York World's Fair,
1939. Library of Congress,
Prints and Photographs
Division, Gottscho-
Schleisner Collection.
LC-G613-T01-38518.

fig. 14
(below)
Morris Lapidus, interior
of the Ansonia Shoe Store,
West Thirty-fourth Street,
New York, 1944.
Library of Congress,
Prints and Photographs
Division, Gottscho-
Schleisner Collection.
LC-G612-T01-47540.

The Four Freedoms by Leo Friedlander (fig. 13). Though American artists and audiences clearly strove to incorporate abstraction into contemporary art and architecture, the countervailing appeal of the literal and sentimental often won out: what was most important was getting the message across. Lapidus took this lesson to heart in his own work.

In his Ansonia Shoe Store in New York City of 1944, for example, Lapidus drew on the movie musicals of Busby Berkeley to create a theatrical space filled with light and fantasy (fig. 14). Here the delicate linear features of

fig. 15
(bottom, left)
Stairway to the first class dining room, S.S. *France*. From the pamphlet *Le Nouveau Pâquebot "France,"* Compagnie Générale Transatlantique, c. 1912. Long-term loan, The Mitchell Wolfson Jr. Private Collection, Miami, Florida. XM2002.06.1.

fig. 16
(bottom, right)
Grand staircase of the S.S. *Paris*. From the pamphlet *The Paris*, Compagnie Générale Transatlantique, c. 1921. The Wolfsonian–Florida International University, Miami Beach, Florida, The Mitchell Wolfson Jr. Collection. XB1990.1191.

his earlier projects give way to more massive forms and exaggerated effects. The showroom was spacious and indeterminate in size, an impression enhanced by a dropped ceiling that had been cut away to create a free-form curve (Lapidus later referred to such shapes as "woggles").[27] At the far end, a glass wall, lighted from behind, drew shoppers into the deep space of the store; the powerful recession from front to back was further underscored by rows of back-lit harp-shaped frames along the side walls and by the placement of a large, abstract sculpture at the furthest point of the room. Three massive columns, each encircled by a spiral garland of light, marched down the center of the space, penetrating circular cutouts in the ceiling, which, together with smaller lights, created a lively pattern overhead.[28] Any one of these devices would have created a dramatic effect, but Lapidus used them all at once, ensuring that his clients and their customers would not only be over-whelmed, but would later recall the experience with amazement.

In the mid-1940s, Lapidus's professional career briefly branched out in a different direction. The commission to design new interiors for a large military transport ship that was being converted to peacetime use offered him the opportunity to explore the world of leisure ocean travel and to become familiar with a new area of product design. Admired for their speed and cutting-edge technology, ocean liners were essentially floating hotels, and they typically offered a wide range of leisure activities and amenities, from sports and spa treatments to elegant boutiques and night-clubs, in distinctive, theatrical settings. The functionalist image of a ship's exterior—the elegant, silhouetted curve of the hull and the massive fun-nels trailing smoke were familiar from travel posters and advertisements—

was thus frequently at odds with the lavish decor of interior spaces, such as dining salons and lounges.[29] Though Lapidus would later employ this same strategy in his resort hotels of the 1950s, it is fascinating that, in his own design for a new cruise ship, he instead advocated the use of a "contemporary" style, seeking to alter what he viewed as an outmoded and inappropriate convention.[30]

No doubt Lapidus was familiar with the neobaroque interiors of the S. S. *France* (1912; fig. 15) and *Paris* (1921; fig. 16) and with the glamorous Art Deco spaces of the *Île de France* (1927; fig. 17) and *Normandie* (1935), yet he proposed a series of strikingly spare, modern spaces (fig. 18), featuring glass walls, and light, unenclosed staircases. For Lapidus, these forms best conveyed the American experience of ocean travel:

> Let us remember that the ship will be used by those who want the sense of freedom that only an ocean voyage can give…. In the ship's public rooms, that freedom from earth-bound cares and encumbrances should persist—no confining walls, but a feeling of freedom, openness, color, light and rich experience that can be found nowhere else…. A real American style should be as forward looking as America is forward looking. Not necessarily modern as French modernists or followers of the German Bauhaus are modern, but characterized by cleanness of line and freshness of color and honesty of construction.[31]

Viewed in the context of his later work, this project reveals a great deal about Lapidus's architectural ambitions. His goals were clearly two-sided: while he believed, in principle, in the appropriateness of modern design for certain building types, he also recognized that he didn't have the luxury of maintaining a position based on architectural theory. Indeed, his success as an architect and interior designer was entirely dependent on creating images that would sell. The hybrid nature of so much of his work seems to have been a compromise forged to satisfy these conflicting demands.

When Lapidus entered the hotel field in the late 1940s, the tastes of his clients, most of whom had little or no previous experience with architecture or design projects, were often disparate and confusing. Although there was a significant audience for the "contemporary style" of architecture, many signals in the retail world suggested that historical elements, with their ornamental richness, also had broad popular appeal. In fashioning an approach, Lapidus seems to have returned to the example of the ocean liners that he knew so well, creating a pastiche that juxtaposed the modern details of exterior architecture with period-style decor and ornament. What further distinguished his hotel designs, apart from the fact that he worked successfully in a variety of modes (refusing, unlike many prominent architects, to declare his exclusive allegiance to Modernism) was the skill with which he created memorable and financially successful projects. Indeed, the highly choreographed hotel spaces he produced had much in common with successful shops and glamorous ocean liners, placing the experience and entertainment of guests and clients ahead of all other priorities.

In 1949 Lapidus was hired to design the interiors for the Sans Souci, his first hotel commission on Miami Beach (fig. 19). Though he had never worked on a building of this type, he was recommended for the job by a friend, Harry Toffel, the vice president of the A. S. Beck shoe store chain, one of his most loyal clients. The project was backed by a trio of investors that included Ben Novack, a developer whose family owned the Laurels, a popular resort hotel in the Catskill Mountains, and Harry Mufson, whose background was in the women's clothing business. Like the Grossinger family and many other Catskill hotel owners, Novack and the others were in the process of expanding their investments and developing new properties in Miami Beach.[32]

What hotel builders sought was both a new look and a fresh approach to appeal to postwar vacationers. Lapidus was brought into the Sans Souci project very late; indeed, the plans for the hotel had already been completed by Roy F. France, one of the most prominent architects of the Art Deco era, whose own Saxony Hotel (1948) had recently been constructed on the adjacent site.[33] Backed by Toffel, Lapidus seized upon the opportunity to take control, muscling his way into the position of "associate architect" by impressing his clients with showy renderings for a new building. Though his memoirs depict his actions in a positive light (blaming his clients for the change), the forced collaboration with France, who remained the architect of record, cannot have been viewed favorably by local professionals.[34] What's more, the pattern was repeated frequently over the next three years, as Lapidus was hired to rework other architects' projects, many of which were already under construction. With stunning effectiveness, Lapidus thus usurped power from the most influential and established figures in the hotel field, including Henry Hohauser (the Algiers) and Albert Anis (the Nautilus and Biltmore Terrace).

He referred to himself as "the hotel doctor" in these years; no doubt others had different terms to describe him.[35]

With these postwar projects, developers broke new ground, both literally and figuratively. Their hotels—or, more properly, hotel complexes—changed the face of Miami Beach, bringing new prosperity and a new clientele to the area. During the 1930s and early 1940s, Miami Beach had become a magnet for Jewish vacationers, refugees from Europe, and retirees, including first-generation immigrants and others of modest means.[36] Though overshadowed by the Holocaust and by a longstanding tradition of anti-Semitism in the hotel industry, these years saw the transformation of the area and the establishment of its strong identification with Jewish culture, particularly in South Beach. Scores of new hotels were constructed, many in the Art Deco style for which Miami Beach is still well known. Most were modest in size, frequently offering guests no other amenities than a small lobby, cocktail bar, and pool. A handful of examples constructed at the end of this period, however—including the streamlined towers of L. Murray Dixon's Grossinger Beach Hotel (1940), France's National (1940), and Polevitzky and Russell's Shelborne (1940–1941)—reflect a trend toward expansion.[37] Following the Second World War, Miami Beach was thus poised to market itself to a younger generation, refashioning its image to keep pace with the increased prosperity and expectations of vacationers.

As historian Deborah Dash Moore has shown, the Second World War and the years immediately following represented a period of introspection and change for a large number of Americans, and for immigrant Jews and their children in particular, both in their view of themselves and in their status in the world. Military service had exposed many young men and women to a wide range of people and places (including Miami Beach, where many servicemen were billeted during the war), holding out the promise of new freedom and new identities. More confident and prosperous than their immigrant parents and eager for new experiences—including, for some, the desire to live as assimilated Americans—these young people began to explore the world beyond the narrow confines of their familiar urban neighborhoods. For many, the prospect of a luxurious vacation, or even perhaps a permanent home in a warm climate where so many others were starting new lives, was extremely compelling.[38]

Fueled by new arrivals from the North, the population of Miami Beach jumped from 28,000 permanent residents before the war to 46,000 in 1950. This pattern of expansion continued throughout the following decade, resulting in the arrival of thousands of new visitors each year and the construction of scores of new hotels.[39] Moreover, from 1947 on, inexpensive package tours and frequent airline flights made a Miami Beach vacation accessible to an even wider public, increasing demand for a range

fig. 20
The Laurels Hotel and
Country Club, Sackett
Lake, Monticello, New
York, postcard, c. 1965.
© Bill Bard Associates.
Photograph by Al Bard.

of visitor services at both ends of the economic spectrum. Although this widening of opportunity was obviously limited in the segregated South, the changes that took place were fundamental to the new image and vibrant culture of the city.[40]

Architects and developers made strenuous efforts to differentiate their new, high-end hotels both from Art Deco precedents and from the resorts of the Catskills.[41] On the basis of location alone, the two areas offered a very different vacation experience—in terms of geography, distance traveled, time, and expense—and as a result, each had its characteristic architecture and activities, despite the fact that there was always significant overlap in both clientele and seasonal workers. After the Second World War, these distinctions became clearer and more pronounced. With their tropical urban setting and expanded size, Miami Beach hotels came to be associated with high-priced entertainment, glamorous nightlife, gambling, and conspicuous consumption of material and physical pleasures. Resorts in the Catskills, on the other hand, remained more informal and rural in character, with meandering golf courses, woods, and open fields surrounding sprawling low-rise buildings (fig. 20). Although almost every hotel or bungalow colony, no matter how modest, offered entertainment in a "casino" or clubhouse, the focus of a vacation in "the mountains" remained on sports, outdoor activities, and visiting with friends, many of whom made the short trip by car from New York City or its suburbs year after year.

Acutely aware of the market share they were losing in the 1950s, particularly in the fall and spring seasons, many of the biggest Catskill hotels added new lobbies, high-rise towers, supper clubs, and pool decks modeled on those of Miami Beach, but the popularity of the Florida resort, with its fast pace and its many shopping venues, continued to grow exponentially.[42] Even after undergoing costly renovations (many of which were overseen

fig. 21
Morris Lapidus, lobby
of the Sans Souci Hotel,
Miami Beach. Courtesy
of the Historical Museum
of Southern Florida.

by Lapidus himself), the architecture of hotels like Grossinger's, the Laurels, Tamarack Lodge, and the Concord was overshadowed by the glamour of Miami Beach. Of course, many other factors contributed to the lasting popularity of the Catskills area as a vacation destination throughout the 1950s and 1960s, but its modern architecture wasn't its primary drawing point.

At the Sans Souci, Lapidus began to give shape to the postwar identity of Miami Beach. He adapted elements of France's Saxony in his design for the exterior (including the stacked horizontal strips of the balcony parapets), adding details like the curved driveway and dramatic, projecting porte cochere to fashion the monumental free-standing hotel type that would become his trademark. On the interior he employed many devices—massive columns, perforated ceilings, dramatic lighting—familiar from the Ansonia store and other retail projects, creating an easy flow of traffic through the lobby (fig. 21) to the supper club, restaurants, "specialty shops," or outdoor terraces. A commercial success from its opening date, the Sans Souci demonstrated Lapidus's ability to transfer both his retail experience and his familiarity with luxury ocean liners to the hotel field, gaining him the respect of potential clients who avidly watched the building take shape.

fig. 22
(above, left)
**Albert Anis and Morris
Lapidus, Biltmore Terrace
Hotel, Collins Avenue and
Eighty-seventh Street,
Miami Beach, 1951.
Library of Congress,
Prints and Photographs
Division, Gottscho-
Schleisner Collection.
LC-G613-T01-62800.**

fig. 23
(above, right)
**Albert Anis and Morris
Lapidus, entrance detail,
Biltmore Terrace Hotel,
Miami Beach. Library of
Congress, Prints and
Photographs Division,
Gottscho-Schleisner
Collection. LC-G613-T01-
62802.**

In 1950, while the Sans Souci was under construction, Lapidus traveled on the S. S. *Brazil* to Argentina and Brazil, where he met Oscar Niemeyer and studied new developments in Latin American Modernism first hand.[43] The effects of this visit were immediately evident in his work. At the Biltmore Terrace of 1950–1951, for example, a project commissioned after an initial scheme by Albert Anis was set aside, he combined a tall pylon, louvered ribbon windows, and *brise-soleils* in a composition that expanded on the distinctive form of the Sans Souci (fig. 22).[44] Early photographs reveal a stark, monumental building surrounded by open space in the manner of work by Niemeyer, Costa, and Affonso Reidy in Rio de Janeiro. A circular driveway and a diagonal porte cochere supported by free-form piers gave the hotel a dramatic entrance sequence (fig. 23). In a distinctively Modernist gesture, Lapidus added a large, semicircular glass pavilion to the right of the entrance stairway, quoting Niemeyer's casino at Pampulha (1940–1942). This element, which would become a familiar feature of Lapidus's work, enhanced the image of the building by emphasizing its separateness from its site, while also affording guests an elevated vantage point onto the street.

The lobby of the Biltmore Terrace is an ebullient pastiche, incorporating many devices characteristic of Lapidus's well-known style (fig. 24). It brings together such disparate elements as multiple light sources and fixtures, dropped ceilings, a bamboo wall perforated with repeated circular patterns (he referred to these as "cheese holes"), a screen of thin diagonal wires (which he called "bean poles"), and a large pier surrounded by radiating vertical fins. This central feature also supports a multipart ornamental light fixture that loosely recalls the gaslights of the fin de siècle. A round banquette, covered in variegated black and white pony skin,

fig. 24
(above, left)
Morris Lapidus,
lobby of the Biltmore
Terrace Hotel, Miami
Beach. Library
of Congress, Prints
and Photographs
Division, Gottscho-
Schleisner Collection.
LC-G613-T01-62812.

fig. 25
(above, right)
Morris Lapidus,
stairway of the Biltmore
Terrace Hotel, Miami
Beach. Library of
Congress, Prints
and Photographs
Division, Gottscho-
Schleisner Collection.
LC-G613-T01-62798.

provides an even more incongruous touch. Here, as in the cruise ship project of 1945, he included a dramatic suspended staircase (fig. 25). Thus the lobby, though rather modest in size, packs in virtually all the glamorous touches that Lapidus had in his "bag of tricks."

The Algiers Hotel (1950–1952), built by David Levinson, the owner of the Tamarack Lodge in Greenfield Park, New York, was perhaps the most distinctive of Lapidus's early works, recalling the grand Miami Beach hotels of the 1920s, such as the Flamingo and the Roney Plaza.[45] Viewed at night across Indian Creek, it resembled a huge, gaily lit cruise ship, with bold ribbon windows, a massive pylon, and a large neon sign on the roof (fig. 26). Jointly designed by Lapidus and Melvin Grossman (following a design by Henry Hohauser, another of the Art Deco–era masters), the L-shaped form of the hotel created a protected enclosure for a substantial pool and sundeck raised well above street level (fig. 27); both architects would frequently return to this approach in their later work. Like other large hotels of the period, the Algiers included ground-floor shops, restaurants, bars, and other entertainment facilities; an ample glass pavilion also provided space for an expanded range of social activities, including weddings, banquets, and receptions. With its high podium and monumental silhouette, the Algiers incorporated many elements of the expanded hotel program into a distinctive new building type. It thus became a model for the resort hotels of the post–Second World War period.

fig. 26
(opposite page, top)
Henry Hohauser,
Morris Lapidus, and
Melvin Grossman,
Algiers Hotel, Miami
Beach, night view, 1952.
Library of Congress,
Prints and Photographs
Division, Gottscho-
Schleisner Collection.
LC-G613-T01-62765.

fig. 27
(opposite page, bottom)
Henry Hohauser, Morris
Lapidus, and Melvin
Grossman, Algiers Hotel,
Miami Beach, postcard,
1952. © Hannau Color
Productions, Miami Beach,
Florida. Photograph by
Hans Hannau.

fig. 28
(this page)
Morris Lapidus, lobby
of the Algiers Hotel,
Miami Beach. Library of
Congress, Prints and
Photographs Division,
Gottscho-Schleisner
Collection. LC-G613-T01-
62757.

Both the exterior and interior suggest new directions in Lapidus's work
and offer a glimpse of things to come: the strong projections and thin
edges of the concrete slabs above the windows, the expansive use of glass,
sinuous shapes, and smooth wall textures all suggest a coherent, contemporary vision strongly influenced by Latin American precedents (fig. 28).
The lack of surface ornament or period detail throughout the hotel is
also notable here, although the lobby featured many brightly colored
surfaces in contrasting patterns, including an oversized tartan on the wall
surrounding the reception desk. This extravagant feature, together with
a large, floor-to-ceiling birdcage filled with parrots (prefiguring the
double-height terrarium at the Americana), added Lapidus's unmistakably
theatrical signature to the project.

The Algiers established Lapidus's reputation as an architect who understood
the demands of the postwar resort industry: It offered guests a carefree
world in which the image of luxury was matched by a wide range of
amenities and efficient back-of-house services. By the time the commission
for the Fontainebleau came his way, giving Lapidus his first chance to design
a hotel from the ground up, he had a very clear idea of how to proceed
(fig. 29). The developer, Ben Novack, with whom he had worked on the
Sans Souci, had purchased the fourteen-acre Firestone estate, a Beaux
Arts–style mansion set on an ample plot of land north of Forty-fourth
Street, which for many symbolized the former glory of the old Miami
Beach elite. Now the house was abandoned and the gardens were
overgrown, offering the newcomers the opportunity to stake their claim
in a highly visible location on the exclusive northern fringes of the city.

fig. 29
(top, right)
Morris Lapidus,
Fontainebleau Hotel,
Miami Beach, 1954.
Library of Congress,
Prints and Photographs
Division, Gottscho-
Schleisner Collection.
LC-G613-T-67000.

fig. 30
(bottom, right)
Morris Lapidus, general
view of the lobby,
Fontainebleau Hotel,
Miami Beach.
Library of Congress,
Prints and Photographs
Division, Gottscho-
Schleisner Collection.
LC-G613-T-66988.

Years before, Novack had traveled in France with his wife, and they had driven by the palace of Fontainebleau. Although they didn't stop to look at it (because, as he told Lapidus, he didn't "go for those foreign châteaux"), he felt that the name sounded "catchy" and he used it to set the theme for his new hotel, directing Lapidus to design interiors in the "modern kind of French Provincial" style.[46] To please his client, whom Lapidus claimed was "just as illiterate and uncultured as many of his guests," he concocted a mixture of "French Renaissance" and contemporary design, drawing on the lexicon of devices and motifs that he had developed in his earlier work.[47] From its spacious lobby to the landscaped grounds, where Renaissance-style parterres stood side by side

fig. 31
(bottom, right)
Morris Lapidus, aerial
view of the hotel and
gardens, Fontainebleau
Hotel, Miami Beach.
Color postcard.
© Gulf Stream Card
and Distributing Co.,
Miami, Florida.

with an enormous, state-of-the-art pool deck, the Fontainebleau offered visitors a seemingly endless array of vistas and entertainments (figs. 30, 31).

In an interview in the early 1970s, Lapidus explained how he set out to appeal to potential hotel guests:

> Who are they? What's their background; their training? They're going to come to Miami. They've heard that on the former Firestone Estate the fabulous Fontainebleau is going to be built. To begin with, it had to be *fabulous*. It had to live up to this dream picture, the dream drawn by the advertising people.[48]

If resort hotels were going to provide their guests with the experience of a glamorous vacation, every movement had to be theatrically staged and choreographed:

> My early training in drama and my experience in store and restaurant design gave me an inkling about what people thought and felt as they came into a room. People love to feel as if they are onstage when traveling or stopping at an elegant hotel.... In the Fontainebleau, I actually have the guests go up three steps to arrive at the platform, walk out on the platform, and then go down three steps.... Everyone loves a dramatic entrance.[49]

The Fontainebleau was thus graced with a "staircase to nowhere," as Lapidus called it, in the manner of the grand salon on an ocean liner (fig. 32). This central feature of the lobby was placed against an oversized Piranesian photomural, which created a theatrical backdrop for guests descending to the lobby from the mezzanine. There was also a wide range of restaurants and coffee shops, each with a themed interior. In the Café Bon Bon, for example, Lapidus and his client sought to re-create a feeling of

**fig. 32
(above, left)
Morris Lapidus,
lobby staircase,
Fontainebleau Hotel,
Miami Beach.
Library of Congress,
Prints and Photographs
Division, Gottscho-
Schleisner Collection.
LC-G613-T-67025.**

**fig. 33
(above, right)
Morris Lapidus,
detail, furniture group
in the lobby,
Fontainebleau Hotel,
Miami Beach.
Library of Congress,
Prints and Photographs
Division, Gottscho-
Schleisner Collection.
LC-G613-T-66985.**

"Old World luxury" with "Dresden figurines, rococo arches, [and] gaslit crystal chandeliers." Neither Lapidus nor Novack had ever been to Europe, he recalled, but they felt they had a pretty clear idea of what a Viennese café *ought* to look like.[50] Theatrical touches were also applied to the Boom Boom Room, with its Guatemalan cloth-covered chairs and large "tribal mask"; at La Ronde, a nightclub entered via an enormous, neon-framed Baroque arch; and at the Fleur de Lys, the hotel's main dining room with its life-size figurines and gilt-encrusted, Louis XV-style furniture.

The hotel immediately created a stir. Few commentators took note of the modern exterior, however; it was the outlandish, over-the-top interior that left visitors in a state of shocked amazement (fig. 33). Although the mayor of Fontainebleau, flown over especially for the opening, called the hotel "a bouillabaisse," a correspondent for *Interiors*, sent by the magazine to review the project, confessed to a certain stupefied pleasure as she surveyed the scene:

> If you are lucky, you arrive at the Fontainebleau at 6 p.m. for the changing of the guard. Six bellboys in gold epaulets march in formation, fall out smartly, and take their stations by the white marble columns. Six bellboys fall in and march out. They are part of the constantly changing show at the Fontainebleau, not the least of which are the patrons of the hotel itself. Architecture, decor and facilities are calculated to amuse, beguile, bemuse, entertain and generally overwhelm the 1,400 patrons who are gladly paying from $35 to $150 a day."[51]

The whole thing was unapologetically ostentatious, a defiant crowd-pleaser filled with transgressions against the canons of good taste. The reviewer provided a catalogue of Lapidus's creations, offering a fascinating glimpse of details only suggested by period photographs. He had bought up good French antiques from estates and New York dealers, stripped the frames, reupholstered them and refinished them with a lot

fig. 34
Morris Lapidus, view
of the lobby from above,
Eden Roc Hotel,
Miami Beach, 1955.
Photograph by
Ezra Stoller © Esto.

of white and gold. He bought up a lot of white statues and stood them on rosewood planters; he made lamps out of bisque figurines and bronze blackamoors; he designed huge brass chandeliers and had them made.... In a typical lobby corner, an antique gilded wood escutcheon bearing the seal of the city of Paris hangs on a Florida coralstone wall over a Lapidus-designed, Valley [a furniture manufacturer]-made cabinet (white leather, brass, rosewood) on which stand a pair of ormolu figurine candelabras and a cupid-topped French clock.[52]

Built at a cost of $13 million, the Fontainebleau was an amazing spectacle that horrified the critics and delighted the public.[53] With the exception of *L'architecture d'aujourd'hui*, the major design magazines refused to publish accounts of either the Fontainebleau or any of Lapidus's other hotel work in Florida.[54] Nevertheless, the project proved consistently profitable and newsworthy, luring a steady stream of clients to Lapidus's practice over the next decade. In the projects that immediately followed, such as the Eden Roc and the Americana in Bal Harbour, Lapidus refined the details of a type that would be successfully re-created in Jamaica, Aruba, and other resort locations, and even, with some significant variations, in New York City, at the Sheraton (1959–1960), Summit (1960–1961), and Americana (1961–1962) hotels.

The client of the Eden Roc—Harry Mufson, another former partner at the Sans Souci—was typical. As Lapidus recalled in his memoirs, he wanted a design that would "make the guy who can afford to pay fifty bucks a day look around and think that a fortune had been spent to create my hotel."[55] The place had to be luxurious, but without the "French stuff" for which the Fontainebleau was known. Lapidus showed him examples of "contemporary design," but he rejected these: "Nothing doing, Morris," he exclaimed, "my guests aren't kids out of school. They don't go for that modern jazz. I want antiques and crystal and marble and fancy woods." Lapidus then suggested designs based on Italian Renaissance themes. The client liked what he saw, except that he wanted Lapidus to "leave out that heavy ornament." When Lapidus replied that perhaps he objected to "the Baroque influence," the confused and exasperated Mufson couldn't stand it any longer: "I don't care if it's Baroque or Brooklyn," he screamed, "just get me plenty of glamor and make sure it screams luxury!"[56] Here, as else-where, Lapidus delivered the goods.

The lobby of the Eden Roc, perhaps Lapidus's most successful and elegant interior, combined brilliant scenography with rather restrained (in comparison to the Fontainebleau) period touches (fig. 34). Fluted wooden columns ringed a sunken lobby lounge; on the floor, a striking pattern of overscaled fleurs-de-lis radiated outward from this circle. As at the Fontainebleau, a marble staircase led to a mezzanine level from which guests could survey the scene before descending to the lobby. The heavy, wooden handrail was supported by a classical balustrade, indicated by armatures of golden wire, which enhanced the sense of drama; this feature reprised a theme established on the exterior, with its elaborate, wrought-iron light fixtures and stone staircases, complete with turned balusters (fig. 35). Adding further variety, the Bacchus Cocktail Lounge, a stream-lined, imitation grotto with trapezoidal windows and leaded glass, managed somehow to set a tone of space-age luxury.

The interior of the Americana in Bal Harbour was even more sensational. Here Lapidus offered guests the spectacle of a giant terrarium filled with tropical vegetation and a pair of torpid alligators in the lobby (the management did not approve his plan to use monkeys). The Medallion Dining Room featured a backdrop of enormous golden coins, embossed with eagles and set against a backdrop of heavy rouched cloth suspended on pointed pikes. The exterior architecture of the hotel, by contrast, was rather more conventional than Lapidus's earlier works had been, substituting a series of modular projecting units stacked up on a diagonal grid for the flowing lines and monumental scale of the Eden Roc and Fontainebleau.[57]

fig. 35
**Morris Lapidus, detail
of the driveway and
entrance, Eden Roc Hotel,
Miami Beach, 1955.
Photograph by
Ezra Stoller © Esto.**

Although the Americana and Lapidus's other hotel architecture would later be championed by Postmodernists for their irreverent use of sources and clever pastiche, it would be wrong to think that contemporaries viewed them in this way. On the contrary, by bringing fantasy and theatricality into the public realm, even in the setting of a resort hotel, Lapidus crossed an invisible line that disqualified his work from serious consideration by architects and theorists. Like television, comic books, and rock 'n' roll, these hotels struck many commentators as childish and self-indulgent.[58] The prevailing attitude is suggested by one of the few serious assessments that was published, a critique of the Summit and Americana in New York that appeared in *Art in America* in 1960:

> We are snobbishly intolerant in New York of the subculture of Florida, and we wish they would keep everything but their pompano and oranges down there where it belongs and not foul our nest with their taste. Ours is bad enough already; we need no help from the provinces.[59]

Lapidus fondly remembered the experience of spending $100,000 on antiques for the Fontainebleau, of buying "beautiful things" that he "could never afford" himself as one of the high points of his career.[60] But for some observers, Lapidus's love of antiques and the brightly colored, ersatz palaces he created with them was deeply disturbing. Class and regional prejudices, combined with deep-seated fears about the corrupting effects of popular taste, cast these hotels, and the culture of Miami Beach as a whole, in a negative light.[61] Critics despaired that the popularity of these and other extravagant entertainments signaled the failure of elite culture to win the battle (inaugurated at the end of the

previous century) to reform the aesthetic sensibilities of "the masses," and of immigrants in particular, by introducing them to proper conduct, high art, and good design.[62] To make matters worse, Lapidus's clients and their customers were wealthy and free to buy whatever they pleased: the power that this conferred on them seriously challenged the traditional authority of elite culture and, by extension, of professional critics.

For many middle-class Americans, taste became a matter of considerable anxiety and confusion.[63] On the one hand, consumers wanted the bright color, texture, and exuberant freeform styling that were the hallmarks of American commercial design, but on the other, critics and designers associated with elite institutions like the Museum of Modern Art and East Coast universities made it clear that the more intelligent and honorable choice was to buy furniture and household objects in the "Bauhaus style" or "Scandinavian modern." Even Colonial Revival, the familiar standby of the social reformers, was better than mass-produced "contemporary" products. Consumers didn't want to appear uneducated or "lower class," but, as Lapidus well understood, many in the postwar period had the ability, often for the first time, to buy new things, and they wanted the pleasure of showing them off.

Concerns about the dangerous effects of consumer culture were expressed in a variety of ways. For example, in many films of the 1940s and 1950s, including Otto Preminger's *Laura* (1944), John Huston's *The Asphalt Jungle* (1950), and other works in the genre of film noir, plot development often centered on greed, consumption, and the ostentatious display of wealth. Through portrayals of upper-class decadence, American moviegoers learned to associate the highly ornamented interiors and fussy tastes of elite women, effete men, and homosexuals with narcissism and ruthless self-interest. In *Laura*, for example, an ornate antique clock not only conceals the murder weapon, but comes to symbolize the perverted lack of masculinity that leads the foppish villain to commit the crime.[64] Postwar consumers were thus offered a diverse set of images on which to hang their anxieties about luxury and pleasure. Mental illness and "sexual deviance" could now be added to the long list of dangers about which social reformers, teachers, journalists, and other commentators had warned.

These assessments also reveal a significant undercurrent of misogyny that coincided with the emergence of consumer culture in the period.[65] Though largely unspoken, and even perhaps unconscious, this prejudice was rooted in the fear that women lacked either the education or the maturity to combat their own acquisitiveness and malleability, characteristics that expressed themselves in rampant consumerism and the ubiquity of advertising imagery and slogans. Like children (and teenagers in particular), they had to be guided to more worthy goals than the marketplace could offer. Moreover, some critics of popular culture implied that the deformations of American taste could be explained, at least in part, by the expansion of women's frivolous (and emotionally based) interests into the culture at large.[66] Thus, as the pleasures of the local movie theater, the shopping mall, and the resort vacation increasingly became the focus of postwar culture, many elements of popular entertainment came to be regarded as threats both to elite values and to traditional definitions of masculine self-discipline. One result of these changes, it was argued, was the commercial success of middlebrow architecture like Lapidus's, which, according to some observers, appealed to the senses without demanding anything of self-restraint or reason and manipulated clients by making them feel like kings and queens, or movie stars, in make-believe palaces.

Though he never expressed his theory in gendered terms, Lapidus viewed his hotels and their appeal to popular audiences as the crowning examples of an approach that he termed the "architecture of emotion."[67] His architecture, he maintained, was successful because it responded to fundamental human desires for pleasure and adornment—motivations that he knew well from his long experience in the commercial realm. Expressive and satisfying, it offered an alternative to the Modern movement, which he claimed would never be accepted beyond a narrow sphere. As he described it in an article published in the *AIA Journal* in 1961, the architecture of his own time was moving toward "the new sensualism" of "motion and emotion." He summed up his position:

> I maintain that no architecture has ever been accepted, nor will it ever be accepted, unless it satisfies that early, ineradicable, primitive emotional craving for enrichment or adornment. Mies van der Rohe cannot change human nature.... No architect will ever be able to root out that primitive emotion, that first love of adornment. And furthermore, unless and until we can accept it and satisfy it we, as architects, will never produce a true architecture of our epoch.[68]

While they were hardly considered worthy of notice when they were first expressed, these contrarian and populist views captured the attention of professionals as early as the mid-1960s. Although many buildings of the 1950s were rejected in the anti-Modernist backlash of succeeding decades (including many of the very projects that had been cast in a positive light by critics), young architects eager for new models championed Lapidus's work. In 1970 he was given a controversial one-man show at the Architectural League in New York City.[69] More recently, thanks in part to the expansion of the travel industry, Lapidus has again become the focus of considerable interest, and his designs continue to be studied by architects, interior designers, and retail specialists eager to follow his lead toward commercial success.

In 1996, having reached his nineties, Lapidus republished his memoirs and embarked on a lecture tour that combined self-promotion, self-parody, and sharp marketing skills. For students and professionals weary of both Modernist orthodoxy and Postmodern cynicism, the achievements of his long career offer a thick playbook of strategies with which to confront the challenges of design for commerce and entertainment in a global culture. Moreover, as historians have gained greater knowledge of his work, Lapidus has emerged not only as a leader in the field of hotel design, but also as a strong voice for change in a period in which women and popular audiences were gaining new visibility and influence. ❖

Acknowledgments

I am grateful to the Wolfsonian–Florida International University for a fellowship in January 2003 that enabled me to pursue my research and consult the collections. My project and this essay were greatly enriched by the collegiality and counsel offered by many members of the Wolfsonian staff: Marianne Lamonaca, Francis X. Luca, Nicholas Blaga, Leslie Sternlieb, and Silvia Ros. I also wish to acknowledge the generosity of Allan Shulman, Randall Robinson, and Dawn Hugh, archives manager of the Historical Society of Southern Florida, in helping me research the history of Miami Beach hotels. Thanks, too, to Wellesley College for awarding me a Faculty Research Grant in support of this research. My colleague in the Department of Art at Wellesley College, Patricia Berman, kindly read and commented on early drafts of this essay.

Notes

1. Lapidus's memoirs appear in two different versions: *An Architecture of Joy* (Miami: E. A. Seemann, 1979) and *Too Much Is Never Enough: An Autobiography* (New York: Rizzoli, 1996). For analysis of his career and works, see Martina Düttmann and Friederike Schneider, eds., *Morris Lapidus: Architect of the American Dream* (Basel: Birkhäuser, 1992) and Alice T. Friedman, "The Luxury of Lapidus: Glamour, Class, and Architecture in Miami Beach," *Harvard Design Magazine* 11 (Summer 2000): 39–47.

2. This new scholarship on mid-century modern architecture includes Sarah Goldhagen and Réjean Legault, eds., *Anxious Modernisms: Experimentation in Postwar Architectural Culture* (Cambridge, MA: MIT Press, 2000); Valerie Fraser, *Building the New World: Studies in the Modern Architecture of Latin America 1930–1960* (London: Verso, 2000); and R. E. Somol, ed., *Autonomy and Ideology: Positioning the Avant-Garde in America* (New York: Monacelli, 1997).

3. Deborah Dash Moore, *To the Golden Cities: Pursuing the American Dream in Miami and Los Angeles* (Cambridge, MA: Harvard University Press, 1994): 25–26, and Ann Ambruster, *The Life and Times of Miami Beach* (New York: Knopf, 1995): 105–106.

4. I am grateful to Randall C. Robinson Jr. for his advice in locating this information. For additional data on specific buildings in Miami Beach, see www.miamibeachfl.gov. The best scholarly treatment of this subject is Jean François Lejeune and Allan T. Shulman, eds., *The Making of Miami Beach: The Architecture of Lawrence Murray Dixon* (New York: Rizzoli, 2000), although the book focuses on the period prior to the Second World War. I have drawn on a number of unpublished sources, including Randall C. Robinson and Carolyn Klepser, tour notes for "Miami Modernism and the Post-War Resort Hotel," Society of Architectural Historians Annual Meeting, June 2000, and Carolyn Klepser, "Ninety Years of North Beach: A Synopsis of the Northern Part of the City of Miami Beach," www.gonorthbeach.com/pdf/nbhist.pdf. Although most of Lapidus's drawings were destroyed in the 1960s, a small but valuable archive is held by the Department of Special Collections, Syracuse University.

5. In this paper, the term "resort hotels" is used to refer to luxury hotels offering an expanded program of activities, both indoor and outdoor, and services, in addition to lodging, especially to vacationers.

6. Contemporary examples include the Caribe Hilton in Puerto Rico by Charles Warner and Oswaldo Luis Toro, the El Panama Hotel by Edward Durell Stone, the Istanbul Hilton by Skidmore, Owings, and Merrill (with Sedad H. Eldem), and Welton Becket's Beverly Hilton. See Annabel Wharton, *Building the Cold War: Hilton International Hotels and Modern Architecture* (Chicago: University of Chicago Press, 2001), esp. the introduction and chaps. 1 and 6. An overview of the subject was published in "New Hotels—Just Because They Are Better," *Architectural Forum* 98 (January 1953): 97–117.

7. For the evolution of the "Tiki Style," see Sven A. Kirsten, *The Book of Tiki: The Cult of Polynesian Pop in Fifties America* (Cologne: Taschen, 2000), 80–105.

8. For the history of the American vacation and the tradition of moral improvement, see Cindy S. Aron, *Working at Play: A History of Vacations in the United States* (New York: Oxford University Press, 1999). A range of views on popular culture and its effects on American society was published in Bernard Rosenberg and Daniel Manning White, eds., *Mass Culture: The Popular Arts in America* (Glencoe, IL: Free Press, 1957). See also Gary Cross, *An All-Consuming Century: Why Commercialism Won in Modern America* (New York: Columbia University Press, 2000).

9. Lapidus, *Architecture of Joy*, 129.

10. Ibid., 77–78.

11. Ibid., 62.

12. Valuable surveys of the history of hotel design include Elaine Denby, *Grand Hotels: An Architectural and Social History* (London: Reaktion Books, 1998) and Jeffrey Limerick, Nancy Fergusson, and Richard Oliver, *America's Grand Resort Hotels* (New York: Pantheon Books, 1979). For the interior decor of nineteenth-century hotels, see Catherine Cocks, *Doing the Town: The Rise of Urban Tourism in the United States, 1850–1915* (Berkeley and Los Angeles: University of California Press, 2001), chap. 3. The role of gender is discussed by Molly W. Berger, "A House Divided: The Culture of the American Luxury Hotel, 1825–1860," in *His and Hers: Gender, Consumption, and Technology*, ed. Roger Horowitz and Arwen Mohun (Charlottesville: University Press of Virginia, 1998), 39–65, and by Carolyn Brucken, "In the Public Eye: Women and the American Luxury Hotel," *Winterthur Portfolio* 31, no. 4 (1996): 203–20.

13. Some of these changes are described by Neil Harris, "Urban Tourism and the Commercial City," in William R. Taylor, ed., *Inventing Times Square: Commerce and Culture at the Crossroads of the World* (New York: Russell Sage Foundation, 1991), 66–82. For definitions of the "commercial aesthetic," which helped to shape the visual culture of the city, see William Leach, "Introductory Essay," in *Land of Desire: Merchants, Power and the Rise of a New American Culture* (New York: Pantheon, 1993), 234–42. For the history of hotel architecture in New York City during this period, see Robert A. M. Stern, Gregory Gilmartin, and Thomas Mellins, *New York 1930: Architecture and Urbanism Between the Two World Wars* (New York: Rizzoli, 1987), 200–25; see also Annabel Wharton, "Two Waldorf Astorias: Spatial Economies as Totem and Fetish," *Art Bulletin* 85, no. 3 (September 2003): 523–43.

14. See, for example, Lapidus, "Store Design: A Merchandising Problem," *Architectural Record* 89 (February 1941): 113–36; "The Retail Store and its Design Problems," *Architectural Record* 97 (February 1945): 96–102, and "Let's Beautify the Selling Machine," *Interiors* 106 (June 1947): 98–99. A complete bibliography and list of works are included in Düttmann and Schneider, *Lapidus*, 246–47.

15. Lapidus, *Architecture of Joy*, 78–79. Photographs of the retail work appear in Düttmann and Schneider, *Lapidus*, 23–70. For the 1925 Exposition des Arts Décoratifs et Industriels Modernes and its influence, see Charlotte Benton, Tim Benton, and Ghislaine Wood, eds., *Art Deco 1910–1939* (London: V & A Publications, 2003), esp. Tag Gronberg, "Paris 1925: Consuming Modernity," 156–63, and Tim Benton, "Art Deco Architecture," 244–59.

16. Cook and Klotz, *Conversations*, 166–67.

17. Ibid., 161–62, 164. For Mendelsohn's commercial architecture, see Kathleen James, *Erich Mendelsohn and the Architecture of German Modernism* (Cambridge, U.K.: Cambridge University Press, 1997), chaps. 5 and 6. For the history of night illumination, see Dietrich Neumann, *Architecture of the Night: The Illuminated Building* (New York: Prestel, 2002).

18. See Morris Ketchum, *Shops and Stores* (New York: Reinhold, 1948) and James Hornbeck, ed., *Designs for Modern Merchandising* (New York: Dodge, 1954).

19. Lapidus, *Architecture of Joy*, 100.

20. See Kathy Peiss, *Cheap Amusements: Working Women and Leisure in Turn-of-the-Century New York* (Philadelphia: Temple University Press, 1986) and Jenna Weissman Joselit, *A Perfect Fit: Clothes, Character and the Promise of America* (New York: Metropolitan Books, 2001).

21. For window displays, see Leach, *Land of Desire*, chap. 10. Women's employment in department stores is analyzed in Susan Porter Benson, *Counter Cultures: Saleswomen, Managers and Customers in American Department Stores, 1890–1940* (Urbana: University of Illinois Press, 1986), chaps. 4 and 6.

22. See David Nasaw, *Going Out: The Rise and Fall of Public Amusements* (Cambridge, MA: Harvard University Press, 1993), esp. chaps. 7, 11, and 16.

23. David Naylor, *American Movie Palaces: The Architecture of Fantasy* (New York: Prentice-Hall, 1981) remains the best source on this subject; for modern architecture in film, see Donald Albrecht, *Designing Dreams: Modern Architecture in the Movies* (New York: Harper & Row, 1986). Images of New York City in film are discussed in Stern et al., *New York 1930*, 78–87.

24. For an early use of the term, see *Glamour of Hollywood: A New Magazine of Fashion, Beauty and Charm*, published by Condé Nast, which first appeared in April 1939; in May 1941 its name was changed to *Glamour*.

25. This point is made by Leach, *Land of Desire*, 298, and *passim*.

26. For the New York World's Fair, see Robert Rydell, *World of Fairs: The Century of Progress Expositions* (Chicago: University of Chicago Press, 1993) and Helen A. Harrison, ed., *Dawn of a New Day: The New York World's Fair 1939/1940* (New York: Queens Museum, 1980). For information on buildings and exhibits, see Richard Wurts and Stanley Appelbaum, eds., *The New York World's Fair 1939* (New York: Dover Press, 1977). Among many original sources, the most detailed are *Official Guide Book of the 1939 World's Fair* (New York: Exposition Publications, 1939) and Frank Monaghan, ed., *Official Souvenir Book: New York World's Fair 1939* (New York: Exposition Publications, 1939).

27. Lapidus explained his use of the terms "woggles," "bean poles," and "cheese holes" in a number of articles and interviews. See, for example, Cook and Klotz, *Conversations*, 159.

28. Ibid., 150–51; see also Lapidus, *Architecture of Joy*, 105–106.

29. For the history of ocean liners, see William H. Miller Jr., *The First Great Ocean Liners in Photographs 1897–1927* (New York: Dover, 1984); *The Great Luxury Liners, 1927–1954: A Photographic Record* (New York: Dover, 1981); and Louis-René Vian, *Pâquebots de légende: Décors de rêve* (Paris: Musée de la Marine, 1991).

30. Morris Lapidus, "Public Rooms for Tomorrow's Ships," *Interiors* 105 (December 1945): 60–65.

31. Ibid., 61, 62–63.

32. Advertisement in the *New York Times*, 18 December 1949, 16. For the Catskills, see Moore, *To the Golden Cities*, 32–34, and Phil Brown, *Catskill Culture: A Mountain Rat's Memories of the Great Jewish Resort Area* (Philadelphia: Temple University Press, 1998), 43–44. Brown also discusses the seasonal movements of workers and the informal networks that existed among hotel people as they traveled back and forth between "the mountains" and Miami Beach, 128–32. For the Grossinger Beach Hotel by L. Murray Dixon, see Lejeune and Shulman, *The Making of Miami Beach*, 118–21, 183, 187.

33. Very little has been published on France or his buildings, which include numerous Miami Beach hotels, such as the St. Moritz (1939), the Sands (1939), the National (1940), the Sea Isle (1940), the Saxony (1948), and the Casablanca (1950), and movie theaters, such as the Carib (1950, with Michael J. Di Angelis), and the Gateway (1952) in Fort Lauderdale. On the theaters, see Michael D. Kinerk and Dennis W. Wilhelm, "Dream Palaces: The Motion Picture Playhouse in the Sunshine State," *Journal of Decorative and Propaganda Arts* 23 (1998): 209–36.

34. Lapidus, *Architecture of Joy*, 125–32.

35. Lapidus, *Too Much*, 150; see also Cook and Klotz, *Conversations*, 150.

36. Moore, *To the Golden Cities*, 154, and Armbruster, *Life and Times*, 77–81. See also *Miami Beach Is Calling You: Hotel and Apartment Book, 1940–41* (Miami Beach Chamber of Commerce, 1940), where advertisements for the Grossinger Beach Hotel appear side by side with other listings specifying "Gentiles only" or "restricted clientele." For a rare discussion by Lapidus of his experience as a Jewish architect, see *Interview* 16 (September 1986): 148–49.

37. For the history of Art Deco hotel design on Miami Beach, see Barbara Baer Capitman, *Deco Delights: Preserving the Beauty and Joy of Miami Beach Architecture* (New York: Dutton, 1988). The period and its architecture are analyzed in Allan T. Shulman, "Building and Rebuilding: The Making of Miami Beach" and "Miami Beach between the World's Fairs: The Visual Culture of a Modern City," both in Lejeune and Shulman, *The Making of Miami Beach*, 8–39 and 40–72. For Polevitzky, see Allan T. Shulman, "Igor Polevitzky's Architectural Vision for a Modern Miami," in *Journal of Decorative and Propaganda Arts* 23 (1998): 334–59.

38. Jewish attitudes toward vacations and leisure are discussed by Andrew R. Heinze, *Adapting to Abundance: Jewish Immigrants, Mass Consumption, and the Search for American Identity* (New York: Columbia University Press, 1990), chap. 7.

39. Ruby Leach Carson, "Forty Years of Miami Beach," *Tequesta: The Journal of the Historical Association of Southern Florida* 15 (1955), 3–28, esp. 4–12; see also Henry Alan Green and Marcia Kerstein Zerivitz, *The Mosaic Project: Jewish Life in Florida, A Documentary Exhibit from 1763 to the Present* (Miami Beach: Sanford L. Ziff Jewish Museum of Florida, 1991).

40. Carson, "Forty Years," 24. For the architecture of Overtown, a largely African American neighborhood where many performers stayed during the period of segregation, see Dorothy Jenkins Fields, "Tracing Overtown's Vernacular Architecture," *Journal of Decorative and Propaganda Arts* 23 (1998): 323–32.

41. The most authoritative scholarship on this subject is Brown, *Catskill Culture*, which contains an up-to-date bibliography; Irwin Richman, *Borscht Belt Bungalows: Memories of Catskill Summers* (Philadelphia: Temple University Press, 1997); and Phil Brown, *In the Catskills* (Philadelphia: Temple University Press, 2002).

42. For the architecture of Catskill hotels, see Alf Evers, Elizabeth Cromley, Betsy Blackmar, and Neil Harris, *Resorts of the Catskills* (New York: St. Martin's Press, 1979) and Irwin Richman, *Catskill Hotels* (Charleston, SC: Arcadia, 2003), esp. 122–25 and chap. 5. Additional information is available at www.brown.edu/Research/Catskills_Institute. For Lapidus's work in the area, see also Lapidus, *Too Much*, 205.

43. Lapidus, *Too Much*, 148–49. Niemeyer's early work was published in Philip Goodwin, *Brazil Builds* (New York: Museum of Modern Art, 1943). Lapidus had an exhibition of his photographs of these buildings at the Architectural League in 1950, *New York Times*, (3 September 1950): 51.

44. The hotel, at Collins Avenue and Eighty-seventh Street, is essentially intact, although many elements are obscured by later additions.

45. The Algiers incorporated elements of nineteenth-century Florida resorts as well; see Susan R. Braden, *The Architecture of Leisure: The Resort Hotels of Henry Flagler and Henry Plant* (Gainesville: University Press of Florida, 2002) .

46. Lapidus, *Architecture of Joy*, 141–43.

47. Cook and Klotz, *Conversations*, 156

48. Ibid.

49. Lapidus, *Architecture of Joy*, 164.

50. Ibid., 146.

51. Marilyn Silverstone, "What One Man Did with $13,000,000: 'Put It Where It Shows,'" *Interiors* 114 (May 1955): 88–95 (quote on 91).

52. Ibid.

53. One of the more positive reviews of Lapidus's work, albeit not by a design critic, was published by Gilbert Millstein, "Architect de luxe of Miami Beach," *New York Times Magazine* (6 January 1957): 26–27, 36.

54. *L'architecture d'aujourd'hui* (September 1955): 46–48.

55. Lapidus, *Architecture of Joy*, 163.

56. Ibid., 164.

57. For the Americana in Bal Harbour, see Lapidus, *Too Much*, 190–96, 212–15, and Allan T. Shulman, "Morris Lapidus and the Search for a Hemispheric Modernism," *Aula 3* (2002): 48–59.

58. I discuss the critical response at greater length in "The Luxury of Lapidus."

59. Russell Lynes, "New York Hotels with Reservations," *Art in America* (April 1963): 58–61.

60. Morris Lapidus, interview with author, Miami Beach, 4 January 2000.

61. See Thomas Hines, *Populuxe* (New York: Knopf, 1986), esp. chaps. 4 and 12.

62. Many examples of writings in this critical voice are included in Rosenberg and White, eds., *Mass Culture*. For more on this subject, see Karal Ann Marling, *As Seen on T.V.: The Visual Culture of Everyday Life in the 1950s* (Cambridge, MA: Harvard University Press, 1994). For tenement interiors and social respectability, see Lizabeth Cohen, "Embellishing a Life of Labor: An Interpretation of American Working-Class Homes, 1885–1915," in Dell Upton and John Michael Vlach, eds., *Common Places: Readings in American Vernacular Architecture* (Athens: University of Georgia Press, 1986), 261–78. See also Joselit, *Wonders of America*, 137–69, and Heinze, *Adapting to Abundance*, 110–12 and chap. 8, "The Parlor and the Piano."

63. Terence Riley and Edward Eigen, "Between the Museum and the Marketplace: Selling Good Design," *Studies in Modern Art* 4 (1994): *The Museum at Mid-Century: At Home and Abroad*, 150–79.

64. For more on the equation of taste with sexuality in *Laura*, see Robert Corber, *Homosexuality in Cold War America: Resistance and the Crisis of Masculinity* (Durham, NC: Duke University Press, 1997), chap. 2.

65. For an elaboration of these ideas, see Andreas Huyssen, "Mass Culture as Woman: Modernism's Other," in *After the Great Divide* (Bloomington: Indiana University Press, 1986), 44–62 and James Livingston, "Modern Subjectivity and Consumer Culture," in Susan Strasser, Charles McGovern, and Mathias Judt, eds., *Getting and Spending: European and American Consumer Societies in the Twentieth Century* (Cambridge: Cambridge University Press, 1998), 413–29.

66. For the changing use and assessment of private and public space in the 1950s, see Lizabeth Cohen, *A Consumer's Republic: The Politics of Mass Consumption in Postwar America* (New York: Knopf, 2003). For anxieties about masculinity in this period, see Barbara Ehrenreich, *The Hearts of Men: American Dreams and the Flight from Commitment* (Garden City, NY: Anchor Press/Doubleday, 1983).

67. Morris Lapidus, "The Architecture of Emotion," *AIA Journal* 36 (November 1961): 55–58.

68. Ibid., 57.

69. Ada Louise Huxtable, "Show Offers 'Joy' of Hotel Architecture," *New York Times* (15 October 1970): 60.

Mitchell Owens

Living Large: The Brash, Bodacious Hotels of Dorothy Draper

Mitchell Owens is a writer and independent scholar of twentieth-century interior design living in Marrakech, Morocco. He writes for the *New York Times*, *Elle Decor*, and *Travel & Leisure*.

Alightly educated blue blood from Tuxedo Park, the famously posh gated community in New York's Ramapo Mountains, Dorothy Draper (born Dorothy Tuckerman, 1889–1969) defined the countenance of the cutting-edge American hotel in the mid-twentieth century. Contemporaries like Eleanor McMillen Brown (1890–1991), Ruby Ross Wood (1881–1950), and Draper's cousin Dorothy "Sister" Parish (1910–1994) focused their considerable skills and often commanding social positions on defining the antiques-laden look of upper-crust residential interiors along the eastern seaboard, but Draper (fig. 1) specialized in improving the interiors of commercial structures, particularly hotels and apartment buildings. It was a skill that her professional peers seem to have acknowledged as Draper's by right, given that her office won some of the nation's most publicized and influential commercial design commissions. "Not one of [her competitors] would know what to do with a dining room for five hundred," wrote her biographer, Carleton Varney (b. 1939). "Their minds thought small scale, and hers thought large scale. It was as simple as that."[1]

Actually, it wasn't that simple at all. What made Draper an acknowledged force in American commercial design from the 1930s until her retirement in 1961 wasn't just an uncommon ability to handle cavernous spaces. She revolutionized the American hotel industry, upending the antiquated notion of hotels as plush but forgettable way stations for monied travelers and reinventing them as camera-ready fantasias where café-society chic met surrealistic set design, top fashion photographers staged elaborate shoots of the latest haute couture, and smart society matrons went for cocktails and dancing, secure in the knowledge that their surroundings were the ultimate place to see and be seen. Draper pioneered the hotel as aesthetic attraction. Each was planned to be a destination in itself, as compelling and, more important, as lucrative as traditional sightseeing landmarks. It was a shrewd, showman-like formula that anticipated by

All interior design by Dorothy Draper, except where noted.

Sitting room, Palácio Quitandinha, Pétropolis, Brazil, decorated 1944. Author's collection. Photograph by Anthony Baratta.

fig. 1
(right)
Dorothy Tuckerman
Draper, 1930. Courtesy
of Dorothy Draper & Co.,
New York.

fig. 2
(below, left)
Main floor lounge, Coty
Salon, Rockefeller Center,
New York. From the
Decorative Furnisher,
August 1941.

fig. 3
(below, right)
Cover of *Decorating Is
Fun! How to Be Your Own
Decorator*, by Dorothy
Draper (New York:
Arts & Decoration Book
Society, 1939).
Author's collection.

decades the 1960s Miami Beach resort hotels of the architect Morris Lapidus (1902–2001) and the trendsetting boutique hotels developed in recent years by the team of Ian Schrager (b. 1947) and Philippe Starck (b. 1949).

Clubs and restaurants like the Versailles and Sherry's, deluxe retail stores like the two-story Coty salon at Rockefeller Center (fig. 2), and public spaces like the cafeteria of the Metropolitan Museum of Art, a Roman-style atrium with giant birdcage light fixtures, were among the Draper firm's much-publicized projects. Assisted by John B. Wisner,[2] Lester Grundy (1914–1985),[3] Ted Stewart, Isabel Thacher Barringer (1911–1970), Glenn Boyles (1910–1982), and Katharine Walton Seaman (d. 1956), Draper decorated hundreds of private residences for clients such as gossip columnist Walter Winchell (1897–1972), philanthropist Mary Woodard Lasker (1901–1994), and playwright-diplomat Clare Boothe Luce (1903–1987). The company produced popular collections of furniture, fabrics, and wallpapers for prominent manufacturers, dabbled in cosmetics packaging, and decorated airplanes. Dorothy Draper's fame was broadcast into America's living rooms through best-selling books about do-it-yourself decorating (fig. 3) and entertaining, ghostwritten syndicated newspaper columns, the monthly generation of home improvement ideas for *Good Housekeeping* magazine, and radio and television programs. Her prime-time interview with Edward R. Murrow (1908–1965) on the television program *Person to Person* in 1957 cemented Draper's reputation as the decorator best known to American housewives.

Decorating Is Fun!
Dorothy Draper

HOW TO BE YOUR OWN DECORATOR

**fig. 4
Corridor, Palácio
Quitandinha, Pétropolis,
Brazil. Author's collection.
Photograph by
Anthony Baratta.**

According to an unnamed associate who was quoted in one of the designer's obituaries, the firm's international celebrity was misleading. "Mrs. Draper's enthusiasm [for making innovations] led to widespread publicity for her, but the company was not a financial success."[4] Still, the firm, which was known as Dorothy Draper Inc. during its founder's lifetime, made a lasting contribution to the American design landscape through the popularization of boldly themed, instantly recognizable decors.

Using what the designer described as "masses of beautiful color, a sense of balance and scale, and an awareness and love of smart accessories," Draper and her associates animated dozens of high-end urban hotels and suburban resorts, from the august Mayflower Hotel in Washington, D.C. (1925, partially decorated by Draper in 1941) to the tony Arrowhead Springs Hotel in Arrowhead Springs, California (built and decorated 1938–1939).

Nearly all of these hotels have been destroyed or significantly altered, but Draper's greatest work still stands largely intact: Palácio Quitandinha (built and decorated 1942–1944), a bizarre hotel and casino in Pétropolis, Brazil, a Palm Beach–style resort town in the mountains northwest of Rio de Janeiro. Inside a colossal building that looks like a Swiss chalet pumped with steroids, Draper conceived the grandest neobaroque interiors of her career and some of the most outlandish details ever to come out of her office. They include a winter garden dominated by a sixteen-foot-tall chinoiserie iron birdcage, molded-plaster door openings that gaped like monstrous mouths, and multicolored terrazzo floors with swirling rococo patterns. Quitandinha (opening image and fig. 4) is a stupendous survivor of an important portfolio of projects.[5]

The Draper touch was about creating a *Gesamtkunstwerk,* or unified work of art, addressing in color- and theme-coordinated fashion a hotel's entire visual character, from guest rooms and dining room china to staff uniforms and matchbook covers. This artistic thoroughness was already a hallmark of Draper's work as early as the 1920s, when she was attracting

attention not only for sleek apartment-house lobbies (fig. 5) but for her apparently singular position as a leader in the male-dominated American residential construction industry.

In 1930 Frances Drewry McMullen wrote what is arguably the first feature-length appreciation of Draper as a professional designer rather than as a society wife and mother. The article appeared in the *Woman's Journal*, a popular general-interest magazine in the Depression years. While the tone of McMullen's text was upbeat and a bit earnest—"Her place in apartment house construction she has made for herself, and in doing so she has opened up new prospects for the qualified woman"—its underlying message was clear. Dorothy Draper was someone any ambitious woman chafing under domesticity's restrictions could admire and even emulate, a shining example of a bright, charming, practical, womanly woman who had established a successful career in a man's world by capitalizing on an aptitude that at the time was considered traditionally feminine: making a home. "Since the fate of a great dwelling building is largely decided by women, who select the family abode, and since women are 'picky' in ways that only their kind comprehend, real estate operators, Mrs. Draper believes, are coming to feel the need of expert feminine advice," McMullen continued. Expert advice or not, even McMullen was aware that Draper's interaction with certified professionals was still controversial in traditional working environments. Draper was not only a woman but an autodidact with an uncommon sense of assuredness, whose early success grew out of a combination of instinct and bravado rather than academic training. It was not the kind of modus operandi held in high regard by men with the perceived superiority that came from earning a degree from the École des Beaux-Arts in Paris, as so many of the era's top architects had. As McMullen pointedly noted, "Architects and builders are not yet ready to take a woman in such capacity into their offices, [Draper] thinks, but they recognize the value of an outside consultant's ideas."[6]

A decorator who preferred to call herself a "real estate stylist," Dorothy Draper was a design revolutionary whose seemingly fanciful ideas were as commercially sound as her influence was nationally renowned.[7] In 1937 Evelyn Roe of the *Christian Science Monitor* wrote about Draper's idiosyncratic success in harnessing interior design and using it to make profitable previously unproductive hotels, apartment buildings, stores, restaurants, and supper clubs. In her interview with Roe, the designer made it perfectly clear that her talent wasn't in creating pretty rooms; she was an expert at merchandising. It was a message that any businessman could appreciate, whether the messenger was a man or a woman. "You can't just let buildings sit, staring the public in the face, and expect that they will rent themselves," Draper said. "Neighborhoods change. Obsolescence gallops on the heels of every former headliner. Americans are notoriously fickle."[8]

Those words surely captured the attention of America's real-estate investors and developers. But in an apparent gesture to connect with the newspaper's female readership, the designer further explained her philosophy of the bottom line by employing a fashion analogy to illustrate how she approached the job of improving the interiors of an outmoded building: "You want your clothes to be of the here and now, not of yesterday, gone and forgotten." It was the perfect sound bite, glib and memorable. On closer examination, however, the carefully rehearsed comment softens Draper's corporate success for mass-market consumption, metaphorically outfitting it in an organdy dress to make her professional standing more palatable, both to chauvinistic men (who might doubt the hard-charging designer's personal femininity) and yearning women (who might wonder how they could launch a career without compromising their womanliness). An empowerment subtext, however simplistic, seems equally clear: that a woman who knows the ins and outs of her wardrobe

fig. 6
Make-up tent, Coty Salon,
Rockefeller Center,
New York. From the
Decorative Furnisher,
August 1941.

can take those sartorial lessons and apply them to a business plan. Practicality, panache, and a highly developed knowledge of what people, i.e., women, want were skills that Draper obviously believed had as much viability in the dressing room as they did in the boardroom.

Established by charter on 27 March 1925 as The Architectural Clearing House[9] and still in operation as Dorothy Draper and Company, the interior design firm this New York socialite founded garnered headlines for its crowd-pleasing, and therefore moneymaking, schemes. Not everyone was delighted with the company's steadfast reliance on dramatic signature effects. These became known as Draperisms: muscle-bound baroque-style plasterwork, walls painted with stripes a foot wide, busily flowered upholstery, and painted furniture crafted more often for its visual impact than as shining examples of cabinetmaking finesse.[10] Carleton Varney, the owner of Dorothy Draper and Company since 1960, has noted that one of Draper's projects, a canopied dining pavilion not unlike the make-up tent she created for Coty's Rockefeller Center shop (fig. 6), was derided as a "posh pup tent" liable to suffocate its inhabitants if the curtains fell closed.[11] When the San Francisco office of Gensler and Associates, an international architecture and interior design firm; Virginia Ball Designs, a design company in Los Angeles; and Wilson and Associates, a design firm in Dallas, were hired to renovate and redecorate the Fairmont

San Francisco in 1999, travel writers and design journalists were quick to proclaim the soon-to-vanish 1945 Draper interiors as "flamboyant," "over the top," "bordello chic," and "garish black-and-red opulence."[12]

Typical of Draper's work, commercial or residential, the Fairmont was the design equivalent of Joan Crawford at mid-career: brash but sophisticated, boldly painted, furbelowed to a fare-thee-well, meticulously crafted to attract maximum attention. What Draper wrought could be frothy, lush, and tough to swallow by today's more streamlined standards, but often even her finest and most surprisingly nuanced interiors failed to get the attention they deserved. *California Arts & Architecture* featured the sensationally suave interiors of the Arrowhead Springs Hotel in a six-page article without once identifying Draper's firm, though it praised Gordon B. Kaufmann (1888–1949) and Paul R. Williams (1894–1980), the architects of the ungainly building, a Regency-style behemoth.[13] Frank Lloyd Wright (1867–1959), for his part, loathed Draper's often-floriferous decors, and given his towering ego, it seems highly probable that the architect was equally annoyed by her household-name status. He once brutally denounced her as an "inferior desecrator" in a speech that he delivered at an American Institute of Decorators dinner held in his honor in 1952 at the Waldorf-Astoria. "She doesn't know anything," he hissed from the podium. "All she knows is God made some flowers."[14] The lady from Tuxedo Park, who was in the audience that evening, blithely ignored Wright's insults, as she apparently did everyone else's. More important, so did the developers who kept hiring her. They were as sure of the star quality of Draper's taste as she was herself.

Long before the designer became the queen of American hotels, the masters of Manhattan's real-estate universe were relying on "Mrs. George Draper,… a society woman and the mother of three lovely children" to play Everywoman in consultation with their architects and contractors.[15] Outfitted by the best dressmakers, married to one of Franklin Delano Roosevelt's doctors, member of all the right ladies' clubs, and frequently featured in national fashion magazines and regional society columns, Dorothy Draper represented "the composite prospective tenant, interpreting with professional insight the needs and desires, sometimes explicit, sometimes vague, of this little understood personage."[16] Men might make the money that kept the home fires burning, but women made the family's aesthetic decisions, including how their families would live, in which building, in which neighborhood. Therefore, they often had considerable power in determining where the family's money would be spent, and residential real estate developers were keen to tap into the market of upper-middle-class women—the wives of bank presidents, stockbrokers, and other white-collar professionals. In Mrs. George Draper, developers had the ultimate weapon: entrée. She was lovely to look at (John Singer Sargent sketched her), widely admired, and best of all, she understood how the tony young wives they wanted to attract actually lived. After all, she was one. It seems likely it was these attributes—along with a close friendship with Douglas L. Elliman (1890–1979), the founder of one of Manhattan's leading real estate companies—resulted in one of Draper's earliest known commissions. Sutton Hall, a cooperative apartment building in New York City, brought the newly minted designer on board to "consult on the plans and decorations from the point of view of 'the lady of the house.'" [17] Evidently the consultation was a success. Within two years, Draper was collaborating on luxury cooperative apartment buildings in Manhattan with some of the city's top residential architects: Rosario Candela (1890–1953), Pleasants Pennington (1889–1942), and blue-chip firms like Warren and Wetmore, Cross and Cross, and McKim, Mead, and White. And in 1928, she and the architect Archibald Manning Brown (1881–1956) broke ground on a development of Bermuda-style suburban houses in Kenilworth, Long Island. [18]

Certainly Draper knew many of these architects socially, but her "feminine" insights obviously were considered invaluable, given her rapid acceptance into the real-estate development ranks and her increasingly high-profile commissions. If the head-shaking tone of contemporary magazines like the *Woman's Journal* are to be believed, many male architects had little concept of precisely how an upscale private residence operated and a tendency to overlook the kind of life-enhancing details that can make a house livable and a hotel a home away from home. Draper, on the other hand, encouraged architects to incorporate novelties like closets deep enough for hangers bearing bulky fur coats and dressing rooms adequately scaled for ladies-who-lunch wardrobes. She felt the utilitarian roofs of high-rise buildings should be put to better use as gardens with lacy trellis-work and potted trees. [19] Some architects may have resented her lack of professional training and having to alter their plans to suit her "improvements," but others joined in fruitful associations with her. [20] In 1937, when Draper was hired to design the interiors of Hampshire House, an apartment hotel on Central Park South in New York City, for example, her relationship with the building's co-architect A. Rollin Caughey was unusually close. The two reportedly worked as a team to combine "the structural design with the decorative style through the building." [21]

In 1928 Draper proved that style equals profit by deftly renovating a block of shabby nineteenth-century brick tenement buildings on Sutton Place South in New York City. Cold-water apartments in the five-story brownstone structures rented for as little as $15 a month, but vacancies abounded. The buildings were so depressed that not even their proximity to Sutton Place—recently made fashionable by the decorator Elsie de Wolfe (1865–1950) and society leaders like banking heiress Anne Tracy Morgan (1873–1952) and theatrical agent Elisabeth Marbury (1856–1933) —could be used as a marketing tool. A friend of Draper's was a tenant,

fig. 7
Advertisement for
50 East Seventy-seventh
Street. From the *New York
Times*, 4 May 1930.

however, and after she saw how creatively and inexpensively he and his wife had decorated their flat, she approached the owners of the property, the Phipps real-estate family, with a renovation plan. Given a modest budget of $15,000 per building and a mandate to attract respectable tenants who could pay higher rents, Draper painted the filthy facades high-gloss black, the window and door frames shiny white, and the front doors shocking primary colors. She also romanticized the industrial-strength fire escapes by giving them a coat of white paint and then bolting on cast-iron ornaments that gave the buildings a New Orleans mien. To brighten the gloomy corridors and stairwells, she installed jaunty flowered wallpapers and carpets in high Victorian style, an idiosyncratic and extremely cozy antidote to the era's growing reliance on edgy Art Deco motifs. The land around the riverside property was improved as well, with fruit trees and flowering shrubs.

A reporter from *Business Week* noted that Draper's revamp "differs from the mill run of modernization by its emphasis on big results from minimum expenditures. It stresses the importance of eye appeal." [22] And, the writer continued, the designer's largely superficial renovations had a surprisingly profound impact on the landlord's pocketbook. The apartments were soon fully occupied at an average of $100 a month, and, fulfilling the Phipps family's mandate, New Yorkers moved into the rechristened Cannon Point Row. The residents included Henry Huddleston Rogers Jr., a Standard Oil heir, and Clarence Francis, the president of Post Products and later chairman of General Foods. [23]

Casual observers may have been amazed, but Draper was not surprised by the buildings' new profitability. "I am convinced that structural alterations and routine modernization would not have done the trick with this property," she told the *Christian Science Monitor*. "They would have had no publicity value—and often, I am sure, the reconversion of a property may hang primarily on clever publicity rather than on anything big, factually accomplished." [24]

Draper's publicity-oriented decoration mirrored the designer's conscious marketing of her own social position and significant personal glamour. Dorothy Draper, soignée socialite turned working woman, was a package that neatly paralleled the era's passion for movies with a high-society theme and the concurrent growth of women in the workplace. Soon Draper became as much an icon of all-American style and feminine independence as the actresses Carole Lombard (1908–1942) and Norma Shearer (1902–1983). She got star billing, her name prominently featured in advertisements that promoted the buildings for which she was a consultant (fig. 7). And like any box-office sensation cultivating her public image, Draper also was keenly aware of the importance of maximizing commercial projects with surgically precise advertising campaigns and coherent public relations plans. "These last years have been difficult for hotels," Draper said in 1937. "Many of them were built in a time of opulence, and there was no provision to withstand the shock of the economic upheaval. I believed that the way to renew the hold on people of these buildings was to impart an idea to them."[25] Central to that idea was her realization that American taste was "turning from the pompous and grand to the elegantly chic."[26]

It was an observation whose moment had come. Just as the still-young movie industry had spawned rapturous fans who read about the supposedly intimate details of stars' lives, wardrobes, and romances in movie magazines, so there was a torrent of shelter and design magazines—including *Country Life in America, House & Garden, House Beautiful,* and a multiplicity of general-interest women's magazines incorporating interior design tips—anointing the latest guru whose unerring taste could change one's life for the better, or, at the very least, make it more beautiful, more streamlined, more comfortable. Given the cult of celebrity that exploded during the interwar years, Draper's family nickname seems almost ridiculously appropriate: her parents called her Star.

In 1938 Draper oversaw the interiors of the Carlyle, an apartment hotel at the intersection of Madison Avenue and East Seventy-six Street on Manhattan's Upper East Side. It was a plum assignment. Despite the welcome publicity, Cannon Point Row had basically been a down-and-dirty renovation, and her architectural consultations and interior design projects for private residential clients were lucrative but rarely newsworthy. The Carlyle, however, was a high-profile opportunity with a significant amount of square footage on one of the city's prime pieces of real estate.

Officially opened on 1 November 1930,[27] the forty-story Carlyle was one of New York City's proliferating number of top-flight, high-rise housing stock: a deluxe rental building equipped with four-star services like a private dining room, a gymnasium, housekeeping staff, and, as an advertisement stated, "kitchenettes for the occasional domestic urge."[28] It was a hotel in all but the strictest definition, an amenities-rich pied-à-terre for the transient rich who could afford neither the taxes nor the hassles associated with maintaining a large private house in the city but who could see the appeal of entertainment and exercise facilities and maids on call. Construction was well under way by the time of the 1929 stock market crash, and though wealthy New Yorkers like millionaire widow Mrs. Ben Ali Haggin and art collector Chester Dale took up residence in the Carlyle, it went into receivership and was sold at a foreclosure sale on 9 May 1932 for $2,655,000.[29]

Brought in as the "style consultant" when new owners decided to revive the depressed property, Draper was on board to attract the "right people" —that is, people with money—by decorating the Carlyle in an eye-catching fashion befitting its deluxe pretensions. For the designer, that meant assembling lobbies and sitting rooms that looked like home, decked out with handsome antiques, up-to-date upholstered furniture, and colors that invigorated the spirit without exhausting the eye. As a contemporary magazine for professional architects and decorators once noted, "Even the ubiquitous traveler feels a certain sense of lonesomeness when he contemplates the average hotel interior, particularly his bedroom." [30] The residential-style decoration that Draper proposed as an alternative to soulless uniformity was not a new concept in hotel design, though she would make it an important component of her company's commercial-design philosophy until her retirement in 1960. [31]

Many other designers promoted hotels with domestic character in the 1920s and 1930s. One of the most prominent was the Ambassador Hotel in New York City, which opened in 1921 and was built to the designs of Warren and Wetmore, co-architects of Grand Central Station. Journalist turned interior designer Ruby Ross Goodnow, then the director of the Belmaison Galleries of John Wanamaker's New York store, and her associate Blanche Falls Shanley (d. 1941) [32] decorated many of the Park Avenue hotel's interiors, which were attractively conventional. Goodnow (better known as Ruby Ross Wood) approached the job as if she were decorating individual apartments for well-mannered, well-monied, but not particularly adventuresome, clients. For the six hundred guest rooms and suites, she and Shanley relied on Wanamaker's fabled stock of eighteenth-century French and English antiques, as well as high-quality reproductions that the department store manufactured especially for the hotel. Fabrics and paint colors also were varied throughout the rooms to avoid the standardization that had become a blight on the industry and a bane to the frequent traveler.

Draper handled her own home-style hotel work with considerably more élan, bypassing milquetoast traditionalism in favor of spirited shots of hearty Victoriana. The cozy confusion of the late nineteenth-century interior was being embraced by design-conscious intellectuals and aesthetes in the 1920s and 1930s, notably in England by the novelist Arnold Bennett (1867–1931) and the enfants-terrible aristocrats Osbert Sitwell (1892–1969) and Sacheverell Sitwell (1897–1988). [33] Draper, on the other hand, had no interest in reviving every dust-catching detail of the Victorian decorations of her childhood or in treating the style ironically, like a slightly despised toy in the hands of a superior child. At Cannon Point Row, for example, she relied on the style for its spiritual comforts: warmth, color, and familiarity. At the Carlyle, however, she imbedded the Victoriana deep inside the outwardly modern building like a chocolatier

fig. 8
(right)
Living room, The Carlyle, New York. From the *New York Times*, 5 April 1931.

fig. 9
(far right)
Baroque fireplace design. From *Decorating Is Fun! How to Be Your Own Decorator* (New York: Arts & Decoration Book Society, 1939). Author's collection.

hides a cordial cherry inside a hard candy shell. So, though the main lobby of the Carlyle would be decorated in a café-society take on imperial Rome—black-and-white checkerboard marble floor, button-tufted satin sofas, French antique tapestries found at the New York shop of the purple-haired courtesan turned decorator Rose Cumming (1887–1968) —Draper indulged her enthusiasm for the previous century in a three-room suite for entertaining, though with a few twentieth-century modifications (fig. 8). One-color wall-to-wall carpeting clarified the confectionary qualities of the apartment's Rococo Revival–style floral wallpaper. For example, the ceilings were painted a bright sky blue, and in a touch that soon would become a Draperism—every door was painted shiny black with bright white panel moldings.[34]

This refreshing combination of old and new, now and then, would remain a linchpin of Draper's commercial interiors for decades, the traditional elements invigorated by lessons, colors, and materials gleaned from modern design movements. The genesis of the designer's overscale moldings, door frames, mirrors, chimneypieces, and other gigantically proportioned architectural elements made of cast plaster or carved stone (fig. 9) is unknown, though a few hints can be gleaned from the lists of reference books she advised her admirers to add to their libraries.[35]

A study of the buildings of Sir John Vanbrugh (1664–1726)—the eighteenth-century playwright and architect who designed Blenheim Palace (1705–1724) in Oxfordshire for war hero John Churchill, the first Duke of Marlborough (1650–1722)—was recommended for its subject's thrilling "sense of scale and drama." The work of some 1920s Danish

fig. 10
Corridor, Hampshire
House, New York,
c. 1930. Courtesy of
Dorothy Draper & Co.,
New York.

architects found favor with Draper, too, particularly their inventive handling of interior details like "great shells over doors." A book about Russian imperial palaces was another favorite. The designer cited her admiration for the Romanov family's passion for kaleidoscopically patterned inlaid floors, whose "dynamic parquetry" she imagined might be effectively reproduced in linoleum or Zenitherm, a synthetic acoustical fiber whose advertising claimed it "Looks like stone—Works like wood."[36] As for the fruit-motif plaster swags and similarly modeled multibranch girandoles (fig. 10) that she frequently hung on mirrored surfaces or applied to brightly painted walls, they were vastly magnified interpretations of naturalistic lime-wood carvings made popular in the late 1600s and early 1700s by the Dutch-born British master craftsman Grinling Gibbons (1648–1721).[37]

Another important influence on the company's much-imitated style was Lester Grundy, a designer who joined the firm in the mid-1930s and eventually moved on to *House & Garden* as decorating editor and eventually to *Architectural Digest* as editor. Given the rococo extravagance of his work for Draper, particularly the fantastical plaster decorations that were created under his direction and became one of the firm's inescapable hallmarks, it seems likely that Grundy was an admirer of two influential

fig. 11
Entrance, Coty Salon,
Rockefeller Center,
New York, c. 1941.
Courtesy of
Dorothy Draper & Co.,
New York.

books that appeared to acclaim in the late 1920s, both written by
Sacheverell Sitwell: *Southern Baroque Art* and *German Baroque Sculpture*.[38]
The first book was particularly admired in artistic circles, and it brought
back into fashion the flamboyance of eighteenth-century Italy—extravagantly cresting fireplaces and door frames, polychrome terrazzo floors,
wedding-cake plasterwork lashed with gilt and silver. It was a pulsating
plastic vocabulary that the British museum curator and design historian
Stephen Calloway claimed captivated a generation of aesthetes because
of "its overwhelming scale, its love of imbalance, its quality of striving,
and for its palpable sense of danger."[39]

Other Draper employees had antiquarian interests that meshed neatly
with Grundy's, and they would take up the banner of the neobaroque
after his departure. One was John B. Wisner, who worked for Draper
from 1940 until 1949. Glenn Boyles, the company's chief designer for
many years, was a teacher and illustrator who spent time in prewar Europe
as a student at the New York School of Fine and Applied Art, sketching
and painting watercolors of baroque masterpieces like the Villa Pisani
at Stra, near Venice, which would be stylistically echoed in the Draper
firm's modern-baroque interiors.

Thanks to the influence of Grundy, Wisner, and Boyles, powerhouse
theatricality became the prevailing Draper leitmotif. Occasionally it could
be astoundingly oppressive, even strangely bilious, as in the Coty salon in
New York City, where the extravagant molded-plaster balustrades seemed

fig. 12
Camellia House,
Drake Hotel, Chicago,
c. 1941. Courtesy of
Dorothy Draper & Co.,
New York.

alternately dispirited and menacing, their voluptuous silhouettes smoth-
ered under pale blue paint (fig. 11).[41] At their best, however, these
past-perfect accents—scallop shells and volutes, arabesques and acanthus
leaves—were blown up to bewitching proportions and then finely cast and
carved by the Cinquini family, a little-known clan of Italian-American
craftsmen in Brooklyn who produced the majority of the plaster details
used in Draper's commercial interiors.[42] The Cinquinis also crafted
extraordinary plaster chandeliers for the Camellia House, a Draper-
designed nightclub that from 1941 until 1970 was a mainstay of the
Drake Hotel (1920) in Chicago (fig. 12).

With its thirty-six stories of gleaming white brick accented with brushed-
metal fittings, Hampshire House on Central Park South in New York City
is inarguably the finest urban example of Draper's excursion into the
exuberant possibilities inherent in the baroque. Hampshire House was yet

fig. 13
Party room, Essex House,
New York, c. 1940.
Courtesy of Dorothy
Draper & Co., New York.

another luxury apartment hotel that had fallen on hard times, though in a more dramatic fashion than the Carlyle. It had stood empty and unfinished since 1931, when the owners went into foreclosure because of the Depression.[43] Draper landed the commission to complete Hampshire House in 1937, after reportedly beating 154 other designers.[44] (Douglas L. Elliman was the hotel's managing agent, as he was for the Carlyle and many of the apartment buildings for which she renovated lobbies, so perhaps the competition was a formality.) It also was reportedly the most expensive decorating job ever entrusted to a woman. The budget was $396,000; Draper's fee was $15,000.[45] That this fact warranted reporting underscored Draper's singular position in the commercial design world. The designer told the *New York Times* that she would be developing an overall color scheme to encompass every detail of the hotel in chromatic unity, "walls, carpets, upholstery, draperies, china, stationery, and servants' uniforms." She also said that there would be nothing modernist about the planned decors, only what the newspaper described as "conservative old English townhouse styles."[46]

fig. 14
(below, left)
The Cottage, Hampshire
House, New York, 1937.
Courtesy of Dorothy
Draper & Co., New York.

fig. 15
(below, right)
Corridor, Hampshire
House, New York, 1937.
Courtesy of Dorothy
Draper & Co., New York.

Draper either misled the newspaper or the reporter misunderstood her intentions. When Hampshire House opened on 15 September 1937, just five months after she signed the contract, it was obvious that she and Grundy had jettisoned the London-traditional plan, if indeed there had been one. Instead, the pair installed a series of magical public rooms that took the muscular formalism of the British architect, painter, and landscape designer William Kent (1685–1747) and spliced it with a sense of whimsy that was two parts carnival fun house to one part surrealism. The result was a high-octane juggling act that an advertisement for the hotel breathlessly but correctly described as "excitingly new,… divertingly different."[47] Several years later, the designer's friend Eleanor Roosevelt (1884–1962) described decorative antics such as these as "showing off," though the First Lady admitted that Draper's work could be "charming and restful."[48] What Roosevelt made of the Grimms' fairy tale artificial trees whose branches slithered across the ceiling of a freakish but alluring party room at Essex House (1931), an Art Deco skyscraper hotel in New York, went unrecorded (fig. 13).

To Draper, her work's raison d'être was the shock of the new and its ability to increase consumer traffic and free spending. "The hold a building will exert on the public is a question of the way that building is presented to the public…. People coming into a building can tell whether it is successful," she said, shortly after winning the Hampshire House competition. "It's in the modeling of the wainscotings, the coloring of its hallways, the fashioning of stair rails."[49] Logic would dictate and balance sheets proved that the more people were dazzled by a building's perceived importance, fashionability, and uncommon attention to detail, the more they would patronize it, whether hotel, restaurant, or supper club.

Draper and Grundy put enormous effort into the decoration of the primary ground-floor corridor of Hampshire House, a much-trafficked passage that led from the public entrance to the main dining room and an adjacent dining room known as the Cottage, a stage-set orangerie where giant painted-metal orange trees stood at attention amid mirrored walls and a sea of lacy wrought-iron chairs (fig. 14).[50] Visitors walked across a long, broad floor paved with Draper's favorite two-foot-square black-and-white marble tiles and past pairs of towering purple-black paneled doors framed with thick clear-glass moldings (fig. 15). Spiky girandoles of white plaster bearing electric candles jutted from the walls, emerging from Grinling Gibbons–style plaster swags of fruit and ribbons, while a pair of grave busts gazed down from grand tapered plinths. On either side of the corridor stood two pairs of button-tufted Georgian-style settees, staggered asymmetrically, their lightly carved frames washed with white paint. It was a sculpted, semisurreal look that Draper would return to frequently, freshly, and sometimes rashly, reinterpreting it for many hotel jobs she and her design team undertook.

Draper and Grundy's modern-baroque work was closely related to the highly influential neoromantic interiors being created in France by the designers Jean-Charles Moreux (1889–1956), Serge Roche (1898–1988), Jean Pascaud (1903–1996), and the design firm Dolt (in operation from 1935 to 1940).[51] Characterized by a fanciful reinvention of baroque motifs, a predatory sense of scale, and an air of aristocratic ennui, neoromanticism was already a dominant aesthetic by the time it was officially codified by the Éxposition des Arts et Techniques dans la Vie Moderne in Paris in 1937. For approximately a decade, it would affect numerous mediums with the gloss of artistic but elegant taste: the fashion photography of Cecil Beaton (1904–1980) and Horst P. Horst (1906–1999); motion pictures like *The Scarlet Empress* (United States, 1934) and *Les enfants du paradis* (France, 1945); and the irreverent haute couture of the Italian-born French designer Elsa Schiaparelli (1890–1973).

More domestically influential than the bulging plasterwork was the rose-patterned chintz upholstery fabric designed by Glenn Boyles, the component of the Hampshire House decor that made its way into homes from coast to coast. Draper lavished it throughout the apartment hotel with Sensurround abandon. Emblazoned with cabbage roses as big as softballs, it was made into curtains, padded dining chairs, and was sewn into panels for four-poster beds. The ubiquitous pattern eventually became the best-selling fabric in the history of F. Schumacher and Company. Variations on this floral motif would be a constant of Draper design, along with flamboyantly veined faux-marble wallpaper, drum-shaped black or green lampshades measuring nearly two feet across, crisp organdy curtains that incorporated as much yardage as an antebellum ball gown (fig. 16), and Syracuse restaurant china blooming with a single plate-size camellia or rose.

fig. 16
(top, right)
Sunroom, Gideon Putman Hotel, Saratoga Springs, New York, 1935.
Courtesy of Dorothy Draper & Co., New York.

fig. 17
(bottom, right)
Gordon B. Kaufmann and Paul R. Williams, Arrowhead Springs Hotel, Arrowhead Springs, California. From the *Decorative Furnisher*, April 1940.

Defiant color schemes were associated with Draper throughout her career, too, and she proselytized about how necessary it was to banish "undecided colors" from the design vocabulary. "There should never be any doubt about what your color has to say, whether it is a pale or a brilliant shade," she wrote. "It may be chalk blue, watermelon pink, lemon yellow, grass green, chocolate brown, café au lait, warm gray—anything on earth you like, just so long as it knows its own mind."[52]

Another of the designer's maxims, one especially suited to the architectural scale of a luxury hotel, was "The wider the curtain and the bigger the cushion, the smarter the effect." She, Lester Grundy, and Katharine Walton Seaman translated that statement of living large into reality for the 150-room Arrowhead Springs Hotel, which was completed in 1939 (fig. 17). Located in Arrowhead Springs, a resort town in the San Bernardino Mountains sixty-odd miles southeast of Los Angeles, the hotel was the fourth constructed on the site. The earlier structures had been destroyed by wildfires, most recently in November 1938.[53] Emboldened by the

fig. 18
Gordon B. Kaufmann and
Paul R. Williams, lobby
sitting area, Arrowhead
Springs Hotel, Arrowhead
Springs, California. From
the *Decorative Furnisher*,
April 1940.

disruptions in international tourism caused by the war in Europe, the
owners of the 1,800-acre property chose to rebuild the complex once
more, this time as a chic mountain retreat and mineral-bath spa for
Hollywood's increasingly homebound stars. Draper, by now the most
famous designer in America, was selected for the interiors. The massive
hotel building and its array of cabanas, guest cottages, garages, dormitories,
and health and recreation facilities was entrusted to two architects admired
by California's new-money elite: Gordon B. Kaufmann, designer of the
nearby Santa Anita Racetrack and the award-winning Los Angeles Times
Building, and Paul R. Williams, a black architect who designed homes in
a "modernized Regency mode"[54] for film-colony eminences like Tyrone
Power, Lon Chaney, Lucille Ball, and Frank Sinatra.

The Arrowhead Springs Hotel opened on 16 December 1939 with a gala
that was broadcast nationally on a radio show hosted by Rudy Vallee and
featuring a seventeen-year-old Judy Garland singing "Comes Love."
It was the Draper firm's most stylistically nuanced project.[55] Still bold,
though airier than the firm's earlier work, it also appears to have been the
only one that magazines for design professionals took seriously. *California
Arts & Architecture, Architect and Engineer*, and the *Decorative Furnisher*
all published glowing articles about the hotel. The latter publication called
Draper's sophisticated decors "full of life and virility, and … unusually gay

and colorful even for a section of the country where color and gayety [*sic*] are expected as a matter of course." Following Kaufmann and Williams's decision to rework Regency architecture "to fit the climate of Southern California with many outside porches and terraces for dining and lounging,"[56] the interior designer, in the sort of dizzy comment sure to enrage enemies like Frank Lloyd Wright, described her interior scheme as "a mythical Georgian mansion on an imaginary island in the Caribbean sea."[57] The open lobby was a characteristically dramatic introduction: black-lacquered support columns, walls and folding screens of bleached oak flexwood (a wood veneer), curtains of quilted emerald-green slipper satin weighted with heavy bullion fringe, and tall Chinese Chippendale– style fretwork niches packed with decorative blue-and-white china. Off the lobby were sitting areas where deep-dish sofas and armchairs upholstered in wide-wale beige chenille were pulled up to graphic Georgian-style fireplaces fashioned of black-and-white marble and built to a fantastic scale unknown to the average eighteenth-century householder (fig. 18).

Working within the *Gesamtkunstwerk* tradition, Draper manipulated the lobby's color scheme throughout the hotel, muted in the guest rooms and pumped up in public spaces intended for constant activity. Between the dining room and the lobby, for example, was a lounge clad in green-and-white wallpaper printed with wildly magnified marble veining and furnished with English rococo-style armchairs painted stark white and pulled up to a ground-hugging green satin sofa (fig. 19). The hotel's sunken dining room daringly combined the floral exuberance of Hampshire House with broad-shouldered, black-lacquered Chinese Modern cabinets and white walls frosted with exaggerated white-plaster girandoles crafted by the Cinquinis. The cavernous cocktail lounge was carpeted in outsize Kelly-green plaid, an adjoining games room had a mirrored fireplace, green leatherette walls, and a Chippendale-style sofa covered in an aggressively sculpted white bird's-eye chenille. These inventive interiors were ideal backgrounds for the hotel's Hollywood habitués, theatrical environments tailor-made for theatrical people. Draper was quick to admit that she had learned a bit about provocative decors from watching her fair share of double features. As she told the actress Alice Faye, "Motion pictures ... have taught us much in scale and value of the dramatic."[58]

A project that the Draper office handled soon after the Arrowhead Springs was the Mayflower Hotel in Washington, D.C. (1925). Instead of decorating the majestic hotel top to bottom, however, Dorothy Draper Inc. was given the fifth floor to renovate. As interior design became increasingly popular in the mid-twentieth century and designers were elevated to cult status, luxury hoteliers frequently hired popular society decorators to rework individual suites that could be hired at a premium, including notables like Elsie de Wolfe (then known as Lady Mendl) at the Plaza (1905–1907; addition 1921), the St. Regis (1901–1904), and Essex

fig. 19
Gordon B. Kaufmann and
Paul R. Williams, lounge,
Arrowhead Springs Hotel,
Arrowhead Springs,
California. From the
Decorative Furnisher,
April 1940.

House (1929–1930), millionaire Spanish tastemaker Carlos de Beistegui (1890–1970) at the St. Regis, and the Paris interior-decorating firm Jansen at the Waldorf-Astoria (1929–1931). The one hundred-odd redecorated rooms that made up the Mayflower's fifth floor, christened the Draper floor, were easily the most modern in the tradition-loving capital and strong evidence that some member of Draper's organization was eager to work in less self-conscious, more rational modes. Nonetheless, the *Decorative Furnisher* noted the company had successfully restyled "ordinary drab hotel rooms into veritable palaces, which are drawing words of admiration from even the most blasé of hotel guests."[59]

What had astonished observers were eccentrically multipurpose rooms outfitted with custom-designed, presto-chango furniture that looked like one thing but could and did behave like quite another. ("I always put in one controversial item," Draper liked to say. "It makes people talk.")[60] In the designer's opinion, Washington's constant flow of business visitors needed hotel accommodations that could be used for meetings as well as daily living, that went from conference room to bedroom in a snap. The multipurpose personality of the project turned out to be more than just a stunt when the Japanese attacked Pearl Harbor on 7 December 1941, a few months after Draper completed the job. Suddenly, the nation's capital was flooded with thousands of additional politicians, bureaucrats,

fig. 20
(below, left)
Bedroom, Mayflower
Hotel, Washington, D.C.,
1941. From the *Decorative
Furnisher*, December 1941.

fig. 21
(below, right)
Bedroom, Mayflower
Hotel, Washington, D.C.,
1941. From the *Decorative
Furnisher*, December 1941.

diplomats, and military personnel, taxing the city's residential and commercial resources, and Draper's concept for the Mayflower's new and improved decor was discovered to be prescient as well.

The focus on day-to-night versatility, something unseen in Draper-designed hostelries to date, inspired the firm's designers to develop several hybrid pieces of furniture for the Mayflower—all of them sensible, each of them clumsily named. The "chesk" combined the drawer space of a chest of drawers with the broad work surface of a desk that concealed a pop-up dressing-table mirror. (A similar piece of furniture was called a "dresk.") The innovation that caught the average public's attention and launched a flood of imitations high and low, however, was the "bed couch," a damask-covered banquette whose back folded down, converting it into a presumably comfortable bed. And coming to the rescue of guests who might be confused by multiple corridors and endless ranks of anonymous doors—a hotel hazard then as now—Draper color-coded the entrances of the rooms with doors painted red, green, or black.

The decor of the guest rooms (figs. 20, 21) was surprisingly calm given the Draper office's cabbage-rose-and-puff-pastry reputation. As the *Decorative Furnisher* carefully explained of the Draper floor's rooms, one of every four walls, sometimes two, was painted gunmetal gray, deep green, pale blue, or white. (Draper claimed the chromatic variety of the walls would help "harmonize with the fluctuating moods of the average occupant.") Ceilings were blue or pink. Gingham checks were deployed on tailored armchairs, and some headboards were dramatically double-humped like a Bactrian camel, then upholstered in tone-on-tone satin woven with zigzag stripes. The "one-bedparlor" rooms—studios designed to "serve the busy industrialists who throng the Mayflower"[61]—had a white painted coffee table with African-style serrated legs (fig. 22), most

likely adapted from a varnished-oak model created in the 1920s by the French designer Jean-Michel Frank (1895–1941) and widely used in the fabled seaside villa of millionaire Georges Sebastian in Hammamet, Tunisia. The Draper firm's decision to decorate the bedrooms with giant framed images of single pansy blossoms (see fig. 20), their Pop Art qualities anticipating the flowers executed decades later by the artist Andy Warhol (1930–1987), was deemed highly unusual, too, observed the *Decorative Furnisher*—"quite unlike the conventional subjects generally found in most hotel rooms."[62]

The Mayflower spaces were tasteful, youthful, and modern in a way that was hinted at in the quiet elegance of the guest rooms of the Arrowhead Springs. In fact, the only real note of typical Draper melodrama was the oversize fittings of most of the Mayflower's storage furniture. From dresks to chesks to the otherwise conventional bedside and lamp tables, nearly all had diagonal drawer handles shaped like larger-than-life-size oak leaves, often brightly gilded.

More illustrative of Draper's preferred taste, and the sort of creativity that American travelers expected of a Draperized hotel, was the 1943–1945 renovation of San Francisco's Fairmont Hotel (1906). Seriously damaged in the earthquake of 1906 and entirely restored by the architect Julia Morgan (1872–1957), the first woman graduate of the École des Beaux-Arts,[63] the hotel remains a prize of Nob Hill, standing near the equally venerable Mark Hopkins Hotel (1926), whose lobby Draper would also decorate (figs. 23, 24).

fig. 24
Lobby, Mark Hopkins Hotel, San Francisco, c. 1945. Courtesy of Dorothy Draper & Co., New York.

In the manner of so many hotel projects associated with Draper, the Fairmont was a dingy landmark that had lost much of its allure through stopgap renovations made by a series of owners. The Swig real-estate family from Boston purchased the hotel at the end of the Second World War and soon informed Draper that her renovation had to fulfill a greater purpose than the merely aesthetic. The hotel was to host the 1945 inaugural meeting of the United Nations, and she would be paid $20,000 to meet the deadline. Intrigued by San Francisco's gold rush past, Draper returned to the Victorian age for inspiration, but this time she chose to execute her updated Diamond Jim Brady imagery in moody colors like ebony and garnet red jolted by accents of geranium pink. Her associate Ted Stewart took care of the details: plump fringed chairs, gilded architectural details, substantial coats of shining black paint, wall-to-wall carpeting woven with a pattern of massive flowers (fig. 25).[64] He also wrapped the lobby's towering columns and pilasters with marble-pattern wallpaper similar to that used in the Arrowhead Springs Hotel. The interiors were a sensation, alternately admired and reviled, for more than fifty years.

After the Fairmont's completion, Draper embarked on her most famous renovation project: the Greenbrier, a monumental resort hotel in the Allegheny Mountains near White Sulphur Springs, West Virginia.

**fig. 25
Lobby, Fairmont
San Francisco, 1945.
Courtesy of Dorothy
Draper & Co., New York.**

A favorite destination of the East Coast and Southern grandees since the original inn opened on the site in 1780—Draper's family were frequent visitors—the hotel and its 6,500 surrounding acres became the property of the Chesapeake and Ohio Railway in 1910. The railroad rebuilt and greatly enlarged the resort in 1929–1930, hiring Small, Smith, Reed, and Draz, an otherwise undistinguished architecture firm in Cleveland.[65] During the Second World War, the Greenbrier, also known as the Old White, was purchased by the U.S. government, like many of the nation's grand hotels, and turned into a two-thousand-bed military hospital "crammed with wounded American boys who have been brought home from North Africa, Sicily, Italy, and elsewhere." (It also briefly held Axis diplomats awaiting deportation.) Examining the wear and tear in 1946, after the hotel was sold back to the railroad by the War Assets Administration, Chesapeake and Ohio chairman Robert R. Young contracted Draper to develop and execute a complete makeover of the multibuilding investment.[66]

The columned hotel's condition was considered dire, "Tara in extremis."[67] The designer's solution to the problem was to underscore, as many times as possible, the Greenbrier's antebellum heritage with a scheme she referred to as "Romance and Rhododendrons," but which might just as easily be called "Scarlett O'Hara Drops Acid." A surprisingly vibrant

**fig. 26
(opposite page)
Lobby, The Greenbrier,
White Sulphur Springs,
West Virginia, 1948.
Courtesy of Dorothy
Draper & Co., New York.**

**fig. 27
(above)
Trellis Lobby, The
Greenbrier, White
Sulphur Springs, West
Virginia,
1948. Courtesy of
Dorothy Draper & Co.,
New York.**

palette was selected for the interiors (figs. 26–28), dominated by felt-green walls, scarlet carpets, flower-splashed chintz fabrics, movable pale blue lattice dividers, clear plastic furniture pulls filled with artificial blossoms, and Syracuse earthenware dishes emblazoned with underglaze transfers of pink rhododendrons. Furniture ranged from spiky Gothic Revival headboards to a white-and-gold center table that recalled William Kent's furniture for the Double Cube Room at Wilton House (c. 1540s, remodeled from 1635, enlarged and altered 1801–1816), seat of the earls of Pembroke and Montgomery. The Cinquinis of Brooklyn produced a dazzling array of three-dimensional molded plasterwork, more stylistically restrained than their work at Hampshire House, but no less heroic. The chimneypiece of a columned reception area, for example, was surmounted by a massive American eagle, its wings spread, its claws clutching plaster swags (fig. 27).

Draper also redecorated the local C & O train station for good measure, in anticipation of a $65,000 opening-weekend party scheduled for three hundred international swells, including Bing Crosby, the Duke and Duchess of Windsor, and John F. Kennedy's sister Kathleen, the Marchioness of Hartington. The event, 15–19 April 1946, was so lavish

fig. 28
Guest room, The
Greenbrier, White Sulphur
Springs, West Virginia,
1948. Courtesy of
Dorothy Draper & Co.,
New York.

that it captivated Hearst newspapers' gossip columnist Cholly Knickerbocker (Igor Cassini) enough to write: "We doubt that even the Sultan of Turkey, the Emperor of China, or the Czar of Russia, when those fabulous courts were at their peak, ever attempted anything on a more colossal scale."[68]

The Greenbrier's $4.2 million refurbishment, for which Draper was paid a reported $120,000, appeared in a wide range of publications, from *Life* to *House Beautiful*, which put on its cover a corner of an "elegantly domestic" writing room decked with leaf-green walls, brilliant white wainscot, multicolored chintz curtains and upholstery, and modern pedestal side tables finished in glossy white paint. The magazine praised Draper's "pairing off of antiques with contemporary tables and upholstered comfort," asserting that "in such charming rooms, sociability flourishes." So, too, did revenue. As *Life* reported, Dorothy Draper had done it again: the Greenbrier was booked solid, "well into 1949."[69]

In combining American traditionalism with European surrealism, a hotel styled by Dorothy Draper acted as an unconscious conduit of contemporary world culture for the average traveler, serving up edgy artistic movements with twenty-four-hour room service. Unlike the stylishly banal hotel interiors that would come to dominate the hotel industry in the 1960s, like those of Conrad Nicholson Hilton (1887–1979), a Draperized hotel took travelers out of their humdrum daily lives and, like the cyclone that brought Dorothy Gale from the plains of Kansas to the Technicolor world of Munchkinland, abruptly inserted them into a special universe that existed only behind a revolving door. The hyper-scale environments transformed every patron into a virtual film star, an experience that neatly intersected with the American public's fascination with Hollywood and the possibility of reinventing one's identity. And by proving that a woman, even without academic training, could decorate a commercial enterprise in a way that encouraged profits, Draper pioneered the then-revolutionary notion that interior decoration—a field that had been long dismissed as a largely domestic endeavor—could be as productive as any advertising campaign at manipulating public opinion.◆

Acknowledgments

I would like to thank Nellie Xinos and Carleton Varney of Dorothy Draper and Company for their help with this article.

Notes

1. Carleton Varney, *The Draper Touch: The High Life and High Style of Dorothy Draper* (New York: Prentice Hall, 1988), 131.

2. Wisner joined Dorothy Draper Inc. in 1941 after working as the art director for the carriage-trade department store W. and J. Sloane in New York. In 1949 he launched the industrial design firm McNab and Wisner with Allan McNab, a British-born artist and illustrator who had worked as design director for the designer Norman Bel Geddes (1893–1958) and as an art director for *Life*.

3. Varney, *The Draper Touch*, 117.

4. "Dorothy Draper, 79, Designer and Interior Decorator, Dies" *New York Times* (12 March 1969): 47.

5. A visiting reporter once described it as "an Errol Flynn movie set" that "looms over an artificial lagoon constructed in the shape of Brazil." James Brooke, "Rio de Janeiro," *New York Times* (17 May 1992): SMA6.

6. Frances Drewry McMullen, "Mrs. Draper, Home Stylist," *Woman's Journal* (March 1930): 17.

7. "Re-Styled Buildings: Dorothy Draper Shows New York Realty Owners How to Rescue Their Properties through Applications Consisting Mainly of Brains and Paint," *Business Week* (5 September 1936): 34–35.

8. Evelyn Roe, "Giving 'Style' to Real Estate," *Christian Science Monitor* (25 August 1937): 6.

9. "New Incorporations: New York Charters," *New York Times* (28 March 1925): 24.

10. The mongrel style of this custom-made furniture has been accurately described as "neo-Victorian-American-Queen Anne." Varney, *The Draper Touch*, 186.

11. Varney, *The Draper Touch*, 264.

12. Suzanne Bohan, "S. F. Hotel Regains Lustrous Past," *Sacramento Bee*, 8 January 2000, www.page-turnbull.com; Mary Scoviak Lerner, "Rewriting History," *Hotels Magazine*, November 2001, www.hotelsmag.com; Zahid Sardar, "FairMontage," *San Francisco Examiner*, 2 April 2000, www.gensler.com; Anne Chalfant, "Fairmont Restores Its Beauty and Elegance," *Bay Area Times*, 26 November 2000, www.bayarea.com.

13. "Arrowhead Springs Hotel," *California Arts & Architecture* (March 1940): 18–21. Though a 25 March 1951 article in the *New York Times* stated that the hotel was being entirely redecorated by Joseph Huston, who was responsible for the Starlight Room of the Waldorf-Astoria, Carlton Varney recently said that Draper's 1939 work remains remarkably intact and that the firm has agreed to refurbish it for new owners.

14. Varney, *The Draper Touch*, 259.

15. McMullen, "Mrs. Draper, Home Stylist," 17.

16. Ibid., 16–17.

17. "A Sutton Place 'Co-op': Point of View of 'the Lady of the House' Being Considered," *New York Times* (18 October 1925): RE19.

18. "Home Buying and Building Active in Suburban Area," *New York Times* (16 December 1928): RE1.

19. McMullen, "Mrs. Draper, Home Stylist," 44.

20. "[I] had no schooling to speak of, except that I was brought up where I had the privilege of being constantly in touch with surroundings of pleasant good taste." Draper, quoted in "Draper, Dorothy (Tuckerman)," *Current Biography 1941*, 237–38.

21. "'Modernism' Rejected in New Apartment; Air of London Town House Is Planned," *New York Times* (13 May 1937): 47. Draper and Caughey would work together again in 1951, when she decorated the lobby and entrance hall of Riverside South, an apartment building on East Eighty-eighth Street in New York. Caughey was its associate architect.

22. "Re-Styled Buildings," 34.

23. Meyer Berger, "About New York," *New York Times* (24 February 1958): 16.

24. Roe, "Giving 'Style' to Real Estate," 6.

25. Ibid.

26. McMullen, "Mrs. Draper, Home Stylist," 44.

27. *New York Times* (1 November 1930): 25.

28. *New York Times* (21 March 1930): 30.

29. "$2,655,000 Is Bid for Hotel Carlyle," *New York Times* (10 May 1932): 39.

30. "The Ambassador Hotel," *American Architect* (June 1921): 644.

31. "Dorothy Draper," *New York Times* (12 March 1969): 47.

32. Later known as the decorator Blanche Falls Storrs.

33. Stephen Calloway, *Twentieth-Century Decoration* (New York: Rizzoli, 1988), 143.

34. Walter Rendell Storey, "Victorian Touches for Modern Homes: The Revival of Interest in the Last Century Makes an Impress on Decorations," *New York Times* (5 April 1931): 80.

35. Dorothy Draper (ghostwriter Betty Thornley), *Decorating Is Fun! How to Be Your Own Decorator* (New York: Doubleday, 1939), 236–40.

36. For a period advertisement, see http://zenitherm.ftldesign.com.

37. Varney, *The Draper Touch*, 116–17.

38. Sacheverell Sitwell, *Southern Baroque Art* (New York: Knopf, 1924); Sitwell and Anthony Ayscough, *German Baroque Sculpture* (London: Duckworth, 1927).

39. Calloway, *Twentieth-Century Decoration*, 12.

40. "Fine Arts Graduation: Students at New York School Will Receive Diplomas Today," *New York Times* (22 May 1936): 21; Edward Alden Jewell, "The Dance in Art Theme of Exhibit," *New York Times* (15 December 1933): 21.

41. "New Coty Salon Has Arabian Nights Splendor," *Decorative Furnisher* (August 1941): 10–13.

42. Varney, *The Draper Touch*, 117.

43. Christopher Gray, "A Case of 'Frenzied Financing,'" *New York Times* (20 May 1990): R12.

44. Roe, "Giving 'Style' to Real Estate," 6.

45. Varney, *The Draper Touch*, 116.

46. "'Modernism' Rejected in New Apartment," 4.

47. *New York Times* (5 December 1937): 96.

48. Eleanor Roosevelt, "My Day," syndicated newspaper column, 28 October 1940.

49. Roe, "Giving 'Style' to Real Estate," 6.

50. The orange trees were illuminated from inside their boughs, allowing them to be used as effective mood lighting. In *Interior Design in the 20th Century* (New York: Harper & Row, 1987), C. Ray Smith called the cottage "one of the most popular rooms in New York for deb parties."

51. Bruno Foucart and Jean-Louis Gaillemin, *Les décorateurs des années 40* (Paris: Éditions Norma, 1998).

52. Draper, *Decorating Is Fun!* 29.

53. "Forest Fires Invade Coast Movie Colonies; Hundreds of Houses Lost Near Santa Monica," *New York Times* (24 November 1938): 1.

54. "Gordon B. Kaufmann," *New York Times* (2 March 1949): 26; Karen Hudson, *Paul R. Williams, Architect: A Legacy of Style* (New York: Rizzoli, 1993), 27.

55. Never a financial success, the Arrowhead Springs became U.S. Public Health Service Hospital No. 54, a naval hospital, during the Second World War, and later a Hilton hotel. It is presently unoccupied though scheduled for renovation by Draper's firm.

56. "Arrowhead Springs Hotel," *California Arts & Architecture* (March 1940): 18–21; "Arrowhead Springs Hotel, San Bernardino," *Architect and Engineer* (June 1940): 20 ff.; "Vivacity in Hotel Decoration," *Decorative Furnisher* (April 1940): 16–20, quotation on 16.

57. Varney, *The Draper Touch*, 137.

58. Ibid., 139.

59. "Dorothy Draper Takes Another Bow," *Decorative Furnisher* (December 1941): 8–11, quotation on 9.

60. Varney, *The Draper Touch*, 127.

61. "Draper Takes Another Bow," 11.

62. Ibid.

63. Morgan would achieve even wider fame by becoming the personal architect of publisher William Randolph Hearst and designer of La Cuesta Encantada (Hearst Castle), his sprawling Hispano-Moorish estate near San Simeon, California.

64. The Fairmont's Wild West lobby decor, much of which survived until 1999, was the silent costar of the 1983–1988 television series *Hotel*.

65. "George C. Smith, 78; Railroad Architect," *New York Times* (18 October 1966): 40.

66. "Government Gets Greenbrier," *New York Times* (30 September 1942): 25; "Greenbrier Hospital Now Army Hospital," *New York Times* (17 October 1943): 12; F. G. Alletson Cook, "Nazi Prisoners Are Nazis Still," *New York Times* (21 November 1943): SM12; "$3,300,000 for Greenbrier: Government Buys White Sulphur Springs Hotel for a Hospital," *New York Times* (29 December 1942): 11; "WAA Sells the Greenbrier Hotel," New York Times (31 December 1946): 20.

67. Varney, *The Draper Touch*, 2.

68. "Business & Finance: Hotels—Housewarming," *Time* 51 (26 April 1948): 85–86.

69. "*Life* Goes to the Big Weekend at White Sulphur," *Life* (10 May 1948): 153–56; Laura Tanner, "Travel to Improve Your Decorating," *House Beautiful* (August 1948): 56–59.

Bernard L. Jim

"Wrecking the Joint": The Razing of City Hotels in the First Half of the Twentieth Century

Bernard L. Jim is a Ph.D. candidate in the history of science, technology, environment, and medicine program at Case Western Reserve University, Cleveland. He is currently finishing his doctoral dissertation, *Ephemeral Containers: A History of Building Demolition*, in which he examines the implications of demolition as a spectacle that masks the social and economic inequities perpetuated by urban renewal while impeding the preservation of the built environment.

The 1942 motion picture *Wrecking Crew* opens with a crowbar-wielding wrecker prying the nameplate from the Great Western Hotel (fig. 1). "Where do you think you're going, Bud?" the wrecker asks a traveling salesman about to enter the hotel. "Why, I've been stopping at the Great Western every trip for the past twenty-eight years," the flustered salesman replies. "Not this trip, Bud," the wrecker explains. "We're wrecking the joint."

Sliding his crowbar behind the Great Western's nameplate, the wrecker drops it to the pavement. Leaning at an angle against the hotel, the nameplate suddenly looks like a tombstone in a country graveyard. Above the fallen nameplate, the year 1902, the hotel's "birthday," is chiseled in the building's stone. Later, the wrecking crew's supervisor describes the Great Western Hotel as "twelve stories of rotten timbers and forty-year-old cement." But this is not a bad lifespan for a hotel, or any building for that matter, in the twentieth century.

The fictional Great Western Hotel, demolished after forty years, was only somewhat older than one of the most famous hotels to be demolished in the first half of the twentieth century. New York City's Waldorf-Astoria Hotel (1891–1893, 1895–1897, demolished 1929), designed by Henry Janeway Hardenbergh, fell thirty-two years after its 1897 completion. The Great Western was only slightly younger than one of Cleveland's most beloved hotels, the Weddell House (architect unknown; built 1845–1847, demolished 1903). The demolition announcements for these two hotels provoked responses that far surpassed the salesman's disbelief. Their current residents and former guests, as well as the local citizenry, had come to see them as more than mere lodgings. What developers viewed as obstacles to progress, New Yorkers and Clevelanders viewed as nearly sacred icons, constructed of personal and collective memories.

fig. 1
Wrecking Crew,
promotional poster,
1942. Courtesy of
Paramount Pictures.

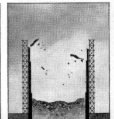

1 After clearing the basement, wreckers work upward from floor to floor, tearing out walls and partitions as they go

2 Debris thrown down from the upper floors accumulates in the basement, the shell of the building serving as a chute

3 After the framework is removed, scaffolding is built outside the walls and they are demolished from the top down

4 When the walls are down to the second story, a power shovel attacks them and scoops up the accumulated debris

The Blowing up of the Ruins of the Phelan Building after the fire of April 18th to 20th 1906. San Francisco, Cal.

Although the population of each city objected to the demolition of structures that they believed played central roles in their cities' identities, they seemed to have little power to prevent their destruction. The Historic American Buildings Survey was not established until 1933, three years after the Waldorf's demolition, and the National Trust for Historic Preservation did not receive its charter from Congress until 1949. New York City's own Landmarks Preservation Commission did not come into existence until 1965, after the demolition of another iconic structure, Pennsylvania Station.

In fact, the New Yorkers who loved the Waldorf-Astoria and the Clevelanders who loved the Weddell House, as well as the developers who demolished them, recognized that destroying a public institution such as a city hotel was not a simple financial transaction. Developers attempted to engineer responses to the two demolitions, but the public proved difficult to manipulate. The widely publicized reaction to the Waldorf-Astoria's 1929 demolition led Clevelanders to resurrect and reconstruct the narrative of their own loss twenty-six years before, an event that had continued to rankle over time. The manner in which residents of the two cities chose to remember their hotels demonstrates the complex and often contentious relationship between the economic elite and the populace of America's

fig. 4
(below, left)
*Razing 'Old' Newport
Stack, Ironwood, Mich.*
From a postcard, c. 1938.
Author's collection.

fig. 5
(below, right)
Watch it Go! The Cleveland
Wrecking Company
demolishing the Walnut
Street Theater, Cincinnati,
1 August 1928. Courtesy of
the National Association of
Demolition Contractors.

cities in the first half of the twentieth century and reminds us of the integral role that culture plays in architectural and urban history.

Demolition Narratives and the Culture of Creative Destruction

Even though few institutional resources were available before the 1930s to prevent an unwanted demolition, powerful cultural currents influenced the way people understood the meaning of "wrecking the joint." Films like *Wrecking Crew* made images of demolition central to the ongoing debate surrounding the relationship between creativity and destruction in the first half of the twentieth century. While the champions of modernity claimed that destroying the old was necessary to make way for the new, other voices argued that sometimes destruction is just that: destructive, not creative. These competing narratives of demolition appeared in professional journals, popular magazines, newspapers, children's literature, the visual arts, and the daily experiences of people living in America's cities. Together these narratives helped shape the way people reacted to the demolition announcements for the Waldorf-Astoria Hotel and the Weddell House.

Using photographs, illustrations, and industry jargon, boosters produced material that instructed the American public how to see, think, and talk about building demolition (fig. 2). A postcard issued after the 1906 San Francisco earthquake and fire, for example, depicted the explosive demolition of a ruined building (fig. 3). The postcard celebrated the controlled destruction wrought by demolition in contrast to the chaos caused by the natural disaster. This second wave of destruction was fabricated, not born of earthquake and fire, and would initiate the rebuilding of the city. In the 1930s a Michigan postcard captured a smokestack undergoing demolition

fig. 6
(above, left)
Great Northern Building
and Hotel, Chicago,
c. 1895. Library of
Congress, Prints and
Photographs Division,
Detroit Publishing
Company Collection.
LC-D4-12550.

fig. 7
(above, right)
The Great Northern Hotel
undergoing demolition,
detail from "Wrecking
A Chicago Landmark,"
Engineering News-Record
(9 May 1940): 76.

in mid-collapse (fig. 4). Here, demolition appeared as spectacle, dangerous and powerful, but safe to watch from a distance. When demolishing Cincinnati's Walnut Street Theatre in 1928, the Cleveland Wrecking Company posted large signs on the doomed building that invited passersby to be spectators to the destruction and "Watch It Go!" (fig. 5).

During this period professional journals for engineers and architects shared the Cleveland Wrecking Company's enthusiasm. In their pages they documented the benefits of demolition. Demolishing hotels, wreckers argued, exposed the materials and techniques employed in the construction of America's first skyscrapers. Chicago's Burnham and Root–designed Great Northern Hotel (1890–1892, demolished 1940) provided one such example (figs. 6, 7). Boosterism extended beyond professional periodicals (fig. 8), however, and it was not uncommon to find articles celebrating the demolition industry in popular magazines as diverse as *Popular Science, Saturday Evening Post, Reader's Digest, Family Circle,* and *Literary Digest.* The cumulative effect was to present demolition as an aggressive, irresistible force that could realize, through brute strength and technological mastery, the ideology of creative destruction.

Early producers of motion pictures also mined such images for more nuanced meanings. The American Mutoscope and Biograph Company produced several demolition films in the first decade of the twentieth century and often employed trick editing to produce startling images.

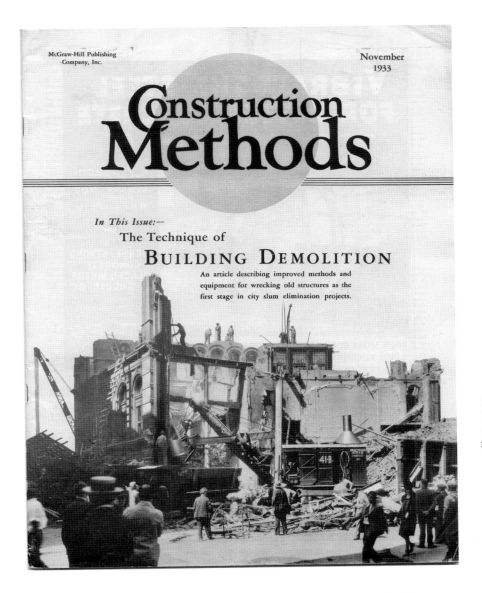

McGraw-Hill Publishing
Company, Inc.

November
1933

Construction Methods

In This Issue:—

The Technique of

BUILDING DEMOLITION

An article describing improved methods and
equipment for wrecking old structures as the
first stage in city slum elimination projects.

Perhaps the most fascinating of these films was *Demolition of the Star
Theatre*. Biograph shot from a single camera position over a period of
thirty days. Using time-lapse photography, the filmmakers compressed
the time required to demolish the structure from thirty days to one and
a half minutes. The accelerated version captured the experience of living
in a city where rapid changes to the built environment challenged turn-
of-the-century Americans to keep pace.

Biograph shrewdly selected a theater as a subject for its demolition film.
Unlike office buildings or factories—places of work where people went
out of necessity—theaters, arenas, and hotels were leisure spaces, places
where people went by choice. While corporations encouraged individualism
and discouraged group activity in the workplace, theaters and arenas were
acceptable places for people to act in unison. As a result, people developed

fig. 9
Waldorf-Astoria Hotel
undergoing demolition,
17 October 1929. Courtesy
of Avery Architectural
and Fine Arts Library,
Columbia University,
New York. The Starrett
Brothers shot more than
one hundred photographs
of the Waldorf-Astoria
from four vantage points
(including this one from
the northeast) over the
course of the nine-month
demolition.

a much deeper connection with these kinds of structures. Because the
public formed collective memories at arenas and theaters—the shared
experience of watching a boxing match, taking one's children to the circus,
or seeing a famous star perform on stage—the demolition of one of these
buildings threatened to sever the bond that existed between the audience
members and the site. The accelerated action of the Star Theatre being
torn down invokes a melancholy tone—images of shadows and fog move
across the site—and remind its admirers that they had little say in the
preservation of a space that had been important in their lives.

The public had similar responses to the demolition of hotels. Like theaters
and arenas, hotels often had distinctive architectural designs, and they
hosted some of the most culturally significant events in their cities. Hotels
played a larger role than any other structure in representing a city to its
visitors. As spaces in which people lived and worked—if temporarily—and
experienced special social activities such as parties and public dinners,

hotels generated personal and collective memories. To demolish a hotel was to risk inviting public furor. Because the possibility of creating enmity was higher than in the demolition of an office building, the demolition of a hotel frequently revealed changing attitudes toward the built environment or tectonic shifts in economic and political power. The demolition announcements for the Waldorf-Astoria and the Weddell House brought these issues to the surface in New York on the eve of the stock market crash and in Cleveland at the beginning of the twentieth century.

When these two buildings faced demolition, each had acquired an undeniable aura that would affect what occurred at the time of their destruction and how they would be remembered. In the case of the Waldorf-Astoria, the developers acknowledged the unique character of the structure and attempted to redirect public sentiment toward the Empire State Building, which would replace it on its site. In Cleveland, the Weddell's owner, Standard Oil magnate John D. Rockefeller (1839–1937), did not share his fellow Clevelanders' attachment to the hotel. Ironically, Rockefeller's disregard for the Weddell helped establish its historical significance and deepened the ambivalence with which he was held in his hometown, especially as he replaced the hotel with a building bearing his name. The Weddell's demolition inspired cities like Cleveland to reexamine their architectural heritage and heightened the significance of narratives that linked citizens to historic buildings. Taking advantage of the federal resources provided in the 1930s, Clevelanders tried to recover the lost history of the Weddell House. The Historic American Buildings Survey, for example, conducted a survey of the Weddell in its inaugural year. Today the Empire State Building has become a more potent icon than the Waldorf-Astoria had ever been, and the Rockefeller Building (1903–1905), designed by Knox and Elliott, has been standing forty years longer than the Weddell House. On the eve of their demolition, however, New Yorkers and Clevelanders pondered the icons they were about to lose, not the ones they were about to gain.

Razing the Waldorf-Astoria: The Cultural Biography of an Iconic Structure

Because architectural historians have included discussions about site preparations in their histories of the Empire State Building, we know many details of the Waldorf-Astoria's demolition (fig. 9).[1] The Starrett Brothers, who managed the construction project, devoted eight pages of a seventy-seven-page notebook to the demolition.[2] Writers who have chronicled the hotel's history also have contributed to our knowledge of its final days.[3] Although these works provide a factual record, they rarely explore the meaning of the event.

By the time of its demolition, the Waldorf-Astoria Hotel had achieved iconic status (fig. 10). The Empire State Building would become an icon, too, but no one knew that during the summer of 1929. In the nineteenth

fig. 10
Waldorf-Astoria Hotel,
New York, c. 1904. Library
of Congress, Prints and
Photographs Division,
Detroit Publishing
Company Collection.
LC-D4-17418. The
building to the right is
the Knickerbocker Trust.

century, the Astor name, like Rockefeller and Carnegie, was synonymous
with wealth. By the twentieth century, visitors from around the world
had made the Waldorf-Astoria nearly synonymous with New York City.
The hotel lent its name to everything it touched: Oscar of the Waldorf,
the Waldorf Crowd, the Waldorf salad, and a number of pre-Prohibition
cocktails. As architectural historian John Tauranac has pointed out,
Waldorf-Astoria was the original name planned for the office building
that would replace the hotel.[4] Hearing the news of the impending demolition, Tauranac tells us, the firm of Thompson-Starrett offered to help
finance the construction of a new hotel, at a new location, under the
Waldorf-Astoria banner.[5]

To New Yorkers, the hotel's current residents, and its former guests from
around the world, the Waldorf-Astoria was not something that could
be bought, sold, or torn down. Neither naïveté about economic realities

nor syrupy sentimentalism could account for the public's reaction to the demolition. Over time, the building had undergone a process of singularization. Described by anthropologist Igor Kopytoff in the essay collection *The Social Life of Things*, singularization and commoditization are two polar forces that act upon a commodity. While singularization works to remove a thing from the commodity sphere, protecting it from being exchanged or put up for sale, commoditization works toward the opposite, "making it [a thing] exchangeable for more and more other things." Culture and individual tastes act as arbiters, preventing either excessive commoditization or excessive singularization. The push and pull of these two forces occurs within the life of any discrete thing and comprises what Kopytoff refers to as a thing's "cultural biography."[6] The Waldorf-Astoria's demolition was the concluding chapter in the hotel's cultural biography.

Kopytoff argues that one of the strongest factors driving a commodity toward singularity is the length of time that it has been possessed. In the case of family heirlooms, for example, "the longevity of the relation assimilates them in some sense to the person and makes parting from them unthinkable."[7] A similar, collective response can be found in the public reaction to the Waldorf-Astoria Hotel. Over its thirty-two-year existence, the Waldorf became more and more singular. With the cumulative effect of every guest's stay, scandal and stock market coup, honeymoon, affair, and group meeting, every stroll down Peacock Alley, and every cocktail sipped in the hotel's Bull and Bear bar, the Waldorf-Astoria's clientele increasingly regarded the hotel as unique, something that should be shielded from the world of exchange. In the wake of the demolition announcement, Virginia Pope wrote in the *New York Times Magazine*, "The hotel has held a place in the lives of many people who regarded it as something more than a mere lodging."[8]

Manhattan's rising real estate values, the hotel's declining business— especially under Prohibition—and its inability to keep pace with modernization and changing standards of luxury worked against the singularity of the Waldorf-Astoria. Where the public saw an aging but beloved institution, developers saw an obstacle to the site's potential. In short, a new skyscraper could generate more revenue than the old hotel. Kopytoff writes, "Anything that can be bought for money is at that point a commodity."[9] To be a commodity, he adds, is to be "common," a direct refutation of a thing's singularity. The year before it was demolished, the Waldorf was "bought for money" twice: in 1928 by the Bethlehem Engineering Corporation for $14 million, then again in August 1929 by the Empire State Corporation for $17.5 million.[10] After years of singularization, its buyers subjected the Waldorf-Astoria to sudden and repeated commoditization.

Because real estate transfers largely exist in the realm of the abstract, sometimes only bankers notice when a hotel changes owners. Momentarily common, the hotel quickly returns to a trajectory of singularity. However, to propose demolition shatters the illusion of singularity and confirms what the sale of a building actually means. While many viewed the Waldorf-Astoria as unique and irreplaceable, its demolition announcement declared the opposite. Historic preservation, which acts as an institutional form of singularization, protects a structure from becoming a terminal commodity. In 1929 no formal obstacles existed to block the Empire State Corporation's plans to clear the site. "Today," wrote architectural historian Carol Willis in 1998, "the old Waldorf-Astoria Hotel would be protected against demolition."[11]

Even though there was no institutionalized resistance to the proposed demolition of the Waldorf-Astoria, the Empire State Building's developers, and the project's boosters, felt an obligation to justify its necessity. In their rhetoric, they tapped into long-held American ideas regarding property and more contemporary notions of waste and efficiency. Both their words and their actions revealed the anxiety that accompanied replacing one icon from the New York City skyline with what they hoped would be another. That the stock market crashed four weeks into the Waldorf-Astoria's demolition could only have aggravated concerns about the wisdom of the project. As a result, barely submerged tensions surfaced in the Empire State Building's promotional campaigns.

The narratives and images produced for the promotional material unintentionally illustrated the tensions created by the "exchange" of the highly singularized Waldorf-Astoria Hotel for the unbuilt Empire State Building. To understand fully why these tensions emerged, Kopytoff's discussion of singularization is again instructive. Singularization, he says, intensifies what Karl Marx called the fetishism of commodities. Marx argued that commodities are "mysterious things" that mask the social relations of the labor that was necessary to produce them. At the moment they are exchanged, they represent those relations to one another.[12] Although it is a difficult concept to simplify, commodity fetishism means that a thing possesses, in addition to its more transparent monetary value, a less frequently acknowledged socially and culturally determined value. While Marx identified the production stage in a commodity's life as the source of its socially determined, fetishlike power, Kopytoff asserts that "some of that power is attributed to commodities *after* they are produced, and this by way of an autonomous cognitive and cultural process of singularization" (emphasis added).[13] To see this cultural process at work, compare the accumulated sentimental value of an object with what the public is willing to pay for it at a garage sale. Cultural value, or singularity, becomes magnified in the case of a public thing such as the Waldorf-Astoria Hotel. For Marxists, hotels and other buildings already possess enormous fetishlike power

fig. 11
Empire State's
first advertisement,
detail from *Empire
State: A History*
(New York: Publicity
Associates, 1931), 29.

(Courtesy Friend-Wiener Advertising Co.)

because of the amount of labor and materials needed to construct them. When one adds the cultural value that the Waldorf-Astoria accumulated, it is clear why the Empire State Corporation felt compelled to create the impression that it was exchanging the hotel for a comparable structure.

The first advertisement for the Empire State Building project betrayed its promoters' desire to transfer the fetishlike power that the Waldorf-Astoria had acquired to the new structure (fig. 11). In the advertisement an ethereal image of the proposed Empire State Building rises out of the Waldorf-Astoria Hotel. The soon to be demolished hotel appears solid and highly detailed. By contrast, the imagined tower lacks detail and is more a column of light and shadows than a building; it exists in the realm of potential. Even more finely drawn—and therefore more real—is the first farm built on the site. In the foreground one can see where the artist sketched the siding of the farmhouse, the rails of the fence surrounding the property, and the leafy branches of the trees. According to the accompanying text, each structure built on this "famous site" has inherited and enhanced its "perpetual prestige." Just as the Thompson farm gave way to the Astor mansion, and the Astor mansion gave way to the Waldorf-Astoria Hotel, the hotel will bow to "a worthy follower."[14]

Empire State Inc. wanted to capture instantaneously the public's regard for the hotel and did not intend to wait several decades for the Empire State Building to achieve singularity. In his dedication speech for the skyscraper, the project's director, former New York Governor Alfred E. Smith (1873–1944), employed a synecdoche that echoed Marx's description of commodity fetishism. Although he was no Marxist, Smith's language revealed his understanding of what Empire State Inc. sought to accomplish. Marx had written that productive activities "are functions of the human organism, and that each such function, whatever may be its nature or form, is essentially the expenditure of human brain, nerves, muscles, &c."[15] Smith said, "Empire State could not be, without the fine individual efforts of *the thousands of arms, the hundreds of brains* that went into its planning and building" (emphasis added).[16] Developers may have failed to diminish the public's veneration of the departed Waldorf-Astoria, but they still could hope to transfer the fetishlike power of the hotel to the Empire State Building.

In addition to invoking Smith's words, promoters turned to photographer Lewis W. Hine (1874–1940) to help expedite the singularization of the Empire State Building. Hine produced images that both complemented Smith's claims and supported his own views about the dignity of humanity and the sanctity of labor. The series of photographs, which Hine later released under the title *Men at Work: Photographic Studies of Modern Men and Machines*, first appeared in the promotional brochure *Empire State: A History*, published on the opening of the Empire State Building. The title reveals the developers' desire to confer a neatly packaged history on the brand-new building. In street-level windows, Empire State Inc. displayed Hine's images, picturing Smith's "thousands of arms" in action high above New York City. He captured riveters standing on narrow beams, derrick men swinging from cables, and welders showered in sparks.[17]

Hine would often show men working at great heights with the thousand-foot-tall Chrysler Building off in the distance, emphasizing that great building's deference to the Empire State. He was one of the finest photographers of his generation, and his images had an undeniable power that contributed to the new building's growing singularity.

Wisely, the Empire State Building's developers had invited the public to participate in the Waldorf-Astoria's farewell. Again they carefully channeled popular sentiment. To purchase something at the month-long auction or to cheer as wreckers drove trucks down Peacock Alley was the appropriate, if engineered, way to say goodbye to the hotel. In their narratives the Empire State boosters demonstrated the proper nostalgia and respect for the inevitability of progress. They provided a model for how developers should handle controversial demolitions in the future, making the job of future preservationists that much more difficult. But they also underestimated the public's ability to subvert their intentions. People made their own peace with the passing of the Waldorf-Astoria and acknowledged the hotel's weakening singularity in surprising ways.

In a luncheon address delivered after the Empire State Building's opening, Al Smith outlined why the Waldorf-Astoria "had to go." A *New York Times* article reported:

> Though there was a great economic waste in the demolition of the Waldorf-Astoria Hotel to make way for the Empire State Building, Mr. Smith said, the hotel had to go because it "did not constitute an adequate improvement commensurate with the importance of the site."[18]

The greater waste would have been for the site not to generate as much money as it was capable of producing. As the environmental historian Ted Steinberg has shown, arguments for "greatest economic prosperity" can be found in the earliest days of American industrialization when mill owners who harnessed waterpower trumped local landowners' concerns over upstream flooding and the rerouting of waterways.[19] In these arguments the terms "economic growth" and "progress" become interchangeable. To be against the option that will make more money places one in the unpopular and irrational position of being against progress.

The argument that the Waldorf-Astoria was guilty of economic waste had more subtle facets as well. Empire State boosters characterized the Waldorf-Astoria as the "social center of New York." The Empire State Building would transform the site into the "business center of New York."[20] "Social" here connoted luxurious spaces, frivolous spending, and leisure time. "Business," by contrast, suggested small offices, serious dealings, and productive use of time. Worse yet, the structure of the Waldorf-Astoria represented its fin-de-siècle excesses. One reason given for the hotel's inability to remain solvent was "too much spaciousness."[21] Wide halls, large dining rooms, and high ceilings meant that the building did not make economically efficient use of its site. How many offices could have been leased in the square footage of Peacock Alley alone? The January 1929 edition of the *Literary Digest* quoted one newspaper writer who believed that the hotel represented "a whole theory of life that pointed to wastefulness."[22] And this was nine months before the stock market crashed!

As wasteful as Empire State Inc. painted the Waldorf-Astoria to be, its first buyers, Bethlehem Engineering Corporation, shared the eventual owner's ideology of efficiency and tried to squeeze every penny out of the hotel before its demolition. When Cleveland's Weddell House was torn down, the Chicago House Wrecking Company purchased its furnishings and salvageable building materials.[23] The company already maintained a large warehouse, published a mail-order catalog of several hundred pages, and built its inventory primarily by demolishing the many fairs and expositions held around the turn of the century. Items that the company obtained through demolition, however, such as those from the Weddell House, were anonymous entries in its catalog. The company advertised every imaginable building supply and fixture without reference to a specific source. Customers purchased types of lumber, but not "Weddell House lumber."

Developers had different plans for the fixtures and furnishings of the Waldorf-Astoria. Bethlehem Engineering decided to hold a public auction inside the shuttered hotel. If their intentions were to exploit the public's love of the hotel, they must have been disappointed when its singularity did not transfer to its constituent parts. The public loved the Waldorf-Astoria, but not at the price that the developers were asking. This became clear as the month-long public auction failed to generate the expected volume of sales. On 1 May 1929, the day that Benjamin Wise of the Wise Auction Company offered the first item for sale—a mahogany dresser with a glass top that went for seventy-seven dollars—the announced value of the total furnishings was $2.5 million.[24] Wise produced an auction catalog and donated a copy to the New York Public Library. The catalog has three sections devoted to furnishings and restaurant equipment, and "the world famous Waldorf collection of art." In addition to outlining the terms of sale, the library's copy of the catalog includes the penciled-in purchase price for each item. A blue upholstered armchair, item number four, went for $22 (the equivalent of $244 in 2004 dollars). Item number 12530, a "Carrara marble life-size figure, 'Diana of the Chase,' signed Benzoni, Roma, 1872" sold for $300 (equaling $3,325 in 2004).[25] By 19 May, during a radio broadcast of the auction in progress, Wise declared that sales had "exceeded expectations" and projected that the total sales "will reach approximately $1,000,000." That number was in fact 60 percent lower than the original appraised value.[26] When the auction closed on 3 June, the actual sales figure dropped to $625,000, or nearly 80 percent below expected returns.[27] Though this public auction was the biggest of its kind to date, it is unfair to measure its success solely on receipts. Its most important function was to provide a socially approved way of saying goodbye to the Waldorf-Astoria. Instead of futilely protesting the "laws of progress" that "demanded" the hotel's demolition, the Empire State Building boosters contended that the public should surrender to nostalgia and purchase a bureau, rug, or mirror.

Rather than participating in the Waldorf-Astoria's auction, people chose their own ways of dealing with the passing of the historic hotel. In the weeks leading up to its closing, guests stole more towels than usual, for example. People made reservations for the hotel's final night. Longtime hotel residents refused to move out until the last possible moment.

New Yorkers who never could have afforded a night's stay walked through the hotel after its closing. Former guests wanted items insignificant to everyone but themselves. One man asked for a brick from the barroom wall to use as a paperweight.[28] An older woman bearing a photograph of herself in her youth that showed her standing beside one of the dining hall's "gilt chairs" wanted one for her home.[29] In another instance, "a man … obtained permission to go to rooms 953 and 954, where he knelt on the floor and offered a prayer for the soul of his mother, who had died in the suite twenty-four years ago."[30] In their construction notebook, the Starrett Brothers recorded the degree of sentiment that the Waldorf-Astoria had inspired. The public auction had not satisfied people who wanted to remember the hotel. As demolition proceeded, the Starretts wrote:

> More than a thousand written requests were received from practically every State in the Union and a few requests from abroad for souvenirs of the hotel before the work of demolition was completed.[31]

Even after its demolition, the Waldorf-Astoria Hotel continued to exist in its relics.

Razing the Weddell House: Power and Naming in the Built Environment

Today, Cleveland's Western Reserve Historical Society holds the relics of the Weddell House in its collection. Among the objects are the three-foot-high letters that spelled the establishment's name, which hung from the hotel's facade when it opened in 1847. In 1903, when John D. Rockefeller demolished two-thirds of the hotel, including its original entrance on the corner of Superior Avenue and Bank Street, the letters moved up the street to the small section of the hotel that remained. Dwarfed by the sixteen-story Rockefeller Building for the next half a century, the last of the hotel was demolished in 1963 to allow for that building's parking lot. The Weddell House's presence was reduced to a brass plaque affixed to the Rockefeller Building's cornerstone.

Clevelanders continued to hold the original Weddell House in high regard, despite its diminishing grandeur over the decades. The highly publicized demolition of the Waldorf-Astoria and the accompanying public heartache caused Americans to reflect on the passing of luxury hotels in their cities. Especially during the years of the Great Depression, Clevelanders looked back fondly on the Weddell. Writing for the *Cleveland Plain Dealer Magazine* in 1931, Ella Grant Wilson recalled "the Glories of the Weddell House": "The famous Weddell House of which Cleveland was so proud in the early days … was considered one of the finest in the middle west."[32] Wilson quoted the nineteenth-century editor and politician Thurlow Weed, who had written: "Among the striking features of the city is the Weddell House, one of the most magnificent hotels in America. The building looms up like the Astor House and is furnished with every attainable luxury."[33] Later in the decade, Cleveland artist Paul Kucharyson, under the auspices of the Works Progress Administration, painted a watercolor of the original hotel (fig. 12). Based on a black-and-white photograph from the turn of the century, Kucharyson's vision of the long-gone Weddell was an idyllic view. He transformed the smoky Cleveland skies of the photograph into rich shades of blue and the hotel's drab exterior into bright yellow. Reminiscent of days gone by, a horse and buggy waits at the unpaved intersection of Superior Avenue and Sixth Street. In an act of historical reversal, Kucharyson placed the Weddell's demolished columned balcony (the hotel's design trademark) in the center of the canvas, but he did not include the portion of the building still standing on Sixth Street. What Rockefeller had demolished, Kucharyson reclaimed, and what Rockefeller saw fit to retain, Kucharyson ignored.

The most extensive reclamation of the Weddell House also came under the umbrella of the federally funded WPA. For *Historic Sites of Cleveland: Hotels and Taverns*, published in 1942—nearly forty years after the main hotel's demolition—the authors compiled news clippings and other pieces of printed information on Cleveland's many social institutions (fig. 13). These entries provide the raw data for the hotel's belated cultural biography, which began with the 1804 sale of "Lot No. 52" and ended with the hotel's demolition, described as a "sad fate" and an "inglorious ending."[34]

Although a portion of the hotel survived the demolition, Rockefeller effectively ended the Weddell House's singularity in 1903. The building that remained was a common structure—bricks and mortar, the Weddell House in name only. The last vestige of the Weddell's legacy would soon disappear. Rockefeller built the city's first skyscraper—the Rockefeller Building, the Cleveland headquarters of Standard Oil—on the parcel of land that the Weddell family had owned for more than eighty years. Designed by the architects Knox and Elliott and based on a design similar to Louis H. Sullivan's Guaranty Bank Building (c. 1894) in Buffalo, the sixteen-story office building was a testament to Rockefeller's success.

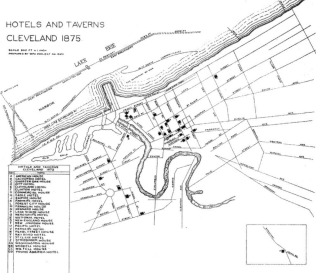

fig. 12
(above, left)
Paul Kucharyson,
Weddell House,
watercolor on paper,
Federal Art Project,
c. 1930s. Department
of Special Collections,
Case Western
Reserve University,
Cleveland, Ohio.

fig. 13
(above, right)
*Hotels and Taverns,
Cleveland, 1875*, map.
From *Historic Sites of
Cleveland: Hotels and
Taverns* (Columbus:
Ohio Historical Records
Survey Project, Service
Division, Work Projects
Administration, 1942): 724.

fig. 14
(right)
The construction of the
Rockefeller Building,
1903. Courtesy of the
Cleveland Public Library,
Cleveland, Ohio. The
remaining portion of the
Weddell House can be
seen to the right of the
building under construction.

Just as his generation of Cleveland businessmen supplanted the previous one, his Rockefeller Building supplanted the Weddell House (fig. 14). Although Clevelanders had embraced the Weddell's contribution to the growth of their city, their reaction to the proposed Rockefeller Building reflected the ambivalence they felt for its owner.

Demolition stories are rarely about deeds and mortgages and are usually about contests of power. Clevelanders had little power but strong sentiment regarding the fate of the Weddell House. Rockefeller, on the other hand, had a great deal of power but a cultivated indifference for the old hotel. He appeared to be simply conducting business. Clevelanders, however, reacted angrily to his decision to build on a site so closely associated with the city's past. The *Cleveland Leader* wrote that "the multi-millionaire's act in ordering the Weddell House torn down seems almost one of sacrilege, of vandalism, the removal of a page of loved history."[35] Because of deeply held personal beliefs, Rockefeller did not participate with his fellow Clevelanders in the singularization of the Weddell House. He did not view the hotel as sacred. When the property fell into his hands, he had no reasons to spare the beloved hotel and at least one good reason to see it go.

Peter M. Weddell (1788–1847), one of the richest men in Cleveland in the middle of the nineteenth century, built the Weddell House in 1847. He had lived and worked in Cleveland for nearly thirty years and had amassed his fortune by wholesaling dry goods and by engaging in a number of real estate deals in and around the city. Although Peter Weddell died the same year that the hotel was to open, his only son and business partner, Horace Weddell (1823–1914), shared his vision for a first-class luxury hotel for the expanding Midwest metropolis they called home. Horace went to great lengths to ensure that the Weddell House met his father's standards. He reinitiated the trip to New York City to shop for furnishings, which had led to his father's death from typhoid fever, and when the Weddell House opened on 26 June 1847, the Cleveland press was unanimous in its praise. The *Plain Dealer* described the hotel as a "beautiful and spacious edifice," "a majestic pile" that was "furnished with the most elegant and costly furniture."[36]

The bounty from the Weddells' shopping excursions did not fail to impress, but Clevelanders saved their highest praise for the furnishings that the hotel had acquired locally. In the spirit of boosterism, the *Plain Dealer* wrote:

> We recognize its more costly carpets, ottomans, divans, and marble work from New York, but the major part of its furniture is from the shops of this city. The upholstery is from Wisdom's, the Cabinet-ware from Gardner and Vincent, the Bed Steads from Duty's, and the mirrors from Sargeant's.... The structure and the furniture reflect the highest credit upon our Cleveland Mechanics.[37]

fig. 15
Weddell House, Cleveland,
c. 1875. Courtesy of the
Cleveland Public Library,
Cleveland, Ohio.

Like Governor Al Smith's "thousands of arms" that had constructed the Empire State Building, the locally made appointments contributed to the singularization of the Weddell House. The Weddell was worthy of Cleveland, Cleveland was worthy of the Weddell, and both were elevated by its presence.

The less extravagant exterior—one author described the hotel's facade as plain—had unique features that reflected its multipurpose design (fig. 15). Five stories high, the Weddell House's street level consisted of a bank and four stores. The second floor of the Superior Avenue side housed two large law offices. The third, fourth, and fifth floors were devoted to the more than two hundred guest rooms. The Bank Street side provided space for three more stores and the hotel's dining room. Dividing the street level and the upper floors, a portico framed in Doric columns drew the eye to the point where the Superior and Bank Street sides of the building converged. This corner balcony was the Weddell House's most distinctive feature. On the roof directly above the portico, a single cupola provided a lookout tower for the arrival of ships on the Cuyahoga River and Lake Erie.[38] While the cupola allowed Cleveland residents and visitors to see the city, the balcony was a way to bring the city into the Weddell House. On the way to his presidential inauguration, Abraham Lincoln spoke from the portico. Between its columns, passersby once caught two lovers in an overlong embrace. The *Plain Dealer* wrote:

> A lady and gentleman were engaged in the most animated forms of love and courtship, such as squeezing, kissing, looking into each other's eyes, leaning on shoulders and other love attitudes too numerous to mention.

308

This style of billing and cooing was indulged in for an hour and a half, the happy pair all the time perfectly oblivious that there was any other person in the city. A photographer was sent for by the lookers-on to immortalize the scene.[39]

Over the years, events such as these tightened the bond between Cleve-landers and the hotel.

Although these incidents and many others recorded in *Historic Sites of Cleveland* helped to singularize the hotel, forces of commoditization also worked against it maintaining that singularity. Among these forces was Rockefeller's relationship with the Weddell family. Although separated by a generation, the senior Weddell and Rockefeller, eventually Cleveland's wealthiest citizen, had much in common. Weddell started in the wholesale business at age fourteen, and the nineteen-year-old Rockefeller took his first job as a clerk with the dry goods wholesalers Hewitt and Tuttle.[40] They both rose within the ranks and eventually became partners in their respective firms. Like Weddell, Rockefeller's early business depended on Lake Erie, the Cuyahoga River, and the canals that led into and out of Cleveland. The elder Weddell died eight years before Rockefeller went into business, so there was no direct competition between the two men. His son, Horace, however, looked to the same lending sources and relied on the same shipping concerns to supply his goods. Early in his profes-sional life, Rockefeller felt no special obligation to the Weddell family business, the city's most respected hotel.

The future of the Weddell House was jeopardized when the third generation of Weddells mortgaged their estate to Rockefeller for $500,000 in 1884. In the late 1880s they radically refaced the hotel, replaced the roof, and added rooms to the interior. Stripped from the building's facade, bricks and lumber littered the Bank Street sidewalk fronting the hotel as testimony to the extent of the overhaul (fig. 16). The owners believed that this aggressive effort to resuscitate the hotel—the project cost upwards of $200,000—would yield a return on their investment.[41] Unfortunately, they made a poor choice in the man they allowed to finance the improvements.

By the 1890s Rockefeller's business was in its ascendance and the Weddells' had waned. Although Rockefeller was a creditor to many interests in Cleveland and beyond, he treated the Weddell House loan in an unusual way. Ron Chernow calls Rockefeller a "forgiving lender" who held many mortgages and rarely, if ever, foreclosed.[42] Rockefeller's director of philanthropies, Frederick T. Gates, wrote of Rockefeller's largesse in his memoirs: "Never have I known Mr. Rockefeller to call a private loan, foreclose a private mortgage, or oppress a debtor."[43] In spite of Rockefeller's reputation—and few men knew him and the inner workings of Standard Oil better than Gates—his motives behind the foreclosure of the Weddell House and the decision to build on the corner of Superior and Bank streets went beyond Rockefeller's typically passionless business deals. In 1903, at a time when the debt, according to contemporary newspaper accounts, had been reduced to $350,000, the "heavy interest" and "diminution in rentals" forced the Weddells to surrender their property to the oil magnate.[44]

Circumstantial evidence suggests that Rockefeller's cultivated indifference to the Weddell House developed because of his religious beliefs and his desire to see his name replace Weddell's in Cleveland's cityscape. Rockefeller was a devout Baptist. Throughout his adult life (though he may have adopted a more liberal attitude in his nineties), Rockefeller strongly disapproved of practices his faith designated as vices. He included on this list theater-going, musical entertainment, gambling, smoking, and drinking alcohol. He also frowned on ostentation, extravagant spending, and over-indulgence in food. One might go so far as to say Rockefeller was against nearly all the things that helped to make the Weddell House a successful and beloved institution.

Throughout its half century of operations, the Weddell House consistently provided a location for activity that Clevelanders embraced but Rockefeller found distasteful. Simply reading the Weddell House menu would have made the milk-and-crackers-eating Rockefeller dyspeptic. Cataloged by the *Plain Dealer*, the fare of Weddell House's 1852 New Year's Eve Banquet represented the kind of meals served during the hotel's heyday:

Oysters, Soup; Oysters, in aspic Jelly; Ham, ornamented; Beef-a-la-mode, decorated; Buffalo tongue; Lobster Salad; Chicken Salad; Boned Turkey, ornamented; Quails, with Jelly; Pigeons, larded; Relishes – Olives, Sardines, Anchovies, Pickles, Celery. Pastry – Cold custards, Grape Jelly Tarts, Boston Cream Cakes, Queen's Puffs, Genoisse Jelly, Wine Jelly, Rum Jelly, Orange Jelly, Charlotte Russe, Charlotte de Pomme, Bavarian Cream, English Cream, Fromage Bavarois, Gateaus de Mille-fleux, Blanc Mange, variegated; Corn Starch Waffles, Orange Meringues, Cream Meringues, Swiss Meringues.[45]

By 1853, the year that Rockefeller started high school in Cleveland, the Weddell was well known as a place to indulge in alcohol. As a longtime advocate of abstention, Rockefeller would have found this report from the Weddell House discouraging:

> We could not help these recollections yesterday, as we sat at the Weddell House table and saw the Heidsick and sparkling Catawba [champagne] going the rounds free as water. The table was bountifully and gorgeously spread with everything to tempt the palate and satisfy the appetite.... This is an every day occurrence at most of our fashionable hotels, and practiced by our most fashionable young men.[46]

Although the Weddell House honored Ohio state laws and forbade alcohol in the late 1850s, during the Civil War and in the relaxed morality of the decades that followed the hotel became known for its wine list, its well-stocked saloon, and its talented bartending staff.

In addition to its dining room and saloon, the Weddell House also was well known for the other diversions it provided the traveler, the meeting attendee, and Cleveland regulars—diversions the devout Rockefeller would have frowned upon. The hotel had a billiard room, described in 1874 as "the most elegant in this part of the West,"[47] with a reputation as a discreet place to play poker. Like any public establishment, the Weddell House had its share of criminal activity and occasional late-night rowdiness, but it maintained a guest list that included the wealthy, foreign dignitaries, and most notably President-elect Lincoln. For Rockefeller, whose sole musical entertainment was religious hymns, the brass bands, costume balls, and billiard demonstrations at the Weddell must have been morally suspect.

As years passed, the Weddell House became more singular in the eyes of every Clevelander but Rockefeller. When the demolition announcement came, Clevelanders clung to hopes that the Weddell House would survive. In September 1903 rumors circulated in the city that in spite of the scheduled demolition a portion of the hotel would remain standing. When asked by the *Plain Dealer*, Rockefeller's agent would neither confirm nor deny the rumor. Because the new Rockefeller Building required only 125 feet of frontage on the Bank Street side, he could not justify the demolition of the entire hotel (fig. 17).[48] Rockefeller now owned the

fig. 17
(top, right)
Peter Weddell House, West Sixth Street and Frankfurt Avenue, Cleveland, detail from first-floor plan showing original and present hotel, 1935. Historic American Buildings Survey line drawing, Library of Congress, Prints and Photographs Division. HABS, OHIO, 18–CLEV, 4.

fig. 18
(below, right)
Rockefeller Building, Cleveland. From a postcard, 1909. Author's collection.

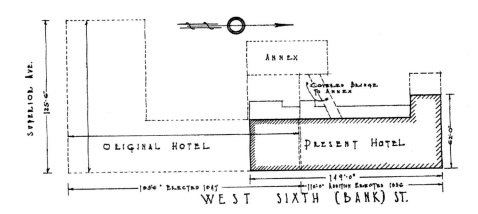

No. 30 ROCKEFELLER BUILDING, CLEVELAND, O.

fig. 19
Rockefeller Building.
From a postcard, 1915.
Author's collection.

hotel that he had tried to destroy. One can imagine his indignation when, less than two months later, Cleveland's new chief of police wrote to him about stopping the gambling that was going on in his hotel.[49] Nevertheless, Rockefeller saw his power realized in concrete and steel. In postcards produced in 1909 and 1915, the sixteen-story building towers over its humbled neighbor, a visual reminder of Rockefeller's preeminence among Cleveland's businessmen (figs. 18, 19).

That Rockefeller had wanted to create an architectural symbol of his power became more evident in the early 1920s. According to Rockefeller historian Grace Goulder, John D. Rockefeller Jr. (1874–1960) sold the Rockefeller Building to Cleveland businessman Josiah Kirby in 1920. John Sr. now divided his time between New York City and Florida and rarely visited Cleveland. Junior must have been surprised, then, at Senior's reaction when the new owner placed the huge letters "K-I-R-B-Y" on the roof of Cleveland's first skyscraper. Because of financial difficulties, Kirby's ownership was short-lived. He was forced to sell the building less than two years later. The letters, however, remained at the top. Senior had Junior buy the building back for nearly $3 million and had the letters promptly removed. When the Rockefellers next sold the building, the new owners, Goulder tells us, had to sign "an agreement that the Rockefeller name be retained."[50] When he tore down the Weddell House twenty years earlier, Rockefeller had replaced the name of one successful generation of Cleveland businessmen with his own. He would not allow the same thing to happen to his building.

Conclusion

The demolition of the Weddell House and the Waldorf-Astoria Hotel occurred amid the ongoing cultural debate about the ideology of creative destruction. Developers like John D. Rockefeller and Empire State Inc. profited from the public's perception of demolition as a servant of modernization and progress. If the old had to give way to the new, beloved landmarks like the Weddell House and the Waldorf-Astoria Hotel would necessarily have to fall. While developers worked to transfer the public's sentiment from the building to be demolished to the one to be constructed, the public had just begun to realize the fetishlike power that a building acquired over time.

Igor Kopytoff identified this process as singularization. Buildings, like personal possessions, can become unique things that their admirers think should be shielded from the world of commodity exchange. In the years before preservation legislation, the public had few means at its disposal to protect such structures. In fact, people often did not recognize the depth of their feelings for a building until it was threatened with destruction. In the case of the Weddell House, the full recognition of its singularity may not have come until nearly thirty years *after* its demolition, when the uproar over the Waldorf-Astoria reminded Clevelanders of their own loss decades before. The advantage lay with builders, who argued, in essence, that singularity resided not in the structure itself but in the history of the property. In their evolutionary schema, singularity passed from the demolished structure to the newly built one. The unfortunate corollary to this argument was that developers and builders who wanted to create an iconic structure felt compelled to look to a site that already contained an iconic structure, virtually dooming the most important buildings in a city's past.

To preserve singular structures, the American public would need to contest the power of wealthy developers and more closely interrogate the cultural productions that espoused the ideology of creative destruction. In the years before historic preservation, the public could not harness the power necessary to protect a structure that had accrued significant cultural meaning. Today, a structure with a rich cultural biography has a chance to escape what the Empire State Building developers called the "laws of progress." Preservation does not block progress; it only asks that we recognize other kinds of value in addition to economics. With hindsight, we know how important both the Rockefeller and Empire State buildings became to their respective cities, but singularized hotels like the Weddell House and the Waldorf-Astoria Hotel were as significant to those cities' histories. In recognizing their contributions to a city's collective memory, buildings such as these no longer need to be sacrificed for the sake of future icons.✧

Acknowledgments
For Charlie.

Notes

1. John Tauranac, *The Empire State Building: The Making of a Landmark* (New York: Scribner's, 1995); and Carol Willis, "Form Follows Finance: The Empire State Building," in *The Landscape of Modernity: Essays on New York City, 1900–1940*, ed. David Ward and Oliver Zunz (New York: Russell Sage Foundation, 1992), 160–90.

2. Carol Willis, ed., *Building the Empire State* (New York: W. W. Norton, 1998).

3. Henry B. Lent, *The Waldorf-Astoria: A Brief Chronicle of a Unique Institution Now Entering Its Fifth Decade* (New York: Currier, 1934); and Albin Pasteur Dearing, *The Elegant Inn: The Waldorf-Astoria Hotel*, 1893–1929 (Secaucus, NJ: Lyle Stuart, 1986).

4. Tauranac, *Empire State Building*, 120.

5. Ibid., 119.

6. Igor Kopytoff, "The Cultural Biography of Things: Commoditization as Process," in *The Social Life of Things: Commodities in Cultural Perspective*, ed. Arjun Appadurai (Cambridge: Cambridge University Press, 1986), 64–94.

7. Ibid., 80.

8. Virginia Pope, "An Epoch Passes With the Waldorf," *New York Times Magazine* (28 April 1929): 6.

9. Kopytoff, "Cultural Biography of Things," 69.

10. John Walker Harrington, "Quarter Mile Climb to Summit of Building Efficiency," *Real Estate Record and Builders' Guide* (May 1931).

11. Willis, "Form Follows Finance," 181.

12. Karl Marx, "The Fetishism of Commodities and the Secret Thereof," in *The Marx-Engels Reader*, 2nd ed., ed. Robert C. Tucker (New York: W. W. Norton, 1978), 319–29.

13. Kopytoff, "Cultural Biography of Things," 83.

14. *Empire State: A History* (New York: Publicity Associates, 1931), 11.

15. Marx, "Fetishism of Commodities," 320.

16. *Empire State: A History*, 5.

17. Ibid., 36; Lewis W. Hine, *Men at Work: Photographic Studies of Modern Men and Machines* (New York: Dover, 1977).

18. "Smith Sees a Halt in Uptown Trend," *New York Times* (2 May 1931).

19. Ted Steinberg, *Down to Earth: Nature's Role in American History* (New York: Oxford University Press, 2002), 59.

20. *Empire State: A History*, 10.

21. "No More Parades in Peacock Alley," *Literary Digest* 100, no. 2 (12 January 1929): 31.

22. Ibid., 32.

23. "$50,000,000.00 Louisiana Purchase Exposition, St. Louis, Mo., Bought By The Chicago House Wrecking Company," *Catalogue No. 145* (Chicago: Chicago House Wrecking Co., 1906).

24. "Waldorf Souvenirs Sought at Auction," *New York Times* (2 May 1929): 3

25. "Catalogue Part One," *The Waldorf-Astoria Hotel: Sales Conducted by the Wise Auction Company, Benjamin S. Wise, Auctioneer*, 1 May 1929.

26. "Waldorf Sale Continues," *New York Times* (19 May 1929): 18; "Waldorf Sale Broadcast," *New York Times* (19 May 1929): 23.

27. "Auction at Waldorf Ends After a Month," *New York Times* (4 June 1929): 15.

28. Pope, "An Epoch Passes With the Waldorf," 23.

29. Ibid., 6.

30. "Waldorf Auction Like 3-Ring Circus," *New York Times* (6 May 1929): 14.

31. "Notes on Construction of Empire State Building," in Willis, *Building the Empire State*, 1.

32. Ella Grant Wilson, "Recalling the Glories of the Weddell House," *Cleveland Plain Dealer* (25 October 1931): 19.

33. Ibid.

34. *Historic Sites of Cleveland: Hotels and Taverns* (Columbus: Ohio Historical Records Survey Project, 1942).

35. Ibid., 700.

36. Ibid., 620–21.

37. Ibid.

38. Ibid., 618.

39. Ibid., 687.

40. Ron Chernow, *Titan: The Life of John D. Rockefeller, Sr.* (New York: Vintage Books, 1998), 44–46.

41. *Historic Sites of Cleveland*, 699.

42. Chernow, *Titan*, 372.

43. Ibid.

44. *Historic Sites of Cleveland*, 701.

45. Ibid., 635.

46. Ibid., 636.

47. Ibid., 687.

48. "Ray of Hope Remains," *Cleveland Plain Dealer* (6 September 1903).

49. "Police to Rockefeller," *New York Times* (24 September 1905): 1.

50. Grace Goulder, *John D. Rockefeller: The Cleveland Years* (Cleveland: Western Reserve Historical Society, 1973), 196.